Making Things See

3D Vision with Kinect, Processing, Arduino, and MakerBot

Greg Borenstein

O'REILLY®

Beijing · Cambridge · Farnham · Köln · Sebastopol · Tokyo

Making Things See

by Greg Borenstein

Published by O'Reilly Media, Inc., 1005 Gravenstein Highway North, Sebastopol, CA 95472.

O'Reilly Media books may be purchased for educational, business, or sales promotional use. Online editions are also available for most titles (*my.safaribooksonline.com*). For more information, contact our corporate/institutional sales department: 800-998-9938 or *corporate@oreilly.com*.

Editors: Andrew Odewahn, Brian Jepson

Production Editor: Holly Bauer

Proofreader: Linley Dolby

Indexer: Fred Brown

Compositor: Nancy Kotary

Cover Designer: Mark Paglietti

Interior Designer: Ron Bilodeau

Illustrator: Rebecca Demarest

January 2012:   First Edition.

Revision History for the First Edition:

2012-01-04   First release

2012-03-16   Second release

See *http://oreilly.com/catalog/errata.csp?isbn=0636920020684* for release details.

ISBN: 978-1-449-30707-3
[TI]

For Jacob and Ellie and Sophie and Amalia. The future is yours.

Contents

Preface

When Microsoft first released the Kinect, Matt Webb, CEO of design and invention firm Berg London, captured the sense of possibility that had so many programmers, hardware hackers, and tinkerers so excited:

> "WW2 and ballistics gave us digital computers.
> Cold War decentralization gave us the Internet.
> Terrorism and mass surveillance: Kinect."

Why the Kinect Matters

The Kinect announces a revolution in technology akin to those that shaped the most fundamental breakthroughs of the 20th century. Just like the premiere of the personal computer or the Internet, the release of the Kinect was another moment when the fruit of billions of dollars and decades of research that had previously only been available to the military and the intelligence community fell into the hands of regular people.

Face recognition, gait analysis, skeletonization, depth imaging—this cohort of technologies that had been developed to detect terrorists in public spaces could now suddenly be used for creative civilian purposes: building gestural interfaces for software, building cheap 3D scanners for personalized fabrication, using motion capture for easy 3D character animation, using biometrics to create customized assistive technologies for people with disabilities, etc.

While this development may seem wide-ranging and diverse, it can be summarized simply: for the first time, computers can see. While we've been able to use computers to process still images and video for decades, simply iterating over red, green, and blue pixels misses most of the amazing capabilities that we take for granted in the human vision system: seeing in stereo, differentiating objects in space, tracking people over time and space, recognizing body language, etc. For the first time, with this revolution in camera and image-processing technology, we're starting to build computing applications that take these same capabilities as a starting point. And, with the arrival of the Kinect, the ability to create these applications is now within the reach of even weekend tinkerers and casual hackers.

Just like the personal computer and Internet revolutions before it, this Vision Revolution will surely also lead to an astounding flowering of creative and productive projects. Comparing the arrival of the Kinect to the personal computer and the Internet may sound absurd. But keep in mind that when the personal computer was first invented, it was a geeky toy for tinkerers and enthusiasts. The Internet began life as a way for government researchers to access one anothers' mainframe computers. All of these technologies only came to assume their critical roles in contemporary life slowly as individuals used them to make creative and innovative applications that eventually became fixtures in our daily lives. Right now it may seem absurd to compare the Kinect with the PC and the Internet, but a few decades from now, we may look back on it and compare it with the Altair or the ARPAnet as the first baby step toward a new technological world.

The purpose of this book is to provide the context and skills needed to build exactly these projects that reveal this newly possible world. Those skills include:

- Working with depth information from 3D cameras
- Analyzing and manipulating point clouds
- Tracking the movement of people's joints
- Background removal and scene analysis
- Pose and gesture detection

The first three chapters of this book will introduce you to all of these skills. You'll learn how to implement each of these techniques in the Processing programming environment. We'll start with the absolute basics of accessing the data from the Kinect and build up your ability to write ever more sophisticated programs throughout the book. Learning these skills means not just mastering a particular software library or API, but understanding the principles behind them so that you can apply them even as the practical details of the technology rapidly evolve.

And yet even mastering these basic skills will not be enough to build the projects that really make the most of this Vision Revolution. To do that, you also need to understand some of the wider context of the fields that will be revolutionized by the cheap, easy availability of depth data and skeleton information. To that end, this book will provide introductions and conceptual overviews of the fields of 3D scanning, digital fabrication, robotic vision, and assistive technology. You can think of these sections as teaching you what you can do with the depth and skeleton information once you've gotten it. They will include topics such as:

- Building meshes

- Preparing 3D models for fabrication

- Defining and detecting gestures

- Displaying and manipulating 3D models

- Designing custom input devices for people with limited ranges of motion

- Forward and inverse kinematics

In covering these topics, our focus will expand outward from simply working with the Kinect to using a whole toolbox of software and techniques. The last three chapters of this book will explore these topics through a series of in-depth projects. We'll write a program that uses the Kinect as a scanner to produce physical objects on a 3D printer, we'll create a game that will help a stroke patient with physical therapy, and we'll construct a robot arm that copies the motions of your actual arm. In these projects, we'll start by introducing the basic principles behind each general field and then seeing how our newfound knowledge of programming with the Kinect can put those principles into action. But we won't stop with Processing and the Kinect. We'll work with whatever tools are necessary to build each application, from 3D modeling programs to microcontrollers.

This book will not be a definitive reference to any of these topics; each is vast, comprehensive, and filled with its own fascinating intricacies. This book aims to serve as a provocative introduction to each area—giving you enough context and techniques to start using the Kinect to make interesting projects and hoping that your progress will inspire you to follow the leads provided to investigate further.

Who This Book Is For

At its core, this book is for anyone who wants to learn more about building creative interactive applications with the Kinect, from interaction and game designers who want to build gestural interfaces to makers who want to work with a 3D scanner to artists who want to get started with computer vision.

That said, you will get the most out of it if you are one of the following: a beginning programmer looking to learn more sophisticated graphics and interactions techniques, specifically how to work in three dimensions, or an advanced programmer who wants a shortcut to learning the ins and outs of working with the Kinect and a guide to some of the specialized areas that it enables.

You don't have to be an expert graphics programmer or experienced user of Processing to get started with this book, but if you've never programmed before, there are probably other much better places to start.

As a starting point, I'll assume that you have some exposure to the Processing creative coding language (or can teach yourself that as you go). You should know the basics from *Getting Started with Processing* by Casey Reas and Ben Fry (*http://shop.oreilly.com/product/0636920000570.do*), *Learning Processing* by Dan Shiffman (*http://learningprocessing.com*), or the equivalent. This book is designed to proceed slowly from introductory topics into more sophisticated code and concepts, giving you a smooth introduction to the fundamentals of making interactive graphical applications while teaching you about the Kinect. At the beginning, I'll explain nearly everything about each example, and as we go I'll leave more and more of the details to you to figure out. The goal is for you to level up from a beginner to a confident intermediate interactive graphics programmer.

The Structure of This Book

The goal of this book is to unlock your ability to build interactive applications with the Kinect. It's meant to make you into a card-carrying member of the Vision Revolution I described at the beginning of this introduction. Membership in this Revolution has a number of benefits. Once you've achieved it, you'll be able to play an invisible drum set that makes real sounds, make 3D scans of objects and print copies of them, and teach robots to copy the motions of your arm.

However, membership in this Revolution does not come for free. To gain entry into its ranks, you'll need to learn a series of fundamental programming concepts and techniques. These skills are the basis of all the more advanced benefits of membership, and all of those cool abilities will be impossible without them. This book is designed to build up those skills one at a time, starting from the simplest and most fundamental and building toward the more complex and sophisticated. We'll start out with humble pixels and work our way up to intricate three-dimensional gestures.

Toward this end, the first half of this book will act as a kind of primer in these programming skills. Before we dive into controlling robots or 3D printing our faces, we need to start with the basics. The first four chapters of this book cover the fundamentals of writing Processing programs that use the data from the Kinect.

Processing is a creative coding environment that uses the Java programming language to make it easy for beginners to write simple interactive applications that include graphics and other rich forms of media. As mentioned previously, this book assumes basic knowledge of Processing (or equivalent programming chops), but as we go through these first four chapters, I'll build up your knowledge of some of the more advanced Processing concepts that are most relevant to working with the Kinect. These concepts include looping through arrays of pixels, basic 3D drawing and orientation, and some simple geometric calculations.

I will attempt to explain each of these concepts clearly and in depth. The idea is for you not to just to have a few project recipes that you can make by rote, but to actually understand enough of the flavor of the basic ingredients to be able to invent your own "dishes" and modify the ones I present here. At times, you may feel that I'm beating some particular subject to death, but stick with it—you'll frequently find that these details become critically important later on when trying to get your own application ideas to work.

One nice side benefit to this approach is that these fundamental skills are relevant to a lot more than just working with the Kinect. If you master them here in the course of your work with the Kinect, they will serve you well throughout all your other work with Processing, unlocking many new possibilities in your work, and really pushing you decisively beyond beginner status.

There are three fundamental techniques that we need to build all of the fancy applications that make the Kinect so exciting: processing the depth image, working in 3D, and accessing the skeleton data. From 3D scanning to robotic vision, all of these applications measure the distance of objects using the depth image, reconstruct the image as a three-dimensional scene, and track the movement of individual parts of a user's body. The first half of this book will serve as an introduction to each of these techniques. I'll explain how the data provided by the Kinect makes these techniques possible, demonstrate how to implement them in code, and walk you through a few simple examples to show what they might be good for.

Working with the Depth Camera

First off, you'll learn how to work with the depth data provided by the Kinect. The Kinect uses an IR projector and camera to produce a "depth image" of the scene in front of it. Unlike conventional images in which each pixel records the color of light that reached the camera from that part of the scene, each pixel of this depth image records the distance of the object in that part of the scene from the Kinect. When we look at depth images, they will look like strangely distorted black and white pictures. They look strange because the color of each part of the image indicates not how bright that object is, but how far away it is. The brightest parts of the image are the closest, and the darkest parts are the farthest away. If we write a Processing program that examines the brightness of each pixel in this depth image, we can figure out the distance of every object in front of the Kinect. Using this same technique and a little bit of clever coding, we can also follow the closest point as it moves, which can be a convenient way of tracking a user for simple interactivity.

Working with Point Clouds

This first approach treats the depth data as if it were only two-dimensional. It looks at the depth information captured by the Kinect as a flat image when really it describes a three-dimensional scene. In the third chapter, we'll start looking at ways to translate from these two-dimensional pixels into points in three-dimensional space. For each pixel in the depth image, we can think of its position within the image as its x-y coordinates. That is, if we're looking at a pixel that's 50 pixels in from the top-left corner and 100 pixels down, it has an x-coordinate of 50 and a y-coordinate of 100. But the pixel also has a grayscale value. And we know from our initial discussion of the depth image that each pixel's grayscale value corresponds to the depth of the image in front of it. Hence, that value will represent the pixel's z-coordinate.

Once we've converted all our two-dimensional grayscale pixels into three-dimensional points in space, we have what is called a *point cloud*—that is, a bunch of disconnected points floating near each other in three-dimensional space in a way that corresponds to the arrangement of the objects and people in front of the Kinect. You can think of this point cloud as the 3D equivalent of a pixelated image. While it might look solid from far away, if we look closely, the image will break down into a bunch of distinct points with space visible between them. If we wanted to convert these points into a smooth continuous surface, we'd need to figure out a way to connect them with a large number of polygons to fill in the gaps. This is a process called *constructing a mesh*, and it's something we'll cover extensively later in the book in the chapters on physical fabrication and animation.

For now, though, there's a lot we can do with the point cloud itself. First of all, the point cloud is just cool. Having a live 3D representation of yourself and your surroundings on your screen that you can manipulate and view from different angles feels a little bit like being in the future. It's the first time in using the Kinect that you'll get a view of the world that feels fundamentally different that those that you're used to seeing through conventional cameras.

To make the most of this new view, you're going to learn some of the fundamentals of writing code that navigates and draws in 3D. When you start working in 3D, there are a number of common pitfalls that I'll try to help you avoid. For example, it's easy to get so disoriented as you navigate in 3D space that the shapes you draw end up not being visible. I'll explain how the 3D axes work in Processing and show you some tools for navigating and drawing within them without getting confused. Another frequent area of confusion in 3D drawing is the concept of the camera. To translate our 3D points from the Kinect into a 2D image that we can actually draw on our flat computer screens, Processing uses the metaphor of a camera. After we've arranged our points in 3D space, we place a virtual camera at a particular spot in that space, aim it at the points we've drawn, and, basically, take a picture. Just as a real camera flattens the objects in front of it into a 2D image, this virtual camera does the same with our 3D geometry. Everything that the camera sees gets rendered onto the screen from the angle and in the way that it sees it. Anything that's out of the camera's view doesn't get rendered. I'll show you how to control the position of the camera so that all of the 3D points from the Kinect that you want to see end up rendered on the screen. I'll also demonstrate how to move the camera around so we can look at our point cloud from different angles without having to ever physically move the Kinect.

Working with the Skeleton Data

The third technique is in some ways both the simplest to work with and the most powerful. In addition to the raw depth information we've been working with so far, the Kinect can, with the help of some additional software, recognize people and tell us where they are in space. Specifically, our Processing code can access the location of each part of a user's body in 3D: we can get the exact position of hands, head, elbows, feet, etc.

One of the big advantages of depth images is that computer vision algorithms work better on them than on conventional color images. The reason Microsoft developed and shipped a depth camera as a controller for the Xbox was not to show players cool looking point clouds, but because they could run software on the Xbox that processes the depth image in order to locate people and find the positions of their body parts. This process is known as *skeletonization* because the software infers the position of a user's skeleton (specifically, his joints and the bones that connect them) from the data in the depth image.

By using the right Processing library, we can get access to this user position data without having to implement this incredibly sophisticated skeletonization algorithm ourself. We can simply ask for the 3D position of any joint we're interested in and then use that data to make our applications interactive. In Chapter 4, I'll demonstrate how to access the skeleton data from the Kinect Processing library and how to use it to make our applications interactive. To create truly rich interactions, we'll need to learn some more sophisticated 3D programming. In Chapter 3, when working with point clouds, we'll cover the basics of 3D drawing and navigation. Then, we'll add to those skills by learning more advanced tools for comparing 3D points with each other, tracking their movement, and even recording it for later playback. These new techniques will serve as the basic vocabulary for some exciting new interfaces we can use in our sketches, letting users communicate with us by striking poses, doing dance moves, and performing exercises (among many other natural human movements).

Once we've covered all three of these fundamental techniques for working with the Kinect, we'll be ready to move on to the cool applications that probably drew you to this book in the first place. This book's premise is that what's truly exciting about the Kinect is that it unlocks areas of computer interaction that were previously only accessible to researchers with labs full of expensive experimental equipment. With the Kinect, things like 3D scanning and advanced robotic vision are suddenly available to anyone with a Kinect and an understanding of the fundamentals described here. But to make the most of these new possibilities, you need a bit of background in the actual application areas. To build robots that mimic human movements, it's not enough just to know how to access the Kinect's skeleton data, you also need some familiarity with inverse kinematics, the study of how to position a robot's joints in order to achieve a particular pose. To create 3D scans that can be used for fabrication or computer graphics, it's not enough to understand how to work with the point cloud from the Kinect, you need to know how to build up a mesh from those points and how to prepare and process it for fabrication on a MakerBot, a CNC machine, or 3D printer.

The final two chapters will provide you with introductions to exactly these topics: 3D scanning for fabrication and 3D vision for robotics.

3D Scanning for Digital Fabrication

In Chapter 5, we'll move from people to objects. We'll use the Kinect as a 3D scanner to capture the geometry of a physical object in digital form and then we'll prepare that data for fabrication on a 3D printer. We'll learn how to process the depth points from the Kinect to turn them into a continuous surface or mesh. Then we'll learn how to export this mesh in a standard file format so we can work with it outside of Processing. I'll introduce you to a few free programs that help you clean up the mesh and prepare it for fabrication. Once our mesh is ready to go, we'll examine what it takes to print it out on a series of different rapid prototyping systems. We'll use a MakerBot to print it out in plastic and we'll submit it to Shapeways, a website that will print out our object in a variety of materials from sandstone to steel.

Computer Vision for Robotics

In Chapter 6, we'll see what the Kinect can do for robotics. Robotic vision is a huge topic that's been around for more than 50 years. Its achievements include robots that have driven on the moon and ones that assemble automobiles. For this chapter, we'll build a simple robot arm that reproduces the position of your real arm as detected by the Kinect. We'll send the joint data from Processing to the robot over a serial connection. Our robot's brain will be an Arduino microcontroller. Arduino is Processing's electronic cousin; it makes it just as easy to create interactive electronics as Processing does interactive graphical applications. The Arduino will listen to the commands from Processing and control the robot's motors to execute them.

We'll approach this project in two different ways. First we'll reproduce the angles of your joints as detected by the Kinect. This approach falls into *forward kinematics*, an approach to robotics in which the robot's final position is the result of setting its joints to a series of known angles. Then we'll reprogram our robot so that it can follow the movement of any of your joints. This will be an experiment in *inverse kinematics*. Rather than knowing exactly how we want our robot to move, we'll only know what we want its final position to be. We'll have to teach it how to calculate all the individual angle changes necessary to get there. This is a much harder problem than the forward kinematic problem. A serious solution to it can involve complex math and confusing code. Ours will be quite simple and not very sophisticated, but will provide an interesting introduction to the problems you'd encounter in more advanced robotics applications.

None of these chapters are meant to be definitive guides to their respective areas, but instead to give you just enough background to get started applying these Kinect fundamentals in order to build your own ideas.

Unlike the first four chapters, which attempt to instill fundamental techniques deeply, these last three are meant to inspire a sense of the breadth and diversity of what's possible with the Kinect. Instead of proceeding slowly and thoroughly through comprehensive explanations of principles, these later chapters are structured as individual projects. They'll take a single project idea from one of these topic areas and execute it completely from beginning to end. In the course of these projects, we'll frequently find ourselves moving beyond just writing Processing code. We'll have to interview occupational therapists, work with assistive technology patients, clean up 3D meshes, use a 3D animation program, solder a circuit, and program an Arduino. Along the way, you'll gain brief exposure to a lot of new ideas and tools, but nothing like the in-depth understanding of the first four chapters. We'll move fast. It will be exciting. You won't believe the things you'll make.

Every step of the way in these projects, we'll rely on your knowledge from the first half of the book. So pay close attention as we proceed through these fundamentals, they're the building blocks of everything else throughout this book, and getting a good grasp on them will make it all the easier for you to build whatever it is you're dreaming of.

Then, at the end of the book, our scope will widen. Having come so far in your 3D programming chops and your understanding of the Kinect, I'll point you toward next steps that you can take to take your applications even further. We'll discuss other environments and programming languages besides Processing where you can work with the Kinect. These range from creative coding libraries in other languages such as C++ to interactive graphical environments such as Max/MSP, Pure Data, and Quartz Composer. And there's also Microsoft's own set of development tools, which let you deeply integrate the Kinect with Windows. I'll explain some of the advantages and opportunities of each environment to give you a sense of why you'd want to try it out. Also, I'll point you toward other resources that you can use to get started in each area.

In addition to exploring other programming environments, you can take your Kinect work further by learning about 3D graphics in general. Under the hood, Processing's 3D drawing code is based on OpenGL, a widely used standard for computer graphics. OpenGL is a huge, complex, and powerful system, and Processing only exposes you to the tiniest bit of it. Learning more about OpenGL itself will unlock all kinds of more advanced possibilities for your Kinect applications. I'll point you toward resources both within Processing and outside of it that will enable you to continue your graphics education and make ever more beautiful and compelling 3D graphics.

Acknowledgments

It's a cliché of acknowledgments to say that all books with solo bylines are really collaborative efforts. In this case, I'll go further and say that I myself am one. Specifically, my possession of the necessary knowledge and abilities to write this book was the direct product of the excellent and patient work of a series of amazing teachers I had at NYU's Interactive Telecommunications Program. This book would have been inconceivable without them.

Dan Shiffman's passion spurred my initial interest in the Kinect; his tireless aid as a professor, technical editor, and friend got me through learning and writing about it; and his inspiring abilities as a teacher and writer gave me a goal to aspire to.

Kyle McDonald and Zach Lieberman taught a short, seven-week class in the spring of 2011 that changed my life. That course introduced me to many of the techniques and concepts I attempt to pass on in this book. I hope my presentation of this material is half as clear and thorough as theirs. Further, Zach came up with the idea for the artist interviews, which ended up as one of my favorite parts of this book. And Kyle was invaluable in helping me translate his work on 3D scanning for fabrication, which makes up the soul of Chapter 5.

Dan O'Sullivan, the chair of ITP, and Red Burns, its founder and patron saint, gave me the space and institutional support to take on this intimidating project and created an environment that gave me the confidence and connections to complete it.

Lily Szajnberg was my first student and ideal reader. The best explanations in this book were forced out of me by her hunger to understand and honesty about when I wasn't making sense.

I'd like to thank Andrew Odewahn and Brian Jepson from O'Reilly. Andrew was the first person—even before me—to believe I could write a book. His early feedback helped turn this project from a very long blog post into a book. Brian's constant and continuous work has made this book better in a thousand ways I'll never be able to fully recount.

Max Rheiner created the SimpleOpenNI library I use throughout this book and acted as a technical editor making sure I got all the details right. This book would have been more difficult and come out worse without his work.

I'd also like to thank all the artists who agreed to be interviewed: Robert Hodgin, Elliot Woods, blablablLAB, Nicolas Burrus, Oliver Kreylos, Alejandro Crawford, Kyle McDonald (again), Josh Blake, and Phil Torrone and Limor Fried from Adafruit. Your work, and the hope of seeing more like it, is why I wrote this book.

Huge thanks to Liz Arum and Matt Griffin from MakerBot as well as Catarina Mota, who helped me get up to speed on making good prints, and Duann Scott from Shapeways, who made sure my prints would arrive in time to be included.

And finally, my family and friends and fellow ITP Residents who put up with me while I was writing: I love you.

Using Code Examples

This book is here to help you get your job done. In general, you may use the code in this book in your programs and documentation. You do not need to contact us for permission unless you're reproducing a significant portion of the code. For example, writing a program that uses several chunks of code from this book does not require permission. Selling or distributing a CD-ROM of examples from O'Reilly books does require permission. Answering a question by citing this book and quoting example code does not require permission. Incorporating a significant amount of example code from this book into your product's documentation does require permission.

We appreciate, but do not require, attribution. An attribution usually includes the title, author, publisher, and ISBN. For example: "*Making Things See* by Greg Borenstein (O'Reilly). Copyright 2012 Greg Borenstein, 978-1-449-30707-3."

If you feel your use of code examples falls outside fair use or the permission given above, feel free to contact us at *permissions@oreilly.com*.

Conventions Used in This Book

The following typographical conventions are used in this book:

Italic
> Indicates new terms, URLs, email addresses, filenames, and file extensions.

`Constant width`
> Used for program listings, as well as within paragraphs to refer to program elements such as variable or function names, databases, data types, environment variables, statements, and keywords.

`Constant width bold`
> Shows commands or other text that should be typed literally by the user.

`Constant width italic`
> Shows text that should be replaced with user-supplied values or by values determined by context.

> *This box signifies a tip, suggestion, or general note.*

Warning

This box indicates a warning or caution.

Safari® Books Online

Safari Books Online is an on-demand digital library that lets you easily search over 7,500 technology and creative reference books and videos to find the answers you need quickly.

With a subscription, you can read any page and watch any video from our library online. Read books on your cell phone and mobile devices. Access new titles before they are available for print, and get exclusive access to manuscripts in development and post feedback for the authors. Copy and paste code samples, organize your favorites, download chapters, bookmark key sections, create notes, print out pages, and benefit from tons of other time-saving features.

O'Reilly Media has uploaded this book to the Safari Books Online service. To have full digital access to this book and others on similar topics from O'Reilly and other publishers, sign up for free at *http://my.safaribooksonline.com*.

How to Contact Us

Please address comments and questions concerning this book to the publisher:

O'Reilly Media, Inc.
1005 Gravenstein Highway North
Sebastopol, CA 95472
800-998-9938 (in the United States or Canada)
707-829-0515 (international or local)
707-829-0104 (fax)

We have a web page for this book, where we list errata, examples, and any additional information. You can access this page at:

http://www.oreilly.com/catalog/9781449307073

To comment or ask technical questions about this book, send email to:

bookquestions@oreilly.com

For more information about our books, courses, conferences, and news, see our website at *http://www.oreilly.com*.

Find us on Facebook: *http://facebook.com/oreilly*

Follow us on Twitter: *http://twitter.com/oreillymedia*

Watch us on YouTube: *http://www.youtube.com/oreillymedia*

What Is the Kinect?

We've talked a little bit about all the amazing applications that depth cameras like the Kinect make possible. But how does the Kinect actually work? What kind of image does it produce and why is it useful? How does the Kinect gather depth data about the scene in front of it? What's inside that sleek little black box?

How Does It Work? Where Did It Come From?

In the next few sections of this introduction, I'll provide some background about where the Kinect came from as well as a little info on how the device works. This issue of the Kinect's provenance may seem like it's only of academic interest. However, as we'll see, it is actually central when deciding which of the many available libraries we should use to write our programs with the Kinect. It's also a fascinating and inspiring story of what the open source community can do.

What Does the Kinect Do?

The Kinect is a *depth camera*. Normal cameras collect the light that bounces off of the objects in front of them. They turn this light into an image that resembles what we see with our own eyes. The Kinect, on the other hand, records the distance of the objects that are placed in front of it. It uses infrared light to create an image (a *depth image*) that captures not what the objects look like, but where they are in space. In the next section of this introduction, I'll explain how the Kinect actually works. I'll describe what hardware it uses to capture this depth image and explain some of its limitations. But first I'd like to explain why you'd actually want a depth image. What can you do with a depth image that you can't with a conventional color image?

First of all, a depth image is much easier for a computer to "understand" than a conventional color image. Any program that's trying to understand an image starts with its pixels and tries to find and recognize the people and objects represented by them. If you're a computer program and you're looking at color pixels, it's very difficult to differentiate objects and people. So much of the color of the pixels is determined by the light in the room at the time the image was captured, the aperture and color shift of the camera, and so on. How would you even know where one object begins and another ends, let alone which object was which and if there were any people present? In a depth image, on the other hand, the color of each pixel tells you how far that part of the image is from the camera. Since these values directly correspond to where the objects are in space, they're much more useful in determining where one object begins, where another ends, and if there are any people around. Also, because of how the Kinect creates its depth image (about which you'll learn more in a second) it is not sensitive to the light conditions in the room at the time it was captured. The Kinect will capture the same depth image in a bright room as in a pitch black one. This makes depth images more reliable and even easier for a computer program to understand.

We'll explore this aspect of depth images much more thoroughly in Chapter 2.

A depth image also contains accurate three-dimensional information about whatever's in front of it. Unlike a conventional camera, which captures how things *look*, a depth camera captures where things *are*. The result is that we can use the data from a depth camera like the Kinect to reconstruct a 3D model of whatever the camera sees. We can then manipulate this model, viewing it from additional angles interactively, combining it with other preexisting 3D models, and even using it as part of a digital fabrication process to produce new physical objects. None of this can be done with conventional color cameras.

We'll begin exploring these possibilities in Chapter 3 and then continue with them in Chapter 5 when we investigate scanning for fabrication.

And finally, since depth images are so much easier to process than conventional color images, we can run some truly cutting-edge processing on them. Specifically, we can use them to detect and track individual people, even locating their individual joints and body parts. In many ways, this is the Kinect's most exciting capability. In fact, Microsoft developed the Kinect specifically for the opportunities this body-detection ability offered to video games (more about this in "Who Made the Kinect?" on page 6). Tracking users' individual body parts creates amazing possibilities for our own interactive applications. Thankfully, we have access to software that can perform this processing and simply give us the location of the users. We don't have to analyze the depth image ourselves in order to obtain this information, but it's only accessible because of the depth image's suitability for processing.

We'll work extensively with the user-tracking data in Chapter 4.

What's Inside? How Does It Work?

If you remove the black plastic casing from the Kinect, what will you find? What are the hardware components that make the Kinect work, and how do they work together to give the Kinect its abilities? Let's take a look. Figure 1-1 shows a picture of a Kinect that's been freed from its case.

Figure 1-1. *A Kinect with its plastic casing removed, revealing (from left to right) its IR projector, RGB camera, and IR camera. (Photo courtesy of iFixit.)*

The first thing I always notice when looking at the Kinect *au natural* is its uncanny resemblance to various cute movie robots. From *Short Circuit*'s Johnny 5 to Pixar's WALL-E, for decades movie designers have been creating human-looking robots with cameras for eyes. It seems somehow appropriate (or maybe just inevitable) that the Kinect, the first computer peripheral to bring cutting-edge computer vision capabilities into our homes, would end up looking so much like one of these robots.

Unlike these movie robots, though, the Kinect seems to actually have three eyes: the two in its center and one off all the way to one side. That "third eye" is the secret to how the Kinect works. Like most robot "eyes," the two protuberances at the center of the Kinect are cameras, but the Kinect's third eye is actually an infrared projector. Infrared light has a wavelength that's longer than that of visible light so we cannot see it with the naked eye. Infrared is perfectly harmless—we're constantly exposed to it every day in the form of sunlight.

The Kinect's infrared projector shines a grid of infrared dots over everything in front of it. These dots are normally invisible to us, but it is possible to capture a picture of them using an IR camera. Figure 1-2 shows an example of what the dots from the Kinect's projector look like.

I captured this image using the Kinect itself. One of those two cameras I pointed out earlier (one of the Kinect's two "eyes") is an IR camera. It's a sensor specifically designed to capture infrared light. In Figure 1-1, an image of the Kinect naked without its outer case, the IR camera is the one on the right. If you look closely, you can see that this camera's lens has a greenish iridescent sheen as compared with the standard visible light camera next to it.

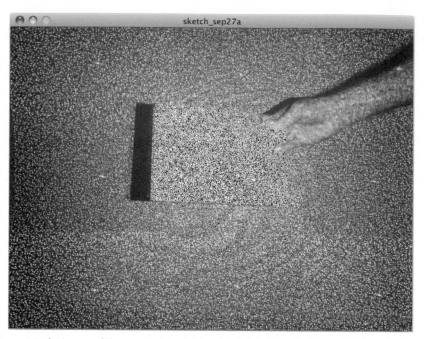

Figure 1-2. *An image of the normally invisible grid of dots from the Kinect's infrared projector. Taken with the Kinect's IR camera.*

So, the Kinect can see the grid of infrared dots that is projecting onto the objects in front of it. But how does it translate this image into information about the distance of those objects? In the factory where it was made, each Kinect is calibrated to know exactly where each dot from its projector appears when projected against a flat wall at a known distance. Look at the image of the IR projection again. Notice how the dots on the notebook I'm holding up in front of the wall seem pushed forward and shifted out of position? Any object that is closer than the Kinect's calibration distance will push these dots out of position in one direction, and any object that's farther away will push them out of position in the other direction. Since the Kinect is calibrated to know the original position of all of these dots, it can use their displacement to figure out the distance of the objects in that part of the scene. In every part of the image that the Kinect captures from the IR camera, each dot will be a little out of position from where the Kinect was expecting to see it. The result is that the Kinect can turn this IR image of a grid of dots into depth data that captures the distance of everything it can see.

There are certain limitations that are inherent in how this system works. For example, notice the black shadow at the edge of the objects in the IR image. None of the dots from the Kinect's infrared projection are reaching that part of the scene. All of them are being stopped and reflected back by a closer object. That means the Kinect won't be able to figure out any depth information about that part of the scene. We'll discuss these limitations in much more detail when we start working with depth images in code. And we'll revisit them again throughout the book every time we introduce a new technique, from drawing 3D point clouds to tracking users. As you learn these techniques, keep in mind how the Kinect is actually gathering its depth data. A lot of the data the Kinect provides seems so magical that it's easy to fall into thinking of it as having a perfect three-dimensional picture of the scene in front of it. If you're ever tempted to think this way, remember this grid of dots. The Kinect can only see what these dots from its projector can hit.

This depth information is the basis of the most fun stuff the Kinect can do, from acting as a 3D scanner to detecting the motion of people. We're going to spend the rest of the book working with it in one way or another. However, capturing depth images isn't the only thing the Kinect can do. There's a lot of other hardware inside this case, and as long as we're in here, it's worth pointing it out.

We've already mentioned the first additional piece of hardware. It's the Kinect's other "eye." Next to the IR camera, the Kinect also has a color camera. This camera has a digital sensor that's similar to the one in many web cams and small digital cameras. It has a relatively low resolution (640 by 480 pixels).

By itself, this color camera is not particularly interesting. It's just a run-of-the mill low-quality web cam. But since it's attached to the Kinect at a known distance from the IR camera, the Kinect can line up the color image from this camera with the depth information captured by its IR camera. That means it's possible to alter the color image based on its depth (for example, hiding anything more than a certain distance away). And, conversely, it's possible to "color in" the 3D images created from the depth information, creating 3D scans or virtual environments with realistic color.

In addition to cameras, the Kinect has four other sensors you might find slightly surprising in a depth camera: microphones. These microphones are distributed around the Kinect much as your ears are distributed around your head. Their purpose is not just to let the Kinect capture sound. For that, one microphone would have been enough. By using many microphones together, the Kinect can not only capture sound, but also locate that sound within the room. For example, if multiple players are speaking voice commands to control a game, the Kinect can tell which commands are coming from which player. This is a powerful and intriguing feature, but we're not going to explore it in this book. Just covering the Kinect's imaging features is a rich enough topic to keep us busy. And also, at the time of this writing, the Kinect's audio features are not available in the library we'll be using to access the Kinect. At the end of the book, we'll discuss ways you can move beyond Processing to work with the Kinect in other environments and languages. One of the options discussed is Microsoft's own Kinect Software Developer Kit, which provides access to the Kinect's spatial audio features. If you are especially intrigued by this possibility, I recommend exploring that route (and sharing what you learn online—the Kinect's audio capabilities are among its less-explored features).

The last feature of the Kinect may seem even more surprising: it can move. Inside the Kinect's plastic base is a small motor and a series of gears. By turning this motor, the Kinect can tilt its cameras and speakers up and down. The motor's range of motion is limited to about 30 degrees. Microsoft added the motor to allow the Kinect to work in a greater variety of rooms. Depending on the size of the room and the position of the furniture, people playing with the Xbox may stand closer to the Kinect or farther away from it and they may be more or less spread out. The motor gives the Kinect the ability to aim itself at

Warning

It is also possible to access the color camera at the higher resolution of 1280 by 1024. However, the trade-off for doing so is that the data arrives at a lower frame rate: 10 frames per second rather than the 30 frames per second that is standard for the 640 by 480 pixel resolution.

the best point for capturing the people who are trying to play with it. Like the Kinect's audio capabilities, control of the motor is not accessible in the library we'll be using throughout this book. However, it is accessible in one of the other open source libraries that lets you work with the Kinect in Processing: Dan Shiffman's Kinect Library (*http://www.shiffman.net/p5/kinect/*).

I'll explain shortly why I chose a library that does not have access to the motor over this one that does for the examples in this book. In fact I'll give you a whole picture of the ins and outs of Kinect development: who created the Kinect in the first place, how it became possible for us to use it in our own applications, and all the different options we have for doing so. But before we complete our discussion of the Kinect's hardware, I want to point out a resource you can use to find out more. iFixit is a website that takes apart new electronic gadgets to document what's inside of them. Whenever a new smartphone or tablet comes out, the staff of iFixit goes out and buys one and carefully disassembles it, photographing and describing everything they find inside, and then posts the results online. On the day of its launch, they performed one of these "teardowns" on the Kinect. If you want to learn more about how the Kinect's hardware works, from the kinds of screws it has to all of its electronic components, their report is the place to look: iFixit's Kinect Teardown (*http://www.ifixit.com/Teardown/Microsoft-Kinect-Teardown/4066*).

Who Made the Kinect?

The Kinect is a Microsoft product. It's a peripheral for Microsoft's Xbox 360 video game system. However, Microsoft did not create the Kinect entirely on its own. In the broad sense, the Kinect is the product of many years of academic research conducted both by Microsoft (at their Microsoft Research division) and elsewhere throughout the computer vision community. If you're mathematically inclined, Richard Szeliski of Microsoft Research created a textbook based on computer vision courses he taught at the University of Washington that covers many of the recent advances that led up to the Kinect: *Computer Vision: Algorithms and Applications* (*http://szeliski.org/Book*).

In a much narrower sense, the Kinect's hardware was developed by PrimeSense, an Israeli company that had previously produced other depth cameras using the same basic IR projection technique. PrimeSense worked closely with Microsoft to produce a depth camera that would work with the software and algorithms Microsoft had developed in their research. PrimeSense licensed the hardware design to Microsoft to create the Kinect but still owns the basic technology themselves. In fact, PrimeSense has already announced that they're working with ASUS to create a product called the Wavi Xtion, a depth camera similar to the Kinect that is meant to integrate with your TV and personal computer for apps and games.

Until November 2010, the combination of Microsoft's software with PrimeSense's hardware was known by its codename, "Project Natal." On November 4, the device was launched as the "Microsoft Kinect" and went on public sale for the first time. At this point, a new chapter began in the life of the project. The Kinect was a major commercial success. It sold upward of 10 million units in the first month after its release, making it the fastest selling computer peripheral in history.

But for our purposes maybe an even more important landmark was the creation of open source drivers for the Kinect. As soon as the Kinect was released, programmers around the world began working on creating open source drivers that would let anyone access the data from the Kinect.

The Kinect plugs into your computer via USB, just like many other devices such as mice, keyboards, and conventional web cams. All USB devices require software "drivers" to operate. Device drivers are special pieces of software that run on your computer and communicate with external hardware on behalf of other programs. Once you have the driver for a particular piece of hardware, no other program needs to understand how to talk to that device. Your chat program doesn't need to know about your particular brand of web cam because your computer has a driver that makes it accessible to every program. Microsoft only intended the Kinect to work with the Xbox 360, so it did not release drivers that let programs access the Kinect on normal personal computers. By creating an open source driver for the Kinect, this group was trying to make the Kinect accessible to all programs on every operating system.

Also on the day of the Kinect's release, Adafruit, a New York–based company that sells kits for open source hardware projects, announced a bounty of $2,000 to the first person who produced open source drivers that would let anyone access the Kinect's data. After a Microsoft spokesperson reacted negatively to the idea of the bounty, Adafruit responded by increasing the total sum to $3,000.

Meanwhile, Josh Blake, a programmer working in the field of Natural User Interfaces, created the OpenKinect community to bring together people working on the project of creating open source drivers into a single collaborative effort. On November 10th, Hector Martin created the first public version of a working driver that could access the depth image from the Kinect and claimed the bounty from Adafruit. He then joined the OpenKinect project, which continues to improve and maintain the drivers to this day.

The creation of an open source driver led to an explosion of libraries that made the Kinect accessible in a variety of environments. Quickly thereafter, the first demonstration projects that used these libraries began to emerge. Among the early exciting projects that demonstrated the possibilities of the Kinect was the work of Oliver Kreylos, a computer researcher at UC Davis. Kreylos had previously worked extensively with various virtual reality and remote presence systems. The Kinect's 3D scanning capabilities fit neatly into his existing work, and he quickly demonstrated sophisticated applications that used the Kinect to reconstruct a full-color 3D scene including integrating animated 3D models and point-of-view controls. Kreylos's demonstrations caught the imagination of many people online and were even featured prominently in a *New York Times* article reporting on early Kinect "hacks."

A WORD ABOUT THE WORD "HACK"

When used to describe a technical project, "hack" has two distinct meanings. It is most commonly used among geeks as a form of endearment to indicate a clever idea that solves a difficult problem. For example, you might say, "Wow, you managed to scan your cat using just a Kinect and a mirror? Nice hack!" This usage is not fully positive. It implies that the solution, though clever, might be a temporary stopgap measure inferior to permanently solving the problem. For example, you might say "I got the app to compile by copying the library into is dependencies folder. It's a hack but it works." In the popular imagination, the word is connected with intentional violation of security systems for nefarious purposes. In that usage, "hack" would refer to politically motivated distributed denial of service attacks or social engineering attempts to steal credit card numbers, rather than clever or creative technical solutions.

Since the release of the OpenKinect driver, the word "hack" has become the default term to refer to most work based on the Kinect, especially in popular media coverage. The trouble with this usage is that it conflates the two definitions of "hack" that I described above. In addition to appreciating clever or creative uses of the Kinect, referring to them as "hacks" implies that they involve nefarious or illicit use of Microsoft's technology. The OpenKinect drivers do not allow programmers to interfere with the Xbox in anyway—to cheat at games, or otherwise violate the security of Microsoft's system. In fact after the initial release of the OpenKinect drivers, Microsoft themselves made public announcements explaining that no "hacking" had taken place and that, while they encouraged players to use the Kinect with their Xbox for "the best possible experience," they would not interfere with the open source effort. So, while many Kinect applications are "hacks" in the sense that they are creative and clever, none are "hacks" in the more popular sense of nefarious or illicit. Therefore, I think it is better not to refer to applications that use the Kinect as "hacks" at all. In addition to avoiding confusion, since this is a book designed to teach you some of the fundamental programming concepts you'll need to work with the Kinect, we don't want our applications to be "hacks" in the sense of badly designed or temporary. They're lessons and starting points, not "hacks."

Not long thereafter, this work started to trickle down from computer researchers to students and others in the creative coding community. Dan Shiffman, a professor at NYU's Interactive Telecommunications Program, built on the work of the OpenKinect project to create a library for working with the Kinect in Processing, a toolkit for software sketching that's used to teach the fundamentals of computer programming to artists and designers.

In response to all of this interest, PrimeSense released their software for working with the Kinect. In addition to drivers that allowed programmers to access the Kinect's depth information, PrimeSense included more sophisticated software that would process the raw depth image to detect users and locate the position of their joints in three dimensions. They called their system OpenNI, for "Natural Interaction." OpenNI represented a major advance in the capabilities available to the enthusiast community working with the Kinect. For the first time, the user data that made the Kinect such a great tool for building interactive projects became available to creative coding projects. While the OpenKinect project spurred interest in the Kinect and created many of the applications that demonstrated the creative possibilities of the device, Open-NI's user data opened a whole new set of opportunities. The user data provided by OpenNI gives an application accurate information on the position of users' joints (head, shoulders, elbows, wrists, chest, hips, knees, ankles, and feet) at all times while they're using the application. This information is the holy grail for interactive applications. If you want your users to be able to control something in your application via hand gestures or dance moves, or their position within the room, by far the best data to have is the precise positions of hands, hips, and feet. While the OpenKinect project may eventually be able to provide this data, and while Microsoft's SDK provides it for developers working on Windows, at this time, OpenNI is the best option for programmers who want to work with this user data (in addition to the depth data) in their choice of platform and programming language.

So now, at the end of the history lesson, we come to the key issue for this book. The reason we care about the many options for working with the Kinect and the diverse history that led to them is that each offers a different set of affordances for the programmer trying to learn to work with the Kinect.

For example, the OpenKinect drivers provide access to the Kinect's servos while OpenNI's do not. Another advantage of OpenKinect is its software license. The contributors to the OpenKinect project released their drivers under a fully open source license, specifically a dual Apache 2.0/GPL 2.0 license. Without getting into the particulars of this license choice, this means that you can use OpenKinect code in your own commercial and open source projects without having to pay a license fee to anyone or worrying about the intellectual property in it belonging to anyone else. For the full details about the particulars of this license choice see the policy page on OpenKinect's wiki (*http://openkinect.org/wiki/Policies*).

The situation with OpenNI, on the other hand, is more complex. PrimeSense has provided two separate pieces of software that are useful to us. First is the OpenNI framework. This includes the drivers for accessing the basic depth data from the Kinect. OpenNI is licensed under the LGPL, a license similar in spirit to OpenKinect's license. (For more about this license, see its page on the GNU site, *http://www.gnu.org/licenses/lgpl.html*.) However, one of OpenNI's most exciting features is its user tracking. This is the feature I discussed above in which an algorithm processes the depth image to determine the position of all of the joints of any users within the camera's range. This feature is not covered by OpenNI LGPL license. Instead, it (along with many of OpenNI's other more advanced capabilities) is provided by an external module, called NITE. NITE is not available under an open source license. It is a commercial product belonging to PrimeSense. Its source code is not available online. PrimeSense does provide a royalty-free license that you can use to make projects that use NITE with OpenNI, but it is not currently clear if you can use this license to produce commercial projects, even though using it for education purposes such as working through the examples of this book is clearly allowed.

> To learn more about the subtleties and complexities involved in open source licensing, consult Understanding Open Source and Free Software Licensing (*http://oreilly.com/openbook/osfreesoft/book/index.html*) by Andrew St. Laurent.

OpenNI is governed by a consortium of companies led by PrimeSense that includes robotics research lab Willow Garage as well as the computer manufacturer Asus. OpenNI is designed to work not just with the Kinect but with other depth cameras. It is already compatible with PrimeSense's reference camera as well as the upcoming Asus Xtion camera, which I mentioned earlier. This is a major advantage because it means code we write using OpenNI to work with the Kinect will continue to work with newer depth cameras as they are released, saving us from needing to rewrite our applications depending on what camera we want to use.

All of these factors add up to a difficult decision about what platform to use. On the one hand, OpenKinect's clear license and the open and friendly community that surrounds the project is very attractive. The speed and enthusiasm with which OpenKinect evolved from Adafruit's bounty to a well-organized and creative community is one of the high points of the recent history of open source software. On the other hand, at this point in time OpenNI offers some compelling technical advantages—most important, the ability to work with user tracking data. Since this feature is maybe the Kinect's single biggest selling point for interactive applications, it seems critical to cover it in this book. Further, for a book author, the possibility that the code examples you use will stay functional for a longer time period is an attractive proposition. By their very nature, technical books like this one begin to go stale the moment they are written. Hence anything that keeps the information fresh and useful to the reader is a major benefit. In this context, the possibility that code written with OpenNI will still work on next year's model of the Kinect, or even a competing depth camera, is hard to pass up.

Taking all of these factors into account, I chose to use OpenNI as the basis of the code in this book. Thankfully, one thing that both OpenNI and Open-Kinect have in common is a good Processing library that works with them. I mentioned above that Dan Shiffman created a Processing library on top of OpenKinect soon after its drivers were first released. Max Rheiner, an artist and lecturer in the interaction design department of Zurich University, created a similar Processing library that works with OpenNI for use by his students. Rheiner's library is called SimpleOpenNI and it supports many of OpenNI's more advanced features. SimpleOpenNI comes with an installer that makes it straightforward to install all of the OpenNI code and modules that you need to get started. I'll walk you through installing it and using it starting at the beginning of Chapter 2. We'll spend much of that chapter and the following two learning all of the functions that SimpleOpenNI provides for working with the Kinect, from accessing the depth image to building a complete three-dimensional scene to tracking users.

Kinect Artists

This book will introduce you to the Kinect in a number of ways. We've already looked at how the Kinect works and how it came into existence. In the next few chapters, we'll cover the technical and programming basics, and we'll build a raft of example applications. In the last three chapters, we'll get into some of the application areas the Kinect has opened, covering the basics of what it takes to work in those fascinating fields.

However, before we dive into all of that, I wanted to give you a sense of some of the work that has gone before you. Ever since its release, a diverse set of artists and technologists has made use of the Kinect to produce a wide range of interesting projects. Many of these practitioners had been working in related fields for years before the release of the Kinect and were able to rapidly integrate it into their work. A few others have come to it from other fields and explored how the possibilities it introduces could transform their own work. All have demonstrated their own portions of the range of creative and technical possibilities opened up by this new technology. Together, they've created a community of people who can inspire and inform you as you begin your own Kinect projects.

In this section, I will introduce the work of several of these practitioners: Kyle McDonald, Robert Hodgin, Elliot Woods, blablabLAB, Nicolas Burrus, Oliver Kreylos, Alejandro Crawford, Josh Blake, and Adafruit. I'll provide some brief background on their work and then the text of an interview that I performed with each of them. In these interviews, I asked the developers to discuss how they came to integrate the Kinect into their own work, how their backgrounds transformed how they wished to apply the Kinect, how they work with it and think about it, and what they're excited about doing with the Kinect and related technologies in the future.

I hope that reading these interviews will give you ideas for your own work and also make you feel like you could become a part of the thriving collaborative community that's formed up around this amazing piece of technology.

Kyle McDonald

Kyle McDonald (Figure 1-3) is an artist, technologist, and teacher living in New York City. He is a core contributor to openFrameworks, a creative coding framework in the C++ programming language. Since 2009 he has conducted extensive work toward democratizing real-time 3D scanning beginning by producing his own DIY structured-light scanner using a projector and a web cam. He has worked widely with the Kinect since its release including as artist-in-residence at MakerBot where he put together a complete toolkit for creating 3D scans with the Kinect and printing them on the MakerBot. Artistically, his work frequently explores ideas of public performance and extremely long duration. In his 2009 "keytweeter" performance, he broadcast every keystroke he entered into his personal computer for a full year via Twitter (http://twitter.com/keytweeter). In 2010, he created "The Janus Machine" with fellow openFrameworks contributors Zach Lieberman and Theo Watson. "The Janus Machine" is a 3D photo booth that turns the user into a two-faced Janus by pairing them with a structured light scan of their own face. Watch a video of The Janus Machine at http://vimeo.com/16197436.

Figure 1-3. *Artist and technologist Kyle McDonald has been building DIY 3D scanners for years.*

How did you first get interested in 3D scanning? What drew you to it as a technique and how did you first set out to learn about it?

At the beginning of 2009, I saw some work called "Body/Traces" from artist Sophie Kahn and dancer/choreographer Lisa Parra. They were using the DA-VID 3D scanning software, with a Lego-driven line laser and a web cam, to scan a dancer. It took about one minute to take a single scan, which meant that one second of stop-motion 3D-scanned video could take 10 to 20 minutes to shoot. I was enamored with the quality of the scans and immediately started dreaming about the possibilities of real-time capture for interaction. So I began working on a practical problem: making a faster 3D scanner. My first scanner was based on a simple intuition about using a projector to display gray codes instead of a laser with its single line. That brought the time down from a few minutes to a few seconds. Then I discovered structured light research while digging around Wikipedia, started reading academic papers, and emailed every researcher who would answer my naive questions. This was months after Radiohead's "House of Cards" video was released, so I should have known about structured light already. But the tagline for that video was "made without cameras," so I assumed it was built on high-end technology that I didn't have access to.

What interactive possibilities do 3D scanning techniques open up? How are the affordances they offer fundamentally different from other forms of digital imaging?

Real-time 3D scanning is fundamentally different from other kinds of imaging in that it focuses on geometry rather than light; or shape rather than texture. This can make a huge difference when trying to accomplish something as simple as presence detection. Having access to information like position, surface normals, or depth edges opens up possibilities for understanding a scene in ways that are otherwise practically impossible. For example, knowing which direction someone's palm is facing can easily be determined by a lenient plane fitting algorithm, or a simple blur across the surface normals. This kind of information has made a huge difference for skeleton tracking research, as our shape is much less variable than the way we look.

Much of the development that led to the Kinect came out of surveillance and security technology. Do you think this provenance makes privacy and surveillance natural themes for creative work that uses the Kinect? How can art and interactive design inform our understanding of these kinds of issues?

Whenever you have a computer making judgements about a scene based on camera input, there is the potential to engage with surveillance as a theme. But if you look at the first demos people made with the Kinect, you'll find an overwhelming majority explore the creative potential and don't address surveillance. I think artists have just as much a responsibility to comment directly on the social context of a technology as they have a responsibility to create their own context. By addressing the creative potential of the Kinect, artists are simultaneously critiquing the social context of the device: they're rejecting the original application and appropriating the technology, working toward the future they want to see.

Chapter 1

Much of your technical work with the Kinect has centered on using it as a 3D scanner for digital fabrication. What are the fundamental challenges involved in using the Kinect in this way? What role do you see for 3D scanners in the future of desktop fabrication?

The Kinect was built for skeleton tracking, not for 3D scanning. As a 3D scanner, it has problems with noise, holes, accuracy, and scale. And in the best case, a depth image is still just a single surface. If you want something that's printable, you need to scan it from all sides and reconstruct a single closed volume. Combining, cleaning, and simplifying the data from a Kinect for 3D printing can be a lot of work. There are other scanners that mostly solve these problems, and I can imagine combining them with desktop printing into something like a 3D "photocopier" or point-and-shoot "Polaroid" replicator.

As part of your artist residency at MakerBot, you disassembled a Kinect to look at its internals. What did you learn in this process that surprised you? Do you think we'll see open source versions of this hardware soon?

I was surprised with how big it is! The whole space inside the Kinect is really filled up with electronics. There's even a fan on one side, which I've only ever heard turn on once: when I removed the Peltier cooler from the IR projector. The tolerance is also really tight: for all the times I've dropped my Kinect, I'm surprised it hasn't gone out of alignment. If you unscrew the infrared projector or the infrared camera and just wiggle them a little bit, you can see that the depth image slowly disappears from the sides of the frame because the chip can't decode it anymore.

I don't expect to see open source versions of the Kinect hardware any time soon, mainly because of the patents surrounding the technique. That said, I'd love to see a software implementation of the decoding algorithm that normally runs on the Kinect. This would allow multiple cameras to capture the same pattern from multiple angles, increasing the resolution and accuracy of the scan.

You've done a lot of interesting work making advanced computer vision research accessible to creative coding environments like openFrameworks. How do you keep up with current research? Where do you look to find new work and how do you overcome the sometimes steep learning curve required to read papers in this area? More generally, how do you think research can and should inform creative coding as a whole?

The easiest way to keep up with the current research is to work on impossible projects. When I get to the edge of what I think is possible, and then go a little further, I discover research from people much smarter than myself who have been thinking about the same problem. The papers can be tough at first, but the more you read, the more you realize they're just full of idiosyncrasies. For example, a lot of image processing papers like to talk about images as continuous when in practice you're always dealing with discrete pixels. Or they'll write huge double summations with lots of subscripts just to be super clear about what kind of blur they're doing. Or they'll use unfamiliar notation for talking about something simple like the distance between two points. As you relate more of these idiosyncrasies to the operations you're already familiar with, the papers become less opaque.

Artists regularly take advantage of current research in order to solve technical problems that come up in the creation of their work. But I feel that it's also important to engage the research on its own terms: try implementing their ideas, tweaking their work, understanding their perspective. It's a kind of political involvement, and it's not for everyone. But if you don't address the algorithms and ideas directly, your work will be governed by their creators' intentions.

If you could do one thing with the Kinect (or a future depth camera) that seems impossible now what would that be?

I want to scan and visualize breaking waves. I grew up in San Diego, near the beach, and I've always felt that there's something incredibly powerful about ocean waves. They're strong, but ephemeral. Built from particles, they're more of a connotation of a form than a solid object. Each is unique and unpredictable. I think it also represents a sort of technical impossibility in my mind: there's no way to project onto it, and the massive discontinuities preclude most stereo approaches. But if studying 3D scanning has taught me anything, it's that there's always some trick to getting the data you want that comes from the place you least expect.

Robert Hodgin

Robert Hodgin is an artist and programmer working in San Francisco. He was one of the founders of the Barbarian Group, a digital marketing and design agency in New York. Hodgin has been a prominent member of the creative coding community since before that community had a name, creating groundbreaking work in Flash, Processing, and the C++ framework, Cinder. He is known for creating beautiful visual experiences using simulations of natural forces and environments. His work tends to have a high degree of visual polish that makes sophisticated use of advanced features of graphical programming techniques such as OpenGL and GLSL shaders. He has produced visuals to accompany the live performances of such well-known musicians as Aphex Twin, Peter Gabriel, and Zoe Keating. Soon after the release of the Kinect, Hodgin released Body Dysmorphia (http://roberthodgin. com/body-dysmorphia/), an interactive application that used the depth data from the Kinect to distort the user's body interactively in real time to make it appear fat and bloated or thin and drawn. Body Dysmorphia was one of the first applications of the Kinect to connect depth imagery with a vivid artist subject and to produce results that had a high degree of visual polish. Hodgin is currently creative director at Bloom, a San Francisco startup working to combine data visualization with game design to create tools for visual discovery.

How did you first hear about the Kinect/Project Natal? Why did it capture your interest?

I first heard about the Kinect when it was making the rounds during E3 in 2009. I am a bit of a video game fan, so I try to keep up-to-date with the latest and greatest. When I saw the Kinect demos, I must admit the whole thing seemed ridiculous to me. The demos were rather odd and didn't make me want to play with the Kinect at all. I had the same reaction I had to the PlayStation Move.

Because of my pessimistic attitude, it is no surprise the Kinect did not capture my interest until right around the time people started posting open source drivers to allow my Mac laptop to get ahold of the depth information. That is when I decided to go buy one. Shortly after the Kinect CinderBlock was released, I hooked up the Kinect and started to play around with the depth data.

Prior to the Kinect's release, I had done some experimentation with augmenting live web cam feeds using hand-made depth maps. I set a camera on the roof of my old office and pointed it towards the Marina district of San Francisco. Since the camera was stationary, I was able to take a still image from the cam and trace out a rudimentary depth map. Using this five-layered depth information, I could add smoke and particle effects to the view so that it looked like a couple buildings were on fire. The effect was fairly basic, but it helped me appreciate how depth information could be very useful for such effects. With it, I could make sure foreground buildings occluded the smoke and particle effects.

Once I bought the Kinect, I knew I wanted to explore these older concepts using proper depth data. That is when I realized how fantastic it was to have access to an extremely affordable, good quality depth camera. After a couple weeks, I had made the Body Dysmorphia project and it got a lot of good reactions. It is one of my favorite projects to date.

I still have not hooked the Kinect up to my Xbox 360.

A lot of your work has involved creating screen-based visuals that are inspired by nature. Flocking and particle systems. Light effects and planet simulations. However, in Body Dysmorphia you used your actual body as an input. How does having input from the physical world alter the way you think about the project? Is part of what you're designing for here your interaction with the app or are you exclusively focused on the final visual result? Have you thought about installing Body Dysmorphia (or any of your other Kinect-based work) in a public exhibition venue or otherwise distributing it in order to share the interaction as well as the visual results?

For all of the Kinect projects I have created, I rarely got to work with a set idea of what I wanted to make. The Body Dysmorphia piece actually came about by accident. I was finding ways to turn the depth map into a normal map because I thought it might be interesting to use virtual lighting to augment the actual lighting in the room. I was getting annoyed by the depth shadow that appears on the left side of all the objects in the Kinect's view. I think this is just a result of the depth camera not being able to be situated in the exact same place as the infrared projection. I wanted to find ways to hide this depth shadow so I tried pushing the geometry out along the normals I had calculated to try and cover up the gap in the depth data. It was one of those surprising *aha* moments and instantly became the focus of the next month of experimentation. The effect was so lush and unexpected.

I am currently working on a Cinder and Kinect tutorial, which I will be releasing soon. It will cover everything from just creating a point cloud from the depth data all the way up to recreating the Body Dysmorphia project. I am doing this for a couple reasons. I wanted to clean up the code and make it more presentable, but I was also approached by a couple different people who want to use Body Dysmorphia as installations for festivals. The code was definitely sloppy and hacked together so I broke it all down and rebuilt it from scratch with extra emphasis on extensibility and ease of implementation. I look forward to releasing the code so that I can see what others can do with it.

You've worked with musicians such as Aphex Twin, Peter Gabriel, and Zoe Keating to produce visuals for live performance. These projects have ranged from prerendered to synced to audio to fully interactive. How do you approach music as a starting point for visual work? Do you think of this work as a visualization of the music or as part of a theatrical performance? Have you considered including music or sound as an accompaniment to your other visual work?

Music has played a really large role in my development as a creative coder. Early on, when I was just getting started with particle engines, I got bored with having to provide all the input. I was just making elaborate cursor trails. I wanted something more automated. So I entered my Perlin noise phase where I let Perlin noise control the behavior of the particles. But eventually, this became a bit frustrating because I wanted something more organic. That is when I tried using live audio data to affect the visuals. I usually listen to music while I code, so if I could use microphone input for the parameterization of the project, I could have a much larger variety of behaviors. I didn't set out to make audio visualizers. I just wanted some robust real-time organic data to control my simulations.

When I need to make an audio visualization, as opposed to just using audio as an easy input data, I try to consider the components of the audio itself. If it is electronica and not too beat heavy and is completely lacking in vocals, the visualizations are very easy. It just works. But once you start adding string instruments or vocals or multilayered drum tracks, the FFT analysis can very quickly start to look like random noise. It becomes very difficult to isolate beats or match vocals.

Zoe Keating and I have worked together a couple times. I love collaborating with her simply because I love her music. The couple times we have collaborated were for live performance. I did very little live audio analysis. String instruments can be challenging to analyze effectively. I ended up doing manually triggered effects so essentially, I played the visuals while she played the audio.

Peter Gabriel was different in that he was performing with a full orchestra. They practiced to a click track and I knew they would not be deviating from this. I was able to make a render that was influenced by the beat on the click track, which made sure the final piece stayed in sync with the vocals.

Aphex Twin visuals were the easiest to make. I made an application using Cinder that took in Kinect data and created a handful of preset modes that could be triggered and modified by Aphex Twin's concert VJ. There was no audio input for that project simply because the deadline was very short.

Chapter 1

I am very excited to start playing around with the OpenNI library. Getting to use the skeleton data is going to be a fantastic addition to the Kinect projects. I will easily be able to determine where the head and hands are in 3D space so I could have the audio emanate out from these points in the form of a environment altering shockwave. The early tests have been very promising. Soon, I will post some test applications that will take advantage of this effect.

You've written eloquently about balancing rigorous technical learning with unstructured exploration and play in creative coding work. How do your technical ideas interact with your creative ones? Which comes first, the chicken or the egg, the technical tools or the creative ideas?

Many people would be surprised to hear I have no idea what I am doing half the time. I just like to experiment. I like to play and I constantly wonder, "what if?" When I first started to learn to code in ActionScript, much of my coding process could be described as experimental trigonometry. I would make something then start slapping sine and cosine on all the variables to see what they did. I didn't know much about trig, so my way of learning was to just start sticking random trig in my code haphazardly until I found something interesting.

The programming tools you use have evolved from Flash to Processing to OpenGL with C++ and shaders. What tools are you interested in starting with now? What do you have your eye on that's intriguing but you haven't played with yet? Also, do you ever think about jumping back to Flash or Processing for a project to see if those constraints might bring out something creative?

I still have an intense love for Processing. Without Processing, I am not sure I would have ever learned enough coding to feel comfortable attempting to learn C++. Casey and Ben and the rest of the Processing community have made something wonderful. I am forever in their debt for making something so approachable and easy to learn, but still so very powerful.

I am pretty set on sticking with Cinder. Thanks to the Cinder creator, Andrew Bell, I have developed a love for C++. I still hate it at times and curses can fly, but I love working with a coding language that has such a long history of refinement. It also helps that I am friends with Andrew so he holds my hand and guides me through the prickly bits. The more I use Cinder, the more in awe I am at the amount of work that went into it. I also plan on continuing to learn GLSL. I am a big fan of shaders.

If you could do one thing with the Kinect that seems impossible now, what would that be?

I would love to be able to revisit the early project where I try and augment a web cam view of a cityscape. If the range of the Kinect could be extended for a couple miles, that would be fantastic. Alternately, I would also love to have a Kinect that is capable of doing high-resolution scans of objects or faces. If the Kinect had an effective range of 1 inch to 2 miles, that would be perfect.

Elliot Woods

Elliot Woods (Figure 1-4) is a programmer, designer, artist, and physicist. He is codirector of Kimchi and Chips, an interdisciplinary art and design studio based in London and Seoul. Kimchi and Chips is known for innovative use of the Kinect as a tool for projection mapping, a technique that matches projected computer graphics to the spatial features of architecture and objects. Woods has pioneered the use of the

Kinect to extend the art of projection mapping to moving dynamic objects. His Kinect Haidouken project (http://vimeo. com/18713117) used the Kinect to give users control of a projected light source. His ˣLit Tree installation (http://www.kimchiandchips.com/littree.php) used the Kinect to perform projection mapping onto the moving leaves of a tree. His work has been exhibited in Yokohama, Manchester, London, Berlin, Milan, and Arhus, Denmark.

Figure 1-4. Programmer and artist Elliot Woods specializes in using the Kinect for projection mapping. Photo courtesy of Elliot Woods.

A lot of your work at Kimchi and Chips uses projection to bring objects and spaces to life. What is about projection that draws you to it as a medium?

We see projection as a great prototyping tool. I think of a projector as a dense array of little colored spotlights laid out in a grid.

Its invention is an artifact of consumer/business/education technology, but it is in itself quite a peculiar machine capable of visually controlling its surroundings. Its general use also means that there's plenty of fantastic affordable stuff that you can plug a projector into (powerful graphics card, video hardware, games consoles, and all that).

Our eyes (our cameras) are obviously very important to us. Most creatures have them, and for decades computer scientists have been dedicated to giving useful eyes to our artificial creatures. They give us a sense of the world around us and are arguably the most visceral. Cameras are our proxy eyes onto the real and virtual worlds, through streaming video, films, television, photos, video conferencing, but also now computer vision systems.

The projector is the antithesis to the camera. It's pretty much exactly the same thing, but acting in an inverse way to the camera. It sends light down millions of little beams, where a camera would collect light along millions of little beams. Through this it can (given enough brightness) affect a scene, as much as a camera can sense a scene. If the camera is the sensor, the projector is the actuator.

Since projectors are so closely matched with cameras, I'm surprised that there aren't known biological instances of the projector. Why wouldn't a creature want to be able to project and see the same way it can speak and listen?

An octopus can create highly convincing visual color images across its skin, demonstrating an evolutionary ability to generate images. But if you had a built-in light engine, what could you do if you had as much control over our local visual environment as a human eye could see?

Since we're cursed with the disability of having no built-in light engine, we have to rationally define what we'd like to achieve so that a computer and an electronic projector can do it for us, this is why I work with projectors.

How did you first start working with the Kinect? What made you excited about using it in your projects?

I heard about the Kinect (at the time Project Natal) around 2009. I wasn't very much believing in it at the time, it sounded too unreal.

I'd been playing with the Wiimote and PS3Eyes as HCI devices, and knew that if Project Natal ever came out, then the first thing to do would be to get that depth data out and into open development environments, and was suggesting to friends that we start a bounty for the hack. Luckily the Adafruit/JCL bounty came out, and the closed doors got busted ajar.

Kinect to me is about giving computers a 3D understanding of the scene in a cheap and easy to process way. The OpenNI/Kinect SDK options obviously allow for automatic understanding of people, but I'm more interested in getting a computer to know as much about its surroundings as it knows about the virtual worlds inside its memory.

A lot of the most prominent uses of projection mapping have taken place outside in public spaces. You tend to use it in more intimate interior spaces where it becomes interactive. How are the challenges different when making a projection interactive? What are the advantages of working in this more intimate setting?

There's a few reasons we keep a lot of our works *indoors*.

To make something big, you quickly lose control of your environment, and need a lot of cash to keep on top of things. The cash element also comes in because big public works attract sponsors/commissions from brands, which makes working in that space quite competitive. We don't want to become another *projection mapping* company who'll push your logo onto a five-story building. The whole field's becoming a little irresponsible and messy, we missed out on the innovation period for projecting onto buildings, and hope that advertising agencies/advertising rhetoric might back out of the field a bit so people can start working on something new.

We want to carry our identity into large scale outdoor works, which includes our research into projecting onto trees. We think this medium carries a lot of challenge and has surprisingly beautiful results, but most importantly is an untouched frontier to explore.

What programming languages and frameworks do you use? Has that changed or evolved over time?

If you fancy the long story…

I started out in Basic when I was about seven, copying code out the back of books. Sometimes I'd get my dad to do the typing for me. I was totally addicted to the idea of being part of the making of a piece of software. It took a while to grasp the basics past PRINT A$ and INPUT A$, and I can't remember much apart from the line numbers and getting quickly bogged down when creating repeatable logic.

After that, QuickBasic, then Visual Basic where I made my RCCI (Resistor Colour Code Interpreter) at the age of about 11. I was so proud of myself, I spent days trying to show off to my family. I'd made something that was useful, visible, and worked. This was the first real feeling of closure, or *deployment*. It's an emotion I still feel today when a project is complete.

At the end of college I was getting more into Visual Basic and started developing games, which felt like a decent career move at the time. Then into university I worked on mathematically driven interfaces and graphical elements for websites (now called generative graphics). Mid-university I started developing visual installations with projectors and Max/MSP with a group of friends, then I discovered VVVV, which blew my world.

On to the short story…

I love to use VVVV. VVVV is a massively underused/overpowered toolkit for media development. While the VVVV plugin system was still in its infancy (and I'd just gotten a Mac), I started developing with openFrameworks in parallel. This development was much slower than with VVVV, but more flexible, and importantly for a new Mac owner, platform independent.

Now that the VVVV plugin system has matured, it's capable of many of the things openFrameworks/Cinder can achieve, while retaining the runtime development paradigm that makes it so strong/quick to use/learn.

What was your background before starting Kimchi and Chips? With one of you based in London and one in Seoul, how did you meet? How do you collaborate remotely on projects that frequently have a physical or site-specific component to them?

I studied physics at Manchester; Mimi was running a successful design firm in Seoul. Then I started working in the digital media design field (multitouch, projection mapping, etc.) and Mimi started studying interaction design in Copenhagen Institute of Interaction Design.

We met at a conference in Aarhus, Denmark. She needed some help with a friend's project and saw that I might be a good person to ask. After that, we took on more projects and founded the company. Mimi moved back to Seoul after studying to be with her family, so the company moved with her.

Working apart, we keep in regular contact but also avoid getting too involved with what the other is doing. Often I'm doing a lot of coding and hardware design, while Mimi works on interaction scenarios, motion design, and communicating with the Korean clients.

How does the Kinect fit into your work? What new possibilities does it open up? Do you think it will be important to your work in the future?

Kinect gives us geometry information about a scene. We've begun to show what we'd love to use that for (see Figure 1-5). Hopefully, we'll get enough time to show all of our ideas.

Figure 1-5. *Elliot Woods projecting onto himself by using the Kinect to build a 3D model of the space. Photo courtesy of Elliot Woods.*

What was the seed of the Kinct Haidouken project? What inspired it? How did it relate to what you'd been working on before?

I knew I had to try getting a projector working with the geometry from the Kinect, to see what the results were like. A light source became a good way to demonstrate how the projection could be sensitive to the scene, and *create* something meaningful to the viewer. After waving the virtual light around with my mouse, I wanted to hold it in my hand. then once I had it in my hand, I wanted to throw it. Then I realised what I'd made.

What language and framework did you use for it?

It was C#/OpenNI.Net for the tracking bits and getting the data into a useful form to shift onto the GPU. Then we go into VVVV, where there's a chain of shaders that perform the normal calculations/filtering/lighting and also some patching for the throw dynamics (and a little C# plug-in for the thrown particles).

Will you talk about some of the challenges of matching the 3D data from the Kinect with the point of view of the projector? How accurately did you have to measure the position of the projector relative to the Kinect? Did you have to take into account lens distortion or any other details like that?

This was all really easy. We use a system a friend and I made called Padé projection mapping. The calibration takes about one minute, and just involves clicking on points on the screen. No measuring tape needed!

Where will you take this technique next?

We're looking into trying this technique out with a stage/audience performance. We want people to experience it, and we want to show what it really means to have all these controllable surfaces in your surroundings.

If you could do one thing with the Kinect that seems impossible now what would that be?

I'd be really interested if we could get a really low latency/high framerate (>100fps) 3D scanner with zero kernel size (so an object of one pixel size can be scanned) that connects over USB. That'd be incredible, and something I'm finding myself fighting to achieve with projectors and structured light.

blablabLAB

blablabLAB is an art and design collective based in Barcelona. They describe themselves as "a structure for transdisciplinary collaboration. It imagines strategies and creates tools to make society face its complex reality (urban, technological, alienated, hyper-consumerist). It works without preset formats nor media and following an extropianist philosophy, approaching the knowledge generation, property and diffusion of it, very close to the DIY principles." Their work explores the impact of technology on public life, from urban space to food. In January 2011, they produced an installation in Barcelona called "Be Your Own Souvenir." The installation (Figure 1-6) offered passersby the opportunity to have their bodies scanned and then receive small plastic figurines 3D printed from the scans on the spot. "Be Your Own Souvenir" won a 2011 Prix Arts at the Ars Electronica festival. blablabLAB expresses a highly pragmatic and hybrid approach to using technology for cultural work, exploring a wide variety of platforms and programming languages.

Was "Be Your Own Souvenir" your first project using the Kinect? What made you excited to work with the Kinect?

We presented the project to a contest in summer 2010. By then, the Kinect was called Project Natal, nobody knew much, and rumors were the camera was based on the Time of Flight principle. Our project was selected and the exhibition was scheduled for January 2011.

When we first thought about scanning people, we knew it could be somehow done, since we had seen Kyle McDonald's app for Processing. We researched a bit and found he had ported the code to openFrameworks.

We were working with some previous implementation of a structured light scanner from Brown University (*http://mesh.brown.edu/byo3d*) when our friend Takahiro (*http://yang02.org*) pointed out the new trend. Everybody out there was developing and doing experiments with the Kinect! We went to the shop and got Theo's first ofxKinect to work. Suddenly we gained a lot of time, and the deadline was achievable.

So, it was the first and until now, the only one project we have done with a Kinect. Maybe the last one. Our focus is not the technology.

Figure 1-6. *Two members of blablabLAB, an art and design collective that produced sou-venir 3D prints of people from Kinect scans on the streets of Barcelona. Photo courtesy of blablabLAB.*

How did people react to the prospect of being scanned? Was everyone excited about it? Was anyone nervous? How did you explain to them what was going to happen?

We showed a video in-place to try to explain what we were doing. It was all about daring to stand still for four minutes in front of a crowd, so most of the people were nervous, but some felt like movie stars. As expected, the reward, the figurine, was in many cases strong enough to leave the shyness aside.

Before the scan, we made them sign a contract authorizing us to capture and store their volumetric data. We wanted to raise their awareness about their private data being collected—something that already happens ubiquitously in our everyday life with other kinds of data, and that may happen in the near future with these new kind of technologies.

Did you show people what their scan was going to look like while they were posing? Did that make a difference in how they posed?

No. The point was to replicate the real street artist, so no visualization was planned in the beginning, neither for the statue nor the public.

We noticed though that many people really enjoyed viewing the 3D data on our screens, so we started displaying our working monitor, but because of the physical configuration we had, still, the statue couldn't see him/herself. This led to a funny situation where the statue would act as a traditional one, while the crowd was enjoying a digital spectacle.

Why did you do this project in a public space?

The project is actually about the public space: about the users of La Rambla (the main pedestrian street in Barcelona), how they interact with each other and the city.

Probably there haven't been many Kinect projects related to the public sphere yet (privacy issues, pervasiveness, etc.), but the technology seems to be in the focus of the marketing and commercial sectors. This is something we wanted to deal with, since we believe unfortunately a pervasion of the public space with this kind of hidden technologies, difficult to notice, may happen soon.

How many people worked on "Be Your Own Souvenir"? What is your background and experience?

We were three people coming from different backgrounds including architecture, electronic engineering, computer science, urban planning, design, cinema, and molecular cuisine.

Tell me a little bit about your workflow. How did you create a 3D file from the Kinect data? What processing did you have to do it to get a file that could print in good quality in a reasonable time? What software did you use to control the printer? What was the biggest obstacle you faced?

All the software used in this project is free and open. Custom software has been developed using openFrameworks and OpenKinect in order to produce a tunable full 360 degree point cloud. We avoid the occlusions using mechanic shutters controlled by Arduino. Using a MIDI controller, the three different input point-clouds (three Kinects) can be adjusted in space and resolution. The resulting combined point cloud is processed by MeshLab to produce a mesh reconstruction. Skeinforge takes the mesh, previously cleaned up and tuned through Blender, and outputs a gcode file, which can feed a CNC machine.

The main problem we faced, and we are still facing, is that the time and quality is different for the scanning part and the printing part. You can scan in less than a second, but you need much more to print, while the scan resolution is pretty low, with the printer, you can get awesome details (Figure 1-7). Tweaking the printer to get the equilibrium between fast and reasonable print quality brought us to a 10 minutes average per figurine.

Besides this trade-off, the mesh reconstruction process is the chain-step most likely to be improved. Instead of a one-step reconstruction operation using the three point-clouds at the same time, a two-step process using high-level information to produce X meshes (X being the number of Kinects), to further zipper them would be a nice way to start.

What gear did you bring with you to do this project? How did you approach setting everything up on a public street? Was it hard to get permission to use public space?

We built ourselves three translucent plastic boxes to keep the cameras protected and shelter the screens, and be able to display vinyl labeling with rear lighting. One of the boxes also hosted the computer we use for the scans (i7 desktop, screen, etc.). The printer was placed inside the museum a few meters away, since one of the goals of the project was also to encourage people to visit this art center.

Chapter 1

Thankfully, we were supervised by a production team that dealt with all the permissions. Barcelona is a really hard place when it comes to public space bureaucracy, unless you are Woody Allen…

Figure 1-7. *A print produced by blablabLAB's "Be Your Own Souvenir" project based on a scan of two lovers holding hands. Photo courtesy of blablabLAB.*

How did people react to the quality of the prints? Could they recognize themselves?

They could recognize themselves only for the pose, by the complexity, or from a characteristic piece of clothing. A few reproached us about it but most of them were amazed with their own souvenir.

It's pretty funny to see yourself without color, even with high resolution scanners, so lot of people were actually kind of impressed. Kids were actually the most shocked.

What possibilities do you see for using the Kinect in future projects?

We've been thinking about the possibilities of combining Kinect and real-time mapping with some sort of feature recognition. The Kinect has been designed for human gesture tracking, so pushing this boundary is always exciting. Maybe in the near future higher specification cameras will be available and the horizon will expand.

If you could do one thing with the Kinect that seems impossible now what would that be?

For us would be synchronize them with software to be able to connect more than one to avoid IR occlusions, but we don't even know whether than can be done with the Windows SDK.

Nicolas Burrus

Nicolas Burrus (Figure 1-8) is a postdoctoral scholar in computer vision at Carlos III University in Madrid. He works on building computer vision systems for robotics, from coordinating the movements of dextrous robotic hands to studying the use of 3D cameras for airplanes for Airbus. Burrus created Kinect RGBDemo (http:// nicolas.burrus.name/index.php/Research/KinectRgbDemoV6), a suite of applications that uses the Kinect to demonstrate advanced computer vision algorithms. These include the ability to construct a complete 3D model of a room by moving a Kinect around it, an application that calibrates the Kinect's color and depth cameras, and an application that can detect objects sitting on a flat surface such as a table. RGBDemo uses the OpenKinect driver to access the Kinect so its applications are completely open source and accessible to everyone.

Figure 1-8. *Researcher Nicolas Burrus captured in a 3D point cloud using his open source RGBDemo software. Burrus's work makes advanced computer vision algorithms accessible to beginner Kinect hackers. Photo courtesy of Nicolas Burrus.*

How would you describe the overall mission of your research? What drew you to computer vision work in the first place?

I have been working on statistical image processing during my PhD thesis and decided to apply these tools to computer vision to give robots the ability to see, interpret, and interact with their environment using visual information, pretty much as humans do. The visual data captured by current sensors is very rich, but their automatic analysis—i.e., getting useful information out of the raw pixels—is still a major and exciting challenge.

One portion of your work before the release of the Kinect was focused on vision systems for robotics, particularly robots that would interact with their environment with artificial hands. How did the release of the Kinect change that work? Are you using the Kinect in your current robotics research or are other 3D capture technologies still more effective in the lab? What do you think the future holds for this kind of research as 3D capture technologies like the Kinect become more widespread?

We had been working with stereo cameras, lasers, and even some depth cameras in our lab for a long time before the release of the Kinect. All these devices were already able to output 3D data of the robot environment. The revolution brought by the Kinect is the combination of the best features of these devices. Stereo cameras can be cheap but have a worse depth estimation and require complex processing to compute depth estimations, especially in homogeneous areas. Lasers are precise but are slow to compute a full scan, and are very expensive. Earlier depth cameras were already attractive but had a significantly worse depth precision, and ours was about 50 times more expensive!

The Kinect camera is the first device capable of delivering real-time, precise, and dense 3D scans for a very cheap price. Its wide availability is also a chance for academics to get more impact, since their results can directly be used and repeated by others. So we progressively switched to Kinect for the perception of our robots, when possible.

Other technologies still have a future, though. The Kinect cannot work outdoors, and is limited to short range (about five to six meters). Its precision also rapidly decreases with the distance, which is not the case for the existing professional devices. But its impressive success will definitely open the door to new generations of cheap 3D cameras, hopefully more compact and even more precise.

Your RGBDemo project is designed to introduce people to all the things that can be done with the data from a depth camera like the Kinect. What advice would you give to programmers who wanted to explore those possibilities further? What skills should they be studying? What fundamentals are most important to master?

I think algorithmic skills are very important, since 3D means a lot of data, and thus naive implementations usually result in unusable programs. A good mathematical background in geometry and linear algebra also helps. I would recommend acquiring a practical knowledge of these fundamentals by trying to program small 3D video games.

The area of GPU programming is also becoming more popular and can offer huge performance increases, and is perfectly adapted to the processing of such big quantities of data.

RGBDemo brings together algorithms and techniques from a number of different research efforts such as the Point Cloud Library. What advice would you give to a programmer who was excited about the Kinect and wanted to learn more about the principles of computer vision and to learn more about the current state of the research?

Research works with communities, so the hardest step is to find an entry point. Then, following the mailing list of major software in the field and having a look at the demos and papers of the major conferences (e.g., CVPR, ICCV) is a good way to keep up-to-date. For example, Willow Garage is definitely one of the main actors of the robotics community, and following the development of its vision software libraries such as PCL or OpenCV is very useful.

What have been some of your favorite projects to come out of the "Kinect hacking" community? Are you inspired at all by the interface and artistic applications of the technology in your research?

I have seen a lot of very inspiring and impressive hacks or projects. This is definitely an additional motivation to bring the latest research results to a wider audience, that will find new ways to apply it, be it for fun, artistic, or medical applications. If I had to mention a few projects, I would probably include the Intel RGBD Project, which did a lot on automatic mapping and object model acquisition, people from Konstanz University who developed a system to guide blind people, the Kinemmings game, which proposed an innovative way to interact with games, the many hacks that used the Kinect to create virtual instruments, such as the Kinect Anywhere virtual piano, and all these nice visual effects we have seen on top of the depth images, such as the Dirty Pearls clip.

What are your plans for continuing your work with the Kinect going forward? Do you plan to continue its use in research or in commercial applications?

Both! I will keep working in the academic world and adding new demos to RGBDemo as part of that work. With the big interest that raised the Kinect for computer vision in the consumer market, we also have plans to help transfer the latest developments from academics to end users through a new consultancy company.

Are there other computer vision technologies that are currently in the research phase that you can imagine having a similar impact to the Kinect if made equally accessible? What's the "next Kinect"? What will be the state of the art in this field in five years?

I think the next phase for the consumer market is in the convergence of devices that output 3D data, devices that display 3D data, and software able to process and analyze all this data. I expect mobile devices to embed 3D screens and cameras in the near future. Interactions with computers will also change significantly with the widespread use of multi-touch and touch-free interfaces. With cameras capable of detecting objects and people in a scene, our homes might also change considerably. Virtual worlds and crowds could also take a new dimension with animated and realistic avatars. Exciting times are waiting for us!

Oliver Kreylos

Oliver Kreylos is a computer scientist at UC Davis. His work focuses on using virtual reality to improve interfaces for data visualization in scientific research. Immediately after the launch of the Kinect in November 2010, Kreylos demonstrated an application that used the Kinect to create a complete live full-color 3D reconstruction of his room including integrating animated digital characters. His results stunned the nascent Kinect-hacking community and gained wide attention including in an article in the New York Times (http://www.nytimes.com/2010/11/22/technology/22hack.html). Kreylos has gone on to integrate the Kinect thoroughly into his virtual reality research and to explore its use in remote communication systems, allowing multiple scientists to inhabit a shared virtual environment where they can manipulate data for collaboration.

You began your work with the Kinect immediately after the open source driver was first released. Why were you excited about the Kinect? What work were you doing at the time and how did the Kinect relate to that work?

I had been using 3D video for several years before the Kinect's release, using a 3D camera system based on clusters of regular (2D) cameras developed at UC Berkeley. We were already using 3D video as an integral component of 3D telecollaborative applications back then, but the Berkeley camera system was tricky to set up, very expensive, and fairly low fidelity (320 by 240 pixels at 15 fps per cluster). I had been looking for a low-cost replacement for a long time, and heard about PrimeSense's goal to develop a consumer 3D camera several years back, at which time I contacted them directly. Turns out they had entered their exclusivity agreement with Microsoft just days prior to me contacting them, so they couldn't provide any test hardware at the time. When Kinect was announced later, I expected that it would employ strong encryption to only work with Xbox (I assumed that Microsoft would sell it under cost, like the Xbox itself). When Hector Marcan's work showed that Kinect was not encrypted after all, I jumped right in. Since I already had the larger 3D video environment in place at the time, all I had to do after picking up my first Kinect was to develop a low-level driver (based on Hector's reverse-engineered USB startup command sequence) and some calibration utilities. That's why I got a full working 3D video application only three days or so later.

Since then, Kinect cameras have replaced our previous 3D video hardware, and I'm currently looking into improving the video quality.

From your videos and your open source code releases, it seems like a lot of your work with the Kinect was directly translated from your existing work with other 3D video capture systems. Will you describe the system you were using before the release of the Kinect? What role does the Kinect play today in your ongoing research? How easy was it to "port" the work you were doing to use the Kinect?

The Berkeley 3D video system uses independent clusters of 2D cameras. Each cluster of three cameras is functionally equivalent to a single Kinect. Instead of structured light, the old system uses multiview stereo reconstruction, or "depth from stereo." Two cameras in each cluster are black and white and reconstruct depth; the third camera is color and captures a texture to map onto the reconstructed geometry. Geometry from multiple clusters is joined just as I do for the Kinect, to increase coverage and reduce occlusion shadows. Compared to structured light, depth from stereo is computationally very complex, and you need one high-end PC to run each cluster, for about 15 fps at a reduced resolution of 320 by 240. Due to the special FireWire cameras, each cluster (including the PC) costs about $5000. That's why I was waiting for Kinect as an affordable replacement, especially for our line of low-cost VR environments.

When I replaced the old system with Kinect, I used the chance to also remove some idiosyncrasies from the old code, so I ended up replacing more than just the bare minimum. In our larger software, 3D video is/was handled by a plug-in to our telecollaboration infrastructure. Instead of adapting that plug-in for Kinect, I wrote a different plug-in from scratch, using an improved network protocol. This has the added benefit that I can use both systems at the same time, to stay compatible with our Berkeley colleagues. But in the larger context of the software, that was still a tiny component of the overall software. So, essentially, the Kinect dropped right in.

The Kinect's, or, more precisely, 3D video's, role in my work is to provide a mechanism for two or more people from distributed locations to work together in a virtual 3D environment as if they were in the same place. Our main targeted display environments are not desktop PCs, but fully immersive VR environments such as CAVEs. In those, the 3D video is not rendered on a screen, but appears as a free-standing life-size virtual hologram, which unfortunately never comes across in any videos or pictures. In those environments, 3D video enables a completely natural way to talk to and work with people that are long distances away.

How would you describe the overall mission of your research? What drew you to computer vision work in the first place?

My overall research is to develop software for interactive visualization and data analysis, particularly in VR environments using virtual reality interaction techniques—that is, using your hands to directly manipulate 3D data instead of using a mouse or other 2D devices as intermediaries.

From observing our scientist users, we learned that data analysis is often a group task, where two to four people work together. It turns out that they spend the majority of the time not actually looking at the data, but talking to each other about the data. So when we started developing a telecollaboration system to allow spatially distributed teams of scientists to work together effectively, without having to travel, we quickly realized that we needed a way to create convincing "avatars" of remote participants to be displayed at each site to support natural interaction. It turned out that 3D video is a great way of doing that—while we haven't done any formal studies, I believe that 3D video, even at low fidelity, is much more natural than animated or even motion-captured, computer-generated avatars. So we were forced to implement a 3D video system, and since we're not computer vision experts, we teamed up with UC Berkeley to integrate their system into our larger software. When Kinect came around, the computer-vision aspects of 3D video were already integrated into the hardware, so I could develop the rest of the necessary driver software myself.

A lot of your work focuses on using depth cameras to integrate 3D footage of people into virtual environments for telepresence and other communications applications. What are the areas of technology that you think will be most altered by the arrival of depth cameras like the Kinect? What application areas do you find to be the most promising?

I think the most immediate transformational aspect of cheap 3D cameras is telepresence. Even if you don't have an immersive virtual reality environment, 3D video is still better at teleconferencing than 2D cameras, due to 3D video's elegant solution to the gaze direction problem. I think that we'll quickly see new videoconferencing software that will use 3D video even in desktop or laptop settings, slowly replacing Skype et al.; alternatively, it would make a whole lot of sense for Skype to have a plug-in for 3D video in the near future. Especially now that it's owned by Microsoft.

Apart from that, there are obvious implications for novel user interfaces. People might not want to have to wave their hands in front of a computer to do most work, as I don't see how typical tasks like web browsing or text editing could really benefit from hands-free interfaces beyond gimmickry, but there are other aspects. One is simple and accurate head tracking for 3D graphics such as in computer games. Combined with stereoscopic displays, that could really change things a lot. As an aside, stereoscopy without head tracking doesn't really work, which is why 3D movies and 3D video games aren't taking off as quickly as one might have thought. But throw in head tracking, and you suddenly have 3D displays that appear just like real holograms, only at much better visual quality. Combined with games or other 3D applications exploiting that fact, this could be a big thing. The other line is for more professional applications, where we're already doing direct 3D interaction. Using Kinect, or a higher-resolution future version of the same, we could do away with some of the gadgets we're using, for an even less intrusive user interface. This kind of stuff is not going to go mainstream any time soon, but it will have huge benefits inside its application areas.

What skills do you think beginning programmers should work on if they want to create interesting projects with 3D capture technologies? What are the current problems in developing the technology further? Is it a matter of user interface? Real-world applications with users? More basic research?

This sounds bad, but from my experience of doing 3D computer graphics research at universities, and having taught 3D CG classes, I have learned that most people, even those working in 3D, don't really "get" 3D. Most people tend to think of 3D as 2D plus depth, but that leads to cumbersome approaches, applications, and, particularly, bad user interfaces. You can see the effects of this mindset in a lot of places, especially in 3D movies and many 3D computer games.

As one concrete example, there are de facto standard ways of using 2D input devices (mouse, keyboard, joystick) to control 3D worlds. Think WASD+mouse look or virtual trackballs. When faced with a true 3D input device, like the extracted skeletons provided by OpenNI or Microsoft's Kinect SDK, many people's first approach is to develop a wrapper that translates body motion into inputs for the existing 2D control metaphors, which really doesn't make any sense whatsoever. 3D input devices, instead, should come with completely new 3D interaction metaphors. These kinds of things have been looked into in the scientific field of virtual reality, and that's where budding Kinect developers should be looking. For example, what I am doing with 3D video and Kinect has already been described, down to some algorithms, in a 1997 VR/multimedia paper by Kanade et al. But who'd have thought to look there?

In a nutshell, what I'm trying to say is that the most important requirement for doing exciting stuff with 3D capture is not anything technical, but a mind-set that fully understands and embraces 3D. The rest are just technicalities.

So I think the most important avenues of further development are two-fold: developing better 3D capture hardware (the Kinect, after all, is a first-generation piece of technology and still quite low-fidelity), and fostering a paradigm that embraces true 3D, and consequently leads to better applications, and better interfaces to use them.

What advice would you give to a programmer who was excited about the Kinect and wanted to learn more about the principles of computer vision and to learn more about the current state of the research?

Not being a computer vision expert myself, I don't have good advice. I'd say the basic requirement is a good understanding of 3D and linear algebra. A good way of following state-of-the-art computer vision research, besides following the literature, is keeping in touch with software projects such as OpenCV, where researchers often implement and release their latest algorithms.

What do you think of all of the "Kinect hacks" that have been published online since the launch of the Kinect? What are some of your favorites? What capabilities do you think have failed to be explored?

This might sound strange, but I haven't really kept up with that scene. Most of the initial hacks were just that, one-off projects showcasing some technical feature or novel idea. It only gets interesting once they move into doing something useful or interesting. In that sense, the "real-time motion capture for 3D CG avatars" ones were showing possibilities for exciting real applications, and the 3D body scanning and rapid prototyping booth that someone built and exhibited to the public was an immediately useful new thing [*Editorial note:* Kreylos is referring to Spanish collective blablabLAB, interviewed earlier in this chapter]. I have not, so far, seen any real progress on novel 3D user interfaces. Some preliminary work like the gestural web browsing interface didn't excite me personally, because I honestly don't believe that anybody would actually do that once the novelty wears off. What I haven't seen, and maybe I haven't been looking in the right places, are true 3D interfaces for 3D modeling or 3D data analysis.

Are there other computer vision technologies that are currently in the research phase that you can imagine having a similar impact to the Kinect if made equally accessible? What's the "next Kinect"? What will be the state of the art in this field in five years?

My crystal ball is in the shop right now, so… I really don't know, not working in the computer vision field. But I hope that the next Kinect will have higher resolution, and the ability to use multiple devices in the same capture space without mutual interference. Those are not very lofty aspirations, but they would really improve my particular use of the technology, and would also improve 3D user interface work, for example by the ability to reliably track individual fingers.

Whose work in this field do you find most exciting? Who else should I be looking at and talking to?

Since they're doing more or less exactly what I'm doing (certain aspects at least), and, in those aspects, arguably do a better job, you could contact the group around Henry Fuchs at UNC Chapel Hill, particularly Andrew Maimone regarding his impressive implementation of 3D videoconferencing.

Alejandro Crawford

Alejandro Crawford (Figure 1-9) is a video artist and a student at NYU's Interactive Telcommunication Program. During 2011 he toured with the indie rock band MGMT creating live visuals for their performances using the Kinect. Crawford used four Kinects to create a psychedelic video projection to accompany the band's shows. The tour visited more than 65 venues in 30 countries and was seen by thousands of fans.

Figure 1-9. *Alejandro Crawford used four Kinect to build a VJ system to accompany the band MGMT on tour.*

What kind of work had you done before being tapped by MGMT to do visuals? How did you get involved with working for the band?

I honestly hadn't done that much. Before I started at ITP, I didn't know what a MAX/MSP Jitter was. I come from a poetry/writing background, and as a kid I wanted to be a director, so a lot of my later "writing" endeavors started to stray away from linguistic language for video — or audio video. Commercial poem (*http://vimeo.com/5649993*) is probably pretty indicative of that time, and in many ways a mock-up for ideas I'd be able to explore through programming a year or so later.

As to my work with the band, it started in undergrad with my friend (and roommate at the time), Hank Sullivant. Hank and Andrew van Wyngarden grew up in Memphis together, and there was a time either during or right after their time at Weslyan that Andrew and Ben Goldwasser came to Athens to party. There'd be a keg party, and at that time, MGMT was like hilarious avant-karaoke, where they'd play their tracks off the iPod. There'd be some mics and lots of everybody dancing and it would be really hot.

Hank was the original lead guitarist of MGMT when James Richardson was the drummer. My first year at ITP Hank and James all lived in a house together in Bushwick off Morgan stop. Hank and I actually shared bunk beds. I'm talking, like Walmart.com build them yourself boi-bunks. Gnarly times.

But I guess things really began at ITP, specifically in Luke DuBois's Live Image Processing and Performance class. Josh Goldberg subbed for Luke and showed us the LFOs that control his work "Dervish," which basically involves video feedback and rotation and oscillators. That blew me away and informed a lot of how I went about learning Jitter (and I'm very much still learning Jitter), messing with video, "What happens when I do this to these numbers and this thing down here?" etc.

James, being my roommate and a close friend, was around for a lot of that. Later I got this really random email from James (who was on tour at the time) saying MGMT had had a meeting and decided they wanted to know if I wanted to do visuals for them. It was then that I asked ITP for a leave of absence. I went down to Athens, GA shortly after that and started writing VJ software, collaborating with Alfredo Lapuz Jr., better known as IMMUZIKATION.

How did you decide to use the Kinect in your work for the band? Was it your idea or theirs? Did you know you wanted to work with the Kinect as a piece of technology or did you choose it to achieve a particular aesthetic result? What did the band want in the visuals? Had you worked with the Kinect before?

I asked Santa for a Kinect Christmas 2010, and after New Years I brought it to Athens. Alfredo's the golden goose DJ of Athens, so it was always nice to be able to test out new prototypes by doing visuals beside him; this is how the Kinect stuff started.

I was already very into and obsessed with Andrew Benson; his HSflow and flowRepos GL shaders (for optical flow distortion) were the most gorgeous, flowy Takeshe Murata-type "data-moshy" impressionistic thing I'd come across. So rad. The idea of working with the Kinect really started with me and Ben Goldwasser (MGMT band member) nerding out. Ben's a rad programmer himself, and we'd talk shop lots, so the "Wouldn't it be cool?" seed was already planted. Plus I had already seen Flight404's Cinder Kinect radness and was hooked on the idea.

The wonderful thing about working for MGMT is the faith they have in me. I basically said to them, wouldn't it be cool if we had a Kinect for every member in the band and I could play psychedelic TV producer: "camera 2, camera5, camera1, go cam 4…." I also wanted to include the Benson shaders and LFO feedback effects, so I started programming, sewing it all together (with one Kinect). Then I got back to New York and one of MGMT's managers and I went to Best Buy and got five Kinects, then at B&H Video, we got a USB hub and this Pelican road case.

Talk about the development process behind this project. What environment or programming language did you use to work with the Kinect? How did you develop the look and interaction of the piece? What was the band's input in the process? How did you test it and prepare it for tour?

I spent about a month getting familiar with the Kinect, a lot of "What happens when I do this?" and Jitter coding. I was particularly interested in the ability to slice the depth mapping into color zones. It was very raw (in the sense that it was arguably employing a very primitive aspect of the Kinect's abilities), but on the other hand, it morphed into this kind of stuff once the Benson shaders took hold.

But that was still one Kinect. Once I had all five, I remember very well the first attempt: placing them all out around me in my home, plugging them all into the USB hub, turning them all on, and…like, nothing. I went white, then went to Google and soon learned all about how much juice these puppies need per port. So I had my first big obstacle. Five Kinects into on MacBook Pro: how? I emailed Luke DuBois and Jean-Marc Pelletier, who made the Jitter Kinect module (among other things including Jitter's computer vision lib). I seem to remember Pelletier saying: not gonna happen. And Luke was like: you need to make sure you can even address that many Kinects.

Express card was not an option. Buying a tower was not an option. USB 3.0 cards were not an option.

Resigning myself to four USB ports and therefore four Kinects, I decided to try running two Kinects into my personal MacBook Pro and then sending their feeds over UDP to the MGMT video MacBook Pro, with two more Kinects jacked into it. There was terrible delay and I felt more and more screwed. Finally I tried out connecting the computers via Cat6 Ethernet cable. The cabled connection was much faster, and I was down to milliseconds of latency between the Kinects coming from the second computer.

Basically the patch allows modular control of many of the parameters pertaining to the optical flow distortion of the color-sliced depth mapping and color tweaking and cross fading between a feedback-driven (shape-rendering side). I also had buttons mapped to switch from one Kinect to another and faders to control tilt, buttons to switch mode, etc.

The band saw it for the first time in Japan. All the testing/building was done in not-site-specific environments (such as inside apartments—mostly, my own). I didn't really realize how much of a factor that was, but we didn't have any production rehearsal days, we hadn't rented a warehouse/stage where I could mock it up, set it up. I was a bit anxious about the first show in this regard. I knew I needed to mount the Kinects on the tops of mic stands, but it'd be the first time I really set it up right.

What was the process like for setting up the Kinects and the rest of your system at each show? Did anything ever go wrong?

I always carry a Folsom Image Pro HD with me (usually it's rack mounted), but for the Asia tour, because there were so many different countries and flights, we were sourcing equipment locally all the time. I didn't want to get in a situation where they told me they didn't have a Folsom, because they're basically like scan converter Swiss Army knives. Good luck not being able to pass your video signal along in whatever format or size. So, in total: scan converter, two MacBook Pros, an apc40, four Kinects, lots of active-USB cabling, daisy-chained, maybe one or two other minor things like projectors.

Every show day I'd build VideoLand, oversee the setting up of projectors, show some stagehands how to do the first Kinect-mounting-to-mic-stand, and then we'd lay all cabling. Then I'd wait until soundcheck to finesse the Kinect positions and distances from the band members. Then I'd "spike" the positions with gaffer tape and remove the Kinects until showtime, unplugging them at the connectors.

Things went wrong all the time in a kind of weird Murphy's law way, from electricity crossovers between video sound and lights to the Jitter patch crashing once (at the outro of a song, luckily). I just restarted the patch for the next song.

The first time I tried using the Kinects during a daylight festival show I thought they were broken until I realized the sun was just blinding them. This blinding effect happened once or twice also with particular lights on stage. And maybe once or twice Matt, the bass player, picked up a Kinect and placed it in front of the crowd. That wasn't so much an error as unaccounted for (distances weren't calibrated for that), but it still looked cool, hands swaying, moving paint on the screen.

Do you have plans to work with the Kinect more in the future in other contexts? What do you wish you could do with the Kinect that it can't do right now or that you haven't figured out yet?

I want to get into skeleton tracking stuff and augmented reality with the next album/tour. I want to build an island video game in Unity3D with lots of cool psychedelic spots. I want the band skeleton tracked and 3D modeled on that island. I want to be able to teleport from one place to another (like cutting back and forth between video sources). I wanna VJ with a video game!

Josh Blake

Josh Blake (Figure 1-10) is the technical director of the InfoStrat Advanced Technology Group and the founder of the OpenKinect community that develops and maintains the open source libfreenect drivers for the Kinect. He is a Microsoft Surface MVP, is the author of Natural User Interfaces in .NET (http://manning.com/blake/), and maintains a prominent blog on NUIs (http://nui.joshland.org). He is an expert in developing with each of the major Kinect APIs and SDKs and specializes in creating advanced Natural User Interfaces for enterprise collaboration, data visualization, and education.

Figure 1-10. *Josh Blake uses the Kinect to build Natural User Interfaces.*

When did you first hear about the Kinect/Project Natal? How did you see its relationship to the user interface work you were already doing?

Project Natal, which later became Kinect, was announced June 1, 2009. I don't remember specifically how I found out, but I was pretty well in tune with the latest tech news via blogs and Twitter, so I'm pretty sure I knew about it within a day or two. I remember having email discussions later that month with my colleagues about how we could use Project Natal beyond gaming in general human-computer interfaces.

At the time, I was working on multi-touch and Microsoft Surface projects and already had a pretty deep understanding of natural user interfaces and the coming NUI revolution, but in practice, most discussions of NUI were centered on multitouch, so it was difficult for people to conceptually distinguish NUI and multitouch as distinct concepts with distinct concerns. As Microsoft released more information and videos about Kinect, it validated my thoughts on NUI and I became more and more excited about the possibilities. Motion-tracking technology like Kinect can let us give our applications the ability to see and understand humans in our own world, which is something that multi-touch technologies can't do by themselves.

You played a major role in bringing together all of the people who were working separately on opening up the Kinect into a single united effort. What was your impetus for doing that and what was the biggest obstacle to that collaboration coming together as well as it finally did?

When Kinect came out, there were a lot of people interested in using Kinect on PC. Several people, including myself, were interested in creating drivers, but initially there was no coordinated effort. There were two things that happened that really motivated me to create an open community for this effort.

The first was the $3,000 bounty placed on publishing open source Kinect drivers by Adafruit and funded by Johnny Chung Lee. Now, I wasn't motivated to win the money, but rather I was motivated by the effect that the bounty had on individuals working on Kinect. The nature of contests and bounties creates a competitive atmosphere and results in people keeping knowledge and source code to themselves, rather than sharing it. I knew that at some point, someone would claim the bounty with a minimal prototype driver, but I wondered what would happen afterward. If there was not a single community in place to support a sustained community effort, there was a large risk of fragmentation of efforts.

The second thing that happened was certain individuals started to commercially exploit the interest in Kinect. I won't name names, but there was one individual who actually created a driver for Kinect and posted a video that met the all requirements for the Adafruit bounty except for open sourcing the drivers. This person was not satisfied with the $3,000 prize offered, so instead decided to ask the community to give an additional $10,000 before the programmer would share work. I saw this was a horrible development that furthered the competitive atmosphere of the bounty.

In the ideal world, I knew the community would band together, pool their talents and knowledge, and create Kinect drivers and share the Kinect driver software under a permissive open source license. Since the need was there and no one else was doing it, I decided to organize the OpenKinect community myself. I began contacting all of the individuals who I knew were working on Kinect drivers and created a mailing list to coordinate the efforts.

It turned out that Hector Martin won the Adafruit bounty but had not joined OpenKinect yet. I contacted him and asked him to join us and he agreed. We combined his working drivers with the group's partially working drivers and then kept going, publishing the first drivers for Kinect on PC for Windows, Mac, and Linux. The mailing list membership grew dramatically and many people started contributing code. To help coordinate the contributions, Kyle Machulis stepped up to play the role of source code integrator, which is a vital role in any effort with many contributors.

Beyond the mailing list and the software itself, I also made sure that the community had a good contribution policy, license, wiki, and logo so the community would be self-sustaining. I didn't do all of these things myself and don't take credit for the work. My role was as a coordinator and builder of consensus. I worked with Hector Martin, Kyle Machulis, and others in the community to create consensus on how to run the community, and today it is a self-sustaining effort with over 2,400 members of the mailing list and a large wiki at openkinect.org with documentation on how Kinect works.

I also served as a point of contact between the community and external organizations. PrimeSense contacted me a few weeks before they published OpenNI and I offered them some advice on how to work with and develop a community like OpenKinect.

It was extremely satisfying to see the wide variety of Kinect hacks that resulted from our work on libfreenect, and also to see the spirit of the community apply to other related projects as well as people working with other drivers such as OpenNI and the Kinect for Windows SDK.

You've worked with the Kinect in a wide variety of platforms. You founded the OpenKinect community that created the open source libfreenect drivers and you also work heavily with PrimeSense's OpenNI software and Microsoft's Kinect for Windows SDK. What do you get out of moving between ecosystems like this?

It is quite interesting and informative to compare the different ecosystems, both the software and the community. Each of the drivers, libfreenect, OpenNI/Sensor/SensorKinect, and the Kinect for Windows SDK have advantages and disadvantages, and have different approaches, architectures, and capabilities. We can learn from each other and improve each of the drivers.

Given my role in the OpenKinect community, I was able to make great contacts within PrimeSense and Microsoft and ended up having some amount of influence in all three worlds. Since I'm familiar with and have used all of the drivers, I can provide interesting insight and feedback for each of the groups.

A lot of your work focuses on using the Kinect and other technologies to create new user interface opportunities. Why is this important? What can't we do with the existing mouse-keyboard-touchscreen options? What businesses and realms of life will be most affected by natural user interfaces?

Natural user interfaces will eventually affect every aspect of our lives. Computing devices are already fairly pervasive, and this will only increase in the future with more devices and a wider variety of devices and form factors. The key to the NUI revolution is that it opens up computing to a much larger world of people and situations where for whatever reason, computing was not possible or appropriate.

Two examples of this phenomenon is using speech recognition to control your phone or GPS in a car, and using multi-touch or motion tracking technology to provide therapeutic applications for special needs children. Both of these examples use NUI in ways that a graphical user interface could not address.

This is the same thing that happened during the transition from command-line interfaces to graphical user interfaces as the default mode of interaction. We still have command-line interfaces today for specialized tasks, and likewise we will still have GUIs in the future for things that they are best suited for, but the vast majority of human-computer interaction in the future will use a natural user interface of some type. People are going to expect every interface to be natural and for computing devices to fit into their lives, so we need to be ready for that.

After the incredible success of the Kinect and the huge amount of attention garnered by the OpenKinect project, both Microsoft and PrimeSense released their own SDKs as well. What is the future of the OpenKinect project now that these other systems for working with the Kinect are available?

I'll admit that there are a lot of people who used libfreenect in the early days but are now using OpenNI or the Kinect for Windows SDK. One of the scenarios where OpenNI or the Kinect SDK is better is when the developer needs skeleton tracking, which is available for both OpenNI and the Kinect SDK but not in libfreenect. Some scenarios, such as object scanning and robotics, don't need skeleton tracking, so libfreenect is still a great option. It's only a matter of time before we have an open source implementation of skeleton tracking and the choice between the drivers becomes less clear.

In general, I think that the OpenKinect community will continue to exist and we'll see our initial focus on the drivers expanded into other related projects. Of course, the mailing list is a great place to discuss Kinect projects and ideas.

What do you wish you could do with the Kinect that it can't do right now? What other breakthrough sensors do you wish for in the future that would contribute to your work as much as the Kinect?

I'd love to have a Kinect with two or three times the resolution in the depth and RGB sensors at the same or higher frame rate. Not only would the data look much better visually, it would open up some new possibilities for accurate hand and face tracking as well as object scanning. Higher frame rates would also reduce the lag between a person's movements and the response on the screen. We would have to deal with issues of USB bandwidth limitations as well as processing all of that data in an efficient way, but I'm sure there are solutions to those problems.

Kinect's microphone array is an underused feature that has a lot of potential. It can detect the direction a sound is coming from and reduce the background noise to improve speech recognition. Once people really start using it, I can imagine a wave of innovation in sound recognition using the microphone array in the same way that skeleton recognition is possible because of the depth camera.

As for other sensors, I still can't quite grasp the implications myself because it still seems like the realm of science fiction, but brain-computer interfaces are likely to take off in a few years. There are already low-fidelity consumer games that use a brain interface today. If they can improve the bandwidth of the sensors but also make the device in a form factor that is socially acceptable to wear, it may spark another wave of human-computer interaction innovation.

Adafruit

Adafruit Industries is an open source hardware company that sells kits and parts for original, open source hardware electronics projects featured on *http://www.adafruit.com* as well as other cool open source tronix that we think are interesting and well-made. All the projects are redesigned specifically to make it easy for beginners to make: nicely silkscreened circuit boards, through-hole parts whenever possible, extra large solder pads, and so on. For some kits, you can purchase just the circuit board. To save paper, the easy-to-follow-with-lotsa-pictures instructions are all available online at *http://www.ladyada.net/make*.

Limor Fried and Phil Torrone

When did you first hear about the Kinect/Project Natal? Why did it capture your interest?

Limor and I had heard about when Microsoft was demoing it at the 2009 E3. At the time we just filed it away in our heads in the "future hack" folder. Our thought was "Hey, this is going to be a low cost RGB + distance camera that someone will probably reverse engineer." We thought it would be really useful for art and robotics projects, we guessed right!

Why did you think it was important that there be open source drivers for the Kinect?

When the Kinect was launched, we received a mysterious email from Johnny Lee (of Wiimote hack fame, now at Google, at the time at Microsoft), and he wanted to chat. I had asked if he could drop an email but he wanted to chat on the phone. After a series of conversations, he really inspired us to create the open source driver bounty (and he helped fund it). It was pretty clear to us Microsoft didn't have any plans, at all, to open any parts of the Kinect, and while we could have just reverse engineered the Kinect on our own and released the drivers, we thought we could really get a lot of community support with an open bounty effort. We didn't want this to be about us (Adafruit); we wanted to celebrate and demonstrate the power of open source. We knew once there were free and open drivers projects, companies, and ideas would flourish.

A lot of Adafruit's efforts are put into supporting hardware hackers through kits and information. How do you see the Kinect's relationship to the world of hardware hacking?

Our goal is show that commodity hardware or subsided hardware from large companies can have a life beyond what they were intended for. I think it became really clear within weeks of the open source drivers that the projects created were more interesting and had more potential for humankind than the shipping games. Companies like Microsoft create businesses; we create causes.

What possibilities does the Kinect open up?

Open source is usually associated with education, so right away any open source drivers for Kinect would be embraced and used in education (and that happened right away). Open source also attracts artists. The most interesting things about Kinect when it launched wasn't the games, it was the amazing projects the hackers and makers released.

What problems does it solve?

It was incredibly expensive to develop a RGB + distance camera; every group that wanted to do this would need to reinvent everything. Now, with the Kinect, you can just grab one at the local big box store for $150.

What do you think about PrimeSense's efforts to open up their tools? What are they getting right? What are they getting wrong? What's the relationship between OpenNI and OpenKinect?

We haven't followed this too much—our general opinion is, "This is good!" They saw all the interest in the Kinect and they want people to do the same thing, and I think they want to make sure they get public credit for their work. Most people assume Microsoft invented the Kinect.

What are the prospects for additional depth cameras coming in the future?

It all depends on how the patents around these things work. Technically it's possible, and there's no reason not see more of them—it might just depend on who owns what.

Will there be an open source depth camera at some point?

Probably not, but every depth-sensing camera that's useful will have open source drivers.

What is the single coolest Kinect hack you've seen? What was the first thing built with OpenKinect that made you say: this was worth it!

Every project has been worth it, that's for sure. But we like this early one the best: Interactive Puppet Prototype by Emily Gobeille and Theo Watson (*http://blog.makezine.com/archive/2010/11/kinect-puppet-show.html*). It captures imagination, art, and what's possible. You can imagine using this to control a surgical robot or just for a kid's video game.

Working with the Depth Image 2

In this chapter we're going to learn how to work with the depth image from the Kinect. As I explained in Chapter 1, the Kinect is a depth camera. This means that it captures the distance of the objects and people in front of it in the form of an image. This depth image is similar to the normal color images we're used to seeing all the time from digital cameras except instead of recording the color of light that reaches the camera, it records the distance of the objects in front of it. I'll show you how we can write Processing programs that access the depth image from the Kinect, display it on the screen, analyze its pixels in order to make measurements of the space in front of the Kinect, and use the results of those measurements as a simple user interface.

We'll start with the very basics. I'll show you how to install the Processing library that lets us access the Kinect, and then we'll use that library to display a depth image as well as a regular color image. Once we've got that up and running, I'll show you how to access individual pixels to determine their color and therefore the depth measurements that they represent. Once you're comfortable with accessing individual pixels, I'll show you how to write code that analyzes all of the pixels in the depth image to do more advanced calculations like finding the closest point in front of the Kinect. We'll then use this ability to build some basic interactive applications: we'll draw by waving our hands around, take some measurements of our room, and browse photos with some basic gestures.

Let's get started!

Images and Pixels

What is an image? Whether it's a depth image from the Kinect, a frame from your computer's built-in web cam, or a high resolution photo from the latest digital SLR, digital images are all simply collections of pixels. A pixel is the smallest unit of an image. Each pixel is a single solid color, and by arranging many pixels next to one another, digital images can create illusions such as smooth gradients and subtle shading. With enough pixels to create smooth enough images, you get the realistic digital images that we see every day.

Depending on the type of image, the variety of possible colors a pixel can be may vary. In a black and white image, each pixel is either black, white, or some shade of gray. In a color image, each pixel has a red, green, and blue component, which are combined in different quantities to create any color. Each component of the color is like a single black and white pixel, but instead of ranging from black to white through hundreds of shades of gray, each color component ranges from black to the full intensity of its color through a spectrum of darker versions. So a red pixel component, for example, can be any color from black through deep maroon, to a bright red. When this red component is combined with similar green and blue pixel components at particular shades in their own spectrums, the pixel can represent any in a large spectrum of colors.

As we start writing programs that process images, we'll see very quickly that each pixel is just a number. Each pixel's number value represents its intensity. In a grayscale image, the number value represents how dark the pixel is, with 0 being black and 255 being white. In a color image, each pixel component (red, green, and blue) can range from 0 to 255, with 0 being black and 255 being the full color.

Where did the number 255 come from? The range of colors a pixel can represent is determined by how big of a number we're willing to use to store its largest value. The larger a number we're willing to accept for each pixel, the more memory each image will take up. And since images can have millions of pixels (and always have at least thousands of them), larger pixel sizes will add up quickly. Images that use big numbers to store each pixel will quickly get unwieldy, taking up huge amounts of memory space and becoming very slow to process. Hence, Processing (and many other programming environments) have chosen a maximum value for pixels that's modest, but still large enough to create nice looking images: 255. This value is known as the image's *bit depth*. Processing stores these pixels as 8-bit numbers that can store values from 0 to 255.

Depending on its resolution, every digital image has thousands or millions of pixels arranged into a grid. This grid consists of columns and rows. Like with any grid, the number of columns is equal to the width of the image, and the numbers of rows is equal to its height. As you learned in Chapter 1, the depth image captured by the Kinect is 640 pixels wide by 480 pixels high. This means that each frame that comes in from the Kinect's depth camera will have a total of 307,200 pixels. And, unlike in the grayscale and color images we've mostly discussed so far, each pixel will be doing double duty. Each pixel's number, between 0 and 255, will represent both a color of gray and a distance in space. We can use that same number to either view the data as an image or calculate the distance to the object that pixel is a part of. We can treat 0 as black and 255 as white, or we can treat 0 as really far away and 255 as close up. This is the magic of the depth image: it's both a picture of the scene in front of the Kinect and a series of measurements of it.

But the Kinect is not just a still camera. In fact, it's more like the web cams we commonly use for online video chat. Like those cameras, the Kinect captures a live movie of the scene in front of it and sends it to our computer so fast that we don't notice the time it took to get there: its image appears to match the movements of the objects and people in front of it in "real time." Of course, unlike those cameras, the movie that the Kinect captures contains information about depth as well as color.

What is a movie? Up to this point, we've only been talking about images and pixels. Well, a movie is just a series of images over time. Just like an old-fashioned film reel consists of thousands of still photos, a digital movie (or live stream) consists of a sequence of these individual frames, one after another. The Kinect captures images one at a time and sends them to our Processing sketch, which then displays the series of images on the screen so quickly that we see the result as a smooth movie.

And since a digital movie is just a series of images over time, our approach to it will be to process each frame as it comes in and then use the results from each frame to update some information that we're tracking over the duration. For example, if we were trying to track the closest point over time, we'd do it by always finding the closest pixel in the current image while we had it around and then we'd use that result to update some object or output that persisted over time, such as the position of a circle. Pixels. Image. Movie.

But now we're starting to get ahead of ourselves. Before we can process the thousands of pixels in each of the endless images streaming in from the Kinect, we need to get our hands on a single pixel. And that means starting at the beginning: plugging in our Kinect and writing our first Kinect program.

Now that we know a little bit about how images and pixels work in theory, we're ready to write our first Kinect program so we can start working with some in practice. Before we can dive into the code, though, we have some administrivia to get through, namely installing the Processing library that will give us access to the Kinect's data. This should only take a couple of minutes, and we'll only have to do it this once.

Project 1: Installing the SimpleOpenNI Processing Library

If you're buying a Kinect just for hacking, make sure that you don't select the version that comes bundled with an Xbox. That version will lack the USB connection on its cable that you need to attach the Kinect to your computer. If you plan on using your Kinect with your Xbox as well (or if you already have a Kinect that came bundled with an Xbox), you can buy the separate power supply and connection cable you need to use the Kinect with your personal computer from Microsoft's online store under the product name Kinect Sensor Power Supply (*www.microsoftstore.com/store/msstore/en_US/pd/productID .221244000/search.true*).

Before we get started writing code and looking at Kinect data, we need to install the Processing library we'll be using throughout this book. As I mentioned in Chapter 1, we'll be using a library called SimpleOpenNI. This library provides access to all of the data from the Kinect that we'll need as well as a series of tools and helpers that will prove invaluable along the way.

Warning

This book is not intended to teach you Processing from scratch. However, if you've had even a little exposure to Processing, you should do fine. I'll start at a beginner level and gradually teach you all of the more advanced concepts and techniques you'll need to work with the Kinect. If you have some experience with another programming language, you should be able to pick up Processing as we go.

If you've never used Processing before, you'll need to install it before you get started. The Processing website (http://processing.org/download/) has downloads available for Mac, Windows, and Linux. At the time of this writing, 1.5.1 is the most recent version of Processing, but version 2.0 is expected soon. All of the examples in this book should work in either of these versions.

The steps for installing a library in Processing differ slightly based on your operating system. I'll provide instructions here for installing SimpleOpenNI on Mac OS X, Windows, and Linux. These instructions may change over time, so if you encounter any problems, please check the SimpleOpenNI Installation Page (*http://code.google.com/p/simple-openni/wiki/Installation*) for up-to-date details.

Installing SimpleOpenNI happens in two phases. First, you install OpenNI itself. This is the software system provided by PrimeSense that communicates with the Kinect to access and process its data. The steps involved in this phase differ based on your operating system. Below I've included step-by-step guides for getting OpenNI installed on each major operating system. Find the guide for your operating system and work through all the steps.

After you've got OpenNI successfully installed, the final step is to install the SimpleOpenNI Processing library itself. This is much easier than installing OpenNI and much more standard across operating systems. I've provided instructions for this as well at the end of this section. Once you've completed the install steps for your specific operating system, jump down to there to finish the process.

Installing OpenNI on OS X

This is the easiest platform on which to install OpenNI. Max Rheiner, the author of SimpleOpenNI, has provided an installer that makes the process straightforward and simple. The installer works best on Mac OS X 10.6 and above. Running it will involve a little bit of work at the command line, but I'll show you just what to do. Here are the steps:

- Go to the SimpleOpenNI Google Code site (*http://code.google.com/p/simple-openni/wiki/Installation*).

- Find the Mac OS X installation section. Click to download the installer.

- Double-click on the *.zip* file you just downloaded to unarchive it. A directory named *OpenNI_NITE_Installer-OSX* will appear.

- Launch the Terminal from the Finder by going to Applications→Utilities→Terminal.

- Change directory to the downloaded folder. To do this, type **cd** (for change directory) followed by a space, and then drag the folder you just unzipped from the Finder into Terminal. This will paste the correct path to that folder into your prompt. Hit return. (Terminal commands for this and the next few steps can be seen in Figure 2-1.)

- Run the installer with the command: sudo ./install.sh. Type your password when asked. (You must be logged in as a user with administrative privileges to do this.)

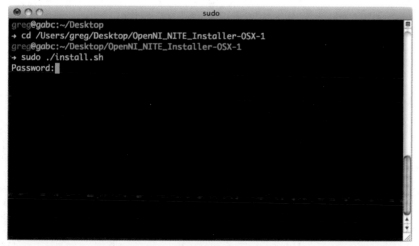

Figure 2-1. *To install OpenNI on OS X, download the installer, unzip it, navigate to that directory, and run the install script as shown here.*

This should successfully complete the installation of OpenNI on Mac OS X. Proceed to the section below on installing the Processing library. If you encounter any errors, visit the SimpleOpenNI Google Code site (*http://code.google.com/p/simple-openni/wiki/Installation*) for debugging tips. Otherwise, proceed with the instructions for installing the Processing library below.

Installing OpenNI on Windows

Installing OpenNI requires a number of pieces of supporting software that all have to be installed for things to work. Thankfully, a company called ZigFu provides a one-click installer that puts all the pieces in place in one shot. You can download the ZigFu installer for Windows from *http://site.zigfu.com/main/downloads*. Select the Zigfu Dev Bundle (not the one labeled "for Mac"). This will provide an *.exe* file you can double-click that should install everything.

However, despite its convenience, the ZigFu installer is still experimental and not officially supported by OpenNI. Hence I've also included instructions for how to install all of these pieces the conventional way directly from OpenNI. These instructions are more complex, but they should work for you if the ZigFu installer fails for some reason. I'll provide the basic steps here along with links to each piece. Make sure you read the pages for each component carefully to ensure that you're following the correct steps to install them for your system.

All of the modules you'll need are available on the OpenNI downloads page (*http://www.openni.org/Downloads/OpenNIModules.aspx*). You'll need to visit that page multiple times to get each of the components one at a time:

Warning

If you've installed the Microsoft Kinect SDK, you need to uninstall it. The OpenNI software does not work with the Microsoft Kinect drivers.

- Start by downloading the hardware drivers. Select OpenNI Compliant Hardware Binaries from the first drop-down menu. In the second drop-down, select Stable. Then, in the final drop-down, you'll need to select the appropriate version for your version of Windows. However, make sure you select the 32-bit version instead of the 64-bit version, even if you're on a 64-bit version of the OS. The Processing library we're using only works in 32-bit mode.

- Double-click the *.msi* installer file you just downloaded and follow the instructions.

- Return to the OpenNI downloads page (*http://www.openni.org/Downloads/OpenNIModules.aspx*) and select OpenNI Compliant Middleware Binaries. Select the Stable version. And then again choose the 32-bit version for your system from the last menu. NITE is the PrimeSense middleware that provides skeleton tracking capabilities. It is necessary for installing SimpleOpenNI and using it in this book.

- Double-click the *.msi* installer file and follow the instructions.

- Some versions of the NITE installer may ask you for a key. If yours does, use this value: `OKOIk2JeIBYClPWVnMoRKn5cdY4=`, including the final equals sign.

- Visit the SensorKinect Github page (*https://github.com/avin2/SensorKinect*).

- Click the "Downloads" tab to the right of the page Files tab and select "Download as zip."

- Open the zip file (named something like *avin2-SensorKinect-2d13967.zip*) and navigate to the Bin folder inside of it.

- Double-click the *.msi* installer for your version of Window, named something like *SensorKinect-Win-OpenSource32-X.msi* where *X* is a dot-separated version number.

Chapter 2

This should successfully complete the install of OpenNI on Windows. Plug your Kinect into your computer's USB port. If everything went smoothly, the device drivers will install automatically, and Kinect should show up in your Device Manager under PrimeSense as Kinect Audio, Kinect Camera, and Kinect Motor. If you encounter any errors, visit the SimpleOpenNI Google Code site (*http://code.google.com/p/simple-openni/wiki/Installation*) for debugging tips. Otherwise, proceed with the instructions for installing the Processing library below.

Installing OpenNI on Linux

If you're a Linux user, you're probably quite comfortable with installing software for your platform. So I'll simply point you towards the SimpleOpenNI install instructions for Linux: *http://code.google.com/p/simple-openni/wiki/Installation#Linux*. The process is relatively similar to the Windows installation process described above, except that you have the choice of downloading and installing binaries for all the packages (OpenNI, NITE, and SensorKinect) or downloading and compiling the source code. You'll need to specify the product key for NITE, which is listed on that page.

Installing the Processing Library

Once you've gotten OpenNI installed (including the NITE middleware and the SensorKinect driver), it's time to install the Processing library. Thankfully, this is dramatically easier than installing OpenNI and pretty much the same for all platforms. Here are the steps:

- Visit the downloads page (*http://code.google.com/p/simple-openni/downloads/list*) on the SimpleOpenNI Google Code site.

- Select the version of SimpleOpenNI that is appropriate for your operating system and download it.

- Unzip the downloaded file (this may happen automatically depending on your browser configuration).

- Locate your Processing *libraries* folder. If you don't already know where that is, you can find out by looking at the Processing Preferences window. As you can see in Figure 2-2, the Processing Preferences window allows you to select your "Sketchbook location." In my case, that location was */Users/greg/Documents/Processing*. Yours may differ based on your operating system and where you installed Processing. Your *libraries* folder will be located inside of this sketchbook folder. For me, it is */Users/greg/Documents/Processing/libraries*. If the *libraries* folder does not exist, create it.

- Drag the unzipped SimpleOpenNI directory to your Processing *libraries* folder.

- Quit and restart Processing.

- SimpleOpenNI should now show up in Processing's list of installed libraries (Figure 2-3). You can confirm this by looking for it under the Sketch→Import Library menu.

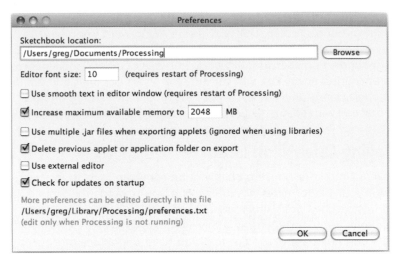

Figure 2-2. *The Processing Preferences window. The "Sketchbook location" entry determines where Processing stores its libraries. You should install the SimpleOpenNI library in a folder called "libraries" inside this directory.*

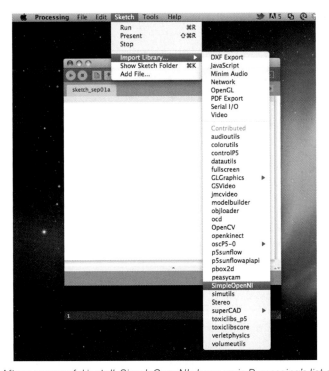

Figure 2-3. *After a successful install, SimpleOpenNI shows up in Processing's list of libraries.*

Now that you've got the library installed, grab your Kinect and plug it in. Plug the electrical plug into a power outlet as shown in Figure 2-4, then plug the Kinect into the female end of the Y-shaped cable coming off of the power cable as demonstrated in Figure 2-5. This should have a glowing green LED on it. The other end of this Y-cable has a standard male USB plug on it. Connect that to your computer as shown in Figure 2-6. Stick the Kinect somewhere convenient, preferably so it's facing you.

Chapter 2

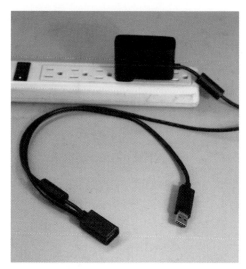

Figure 2-4. *The Kinect's power plug has a y-connector on the end of it. One leg of that connector has a female plug for an Xbox connector and the other has a male USB plug.*

Figure 2-5. *The Kinect has one wire coming off of it with a male Xbox connector at the end. This plugs into the female Xbox connector attached to the power plug.*

Figure 2-6. *The male USB connector from the power supply plugs into your computer's USB port. With the Kinect plugged into the Xbox plug and the power plug in a socket, this completes the physical setup for the Kinect.*

You can test out your install by running one of the built-in examples that ships with SimpleOpenNI. Within Processing, navigate to the File menu and select Examples. This will cause a window to pop up with all of Processing's built-in sketches as well as examples from all of the external libraries such as SimpleOpenNI. Figure 2-7 shows you where to look. Scroll down the list until you hit the entry for Contributed Libraries; open that entry and look for an entry named SimpleOpenNI. Inside, there will be folders for NITE and OpenNI. Inside of OpenNI, find DepthImage and double-click it.

Figure 2-7. *The SimpleOpenNI Processing library includes a number of example sketches. These sketches are a great way to test to see if your installation of the library is working successfully.*

This will cause Processing to open the DepthImage example sketch that is provided with SimpleOpenNI. This is a basic sketch, quite similar to what we'll construct in the next section of this chapter. You'll learn more about this code soon. For now, just hit the play button in the top-left corner of the Processing window to run the sketch (see Figure 2-8).

If everything installed correctly, a new window will pop up, and eventually, you'll see a color image and a grayscale image side by side, representing the Kinect's view of the room. If it takes your sketch a little while to start up, don't worry about it. Slow startup is normal when using SimpleOpenNI.

However, your sketch may raise an error and fail to start. If it does it will print out a message in the Processing window. The most common of these messages is this:

```
Invalid memory access of location 0x8 eip=0xb48d8fda
```

Figure 2-8. *Click the play button to run a Processing sketch. Here we're running one of SimpleOpenNI's built-in example sketches.*

If you see that it most likely means that your Kinect is not plugged in or not fully powered. Make sure your Kinect is connected to a power outlet and plugged into your computer's USB port. If you're working on a laptop, also make sure that your laptop is plugged into power. Some laptops (especially Macs of recent vintage) will provide inadequate power to their USB ports when running off a battery.

If you encounter other errors, consult the SimpleOpenNI Google Code site or review the install instructions provided here to make sure that you didn't skip any steps. If all else fails, try sending an email to the SimpleOpenNI mailing list (accessibly through the Google Code site). The project's maintainers are friendly and quite capable of helping you debug your particular situation. You should search the mailing list archives before you post, just in case someone else has had the same problem as you.

Project 2: Your First Kinect Program

That's it for setup. Now we're ready to start writing our own code. Our first program is going to be pretty simple. It's just going to access the Kinect, read the images from both its depth camera and its color camera, and then display them both on the screen side by side. Once that's working, we'll gradually add to this program to explore the pixels of both images.

You've got the Kinect library installed and your Kinect plugged into your computer, so launch Processing and run the program below. Read through it, run it, and take a look at what it displays. Spend some time waving your hands around in front of your Kinect (this, you'll find, is one of the core activities that make up the process of Kinect development) and then, when you're ready, meet me after the code listing. I'll walk through each line of this first program and make sure you understand everything about how it works.

```
import SimpleOpenNI.*;
SimpleOpenNI kinect;

void setup()
{
  size(640*2, 480);
  kinect = new SimpleOpenNI(this);

  kinect.enableDepth();
  kinect.enableRGB();
}

void draw()
{
  kinect.update();

  image(kinect.depthImage(), 0, 0);
  image(kinect.rgbImage(), 640, 0);
}
```

When you run this sketch, you'll have a cool moment that's worth noting: your first time looking at a live depth image. Not to get too cheesy, but this is a bit of a landmark like the first time your parents or grandparents saw color television. This is your first experience with a new way of seeing, and it's a cool sign that you're living in the future! Shortly, we'll go through this code line by line. I'll explain each part of how it works and start introducing you to the SimpleOpenNI library we'll be using to access the Kinect throughout this book.

Minimum range

As I explained in Chapter 1, the Kinect's depth camera has some limitations due to how it works. We're seeing evidence of one of these here. The Kinect's depth camera has a minimum range of about 20 inches. Closer than that, the Kinect can't accurately calculate distances based on the displacement of the infrared dots. Since it can't figure out an accurate depth, the Kinect just treats anything closer than this minimum range as if it had a depth value of 0—in other words, as if it was infinitely far away. That's why my forearm shows up as black in the depth image—it's closer than the Kinect's minimum range.

Noise at edges

First, what's with splotches around the edges of my shoulders? Whenever you look at a moving depth image from the Kinect you'll tend to see splotches of black appearing and disappearing at the edges of objects that should really be some solid shade of gray. This happens because the Kinect can only calculate depth where the dots from its infrared projector are reflected back to it. The edges of objects like my shoulders or the side of my face tend to deflect some of the dots away at odd angles so that they don't actually make it back to the Kinect's infrared camera at all. Where no IR dots reach the infrared camera, the Kinect can't calculate the depth of the object and so, just like in the case of objects closer than 20 inches, there's a hole in the Kinect's data and the depth image turns black. We'll see later on in the book that if we want to work around this problem, we can use the data from many depth images over time to smooth out the gaps in these edges. However, this method only works if we've got an object that's sitting still.

OBSERVATIONS ABOUT THE DEPTH IMAGE

What do you notice when you look at the output from the Kinect? I'd like to point out a few observations that are worth paying attention to because they illustrate some key properties and limitations of the Kinect that you'll have to understand to build effective applications with it. For reference, Figure 2-9 shows a screen capture of what I see when I run this app.

Figure 2-9. *A screen capture of our first Processing sketch showing the depth image side by side with a color image from the Kinect.*

What do you notice about this image besides my goofy haircut and awkward grin?

First of all, look at the right side of the depth image, where my arm disappears off camera toward the Kinect. Things tend to get brighter as they come toward the camera: my shoulder and upper arm are brighter than my neck, which is brighter than the chair, which is much brighter than the distant kitchen wall. This makes sense. We know by now that the color of the pixels in the depth image represent how far away things are, with brighter things being closer and darker things farther away. If that's the case, then why is my forearm, the thing in the image closest to the camera, black?

There are some other parts of the image that also look black when we might not expect them to. While it makes sense that the back wall of the kitchen would be black as it's quite far away from the Kinect, what's with all the black splotches on the edges of my shoulders and on my shirt? And while we're at it, why is the mirror in the top-left corner of the image so dark? It's certainly not any farther away than the wall that it's mounted on. And finally, what's with the heavy dark shadow behind my head?

I'll answer these questions one at a time, as they each demonstrate an interesting aspect of depth images that we'll see coming up constantly as we work with them throughout this book.

Reflection causes distortion

Next, why does the mirror look so weird? If you look at the color image, you can see that the mirror in the top left corner of the frame is just a thin slab of glass sitting on the wall. Why then does it appear so much darker than the wall it's on? Instead of the wall's even middle gray, the mirror shows up in the depth image as a thick band of full black and then, inside of that, a gradient that shifts from dark gray down to black again. What is happening here?

Well, being reflective, the mirror bounces away the infrared dots that are coming from the Kinect's projector. These then travel across the room until they hit some wall or other nonreflective surface. At that point, they bounce off, travel back to the mirror, reflect off of it, and eventually make their way to the Kinect's infrared camera. This is exactly how mirrors normally work with visible light to allow you to see reflections. If you look at the RGB image closely, you'll realize that the mirror is reflecting a piece of the white wall on the opposite side of the room in front of me.

In the case of a depth image, however, there's a twist. Since the IR dots were displaced farther, the Kinect calculates the depth of the mirror to be the distance between the Kinect and the mirror plus the distance between the mirror and the part of the room reflected in it. It's like the portion of the wall reflected in the mirror had been picked up and moved so that it was actually behind the mirror instead of in front of it.

This effect can be inconvenient at times when reflective surfaces show up accidentally in spaces you're trying to map with the Kinect, for example windows and glass doors. If you don't plan around them, these can cause strange distortions that can screw up the data from the Kinect and frustrate your plans. However, if you account for this reflective effect by getting the angle just right between the Kinect and any partially reflective surface, you can usually work around them without too much difficulty.

Further, some people have actually taken advantage of this reflective effect to do clever things. For example, artist and researcher Kyle McDonald set up a series of mirrors similar to what you might see in a tailor's shop around a single object, reflecting it so that all of its sides are visible simultaneously from the Kinect, letting him make a full 360 degree scan of the object all at once without having to rotate it or move it. Figure 2-10 shows Kyle's setup and the depth image that results.

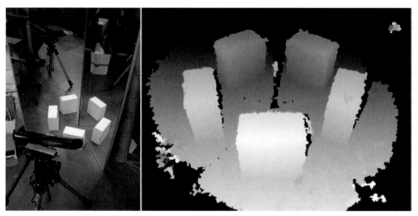

Figure 2-10. *Artist Kyle McDonald's setup using mirrors to turn the Kinect into a 360 degree 3D scanner. Photos courtesy of Kyle McDonald.*

Occlusion and depth shadows

Finally, what's up with that shadow behind my head? If you look at the depth image I captured you can see a solid black area to the left of my head, neck, and shoulder that looks like a shadow. But if we look at the color image, we see no shadow at all there. What's going on? The Kinect's projector shoots out a pattern of IR dots. Each dot travels until it reaches an object and then it bounces back to the Kinect to be read by the infrared camera and used in the depth calculation. But what about other objects in the scene that were behind that first object? No IR dots will ever reach

Chapter 2

those objects. They're stuck in the closer object's IR shadow. And since no IR dots ever reach them, the Kinect won't get any depth information about them, and they'll be another black hole in the depth image.

This problem is called *occlusion*. Since the Kinect can't see through or around objects, there will always be parts of the scene that are occluded or blocked from view and that we don't have any depth data about. What parts of the scene will be occluded is determined by the position and angle of the Kinect relative to the objects in the scene.

One useful way to think about occlusion is that the Kinect's way of seeing is like lowering a very thin and delicate blanket over a complicated pile of objects. The blanket only comes down from one direction and if it settles on a taller object in one area, then the objects underneath that won't ever make contact with the blanket unless they extend out from underneath the section of the blanket that's touching the taller object. The blanket is like the grid of IR dots, only instead of being lowered onto an object, the dots are spreading out away from the Kinect to cover the scene.

Misalignment between the color and depth images

Finally, before we move on to looking more closely at the code, there's one other subtle thing I wanted to point out about this example. Look closely at the depth image and the color image. Are they framed the same? In other words, do they capture the scene from exactly the same point of view? Look at my arm, for example. In the color image, it seems to come off camera to the right at the very bottom of the frame, not extending more than about a third of the way up. In the depth image, however, it's quite a bit higher. My arm looks like it's bent at a more dramatic angle and it leaves the frame clearly about halfway up. Now, look at the mirror in both images. A lot more of the mirror is visible in the RGB image than the depth image. It extends farther down into the frame and farther to the right. The visible portion of it is taller than it is wide. In the depth image on the other hand, the visible part of the mirror is nothing more than a small square in the upper-left corner.

What is going on here? As we know from the introduction, the Kinect captures the depth image and the color image from two different cameras. These two cameras are separated from each other on the front of the Kinect by a couple of inches. Because of this difference in position, the two cameras will necessarily see slightly different parts of the scene, and they will see them from slightly different angles. This difference is a little bit like the difference between your two eyes. If you close each of your eyes one at a time and make some careful observations, you'll notice similar types of differences of angle and framing that we're seeing between the depth image and the color image.

These differences between these two images are more than just a subtle technical footnote. As we'll see later in the book, aligning the color and depth images, in other words overcoming the differences we're observing here with code that takes them into account, allows us to do all kinds of cool things like automatically removing the background from the color image or producing a full-color three-dimensional scan of the scene. But that alignment is an advanced topic we won't get into until later.

Understanding the Code

Now that we've gotten a feel for the depth image, let's take a closer look at the code that displayed it.

I'm going to walk through each line of this example rather thoroughly. Since it's our first time working with the Kinect library, it's important for you to understand this example in as much detail as possible. As the book goes on and you get more comfortable with using this library, I'll progress through examples more quickly, only discussing whatever is newest or trickiest. But the concepts in this example are going to be the foundation of everything we do throughout this book and we're right at the beginning so, for now, I'll go slowly and thoroughly through everything.

On line 1 of this sketch, we start by importing the library:

```
import SimpleOpenNI.*;
```

This works just like importing any other Processing library and should be familiar to anyone who's worked with Processing (if you're new to Processing, check out *Getting Started with Processing* from O'Reilly). The library is called *SimpleOpenNI* because it's a Processing wrapper for the OpenNI toolkit provided by PrimeSense that I discussed earlier. As a wrapper, SimpleOpenNI just makes the capabilities of OpenNI available in Processing, letting us write code that takes advantage of all of the powerful stuff PrimeSense has built into their framework. That's why we had to install OpenNI and NITE as part of the setup process for working with this library: when we call our Processing code, the real heavy lifting is going to be done by OpenNI itself. We won't have to worry about the details of that too frequently as we write our code, but it's worth noting here at the beginning.

The next line declares our SimpleOpenNI object and names it `kinect`:

```
SimpleOpenNI kinect;
```

This is the object we'll use to access all of the Kinect's data. We'll call functions on it to get the depth and color images and, eventually, the user skeleton data as well. Here we've just declared it but not instantiated it, so that's something we'll have to look out for in the `setup` function.

Now we're into the `setup` function. The first thing we do here is declare the size of our app:

```
void setup()
{
  size(640*2, 480);
```

I mentioned earlier that the images that come from the Kinect are 640 pixels wide by 480 tall. In this example, we're going to display two images from the Kinect side by side: the depth image and the RGB image. Hence, we need an app that's 480 pixels tall to match the Kinect's images in height, but is twice as wide so it can contain two of them next to each other; that's why we set the width to `640*2`.

Once that's done, as promised earlier, we need to actually instantiate the `SimpleOpenNI` instance that we declared at the top of the sketch, which we do here:

```
kinect = new SimpleOpenNI(this);
```

Having that in hand, we then proceed to call two methods on our instance: enableDepth and enableRGB, and that's the end of the setup function, so we close that out with a }:

```
    kinect.enableDepth();
    kinect.enableRGB();
}
```

These two methods are our way of telling the library that we will want to access both the depth image and the RGB image from the Kinect. Depending on our application, we might only want one, or even neither of these. By telling the library in advance what kind of data we'll want to access, we give it a chance to do just enough work to provide us what we need. The library only has to ask the Kinect for the data we actually plan to use in our application and so it's able to update faster, letting our app run faster and smoother in turn.

At this point, we're done setting up. We've created an object for accessing the Kinect, and we've told it that we're going to want both the RGB data and the depth data. Now, let's look at the draw loop to see how we actually access that data and do something with it.

We kick off the draw loop by calling the update function on our Kinect object:

```
void draw()
{
    kinect.update();
```

This tells the library to get fresh data from the Kinect so that we can work with it. It'll pull in different data depending on which enable functions we called in setup; in our case, here that means we'll now have fresh depth and RGB images to work with.

We're down to the last two lines, which are the heart of this example. Let's take the first one:

```
    image(kinect.depthImage(), 0, 0);
```

Starting from the inside out, we first call kinect.depthImage, which asks the library for the most recently available depth image. This image is then handed to Processing's built-in image function along with two other arguments both set to 0. This tells processing to draw the depth image at 0,0 in our sketch, or at the very top left of our app's window.

The next line does nearly the same exact thing except with two important differences:

```
    image(kinect.rgbImage(), 640, 0);
}
```

It calls kinect.rgbImage to get the color image from the Kinect and it passes 640,0 to image instead of 0,0, which means that it will place the color image at the top of the app's window, but 640 pixels from the left side. In other words, the depth image will occupy the leftmost 640 pixels in our app and the color image the rightmost ones.

FRAME RATES

The Kinect camera captures data at a rate of 30 frames per second. In other words, every 1/30 of a second, the Kinect makes a new depth and RGB image available for us to read. If our app runs faster than 30 frames a second, the draw function will get called multiple times before a new set of depth and RGB images is available from the Kinect. If our app runs slower than 30 frames a second, we'll miss some images. But how fast does our app actually run? What is our frame rate? The answer is that we don't know. By default, Processing tries to run our draw function 60 times per second. You can change this target by calling Processing's frameRate function and passing it the frame rate at which you'd like your sketch to run. However, in practice, the actual frame rate of your sketch will depend on what your sketch is actually doing. How long each run of the draw function takes depends on a lot of factors including what we're asking it to do and how much of our computer's resources are available for Processing to use. For example, if we had an ancient really slow computer and we were asking Processing to print out every word of Dickens' *A Tale of Two Cities* on every run of the draw function, we'd likely have a very low frame rate. On the other hand, when running Processing on a typical modern computer with a draw loop that only does some basic operations, we might have a frame rate significantly above 30 frames per second. And further, in either of these situations, our frame rate might vary over time both as our app's level of exertion varied with user input and the resources available to it varied with what else was running on our computer.

For now in these beginning examples, you won't have to worry too much about the frame rate, but as we start to build more sophisticated applications, this will be a constant concern. If we try to do too much work on each run of our draw function, our interactions may get slow and jerky, but if we're clever, we'll be able to keep all our apps just as smooth as this initial example.

One more note about how these lines work. By calling kinect.depthImage and kinect.rgbImage inline within the arguments to image we're hiding one important part of how these functions work together: we're never seeing the return value from kinect.depthImage or kinect.rgbImage. This is an elegant and concise way to write a simple example like this, but right now we're trying for understanding rather than elegance, so we might learn something by rewriting our examples like this:

```
import SimpleOpenNI.*;
SimpleOpenNI  kinect;

void setup()
{
  // double the width to display two images side by side
  size(640*2, 480);
  kinect = new SimpleOpenNI(this);

  kinect.enableDepth();
  kinect.enableRGB();
}
```

Chapter 2

```
void draw()
{
  kinect.update();

  PImage depthImage = kinect.depthImage();
  PImage rgbImage = kinect.rgbImage();

  image(depthImage, 0, 0);
  image(rgbImage, 640, 0);
}
```

In this altered example, we've introduced two new lines to our sketch's draw function. Instead of implicitly passing the return values from kinect.depthImage and kinect.rgbImage to Processing's image function, we're now storing them in local variables and then passing those variables to image. This has not changed the functionality of our sketch at all, and if you run it, you'll see no difference in the behavior. What it does is make the return type of our two image-accessing functions explicit: both kinect.depthImage and kinect.rgbImage return a PImage, Processing's class for storing image data. This class provides all kinds of useful functions for working with images such as the ability to access the image's individual pixels and to alter them, something we're going to be doing later on in this chapter. Having the Kinect data in the form of a PImage is also a big advantage because it means that we can automatically use the Kinect data with other libraries that don't know anything at all about the Kinect but do know how to process PImages.

Project 3: Looking at a Pixel

At this point, we've worked our way completely through this first basic example. You've learned how to include the Kinect SimpleOpenNI library in a Processing sketch, how to turn on access to both the RGB and depth images, how to update these images from the Kinect and how to draw them to the screen.

Now that we've got all that under our belt, it's time to start learning more about the individual pixels that make up these images. I told you in the intro to this section that the color of each pixel in the depth image represents the distance of that part of the scene. And, on the other hand, each pixel of the color image will have three components, one each for red, green, and blue. Since we've now got an app running that displays both of these types of images, we can make a simple addition to it that will let us explore both sets of pixels so we can start to get some hands-on experience with them. Once you're starting to feel comfortable with individual pixels, we'll move on to operations that process every pixel in an image so that we can do things like finding the closest part of the depth image. And once we're at that point, we'll be ready to build our first truly interactive projects with the Kinect.

Let's grab some pixels! We'll start by modifying our existing sketch to give us some more information about the pixels of the depth and color images. Specifically, we're going to make it so that whenever you click on one of these images, Processing will print out information about the particular pixel you clicked on.

Here's the code:

```
import SimpleOpenNI.*;
SimpleOpenNI  kinect;

void setup()
{
  size(640*2, 480);
  kinect = new SimpleOpenNI(this);

  kinect.enableDepth();
  kinect.enableRGB();
}

void draw()
{
  kinect.update();

  PImage depthImage = kinect.depthImage();
  PImage rgbImage = kinect.rgbImage();

  image(depthImage, 0, 0);
  image(rgbImage, 640, 0);
}

void mousePressed(){
  color c = get(mouseX, mouseY);
  println("r: " + red(c) + " g: " + green(c) + " b: " + blue(c));
}
```

The new lines are the last four at the bottom, the mousePressed function. Add that to your sketch and run it. Arrange the windows on your computer so that you can see your running sketch as well as the Processing development environment. Click around in a few different places in the depth image and the color image. You should see a line of text appear in the output area at the bottom of the Processing editor every time you click. This is the output from our new mousePressed function. Experiment a bit until you've gotten a feel for these numbers and then come back here and I'll explain this new function, the data it's showing us, and what we might learn from it.

As you've probably figured out by now, this new function gets called whenever you click your mouse within the running Processing app. You've probably seen something like this before, but I'll go through this example just in case you haven't and also so you understand exactly what data we're seeing here about the depth and color images.

Our implementation of the mousePressed function does two things: it figures out the color of the pixel you click on and it prints out some information about that pixel. Unsurprisingly, then, mousePressed only has two lines in it, one to accomplish each of these things. Let's look at how they work.

The first line of mousePressed calls get, which is a function that Processing provides to let us access the value of any pixel that we've already drawn on the screen. In this case, all the pixels that we've drawn to the screen are from the Kinect's depth and color images, so that's what we'll be accessing. This function takes two arguments, the x- and y-coordinates of the pixel whose value we'd like to view. In this case, we want to inspect a different pixel with every

Chapter 2

click (whichever pixel happens to be under the mouse) so instead of using constants for x and y, we use mouseX and mouseY, which are special variables that Processing automatically prepopulates with the current coordinates of the mouse. Calling get within the mousePressed function with these arguments will tell us exactly the color of the pixel the user just clicked on. And, since get returns a color, we store its return value in a local variable, c, that is declared as a color—the Processing type for storing, you guessed it: colors.

Once we've got that color, all we have left to do is print out some information about it. And we know from our discussion about pixels at the start of this chapter that we want the red, green, and blue components if those are available. So the second line of mousePressed calls more built-in Processing functions to extract each component value from our color. We call red, green, and blue one at a time, passing c as an argument, the color we extracted from the clicked pixel. Once we've got those values, we just combine them into one long string (using +) that we can print to the Processing output window with println.

Now that we've got the ability to print out information about any pixel in either the depth or color image at will, let's use it to do some concrete experiments to see how the pixels work in each type of image. We'll start with the color image.

Figure 2-11 shows a screen capture I took of this new version of the app.

Figure 2-11. *Depth and RGB images of the old chair where I wrote this book. Clicking around on this image in our sketch will reveal its depth values.*

It shows my favorite old beaten-up red chair where I wrote much of this book. I'll use this image to illustrate the pixel values shown by our new mousePressed function. You can follow along with whatever your own Kinect is seeing.

Color Pixels

I started by clicking on the color image right in the middle of the chair's back, the part that's been worn shiny by my squirming against it. When I clicked there, I saw the following print out in the Processing output area: r: 124.0 g: 3.0 b: 9.0. Since the pixel under my mouse was part of a color image, the red, blue, and green functions each extracted a different component of the pixel, telling me out of a range of 0–255 how much red, blue, and green there was in the image.

The resulting data has a couple of surprises. First of all, to my eye, the back of the chair where I clicked looks almost perfectly red, but the red component of the pixel was only 124, or less than half the possible total of 255. This shows a key difference between how we see as people with eyes and the pixel values that a computer calculates by processing the data from a digital camera. As people, our impressions of what we see are relative. We focus on the differences between the parts of whatever we're seeing rather than their absolute levels. We think the back of the chair is fully red not because it has a red value close to some theoretical absolute limit, but because its red value is so much higher than its green and blue values. With just 3 for green and 9 for blue, that 124 for red looks like pure red to us.

Now, let's look at a couple of other parts of the color image to explore these ideas further before turning our attention to the depth image. To my eye, the brightest whitest part of the image is the strip of wall on the right side of the image. When I click there, I get these pixel components printed out by the sketch: `r: 245.0 g: 238.0 b: 245.0`. So, what does white look like in a color image? A perfectly white pixel would be one that has all three of the red, green, and blue components at values of 255. This pixel on the white wall is nearly there; it has very high values for all three components and all three components are nearly equal.

Let's compare this perfectly white wall with the slightly dimmer refrigerator door just behind it. When I click there, I get `r: 182.0 g: 165.0 b: 182.0`. These values are still very close to equal with each other, but are now each slightly further from 255.

So, what have we learned about color pixels? First of all, we've learned that color itself comes from there being a difference between the individual color components. A pixel that has all three of its components nearly equal will look white or some shade of gray. Further, while it's the relative levels of the color components that determine which color we perceive, it's the sum total between the levels of all three of the pixels that determines its brightness. The white that had all three values close to 255 was brighter than the one that had all three values clustered around 180.

Let's look at an even darker part of the image to get one more interesting piece of data. When I click on the green curtains that are deep in the shade of my kitchen, I get pixel values that look like this: `r: 15.0 g: 6.0 b: 3.0`. From what we just learned about brightness, we might've expected to see very low numbers like these for each of the pixel components. But, it's surprising that the red pixel has the highest value of the three when the curtains are obviously green or, in their darkest parts, black. What's going on here? Well, if you look at the image for awhile, or if you click around on other parts that appear to be white or neutral (for example, the white wall behind the chair), you'll find that the whole image actually has a reddish or purplish hue. That is, the red and blue components of each pixel will always have slightly higher values than we'd expect.

Again, a color shift like this is one of those qualities that it's very easy for our eye to ignore, but makes a really big impact on the pixel values that our Processing code will see when looking at a color image. You can look at this picture of those curtains and in an instant know that they were green. Your brain automatically eliminates information like the darker lighting and the red-shifted image. It's not confused by them. But imagine if I gave you the assignment of writing a program to figure out the color of those curtains. Imagine if I gave you all the pixels that corresponded to the curtain and you had to use only their component color values to identify the curtain's real color. Since most of the pixels have very low red, green, and blue values and many of them have red as their leading component, nearly any approach that you came up with would end up concluding that the curtains were black with shades of red.

To get a better answer, you'd need access to all of the pixels in the image in order to compare the colors in different areas (so you could do things like detect the red shift), and you might even need a lot of data from other similar images so you'd know what other kinds of distortions and aberrations to expect. In the end, you'd be faced with the extremely difficult problem of inventing a whole system of heuristics, assumptions, and fiendishly complex algorithms in an attempt to extract the kind of information our brain can produce effortlessly on seeing nearly any image. And even if you went ahead and got a degree in computer vision, the academic field dedicated to doing exactly this kind of thing, you could still only achieve limited success while working with badly lit, low-resolution color images like these.

Conventional color images are just fundamentally ill-suited to being processed by computer programs. Sure applications like Photoshop can manipulate and alter these types of images in a million ways to change their appearance, but trying to write programs that understand these images, that extract from them something like our own understanding of our physical environment (how far away things are from us, where one object ends and another begins, etc.), is a fool's errand. In fact, color images are so bad for this task that we're basically never going to look at them again in this book. (The only exceptions to this will be when we're talking about ways of aligning color images with depth images so that we can apply realistic color to our visualizations after we've done the heavy lifting by processing the depth data.)

Depth Pixels

If you were a computer vision researcher, frustrated by these limitations, you'd quickly find yourself wanting a whole different kind of image that didn't suffer from these kinds of problems. You'd want something like a depth image.

Thankfully, even though we're not computer vision researchers (or, at least we're only amateurs), we do happen to have a depth image sitting right here in our Processing sketch next to our color image. Let's click around on that image some to get a feel for its pixel values and how they might be easier to work with than those we've seen so far.

I'll start at the same place I started in the color image: by clicking on the back of my comfy red chair. Only this time, I'll obviously make my click on the left side of the sketch, within the depth image, rather than in the color image. When I click on the back of my chair in the depth image, our `mousePressed` code prints the following output: `r: 96.0 g: 96.0 b: 96.0`.

A couple of things should jump out at you immediately about this. In contrast to any of the color pixels we looked at, all three of the components of this pixel are exactly the same. Not nearly the same as was the case in the parts of the white wall we examined, but exactly the same. After our discussion of color pixels, this should make total sense. We know that the color of a pixel is determined by the difference between its red, blue, and green components. Since the depth image is grayscale, its pixels don't have color, and hence its components are all exactly identical. A grayscale pixel does, however, have brightness. In fact, brightness is just about all a grayscale pixel has, since in this case, *brightness* really means "distance between white and black."

As you saw earlier, brightness is determined by the combination of all three of the pixel components. And since all three components of each grayscale pixel are always going to be exactly equal, the brightness of a grayscale pixel will be equal to this same value we're seeing for each of the components, in the case of this pixel from the back of my chair, 96. In fact, Processing actually has a brightness function that we can use instead of red, blue, or green that will give us the exact same result as any of these when used on grayscale images. As we go forward and start to work more exclusively with depth images, we'll use brightness instead of red, green, or blue to access the value of pixels, because it's silly to talk about the red or green component of an image that is obviously black and white.

Now, let's click around on a few other parts of the depth image to see how the brightness of these depth pixels vary. If I click on those pesky dark green window curtains, I get a brightness reading of 8.0 (technically, Processing prints out r: 8.0 g: 8.0 b: 8.0, but we now know that we can summarize that as brightness). In the depth image, the curtains look nearly completely black. They are, in fact, so dark that they're actually hard to even distinguish from their surroundings with the naked eye. However, if I click around that area of the image, I get a different brightness reading each time. There's detailed depth information even in parts of the image where the eye can't see different shades of gray.

Let's look at a part of the depth image that has some dramatic difference from the color images: my comfy old red chair. By comparing some depth and color readings from different parts of the chair, we can really start to see the advantages of the depth image in overcoming the limitations of the color image we so vividly encountered above.

If I click on different parts of the chair in the color image, the pixel values I measure don't change that much. For example, a pixel from the front of the chair (the part of the seat that's facing forward toward the Kinect) has components r: 109.0 g: 1.0 b: 0.0; while a pixel from low on the chair's back, just above the seat has components r: 112.0 g: 4.0 b: 2.0. These values are barely different from each other, and if I clicked around more in each of these parts of the image, I'd certainly find a pixel reading r: 109.0 g: 1.0 b: 0.0 on the chair's back, and vice versa. There's nothing in these color pixels that tells me that the chair's seat and its back are physically or spatially different.

But what about depth pixels from the same parts of the chair? Clicking on the front of the chair in the depth image, I get a pixel value of 224.0; and on the lower back, I get one of 115.0. Now these are dramatically different. Unlike with the color pixels, there's a big jump in values that corresponds clearly to the two or three feet of depth between the front and back of this chair. Imagine I gave you a similar assignment as the one above with the green curtain, but this time I handed you all the pixels representing the chair and asked you to separate it in space, to distinguish the seat from the back, using depth pixels. Now you'd be able to do it. The pixels on the front of the chair all cluster between 220 and 230 while the pixels on the back of the chair range from about 90 to 120. If you sorted the pixels by brightness, there'd be a big jump at some point in the lineup. All the pixels above that jump would be part of the front of the chair and all the pixels below it would be part of the back. Easy.

For basic problems like this, the information in the depth image is so good that we don't need any super sophisticated computer vision algorithms to accomplish useful work. Basic logic like looking for gaps in the pixels' brightness, or (like we'll see extensively later in this chapter) looking for the brightest pixel, can achieve surprisingly complex and effective applications. And just imagine what we could do once we start using some of those super sophisticated algorithms, which we'll dive into in the next chapter.

Converting to Real-World Distances

But what about these pixels' actual depth? We know that the color of each pixel in the depth image is supposed to relate to the distance of that part of the scene, but how far away is 96 or 115 or 224? How do we translate from these brightness values to a distance measurement in some kind of useful units like inches or centimeters?

Well, let's start with some basic proportions. We know from our experiments earlier in this chapter that the Kinect can detect objects within a range of about 20 inches to 25 feet. And we know that the pixels in our depth image have brightness values that range between 255 and 0. So, logically, it must be the case that pixels in the depth image that have a brightness of 255 must correspond to objects that are 20 inches away, pixels with a value of 0 must be at least 25 feet away, and values in between must represent the range in between, getting farther away as their values descend toward 0.

So, how far away is the back of our chair with the depth pixel reading of 96? Given the logic just described, we can make an estimate. Doing a bit of back-of-the-envelope calculation tells me that 96 is approximately 37% of the way between 0 and 255. Hence the simplest possible distance calculation would hold that the chair back is 37% of the way between 25 feet and 20 inches, or about 14 and a half feet. This is clearly not right. I'm sitting in front of the chair now and it's no more than 8 or 10 feet away from the Kinect.

Did we go wrong somewhere in our calculation? Is our Kinect broken? No. The answer is much simpler. The relationship between the brightness value of the depth pixel and the real-world distance it represents is more complicated than a simple linear ratio. There are really good reasons for this to be the case.

First of all, consider the two ranges of values being covered. As we've thoroughly discussed, the depth pixels represent grayscale values between 0 and 255. The real-world distance covered by the Kinect, on the other hand, ranges between 20 inches and 25 feet. Further, the Kinect's depth readings have millimeter precision. That means they need to report not just a number ranging from 0 to a few hundred inches, but a number ranging from 0 to around 8,000 millimeters to cover the entirety of the distance the Kinect can see. That's obviously a much larger range than can fit in the bit depth of the pixels in our depth image.

Now, given these differences in range, we could still think of some simple ways of converting between the two. For example, it might have occurred to you to use Processing's map function, which scales a variable from an expected range of input values to a different set of output values. However, using map is a little bit like pulling on a piece of stretchy cloth to get it to cover a larger area: you're not actually creating more cloth, you're just pulling the individual strands of the cloth apart, putting space between them to increase the area covered by the whole. If there were a pattern on the surface of the cloth, it would get bigger, but you'd also start to see spaces within it where the strands separated. Processing's map function does something similar. When you use it to convert from a small range of input values to a larger output, it can't create new values out of thin air—it just stretches out the existing values so that they cover the new range. Your highest input values will get stretched up to your highest output value and your lowest input to your lowest output, but just like with the piece of cloth, there won't be enough material to cover all the intermediate values. There will be holes. And in the case of mapping our depth pixels from their brightness range of 0 to 255 to the physical range of 0 to 8,000 millimeters, there will be a lot of holes. Those 256 brightness values will only cover a small minority of the 8,000 possible distance values.

To cover all of those distance values without holes, we'd need to access the depth data from the Kinect in some higher resolution form. As I mentioned in the introduction, the Kinect actually captures the depth information at a resolution of 11 bits per pixel. This means that these raw depth readings have a range of 0 to 2,047—much better than the 0 to 255 available in the depth pixels we've looked at so far. And the SimpleOpenNI library gives us a way to access these raw depth values.

But wait! Have we been cheated? Why don't the depth image pixels have this full range of values? Why haven't we been working with them all along?

Remember the discussion of images and pixels at the start of this chapter? Back then, I explained that the bigger of a number we use to store each pixel in an image, the more memory it takes to store that image and the slower any code runs that has to work with it. Also, it's very hard for people to visually distinguish between more shades of gray than that anyway. Think back to our investigations of the depth image. There were areas in the back of the scene that looked like flat expanses of black pixels, but when we clicked around on them to investigate, it turned out that even they had different brightness values, simply with differences that were too small for us to see. For all of these reasons, all images in Processing have pixels that are 8 bits in depth—i.e., whose values only range from 0 to 255. The `PImage` class we've used in our examples that allows us to load images from the Kinect library and display them on the screen enforces the use of these smaller pixels.

What it really comes down to is this: when we're displaying depth information on the screen as images, we make a set of trade-offs. We use a rougher representation of the data because it's easier to work with and we can't really see the differences anyway. But now that we want to use the Kinect to make precise distance measurements, we want to make a different set of trade-offs. We need the full-resolution data in order to make more accurate measurements, but since that's more unwieldy to work with, we're going to use it more sparingly.

Let's make a new version of our Processing sketch that uses the higher-resolution depth data to turn our Kinect into a wireless tape measure. With this higher-resolution data, we actually have enough information to calculate the precise distance between our Kinect and any object in its field of view and to display it in real-world units like inches and millimeters.

Project 4: A Wireless Tape Measure

The code in this section is going to introduce a new programming concept that I haven't mentioned before and that might not be completely familiar to you from your previous work in Processing: accessing arrays of pixels. Specifically, we'll be learning how to translate between a one-dimensional array of pixels and the two-dimensional image that it represents. I'll explain how to do all of the calculations necessary to access the entry in the array that corresponds to any location in the image. And, more important, I'll explain how to think about the relationship between the image and the array so that these calculations are intuitive and easy to remember.

At first, this discussion of pixels and arrays may feel like a diversion from our core focus on working with the Kinect. But the Kinect is, first and foremost, a camera, so much of our work with it will be based on processing its pixels.

Up to this point, whenever we've wanted to access the Kinect's pixels, we've first displayed them on the screen in the form of images. However, as we just discussed, this becomes impractical when we want to access the Kinect's data at a higher resolution or when we want to access more of it than a single pixel's worth. Therefore, we need to access the data in a manner that doesn't first require us to display it on the screen. In Processing (and most other graphics programming environments) this image data is stored as arrays of pixels behind the scenes. Accessing these arrays of pixels directly (while they are still off stage) will let our programs run fast enough to do some really interesting things like working with the higher resolution data and processing more than one pixel at a time.

Even though Processing stores images as flat arrays of pixels, we still want the ability to think of them two-dimensionally. We want to be able to figure out which pixel a user clicked on or draw something on the screen where we found a particular depth value. In this section, I'll teach you how to make these kinds of translations. We'll learn how to convert between the array the pixels are stored in and their position on the screen.

In this section, I'll introduce this conversion technique by showing you how to access an array of higher resolution values from the Kinect. Then we'll use that to turn the Kinect into a wireless tape measure, converting these depth values into accurate real-world units. Once we've got this down, we'll be ready to take things one step further and start working with all of the pixels coming from the Kinect.

We'll start our tape measure with a new version of our Processing sketch. This version will be along the same lines as the sketch we've been working with but with a few important differences. The basic structure will be the same. We'll still display images from the Kinect and then output information about them when we click, but we'll change what we display, both on the screen and in the output when we click.

First of all, let's forget about the color image from the Kinect. We've learned all that it has to teach us for now and so we're banishing it to focus more on the depth image. Second, we'll rewrite our `mousePressed` function to access and display the higher resolution depth data from the Kinect. I'll explain how this works in some detail, but first take a look at the full code, noticing the changes to `setup` and `draw` that come from eliminating the color image:

```
import SimpleOpenNI.*;
SimpleOpenNI  kinect;

void setup()
{
  size(640, 480);
  kinect = new SimpleOpenNI(this);
  kinect.enableDepth();
}

void draw()
{
  kinect.update();

  PImage depthImage = kinect.depthImage();
  image(depthImage, 0, 0);
}

void mousePressed(){
  int[] depthValues = kinect.depthMap();
  int clickPosition = mouseX + (mouseY * 640);
  int clickedDepth = depthValues[clickPosition];

  float inches = clickedDepth / 25.4;

  println("inches: " + inches);
}
```

The changes to `setup` and `draw` are minimal: I'm no longer accessing the RGB image from the Kinect and no longer displaying it. And since we're now only displaying one image, I made the whole sketch smaller, because we don't need all that horizontal real estate just to show the depth image.

Now, let's talk about the real substantial difference here: the changes I've made to `mousePressed`. First of all, `mousePressed` calls a new function on our `kinect` object that we haven't seen before: `depthMap`. This is one of a few functions that SimpleOpenNI provides that give us access to the higher resolution depth data. This is the simplest one. It returns all of the higher resolution depth values unmodified—neither converted or processed.

In what form does `kinect.depthMap` return these depth values? Up until now, all the depth data we've seen has reached us in the form of images. We know that the higher-resolution values that `kinect.depthMap` returns can't be stored as the pixels of an image. So, then, in what form are they stored? The answer is: as an array of integers. We have one integer for each depth value that the Kinect recorded, and they're all stored in one array. That's why the variable we use to save the results of `kinect.depthMap` is declared thusly: `int[] depthValues`. That `int[]` means that our `depthValues` variable will store an array of integers. If you have a hard time remembering how array declarations like this one work in Processing (as I often do), you can think of the square brackets as being a box that will contain all the values of the array and the `int` that comes before it as a label telling us that everything that goes in this box must be an integer.

So, we have an array of integers. How can this box full of numbers store the same kind of information we've so far seen in the pixels of an image? The Kinect is, after all, a camera. The data that comes from it is two-dimensional, representing all the depth values in its rectangular field of view, whereas an array is one-dimensional, it can only store a single stack of numbers. How do you represent an image as a box full of numbers?

Here's how. Start with the pixel in the top-leftmost corner of the image. Put it in the box. Then, moving to the right along the top row of pixels, put each pixel into the box on top of the previous ones. When you get to the end of the row, jump back to left side of the image, move down one row, and repeat the procedure, continuing to stick the pixels from the second row on top of the ever-growing stack you began in the first row. Continue this procedure for each row of pixels in the image until you reach the very last pixel in the bottom right. Now, instead of a rectangular image, you'll have a single stack of pixels: a one-dimensional array. All the pixels from each row will be stacked together, and the last pixel from each row will be right in front of the first pixel from the next row, as Figure 2-12 shows.

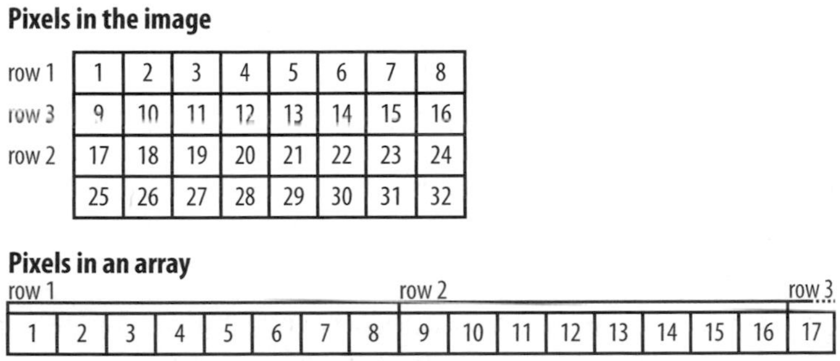

Pixels in the image

row 1	1	2	3	4	5	6	7	8
row 3	9	10	11	12	13	14	15	16
row 2	17	18	19	20	21	22	23	24
	25	26	27	28	29	30	31	32

Pixels in an array

row 1   row 2   row 3

1	2	3	4	5	6	7	8	9	10	11	12	13	14	15	16	17

Figure 2-12. *Pixels in a two-dimensional image get stored as a flat array. Understanding how to split this array back into rows is key to processing images.*

This is exactly how the array returned by `kinect.depthMap` is structured. It has one high-resolution depth value for each pixel in the depth image. Remember that the depth image's resolution is 640 by 480 pixels. That means that it has 480 rows of pixels each of which is 640 pixels across. So, from the logic above, we know that the array `kinect.depthMap` returns contains 307,200 (or 640 times 480) integers arranged in a single linear stack. The first integer in this stack corresponds to the top left pixel in the image. Each following value corresponds to the next pixel across each row until the last value finally corresponds to the last pixel in the bottom right.

But how do we access the values of this array? More specifically, how do we pull out the integer value that corresponds to the part of the image that the user actually clicked on? This is the `mousePressed` event, after all, and so all we have available to us is the position of the mouse at the time that the user clicked. As we've seen, that position is expressed as an x-y coordinate in the variables `mouseX` and `mouseY`. In the past versions of the sketch, we used these coordinates to access the color value of a given pixel in our sketch using `get`, which specifically accepted x-y coordinates as its arguments. However, now we have a stack of integers in an array instead of a set of pixels arranged into a rectangle. Put another way, instead of having a set of x-y coordinates in two axes, we only have a single axis: the integers in our single array. To access data from the array, we need not a pair of x-y coordinates, but an *index*: a number that tells us the position in the array of the value we're looking for. How do we translate from the two axes in which the depth image is displayed and the user interacts with to the single axis of our integer array? In other words, how do we convert `mouseX` and `mouseY` into the single position in the array that corresponds to the user's click?

To accomplish this, we'll have to do something that takes into account how the values were put into the array in the first place. In filling the array, we started at the top-left corner of the image, went down each pixel in each row to the end adding values, and then jumped back to the beginning of the next row when we reached the edge of the image. Imagine that you were counting values as we did this, adding one to your count with each pixel that got converted into a value and added to the array. What would your count look like as we progressed through the image?

For the first row, it's pretty obvious. You'd start your count at 0 (programmers always start counting at 0) and work your way up as you go across the first row. When you reach the last pixel in the first row, your count will be 639 (there are 640 pixels in the row and you started counting at 0 for the first pixel). Then, you'd jump back to the left side of the image to continue on the second row and keep counting. So pixel one on row two would be 640, pixel two would be 641, and so on until you reach the end of row two. At the last pixel of row two, you'd be up to 1279, which means that the first pixel in row three would be 1280. If you continue for another row, you'd finish row three at 1919, and the first pixel of row four would be 1920.

Notice how the first pixel of every row is always a multiple of 640? If I asked what the number would be for the first pixel in the 20th row in the image, instead of counting, you could just multiply: 640 times 20 is 12,800. In other words, the number for the first pixel in each row is the width of the image (i.e., 640) multiplied by which row we're on (i.e., how far down we are from the top of the image).

Let's come back to our mousePressed function for a second. In that function, we happen to have a variable that's always set to exactly how far down the mouse is from the top of the image: mouseY. Our goal is to translate from mouseX and mouseY to the number in our count corresponding to the pixel the mouse is over. With mouseY and the observation we just made, we're now half-way there. We can translate our calculation of the first pixel of each row to use mouseY: mouseY times 640 (the width of the row) will always get us the value of the array corresponding to the first pixel in the row.

But what about all the other pixels? Now that we've figured out what row a pixel is in how can we figure out how far to the left or right that pixel is in the row? We need to take mouseX into account.

Pick out a pixel in the middle of a row, say row 12. Imagine that you clicked the mouse on a pixel somewhere in this row. We know that the pixel's position in the array must be greater than the first pixel in that row. Since we count up as we move across rows, this pixel's position must be the position of the first pixel in its row plus the number of pixels between the start of the row and this pixel. Well, we happen to know the position of the first pixel on the previous row. It's just 12 times 640, the number of the row times the number of pixels in each row. But what about the number of pixels to the left of the pixel we're looking at? Well, in mousePressed, we have a variable that tells us exactly how far the mouse is from the left side of the sketch: mouseX. All we have to do is add mouseX to the value at the start of the row: mouseY times 640.

And, lo and behold, we now have our answer. The position in the array of a given pixel will be mouseX + (mouseY * 640). If at any point in this circuitous discussion you happened to peek at the next line in mousePressed, you would have ruined the surprise because look what that line does—performs this exact calculation:

```
int clickPosition = mouseX + (mouseY * 640);
```

And then the line after that uses its result to access the array of depthValues to pull out the value at the point where the user clicked. That line uses click-Position, the result of our calculation, as an index to access the array. Just like int[] depthValues declared depthValues as an array—a box into which we could put a lot of integers—depthValues[clickPosition] reaches into that box and pulls out a particular integer. The value of clickPosition tells us how far to reach into the box and which integer to pull out.

Higher-Resolution Depth Data

That integer we found in the box is one of our new higher-resolution depth values. As we've been working toward all this time, it's exactly the value that corresponds to the position in the image where the user clicked. Once we've accessed it, we store it in another variable `clickedDepth` and use that to print it to Processing's output window.

If you haven't already, run this sketch and click around on various parts of the depth image. You'll see values printing out to the Processing output area much like they did in all of our previous examples, only this time they'll cover a different range. When I run the sketch, I see values around 450 for the brightest parts of the image (i.e., the closest parts of the scene) and around 8000 for the darkest (i.e., farthest) parts. The parts of the image that are within the Kinect's minimum range or hidden in the shadows of closer images give back readings of 0. That's the Kinect's way of saying that there is no data available for those points.

This is obviously a higher range than the pixel values of 0 to 255 we'd previously seen. In fact, it's actually spookily close to the 0 to 8000 range we were hoping to see to cover the Kinect's full 25-foot physical range at millimeter precision. This is extremely promising for our overall project of trying to convert the Kinect's depth readings to accurate real-world measurements. In fact, it sounds an awful lot like the values we're pulling out of `kinect.depthMap` are the accurate distance measurements in millimeters. In other words, each integer in our new depth readings might actually correspond to a single millimeter of physical distance.

With a few alterations to our `mousePressed` function (and the use of a handy tape measure) we can test out this hypothesis. Here's the new version of the code:

```
import SimpleOpenNI.*;
SimpleOpenNI  kinect;

void setup()
{
  size(640, 480);
  kinect = new SimpleOpenNI(this);

  kinect.enableDepth();
}

void draw()
{
  kinect.update();

  PImage depthImage = kinect.depthImage();

  image(depthImage, 0, 0);
}

void mousePressed(){
  int[] depthValues = kinect.depthMap();
  int clickPosition = mouseX + (mouseY * 640);

  int millimeters = depthValues[clickPosition];
  float inches = millimeters / 25.4;

  println("mm: " + millimeters + " in: " + inches);
}
```

First of all, I renamed our `clickDepth` variable to `millimeters` since our theory is that it actually represents the distance from the Kinect to the object clicked as measured in millimeters. Second, I went ahead and wrote another line of code to convert our millimeter reading to inches. Being American, I think in inches, so it helps me to have these units on hand as well. A few seconds Googling taught me that to convert from millimeters to inches, all you have to do is divide your value by 25.4. Finally, I updated the `println` statement to output both the millimeter and inch versions of our measurement.

Once I had this new code in place, I grabbed my tape measure. I put one end of it under the Kinect and extended it toward myself, as you can see in Figure 2-13.

Figure 2-13. *I held up a tape measure in front of my Kinect to check our depth measurements against the real world.*

The tape shows up as a black line because most of it is inside of the Kinect's minimum range and because all of it is reflective. Once I had the tape measure extended, I locked it down at 32 inches (or about 810 millimeters). Then I could use my free hand to click on the depth image to print out measurements to the Processing output area. It was a little bit hard to distinguish between my hand and the tape measure itself, so I just clicked in that general vicinity. When I did that, Processing printed out: `mms: 806 in: 31.732285`. Dead on! Taking into account the sag in the measuring tape as well as my poorly aimed clicking, this is an extremely accurate result. And more clicking around at different distances confirmed it: our distance calculations lined up with the tape measure every time. We've now turned out Kinect into an accurate digital "tape-less" measuring tape!

Try it out yourself. Get out a tape measure, run this sketch, and double-check my results. Then, once you've convinced yourself that it's accurate, use the Kinect to take some measurements of your room, your furniture, your pets, whatever you have handy.

In this section, you learned two fundamental skills: how to access the Kinect's data as an array of values and how to translate between that array and the position of a particular value in the image.

We're now going to extend those skills to let us work with all of the depth data coming from the Kinect. Instead of translating from a single x-y coordinate to a single array index, we're going to loop through all of the values in the array in order to make general conclusions about the depth data by comparing all of the values. This technique will let us do things like finding and tracking the closest part of the image. At that point, we'll be ready to use the Kinect to build our first real user interfaces. We'll be able to start doing something more interesting than printing numbers in Processing's output area.

This chapter will conclude with a couple of projects that explore some of the possibilities that are opened up by our ability to track the closest point. We'll write a sketch that lets us draw a line by waving our hands and other body parts around. Then we'll go even further and make a sketch that lets us lay out photos by dragging them around in midair *Minority Report*–style.

Project 5: Tracking the Nearest Object

In order to build useful interactive applications with the Kinect, we need to write sketches that respond to the scene in a way that people find intuitive and clear. People have an inherent instinct for the objects and spaces around them. When you walk through a doorway, you don't have to think about how to position yourself so you don't bump into the doorframe. If I asked you to extend your arm toward me or toward some other object, you could do it without thinking. When you walk up to an object, you know when it's within reach before you even extend your arm to pick it up.

Because people have such a powerful understanding of their surrounding spaces, physical interfaces are radically easier for them to understand than abstract, screen-based ones. And this is especially true for physical interfaces that provide simple and direct feedback where the user's movements immediately translate into action.

Having a depth camera gives us the opportunity to provide interfaces like these without needing to add anything physical to the computer. With just some simple processing of the depth data coming in from the Kinect, we can give the user the feeling of directly controlling something on the screen.

The simplest way to achieve this effect is by tracking the point that is closest to the Kinect. Imagine that you're standing in front of the Kinect with nothing between you and it. If you extend your arm toward the Kinect then your hand will be the closest point that the Kinect sees. If our code is tracking the closest point, then suddenly your hand will be controlling something on screen. If our sketch draws a line based on how you move your hand, then the interface should feel as intuitive as painting with a brush. If your sketch moves photos around to follow your hand, it should feel as intuitive as a table covered in prints.

Regardless of the application, though, all of these intuitive interfaces begin by tracking the point closest to the Kinect. How would we start going about that? What are the steps between accessing the depth value of a single point

Chapter 2

and looking through all of the points to find the closest one? Further, all of these interfaces translate the closest point into some kind of visible output. So, once we've found the closest point, how do we translate that position into something that the user can see?

Later in this chapter, you're going to write a sketch that accomplishes all of these things. But before we dive into writing real code, I want to give you a sense of the overall procedure that we're going to follow for finding the closest pixel. This is something that you'll need over and over in the future when you make your own Kinect apps and so rather than simply memorizing or copy-and-pasting code, it's best to understand the ideas behind it so that you can reinvent the code yourself when you need it. To that end, I'm going to start by explaining the individual steps involved in plain English so that you can get an idea of what we're trying to do before we dive into the forest of variables, for loops, and type declarations. Hopefully this *pseudocode*, as its known, will act as a map so you don't get lost in these nitty gritty details when they do arise.

So now: the plan. First, a high-level overview.

Finding the Closest Pixel

Look at every pixel that comes from the Kinect one at a time. When looking at a single pixel, if that pixel is the closest one we've seen so far, save its depth value to compare against later pixels and save its position. Once we've finished looking through all the pixels, what we'll be left with is the depth value of the closest pixel and its position. Then we can use those to display a simple circle on the screen that will follow the user's hand (or whatever else she waves at her Kinect).

Sounds pretty straightforward. Let's break it down into a slightly more concrete form to make sure we understand it:

```
get the depth array from the kinect

for each row in the depth image
  look at each pixel in the row
    for each pixel, pull out the corresponding value from the depth array
      if that pixel is the closest one we've seen so far
        save its value
        and save its position (both X and Y coordinates)

then, once we've looked at every pixel in the image, whatever value
we saved last:
    will be the closest depth reading in the array and whatever position
    we saved last
    will be the position of the closest pixel.

draw the depth image on the screen

draw a red circle over it, positioned at the X and Y coordinates we saved
of the closest pixel.
```

Now this version is starting to look a little bit more like code. I've even indented it like it's code. In fact, we could start to write our code by replacing each line in this pseudocode with a real line of code, and we'd be pretty much on the right track.

But before we do that, let's make sure that we understand some of the subtleties of this plan and how it will actually find us the closest point. The main idea here is that we're going to loop over every point in the depth array comparing depth values as we go. If the depth value of any point is closer than the closest one we've seen before, then we save that new value and compare all future points against it instead.

It's a bit like keeping track of the leader during an Olympic competition. The event starts without a leader. By definition whoever goes first becomes the leader. Their distance or speed becomes the number to beat. During the event, if any athlete runs a faster time or jumps a farther distance, then he becomes the new leader and his score becomes the one to beat. At the end of the event, after all the athletes have had their turns, whoever has the best score is the winner and whatever his score is becomes the winning time or distance.

Our code is going to work exactly like the judges in that Olympic competition. But instead of looking for the fastest time or farthest distance, we're looking for the closest point. As we go through the loop, we'll check each point's distance, and if it's closer than the closest one we've seen so far, that point will become our leader and its distance will be the one to beat. And then, when we get to the end of the loop, after we've seen all the points, whichever one is left as the leader will be the winner, we'll have found our closest point.

OK. At this point you should understand the plan for our code and be ready to look at the actual sketch. I'm presenting it here with the pseudocode included as comments directly above the lines that implement the corresponding idea. Read through it, run it, see what it does, and then I'll explain a few of the nitty-gritty details that we haven't covered yet.

```
import SimpleOpenNI.*;
SimpleOpenNI kinect;

int closestValue; ❶
int closestX;
int closestY;

void setup()
{
  size(640, 480);
  kinect = new SimpleOpenNI(this);
  kinect.enableDepth();
}

void draw()
{
  closestValue = 8000; ❷

  kinect.update();

  // get the depth array from the kinect
  int[] depthValues = kinect.depthMap();

  // for each row in the depth image
  for(int y = 0; y < 480; y++){ ❸

    // look at each pixel in the row
    for(int x = 0; x < 640; x++){ ❹
```

Chapter 2

```
      // pull out the corresponding value from the depth array
      int i = x + y * 640; ❺
      int currentDepthValue = depthValues[i];

      // if that pixel is the closest one we've seen so far
      if(currentDepthValue > 0 && currentDepthValue < closestValue){ ❻
        // save its value
        closestValue = currentDepthValue;
        // and save its position (both X and Y coordinates)
        closestX = x;
        closestY = y;
      }
    }
  }

  //draw the depth image on the screen
  image(kinect.depthImage(),0,0);

  // draw a red circle over it,
  // positioned at the X and Y coordinates
  // we saved of the closest pixel.
  fill(255,0,0);
  ellipse(closestX, closestY, 25, 25);
}
```

Hey, a sketch that's actually interactive! When you run this sketch, you should see a red dot floating over the depth image following whatever is closest to the Kinect. If you face the Kinect so that there's nothing between you and the camera and extend your hand, the red dot should follow your hand around when you move it.

For example, Figure 2-14 shows the red dot following my extended fist when I run the sketch.

The tracking is good enough that if you point a single finger at the Kinect and wag it back and forth disapprovingly, the dot should even stick to the tip of your outstretched finger.

Now you should understand most of what's going in this code based on our discussion of the pseudocode, but there are a few details that are worth pointing out and clarifying.

❶ First, let's look at closestValue. This is going to be the variable that holds the current record holder for closest pixel as we work our way though the image. Ironically, the winner of this competition will be the pixel with the lowest value, not the highest. As we saw in Example 5, the depth values range from about 450 to just under 8000, and lower depth values correspond to closer points.

❷ At the beginning of draw, we set closestValue to 8000. That number is so high that it's actually outside of the range of possible of values that we'll see from the depth map. Hence, all of our actual points within the depth image will have lower values. This guarantees that all our pixels will be considered in the competition for closest point and that one of them will actually win.

Figure 2-14. *Our red circle following my outstretched fist.*

❸ Next, let's look at our two `for` loops. We know from our pseudocode that we want to go through every row in the image, and within every row we want to look at every point in that row. How did we translate that into code?

What we've got here is two `for` loops, one inside the other. The outer one increments a variable y from 0 up to 479. We know that the depth image from the Kinect is 480 pixels tall. In other words, it consists of 480 rows of pixels. This outer loop will run once for each one of those rows, setting y to the number of the current row (starting at 0).

❹ This line kicks off a `for` loop that does almost the same thing, but with a different variable, x, and a different constraint, 640. This inner loop will run once per row. We want it to cover every pixel in the row. Since the depth image from the Kinect is 640 pixels wide, we know that it'll have to run 640 times in order to do so.

The code inside of this inner loop, then, will run once per pixel in the image. It will proceed across each row in turn, left to right, before jumping down to the next row until it reaches the bottom-right corner of the image and stops.

Chapter 2

❺   But as we well know from our previous experience with `kinect.depth-Map`, our `depthValues` array doesn't store rows of pixels; it's just a single flat stack. Hence we need to invoke the same logic we just learned for converting between the x-y coordinate of the image and the position of a value in the array. And that's exactly what we do inside the inner `for` loop.

That line should look familiar to you from the example shown in "Higher-Resolution Depth Data" on page 74. It converts the x-y coordinates of a pixel in the image to the index of the corresponding value in the array. And once we've got that index, we can use it to access the `depthValues` array and pull out the value for the current point, which is exactly what we do on the next line. This again, should look familiar from our previous work.

❻   Another interesting twist comes up with this line near the middle of `draw`. Here we're comparing the depth reading of the current point with `closestValue`, the current record holder, to see if the current point should be crowned as the new closest point. However, we don't just compare `currentDepthValue` with closest value, we also check to see if it is greater than 0. Why?

In general, we know that the lower a point's depth value, the closer that point is to the Kinect. But back in "Higher-Resolution Depth Data"— when we were first exploring these depth map readings—we discovered an exception to this rule. The closest points in the image have depth readings of around 450, but there are some other points that have readings of 0. These are the points that the Kinect can't see and hence doesn't have data for. They might be so close that their within the Kinect's minimum range or obscured by the shadow of some closer object. Either way, we know that none of these points are the closest one and so we need to discard them. That's why we added the check for `currentDepthValue > 0` to our `if` statement.

Now, at this point you've made the big transition. You've switched from working with a single depth pixel at a time to processing the entire depth image. You understand how to write the nested loops that let your code run over every point in the depth image.

Once you've got that down, the only other challenge in this sketch is understanding how we use that ability to answer questions about the entire depth image as a whole. In this case, the question we're answering is: which point in the depth image is closest to the Kinect? In order to answer that question, we need to translate from code that runs on a series of individual points to information that holds up for all points in the image. In this sketch, our answer to that question is contained in our three main variables: `closestValue`, `closestX`, and `closestY`. They're where we store the information that we build up from processing each individual depth point.

Using Variable Scope

To understand how this works, how these variables can aggregate data from individual pixels into a more widely useful form, we need to talk about *scope*. When it comes to code, *scope* describes how long a variable sticks around. Does it exist only inside of a particular `for` loop? Does it exist only in a single function? Or does it persist for the entire sketch? In this example, we have variables that have all three of these different scopes and these variables work together to aggregate data from each pixel to create useful information about the entire depth image. The data tunnels its way out from the innermost scope where it relates only to single pixels to the outer scope where it contains information about the entire depth image: the location and distance of its closest point.

Our Processing sketch is like an onion. It has many layers and each scope covers a different set of these layers. Once a variable is assigned, it stays set for all of the layers inside of the one on which it was originally defined. So, variables defined outside of any function are available everywhere in the sketch. For example, `kinect` is defined at the top of this sketch and we use it in both our `setup` and `draw` functions. We don't have to reset our `kinect` variable at the start of `draw` each time, we can just use it.

Variables defined on inner layers, on the other hand, disappear whenever we leave that layer. Our variable `i`, for example, which gets declared just inside the inner `for` loop—at the innermost core of the onion—represents the array index for each individual point in the `depthMap`. It disappears and gets reset for each pixel *every time* our inner loop runs. We wouldn't want its value to persist because each pixel's array index is independent of all the ones that came before. We want to start that calculation from scratch each time, not build it up over time.

Another piece of information that we want to change with every pixel is `currentDepthValue`. That's the high-resolution depth reading that corresponds to each pixel. Every time the inner loop runs, we want to pull a new depth reading out of the `depthValues` array for each new pixel, we don't care about the old ones. That's why both `i` and `currentDepthValue` are declared in this most inner scope. We want them to constantly change with each pixel.

There's also some data that we want to change every time `draw` runs, but stay the same through both of our `for` loops. This data lives on an intermediate layer of the onion. The key variable here is `depthValues`, which stores the array of depth readings from the Kinect. We want to pull in a new frame from the Kinect every time `draw` runs. Hence, this variable should get reset every time the `draw` function restarts. But we also want the `depthValues` array to stick around long enough so that we can process all of its points. It needs to be available inside of our inner `for` loop so we can access each point to read out its value and do our calculations. That's why `depthValues` is in this intermediate scope, available throughout each run of draw, but not across the entire sketch.

And finally, moving to the outermost layer of the onion, we find our three key variables: `closestValue`, `closestX`, and `closestY`. Just like `kinect`, we declared these at the very top of our sketch, outside of either the `setup` or `draw` function, so they are available everywhere. And, more than that, they persist over time. No matter how many times the inner pixel-processing loop runs, no matter how many times the `draw` function itself runs, these variables will retain their values until we intentionally change them. That's why we can use them to build up an answer to find the closest pixel. Even though the inner loop only knows the distance of the current pixel, it can constantly compare this distance with the closestValue, changing the closestValue if necessary. And we've seen in our discussion of the pseudocode (and of Olympic records) how that ability leads to eventually finding the closest point in the whole depth image. This all works because of the difference in scope. If closestValue didn't stick around as we processed all of the pixels, it wouldn't end up with the right value when we were done processing them.

Do we actually need closestValue, closestX, and closestY to be global variables, available everywhere, just like kinect? Unlike our kinect object, we don't access any of these three in our setup function, we only use them within draw. Having them be global also allows their values to persist across multiple runs of draw. Are we taking advantage of this?

Well, certainly not for closestValue. The very first line of draw sets closest-Value to 8000, discarding whatever value it ended up with after the last run through all of the depth image's pixels. If we didn't reset closestValue, we would end up comparing every pixel in each new frame from the Kinect to the closest pixel that we'd ever seen since our sketch started running. Instead of constantly tracking the closest point in our scene, causing the red circle to track your extended hand, the sketch would lock onto the closest point and only move if some closer point emerged in the future. If you walked up to the Kinect and you were the closest thing in the scene, the red circle might track you, but then, when you walked away, it would get stuck at your closest point to the Kinect.

By resetting closestValue for each run of draw we ensure that we find the closest point in each frame from the Kinect no matter what happened in the past. This tells us that we could move the scope of closestValue to be contained within draw without changing how our sketch works.

But what about closestX and closestY? We don't set these to a default value at the top of draw. They enter our nested for loops still containing their values from the previous frame. But what happens then? Since closestValue is set above the range of possible depth values, any point in the depth map that has an actual depth value will cause closestX and closestY to change, getting set to that point's x- and y-coordinates. Some point in the depth image has to be the closest one.

The only way that closestX and closestY could make it all the way through our for loops without changing their values would be if every single point in the depth map had a value of 0. This can only happen if you've covered the Kinect with a cloth or pointed it face-first up against a wall or done something else to make sure that its entire field of view is covered by something within the Kinect's minimum range. This is a rare, and clearly not very useful, situation. So, in any practical scenario, closestX and closestY will always get changed somewhere within each run of draw. That means that closestX and closestY don't need to be global variables either. In practice, their values will never actually persist between multiple runs of draw. We could declare them within draw without changing how our sketch works.

So, then, why did we declare all three of these variables at the top of the sketch? There are two reasons. First of all, it's nice to have them at the top of the sketch because they're important. Having them at the top of the sketch means that you see them on first glance when looking at the code. You can look at just those first six lines of this Processing sketch and have a pretty good idea of what it's going to be doing. It imports the Kinect library and it defines some variables that are clearly meant to store the value and location of the closest point. Obviously, this code is going to be using the Kinect to track the closest point in front of it. Having these variables at the top of the sketch doesn't just declare their scope, it also declares the sketch's intention.

Also, if we wanted to make this sketch more sophisticated, we'd immediately start taking advantage of the global scope of these variables. For example, imagine we wanted to add some smoothing to the movement of our red circle: instead of just jumping from point to point as the closest object in the scene shifted, we wanted it to make a more gradual transition. To accomplish this we'd want `closestX` and `closestY` to not simply get reset with every frame. We'd want them to be more like a running average so if the closest point suddenly jumped, they would fill in the intermediate values keeping things smooth and continuous. To make our sketch work like this, we'd need to use the global scope of `closestX` and `closestY` explicitly, updating them between each run of `draw` rather than resetting them.

There are similar things we might want to do with `closestValue`. Imagine if you wanted the circle to track the user's hand only if it moved by more than a certain amount. This might allow the user to draw straight lines in a drawing app or allow you to ignore a user who wasn't moving at all. To do something like that, you'd need to start taking advantage of the global scope of `closestValue` so that you could compare data across multiple runs of `draw`. You'd still calculate the closest value of the depth map in each new run of `draw` but then you'd compare what you found to the persistent global `closestValue` and only update `closestValue` if that difference was more than some minimum threshold.

For an example of a sketch that uses global scope in this way, take a look at `closest_pixel_running_average.pde` in the Appendix. That sketch uses the global scope of `closestX` and `closestY` to implement the smoothing example I discussed above.

Projects

To finish up this chapter, we're going to make a couple of small projects that use what we've learned about processing the depth data to create actual fun applications. Each builds on the techniques you've already learned: looping through the depth map to find the closest pixel, persisting data across multiple runs of the `draw` function, and using that data to provide an actual user interface.

For each of the applications, we'll start with a basic version that just takes a small next step beyond the code we've already seen. Once we have that working, we'll add a few refinements and advanced features and then conclude with a discussion of future possibilities that you can explore yourself.

First, we're going to build an "invisible pencil" (Figure 2-15): a sketch that lets you draw by waving your hand around in front of the Kinect. This sketch will use the tracking we've already done to generate a line that follows your hand. In the advanced version, we'll learn how to smooth out the movement of the line to give you more control of the drawing and how to save the final drawing as an image.

Figure 2-15. *The final output of the Invisible Pencil project: smooth handwriting created by waving your hand around in space.*

Second, we'll create a photo layout program that lets you drag a series of images around to arrange them on the screen by moving your hands in space a la Tom Cruise in *Minority Report* (Figure 2-16). We'll build on the tracking and smoothing of the invisible pencil example, but this time, we'll learn how to display and manipulate images. In the advanced version, we'll add the ability to cycle through control of multiple images in order to lay them out like snapshots on a table top.

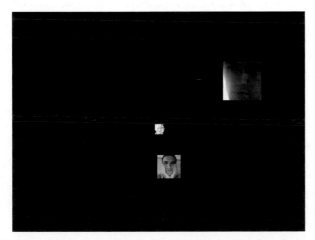

Figure 2-16. *The final output of the Minority Report project: controlling the position and size of three images, one at a time with our closest point.*

Project 6: Invisible Pencil

This application is going to take the tracking interface we created in the last section and turn it into a drawing program. We'll still track the closest point that the Kinect can see, but now instead of simply displaying it as a circle on top of the depth image, we'll use that point to draw a line.

To draw a line in Processing, you need two points. Processing's line function takes four values: the x- and y-coordinates of the first point followed the x- and y-coordinates of the second point. It draws a line on the screen that connects these two points that you give it. To transform our closest point tracking code into drawing code, we'll need to draw a line on each frame instead of a circle. And we'll want our line to connect the current closest point to the previous one. That way, we'll get a series of short lines that connect the positions of our closest point over time. Since the end of each of these individual lines will also be the start of the next one, together they'll join up to create a single line that flows around our sketch following the closest point over time.

To get the two points we need to draw our line, we'll need more than just the closest point we've tracked in any individual frame of the depth image. We'll also need the previous closest point, the one we just tracked in the last frame. Our line will connect this older point to the new one.

At the end of the last section, we discussed strategies for building up information about the depth image across multiple frames. We explored using global variables to save the closest point in a particular depth image so that it would be available when we were processing the depth image. We then showed how you could use that older point to smooth out the movement of the red circle around the screen by averaging the current closest point with the previous closest one (check out the Appendix if you don't remember that discussion).

This time we're going to use that same logic to keep track of the current closest point and the previous one, but instead of using them for smoothing, we'll use them as the start and end of each our line segments.

Let's take a look at the code. This code picks up exactly where the last example we discussed ("Finding the Closest Pixel" on page 77) left off. I've included comments about all the new lines that differ from that older example. Read through this code and see if you can understand how it implements the line drawing strategy I just described.

```
import SimpleOpenNI.*;
SimpleOpenNI kinect;

int closestValue;
int closestX;
int closestY;

// declare global variables for the
// previous x and y coordinates
int previousX;
int previousY;

void setup()
{
  size(640, 480);
```

```
    kinect = new SimpleOpenNI(this);
    kinect.enableDepth();
}

void draw()
{
    closestValue = 8000;

    kinect.update();

    int[] depthValues = kinect.depthMap();

    for(int y = 0; y < 480; y++){
        for(int x = 0; x < 640; x++){
            int i = x + y * 640;
            int currentDepthValue = depthValues[i];

            if(currentDepthValue > 0 && currentDepthValue < closestValue){

                closestValue = currentDepthValue;
                closestX = x;
                closestY = y;
            }
        }
    }

    image(kinect.depthImage(),0,0);

    // set the line drawing color to red
    stroke(255,0,0);

    // draw a line from the previous point to the new closest one
    line(previousX, previousY, closestX, closestY);

    // save the closest point as the new previous one
    previousX = closestX;
    previousY = closestY;
}
```

So, how did we do it? Well, first we added two new global variables, previousX and previousY. These are going to hold the coordinates of the closest point before the current frame of the depth image, the one our line will connect with the new closest point.

After that, our setup function didn't change and neither did our code that loops through all the points to find the closest one. The only other addition is four new lines at the bottom of the sketch. The first of these, stroke(255,0,0) tells Processing to set the color for line drawing to red. This is like dipping our pen in red ink, it means that any lines we draw after this will take that color. In our previous sketch we'd used fill in a similar manner to set the color of our circle; stroke is like fill for lines. The next line actually draws the line between the previous closest point and the new closest point. This works just how we expected from the description above of Processing's line function.

Now, the final two lines here are a bit subtle, but are important for understanding how this sketch works. Right before the end of the draw function, we set previousX equal to closestX and previousY equal to closestY. This is our way of holding onto the current x- and y-coordinates of the closest point so that they'll be available on the next run of the draw function to compare with the next closest point that we find. Remember that previousX and previousY are global variables. That means that they stick around across runs of the draw function. That's what makes it possible to connect each previous point with each new one. If we didn't set previousX and previousY like this every time, instead of drawing a series of line segments that were connected end-to-end and followed the track of the closest point, previousX and previousY would never change. You'd end up with a bunch of lines that all radiated out from a shared starting point. Not a very good drawing interface.

Now let's run this code. We should see a line on top of the depth image tracking the closest point, right?

But wait, what's going on? Instead of a continuous line being drawn over the image, when I run this code, I get a flickering tiny scrap of red that disappears and reappears in each frame. You can see the effect in Figure 2-17.

Figure 2-17. A tiny line of red flickers over the depth image. The depth image is covering our line so we can't see it build up.

Why don't we see the whole line? Why are we only seeing the last line segment at any given frame? Let's look at our sketch again. In addition to drawing the line segment connecting the current closest point to the previous one, there's something else we're drawing as well: the depth image itself. On this line (just after the for loops), we display the depth image from the Kinect:

```
image(kinect.depthImage(),0,0);
```

In Processing, every new thing that you display goes down right on top of what was there previously. Therefore an image that fills the whole sketch will cover over all the drawing that had been done up to that point, essentially clearing the sketch. Think of Processing like a piece of paper on which you're making an ongoing collage. If you draw some lines and then paste down a photograph, the photograph will cover over the lines, making them invisible. You'll only see the lines you scribble over the top of that photograph. That's exactly what's happening here with each frame of the depth image. We're laying down one frame of the depth image then drawing the appropriate line segment for that frame, but then the next frame immediately comes in and covers this.

To fix this, we need to stop displaying our depth image. Let's comment out that line (put `//` in front of `image(kinect.depthImage,0,0);`) and run the sketch again. Now you should see a red line moving around the sketch, following the closest point in front of the Kinect. Try waving your hand around a bit to see if you can draw something. Note how the line moves around and rapidly builds up filling the sketch.

I don't know about you, but my sketch is getting messy quickly, filling up with skittering red lines. Let's add a function to clear the screen when we click the mouse. We'll use Processing's `mousePressed` function to do this. The code is very simple. Add this to the bottom of your sketch:

```
void mousePressed(){
  background(0);
}
```

Stop your sketch and run it again. Now, when you click anywhere within your sketch's window, your drawing should disappear and be replaced with a clean black screen.

So, at this point, we've got a working drawing app. You wave your hand around and you can control a line showing up on your screen. However, it has some limitations. First of all, our line is quite skittery. It's very sensitive to even very small movements of the closest point in the image. And it has a tendency to make big jumps even when you're not consciously moving around the point you think it's tracking. When I run it, my output looks something like Figure 2-18.

Figure 2-18. *Our hand-tracking drawing app's first output.*

All I did to create this drawing was extend my hand toward the Kinect so that it would be tracked as the closest point and then raise and lower it in an arc to my right. The jittery lines in the center of the sketch are where it first started tracking my hand while it was remaining still. The rest of the line is where it followed my hand along the arc.

One of the hallmarks of a good user interface is responsiveness. Users should feel a tight connection between their actions and the results in the application. There shouldn't be any delay between a user's input and the resulting action, and everything that happens within the app should be the result of an intentional action on the part of the user. So far, our app is fairly responsive in the sense that there's nearly no delay between our movement and the movement of the line. However, the line also seems to move quite a bit on its own. In addition to the user's intentional action, there's some randomness in the controls as the closest point hops to unexpected spots or even simply makes tiny shifts within individual points within the user's out-stretched hand. As a user of this sketch, I find this lack of control quite frustrating.

To eliminate these large random jumps, we need to tighten the focus of our tracking. Instead of considering any part of the scene, we want to focus on the area that is most likely to have the user in it: the distance from about two feet to about five feet.

To eliminate the tiny jitters, we need to smooth out the movement of the line. We can do this by not simply jumping directly to the closest point on every frame, but instead "interpolating" between each previous point and each new one that comes in. Interpolation is the process of filling in the missing space between two known points. In other words, instead of jumping to the next point, we'll orient our line toward that next point but only take the first step in that direction. If we do this for every new closest point, we'll always be following the user's input, but we'll do so along a much smoother path.

The second big problem with this basic version is that it's backward. That is, when you move your hand to your left, the line moves to the right on the screen and vice versa. This happens because the Kinect's depth camera is facing you. It sees you the way other people do: your left hand is on its right. What we'd really like is for the sketch to act like a piece of paper: if you move your hand to the left, the line should also move to the left. That would make for a much more intuitive interface.

To achieve this, we need to mirror the image coming in from the Kinect. In a mirror, the image of your left hand is on your left and that of your right hand is on the right. It's just the reverse of what a camera looking at you normally sees. So, to convert the Kinect's image into a mirror image, we need to flip the order of the Kinect depth points on the x-axis.

Let's take a look at an advanced version of the sketch that corrects both of these problems and adds one more nice feature: saving an image of your drawing when you clear it.

```
import SimpleOpenNI.*;
SimpleOpenNI kinect;
```

```
int closestValue;
int closestX;
int closestY;

float lastX;
float lastY;

void setup()
{
  size(640, 480);
  kinect = new SimpleOpenNI(this);
  kinect.enableDepth();

  // start out with a black background
  background(0);
}

void draw()
{
  closestValue = 8000;

  kinect.update();

  int[] depthValues = kinect.depthMap();

    for(int y = 0; y < 480; y++){
      for(int x = 0; x < 640; x++){ ❶

        // reverse x by moving in from
        // the right side of the image
        int reversedX = 640-x-1; ❷

        // use reversedX to calculate
        // the array index
        int i = reversedX + y * 640;
        int currentDepthValue = depthValues[i];

        // only look for the closestValue within a range
        // 610 (or 2 feet) is the minimum
        // 1525 (or 5 feet) is the maximum
        if(currentDepthValue > 610 && currentDepthValue < 1525 ❸
          && currentDepthValue < closestValue){

          closestValue = currentDepthValue;
          closestX = x;
          closestY = y;
        }
      }
    }

  // "linear interpolation", i.e.
  // smooth transition between last point
  // and new closest point
  float interpolatedX = lerp(lastX, closestX, 0.3f); ❹
  float interpolatedY = lerp(lastY, closestY, 0.3f);

  stroke(255,0,0);
```

```
// make a thicker line, which looks nicer
strokeWeight(3);

line(lastX, lastY, interpolatedX, interpolatedY); ❺
lastX = interpolatedX;
lastY = interpolatedY;

}

void mousePressed(){
    // save image to a file
    // then clear it on the screen
    save("drawing.png");
    background(0);
}
```

This code makes a number of improvements over the basic version. Some of them are simple and cosmetic and a couple of them are more sophisticated. Again, I've added comments in the code to every line that I've changed from the previous version. Run the app and see how it behaves and then I'll explain how these changes address the problems we identified above.

First off, I made a couple of simple cosmetic changes that improve the appearance of the sketch. In setup, I start the sketch off with a black background. In the basic version, we were already clearing the app to black so I added this call to background(0) to keep the background for our drawing consistent.

Second, I increased the thickness of the line that we draw. In the fourth line from the bottom of draw, I called Processing's strokeWeight function, which sets the thickness. This defaults to one, so giving it a value of three triples the line's thickness. This makes the line more visible from farther away from the screen (which you tend to be when waving your hand around in front of the Kinect) and also makes the image look better when you save it. Which brings me to the third cosmetic improvement: I modified our mousePressed event so that it saves a copy of the drawing to a file before clearing the screen. The code there simply calls save to save the image into the Sketch folder (choose Sketch→Show Sketch Folder to see it). It's worth noting that if you save more than once, this sketch will overwrite the earlier images with the newer ones, and you'll only end up with the most recent. To prevent this, when you save an image, move or rename it before saving a new one.

So those are the cosmetic improvements, but what about the substantial ones? What have I done to address the erratic movement of our line and to mirror it to improve our app's usability?

Let's discuss the mirroring technique first as it's actually quite simple. To create a mirror image of the depth data, all we need to do is reverse the x-coordinate from the one we've currently been calculating from our point array. Think back to our technique for converting from x-y coordinates to the correct position within our linear array of depth points. To make that conversion, we multiply the number of row we're on (the y-coordinate) by the width of the row and then add the x-coordinate. The first number gets us the number of points already accounted for on previous rows, and the second one gets us the distance between this point and the row's left edge.

This time, though, we want to flip the image over from left to right. Instead of calculating the point's distance from the left edge, we want to translate it into a distance from the right edge, so we can grab the equivalent pixel on the opposite side of the image. If we do this for every pixel across every row, we'll have a mirror image.

❶ You can see from our loop that our x-coordinate counts up from 0 to 639 (x < 640 in our loop declaration means that x stops just before reaching 640). When we used it directly, this progression of values meant that our position in each row marched directly from left to right. To reverse this march, we need to calculate a new number that starts at 639 and then counts down to 0. And given our current x, this is very easy to do: our new reversedX will simply be 640-x-1 (as you can see on line 34). When x is at 0 (i.e., the very left of the row), reversedX will be at 639 (the very right). As x increases, reversedX will decrease until it reaches 0 and jumps to the next row. Just what we want.

❷ Once we've calculated reversedX, all we have to do is swap it into the original formula for calculating the array index in place of x. Boom. with this simple change, we've reversed our image. If you ran the sketch with just this change, you'd see that it now acted as a mirror with the line moving to your left as you moved your hand that way, and vice versa. Much more intuitive.

❸ Now let's get to smoothing. As I mentioned above, there are actually two improvements in this version of the app that eliminate jitter. The first one is to only care about points within a certain depth. We know we only want the user to control the drawing, not bits of the wall or ceiling behind them, not cats that happen to walk by between them and the camera. Hence, if we make an assumption about how far away the user is likely to be from the Kinect, we can eliminate most of the points in the depth image from our closest point calculation. This will eliminate the occasional big jumps we detected in the basic version of the sketch.

But how to chose this range? We want it to be big enough that it's easy to access, but small enough that it limits the scene to the portion the user is most likely to occupy. After some experimentation, I found that a range of two to five feet was appropriate for this. To perform that experimentation, I wrote an sketch that only displays points from the depth image that are within a given range (you can see the code in the Appendix if you're interested). After trying some different values, Figure 2-19 shows what things looked like with the two- to five-foot range.

You can see that my hand is close enough that it's going black and the back of the chair is partially black as well. That should give you a sense of the size of the range: about the length of my outstretched arm.

Having found this range, I moved my furniture around a bit so I could get just my arm into the range. When just my arm and hand started showing up, I knew I had things just right. Figure 2-20 shows the result.

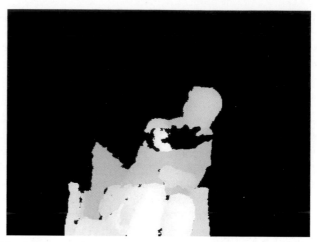

Figure 2-19. *The depth image with its range limited to only show the part of the scene that's likely to include the user.*

Figure 2-20. *The depth image range is calibrated to capture only my hand.*

Once I'd found the correct range, I went ahead and added it to our advanced drawing sketch. This range is enforced on this line.

The first two criteria of that `if` statement are new. They say we should only consider a point as a potential `closestValue` if its depth reading is greater than 610 and less than 1525. I determined these numbers using what we learned in "Higher-Resolution Depth Data" on page 74: these raw numbers are millimeters and there are 25.4 millimeters per inch. Hence, these criteria will limit our search to the area between two ($2 * 12 * 25.4 = 609.6$) and five ($5 * 12 * 25.4 = 1524.0$) feet away from the Kinect. If the user positions himself correctly, this will limit our search to just the points on his hand and arm, eliminating some of the jitter we'd previously seen.

❹ OK, so that's one source of jitter. But what about the other one? What about the constant back-and-forth scribbling? I said above that we were going to use interpolation to create a smooth line rather than just jumping straight between points like we had up to now.

Luckily for us, Processing has an interpolation function built right into it. Processing calls this function `lerp` for "linear interpolation." This function takes three arguments: the first two are the two numbers to interpolate between and the last is a float that tells you how much to move between the two points (with 1.0 being all the way to the second point and 0.0 being none of the way).

These interpolated values will be part of the way between our last position and the new closest point. Only going part of the way to each new point means that erratic values will have less of an impact on the line, introducing fewer jagged turns. As I explained above, interpolating is like constantly shifting your direction toward a new point while continuing to move in an unbroken line instead of just jumping to the new point like we'd previously been doing.

❺ After we've calculated these interpolated values, we use them where we previously had used `closestX` and `closestY` for the rest of the sketch: as coordinates in `line` and when we reset `lastX` and `lastY` after that.

With this change, our sketch is now smooth enough that you can actually use it to draw something intentionally. For example, as you can see in Figure 2-21, I wrote my name.

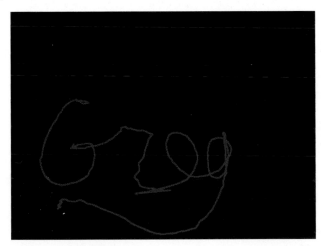

Figure 2-21. *With smoothing and range limiting, I had enough control to be able to write my name by waving my hand around.*

Once you've got everything working, try to add some more features. Can you change the color of the line based on the depth value that comes in? Can you add the ability to "lift the pen," that is, turn drawing the line on and off with the `mousePressed` event so you don't have to only draw one continuous line? Can you think of something else fun you'd like the sketch to do?

If you're still seeing erratic results, make sure you've got all of your furniture (and pets and roommates) moved out of the way. If you're having a hard time telling if you've eliminated everything and if you're standing in the right spot, you can use the code in the Appendix to see the thresholded image from your Kinect to get everything set up.

Project 7: Minority Report Photos

This next project is going to build on what we just learned with the Invisible Pencil in order to implement an interface similar to the one that helped define the idea of gesture-controlled technology in popular culture. In the 2002 sci-fi movie *Minority Report* (based on a Philip K. Dick short story), Tom Cruise played a "pre-crime" policeman who uses the predictions of psychics to anticipate and prevent violent crimes. Cruise accesses these predictions as a series of images on a projected screen that he navigates with gestures. He drags his hands to pull in new images, spreads them apart to zoom in on a telling detail, pinches to zoom out to the big picture.

Watching the movie now, many of the gestures will seem familiar from contemporary touchscreen interfaces that have come to market since the movie premiered. And now, with the Kinect, we can move beyond the touchscreen and build a photo browsing application that looks almost exactly like the interface from the movie. With just Processing and the Kinect, we can make this sci-fi dream come true.

To do this, we're going to build on the code we've already written. Our advanced drawing example already smoothly tracks the user's hand. Now we're going to translate that motion into the position of photographs on the screen. Instead of drawing a line, we're going to let the user pick up and move around photographs.

Just like in the drawing app, we'll build two versions of this sketch. We'll start with a basic version that positions a single photo. Then we'll move on to an advanced version that displays multiple photos and lets us scale them up and down.

> The gestural and touch interfaces demonstrated in Minority Report were heavily based on the work of John Underkoffler (http://oblong.com/) from the Center for Tangible Bits at the MIT Media Lab.

Basic Version: One Image

For the basic version of this app, we only need to make a few additions to our existing drawing app. We're still going to use all our same code for finding the closest point and interpolating its position as it moves. What we need to add is code related to images. We need to load an image from a file and use the interpolated coordinates of the closest point to position that image. And we need to give the user the ability to "drop" the image, to stop it moving by clicking the mouse.

Here's the code. It may look long, but it's actually mostly identical to our advanced drawing app. As usual, I've written comments on all the new lines.

```
import SimpleOpenNI.*;
SimpleOpenNI kinect;

int closestValue;
int closestX;
int closestY;

float lastX;
float lastY;

// declare x-y coordinates for the image
float image1X;
float image1Y;
```

```
// declare a boolean to store whether or not the image is moving
boolean imageMoving;

// declare a variable
// to store the image
PImage image1; ❶

void setup()
{
  size(640, 480);
  kinect = new SimpleOpenNI(this);
  kinect.enableDepth();

  // start the image out moving
  // so mouse press will drop it
  imageMoving = true;

  // load the image from a file
  image1 = loadImage("image1.jpg");

  background(0);
}

void draw()
{
  closestValue = 8000;

  kinect.update();

  int[] depthValues = kinect.depthMap();

    for(int y = 0; y < 480; y++){
      for(int x = 0; x < 640; x++){

        int reversedX = 640-x-1;
        int i = reversedX + y * 640;
        int currentDepthValue = depthValues[i];

        if(currentDepthValue > 610
          && currentDepthValue < 1525
          && currentDepthValue < closestValue) ❷
        {

          closestValue = currentDepthValue;
          closestX = x;
          closestY = y;
        }
      }
    }

  float interpolatedX = lerp(lastX, closestX, 0.3);
  float interpolatedY = lerp(lastY, closestY, 0.3);

  // clear the previous drawing
  background(0); ❸

  // only update image position
  // if image is in moving state
  if(imageMoving){
      image1X = interpolatedX;
```

```
        image1Y = interpolatedY;
    }

    //draw the image on the screen
    image(image1,image1X,image1Y);

    lastX = interpolatedX;
    lastY = interpolatedY;
}

void mousePressed(){
    // if the image is moving, drop it
    // if the image is dropped, pick it up
    imageMoving = !imageMoving;
}
```

To run this app, you'll need to add your own image file to it. Save your Processing sketch and give it a name. Then you'll be able to find the sketch's folder on your computer (Sketch→Show Sketch Folder). Move the image you want to play with into this folder and rename it *image1.jpg* (or change the second-to-last line in setup to refer to your image's existing filename). Once you've added your image, run the sketch and you should see your image floating around the screen, following your outstretched hand.

❶ So, how does this sketch work? The first few additions, declaring and loading an image, should be familiar to you from your previous work in Processing.

At the top of the sketch, we also declare a few other new variables: image1X and image1Y, which will hold the position of our image and a Boolean called imageMoving, which will keep track of whether or not the user has "dropped" the image.

At the very bottom of the sketch, we also rewrote our mousePressed function. Now it simply toggles that imageMoving variable. So if image-Moving is true, clicking the mouse will set it to false, and vice versa. That way the mouse button will act to drop the image if the user is currently moving it around and to start it moving around again if it's dropped.

❷ The real action here is at the end of the draw function, after we've calculated interpolatedX and interpolatedY.

If our imageMoving variable is true, we update our image's x-y coordinates based on interpolatedX and interpolatedY. And then we draw the image using those x-y coordinates. Actually we draw the image using those coordinates whether or not it is currently being moved. If the image is being moved, image1X and image1Y will always be set to the most recent values of interpolatedX and interpolatedY. The image will move around the screen tracking your hand. When you click the mouse and set imageMoving to false, image1X and image1Y will stop updating from the interpolated coordinates. However, we'll still go ahead and draw the image using the most recent values of image1X and image1Y. In other words, we still display the image, we just stop changing its position based on our tracking of the closest point. It's like we've dropped the image onto the table. It will stay still no matter how you move around in front of the Kinect.

Chapter 2

❸ The one other detail worth noting here is this. This clears the whole sketch to black. If we didn't do that, we'd end up seeing trails of our image as we moved it around. Remember, Processing always just draws on top of whatever is already there. If we don't clear our sketch to black, we'll end up constantly displaying our image on top of old copies of itself in slightly different positions. This will make a smeary mess (or a cool psychedelic effect, depending on your taste). Figure 2-22 shows what my version of the sketch looks like without that line. And Figure 2-23 shows what it looks like with the line back in.

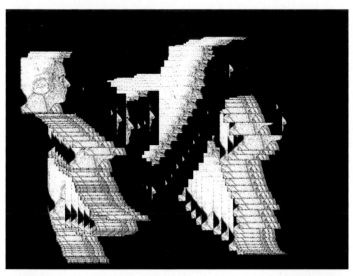

Figure 2-22. *If we don't clear the background to black when moving an image around, the result will be a smeary mess.*

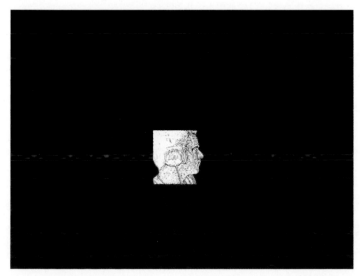

Figure 2-23. *Clearing the sketch's background to black prevents redrawing the image every time and creating a smeary mess.*

Advanced Version: Multiple Images and Scale

That's the basic version. There really wasn't a lot to it beyond the smooth hand tracking we already had working from our drawing example. Let's move on to the advanced version. This version of the sketch is going to build on what we have in two ways. First, it'll control multiple images (Figure 2-24). That change is not going to introduce any new concepts, but will simply be a matter of managing more variables to keep track of the location of all of our images and remembering which image the user is currently controlling. The second change will be more substantial. We'll give the user the ability to scale each image up and down by moving her hand closer to or farther from the Kinect. To do this, we'll need to use `closestValue`, the actual distance of the closest point detected in the image. Up to this point, we've basically been ignoring `closestValue` once we've found the closest point, but in this version of the sketch, it's going to become part of the interface: its value will be used to set the size of the current image.

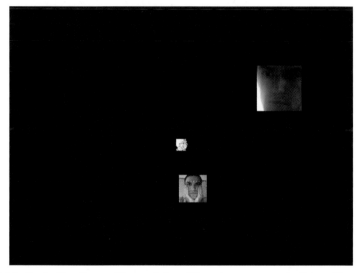

Figure 2-24. *Controlling the position and size of three images, one at a time with our closest point.*

OK, let's see the code.

```
import SimpleOpenNI.*;
SimpleOpenNI kinect;

int closestValue;
int closestX;
int closestY;

float lastX;
float lastY;

float image1X;
float image1Y;
// declare variables for
// image scale and dimensions
float image1scale;
int image1width = 100;
int image1height = 100;
```

Chapter 2

```
float image2X;
float image2Y;
float image2scale;
int image2width = 100;
int image2height = 100;

float image3X;
float image3Y;
float image3scale;
int image3width = 100;
int image3height = 100;
// keep track of which image is moving
int currentImage = 1;

// declare variables
// to store the images
PImage image1;
PImage image2;
PImage image3;


void setup()
{
  size(640, 480);
  kinect = new SimpleOpenNI(this);
  kinect.enableDepth();

  // load the images
  image1 = loadImage("image1.jpg");
  image2 = loadImage("image2.jpg");
  image3 = loadImage("image3.jpg");

}

void draw(){
  background(0);

  closestValue = 8000;

  kinect.update();

  int[] depthValues = kinect.depthMap();

    for(int y = 0; y < 480; y++){
      for(int x = 0; x < 640; x++){

        int reversedX = 640-x-1;
        int i = reversedX + y * 640;
        int currentDepthValue = depthValues[i];

        if(currentDepthValue > 610 && currentDepthValue < 1525
                        && currentDepthValue < closestValue){

          closestValue = currentDepthValue;
          closestX = x;
          closestY = y;
        }
      }
    }
```

```
        float interpolatedX = lerp(lastX, closestX, 0.3);
        float interpolatedY = lerp(lastY, closestY, 0.3);

        // select the current image
        switch(currentImage){ ❶
          case 1:
            // update its x-y coordinates
            // from the interpolated coordinates
            image1X = interpolatedX; ❷
            image1Y = interpolatedY;

            // update its scale
            // from closestValue
            // 0 means invisible, 4 means quadruple size
            image1scale = map(closestValue, 610,1525, 0,4);
          break;
          case 2:
            image2X = interpolatedX;
            image2Y = interpolatedY;
            image2scale = map(closestValue, 610,1525, 0,4);

          break;
          case 3:
            image3X = interpolatedX;
            image3Y = interpolatedY;
            image3scale = map(closestValue, 610,1525, 0,4);
          break;
        }

        // draw all the image on the screen
        // use their saved scale variables to set their dimensions
        image(image1,image1X,image1Y,
              image1width * image1scale, image1height * image1scale); ❸
        image(image2,image2X,image2Y,
              image2width * image2scale, image2height * image2scale);
        image(image3,image3X,image3Y,
              image3width * image3scale, image3height * image3scale);

        lastX = interpolatedX;
        lastY = interpolatedY;
}

void mousePressed(){
  // increase current image
  currentImage++;
  // but bump it back down to 0
  // if it goes above 3
  if(currentImage > 3){
    currentImage = 1;
  }
  println(currentImage);
}
```

To run this code, you'll need to use three images of your own. Just like with the basic example, you'll have to save your sketch so that Processing will create a sketch folder for it. Then you can move your three images into that folder so that your sketch will be able to find them. Make sure they're named *image1.jpg*, *image2.jpg*, and *image3.jpg* so that our code will be able to find them.

Once you've set up your images, you'll be ready to run this sketch. Set up your Kinect so that you're three or four feet away from it and there's nothing between it and you. Just like the last few examples, we'll be tracking the closest point and we want that to be your outstretched hand. When you first run the sketch you should see one image moving around, following the motions of your hand just like before. However, this time try moving your hand closer and farther from the Kinect. You'll notice that the image grows as you get farther away and shrinks as you approach. Now, click your mouse. The image you were manipulating will freeze in place. It will hold whatever size and position it had at the moment you clicked, and your second image will appear. It will also follow your hand, growing and shrinking with your distance from the Kinect. A second click of the mouse will bring out the third image for you to scale and position. A fourth will cycle back around to the first image, and so on.

We'll break our analysis of this sketch up into two parts. First, we'll look at how this sketch works with multiple images. We'll see how it remembers where to position each image and how it decides which image should be controlled by your current movements. Then, we'll move on to looking at how this sketch uses the distance of the `closestPoint` to scale the images.

The changes involved in controlling multiple images start at the top of the sketch. The first thing we need is new variables for our new images. In the old version of this sketch we declared two variables for the position of the image: `image1X` and `image1Y`. Now we have two more pairs of variables to keep track of the location of the other two images: `image2X`, `image2Y`, `image3X`, and `image3Y`. In the basic version, we simply assigned `image1X` and `image1Y` to `closestX` and `closestY` whenever we wanted to update the position of the image to match the user's movement. Now, the situation is a little bit more complicated. We need to give the user the ability to move any of the three images without moving the other two. This means that we need to decide which of the pairs of image position x-y variables to update based on which image is currently being moved. We use a variable called `currentImage` to keep track of this. At the top of the sketch, we initialize that variable to one so that the user controls the first image when the sketch starts up.

`currentImage` gets updated whenever the user clicks the mouse. To make this happen we use the `mousePressed` callback function at the bottom of the sketch. Let's take a look at that function to see how it cycles through the images, letting our sketch control each one in turn. Here's the code for `mousePressed`:

```
void mousePressed(){
  currentImage++;
  if(currentImage > 3){
    currentImage = 1;
  }
}
```

We only have three images, and `currentImage` indicates which one we're supposed to be controlling. So the only valid values for `currentImage` are 1, 2, or 3. If `currentImage` ended up as 0 or any number higher than 3, our sketch would end up controlling none of our images. The first line of `mousePressed` increments the value of `currentImage`. Since we initialized `currentImage` to 1,

Warning

Make sure that you tell the sketch about the dimensions of the images you're using. I'll explain the process in detail below, but in order to scale your images, this sketch needs to know their starting size. Look through the top of the sketch for six variables: `image1width`, `image1height`, `image2width`, `image2height`, `image3width`, and `image3height`. *Set each of those to the appropriate value based on the real size of your images before running your sketch.*

the first time the user clicks the mouse it will go up to 2. Two is less than 3 so the `if` statement here won't fire and `currentImage` will stay as 2. The next time `draw` runs, we'll be controlling the second image and we'll keep doing so until the next time the user clicks the mouse. Shortly, we'll examine how `draw` uses `currentImage` to determine which image to control, but first let's look at what happens when the user clicks the mouse a couple more times. A second click will increment `currentImage` again, setting it to 3 and again skipping the `if` statement. Now our third image appears and begins moving. On the third click, however, incrementing `currentImage` leaves its value as 4. We have no fourth image to move, but thankfully the `if` statement here kicks in and we reset the value of `currentImage` back to one. The next time `draw` runs, our first image will move around again for a second time.

Using this reset-to-one method, we've ensured that the user can cycle through the images and control each one in turn. However, this means that one of the images will always be moving. What if we want to give the user the option to freeze all three of the images in place simultaneously once he's gotten them positioned how he wants? If we change the line inside our `if` statement from `currentImage = 1` to `currentImage = 0`, that will do the trick. Now, when the user hits the mouse for the third time, no image will be selected. There's no image that corresponds to the number 0, so all the images will stay still. When he hits the mouse again, `currentImage` will get incremented back to one, and he'll be in control again. Go ahead and make that change and test out the sketch to see for yourself.

But how does our `draw` function use `currentImage` to decide which image to control? Just keeping `currentImage` set to the right value doesn't do anything by itself. We need to use its value to change the position of the corresponding image.

❶ To do this, we use a new technique called a `switch` statement, which is a tool for controlling the flow of our sketch much like an `if` statement. `if` statements decide whether or not to take some particular set of actions based on the value of a particular variable. `switch` statements, on the other hand, choose between a number of different options. With an `if` statement, we can decide whether or not to reset our `currentImage` variable as we just saw in our `mousePressed` function. With a `switch` statement, we can choose which image position to update based on the value of our `currentImage` variable. Let's take a look at the `switch` statement in this sketch. I'll explain the basic anatomy of a `switch` statement and then show you how we use this one in particular to give our user control of all three images.

A `switch` statement has two parts: the `switch`, which sets the value the statement will examine, and the cases, which tell Processing what to do with each different value that comes into the switch. We start off by passing `currentImage` to `switch`, that's the value we'll be using to determine what to do. We want to set different variables based on which image the user is currently controlling. After calling `switch`, we have three `case` statements, each determining a set of actions to take for a different value of `currentImage`. Each instance of `case` takes an argument in the form of a possible value for `currentImage`: 1, 2, or 3. The code for each case will run when `currentImage` is set to its argument. For example, when `currentImage` is set to one, we'll set the value of `image1X`, `image1Y`, and `image1scale`. Then we'll `break`—we'll exit the `switch` statement. None of the other code will run after the `break`. We won't update the positions or scales of any of the other images. That's how the `switch` statement works to enforce our `currentImage` variable: it only lets one set of code run at a time depending on the variable's value.

❷ Now, let's look inside each of these cases at how this `switch` statement actually sets the position of the image once we've selected the right one. Inside of each case we use the interpolated value of the closest point to set the x- and y-values of the selected image. Before this point in the sketch, we found the closest point for this run of the sketch and interpolated it with the most recent value to create a smoothly moving position. This code is just the same as we've seen throughout the basic version of this project and the entirety of our Invisible Pencil project. Now, we simply assign these `interpolatedX` and `interpolatedY` values to the correct variables for the current image: `image1X` and `image1Y`, `image2X` and `image2Y`, or `image3X` and `image3Y`. Which one we choose will be determined by which case of our `switch` statement we entered.

❸ The images that aren't current will have their x- and y-coordinates unchanged. Here, we display all three images, using the variables with their x- and y-coordinates to position them.

The image that's currently selected will get set to its new position and the other two will stay where they are, using whatever value their coordinates were set to the last time the user controlled them. The result will be one image that follows the user's hand and two that stay still wherever the user last left them.

That concludes the code needed to control the location of the images and the decision about which image the user controls. But what about the images' size? We saw when we ran the sketch that the current image scaled up and down based on the user's distance from the Kinect. How do we make this work? Processing's `image` function lets us set the size to display each image by passing in a width and a height. So, our strategy for controlling the size of each image will be to create two more variables for each image to store the image's width and height. We'll set these variables at the start of our sketch to correspond to each image's actual size. Then, when the user is controlling an image, we'll use the depth of the closest pixel to scale these values up and down. We'll only update the scale of the image that the user is actively controlling so the other images will stick at whatever size the user left them. Finally, when we call `image`, we'll pass in the scaled values for each image's width and height to set them to the right size. And voilà: scaled images controlled by depth.

Let's take a look at the details of how this actually works in practice. We'll start at the top of the sketch with variable declarations.

We declare three additional variables for each image: `image1width`, `image1height`, and `image1scale` are the examples for image one; there are parallel width, height, and scale variables for images two and three as well. We initialize the width and height variables to the actual sizes of the images we'll be using. In my case, I chose three images that are each 100 pixels square. So I set the widths and heights of all of the images to be 100. You should set these to match the dimensions of the images you're actually using. These values will never change throughout our sketch. They'll just get multiplied by our scale values to determine the size at which we'll display each image. Let's look at how those scale variables get set.

We've actually already seen where this happens: inside of our `switch` statement. In addition to setting the x- and y-coordinates of our current image, we set the scale in each `case` statement:

```
case 1:
  image1X = interpolatedX;
  image1Y = interpolatedY;
  image1scale = map(closestValue, 610,1525, 0,4);
break;
```

You can see from that example controlling `image1` that we use `map` to scale `closestValue` from 0 to 4. The incoming range of depth values we're looking for here, 610 to 1525, were determined experimentally. I printed out `closestValue` using `println`, waved my hand around in front of the Kinect, and examined the numbers that resulted. I chose these values as a reasonable minimum and maximum based on that experiment. So, when the `closestValue` seen by the Kinect was around 610, the image will scale down to nothing, and as the closest point moves farther away, the image will grow toward four times its original size. Just like with our position variables, the `case` statement will ensure that only the scale of the current image is altered. Other images will retain the scale set by the user until the next time they become current.

But, again, just setting the value of `image1scale` (or `image2scale` or `image3scale`) is not enough. We have to use it when we call `image` to determine the actual size at which each image is displayed. Let's look again at the arguments we pass to `image`:

```
image(image1,image1X,image1Y,
    image1width * image1scale, image1height * image1scale);
image(image2,image2X,image2Y,
    image2width * image2scale, image2height * image2scale);
image(image3,image3X,image3Y,
    image3width * image3scale, image3height * image3scale);
```

For the width and height values for each image, we multiply their scale by their original width and height. The result will proportionally scale each image based on the value we just set from the user's distance to the Kinect. Now the image that the user controls will scale up and down as she moves her hand in front of the Kinect, and each image will freeze at its current size whenever the user hits the mouse button to cycle along to the next image.

This completes our *Minority Report* project. You now have hands-free control over the position and size of three images. You've created a sophisticated application that uses the depth data from the Kinect in multiple ways at once. You found the closest pixel to the Kinect and used its x- and y-coordinates as a control point for the user. You used the distance of this closest pixel to scale the size of images up and down. And you wrapped it all within a complex control flow that has multiple states and keeps track of a bunch of data to do it.

Chapter 2

You're now ready to move on to the next chapter. There, we'll start to tackle working with the data from the Kinect in 3D. We'll learn how to navigate and draw in three dimensions and we'll learn some techniques for making sketches interactive based on the user's position in space.

Exercises

Here are some exercises you can do to extend and improve this project. Some of them assume advanced skills that you might not have yet. If that's the case, don't worry. These exercises are just suggestions for things you could do to expand the project and practice your skills.

- Give all of the images starting positions so that they're visible when the sketch starts up.

- Add the ability to capture a screen grab of the current position of the images using Processing's `keyPressed` callback.

- Write a `ScalableImage` class that remembers the position, size, and scale of each image. Using multiple instances of your class should dramatically clean up the repetitive variables in the project as it currently exists and make it easier to add multiple images.

Working with Point Clouds

Up to this point, we've basically been treating the Kinect as a two-dimensional camera. Yes, we've looked at the depth data that the Kinect provides, but so far we've only used it to extract information from the image itself. We've treated the depth information almost as a kind of metadata about a two-dimensional image: we've processed it in order to draw conclusions about the image, such as locating its closest point, but that's as far as we've gone. The interfaces we've built with this data have been two-dimensional as well: a line drawing moving through our flat processing window, flat images rearranged within it.

However, there's another way to think about the data coming in from the Kinect. Rather than treating the Kinect's data as a two-dimensional depth image, we can think of it as a set of points in three-dimensional space. If we treat it this way, the depth data goes from being "metadata" about a flat image, simply the color of a pixel, to being one full dimension of each of our three-dimensional points. And once we've got three-dimensional points, we can start to display them in 3D. Rather than drawing a flat image on the screen, we can create a 3D model of our scene that we can view from different perspectives interactively.

Now, even though I said we'll be displaying the Kinect's data in 3D, there's no need to reach for your polarized glasses. We won't be creating a "stereoptic" display. Stereoptic displays send a different image to each of your eyes in order to create the illusion of an actual physical object that jumps off of the flat plane of your screen. Instead what we'll be doing is a lot more like creating a realistic perspective drawing. We'll take the three-dimensional data that's coming in from the Kinect, we'll process it and position it, and then we'll present the user with a picture of it from one particular point of view. We'll be able to present them with any point of view, even ones that don't correspond to the position of the Kinect within the actual room. In fact, we'll be able to look at the scene from any angle without moving the Kinect around at all. Further, if we move the point of view around on each frame of our sketch, we can create the illusion that the viewer is flying through the scene, navigating freely from one point to another.

Working this way, we can also create more sophisticated interfaces that both detect the user in 3D and give him visual feedback in 3D as well. For example, we can turn portions of space into 3D "hot spots": spatial buttons that are only triggered when the user moves part of his body (or an object) into a specific portion of the room. Imagine using these to create "air drums," an invisible drum kit that you can play by waving your hands at spots in the air in front of you. Or, going in another direction, we can load existing 3D models and display them within the scene so they appear to be integrated into it. Imagine towering over a tiny version of the Empire State Building or cowering beneath a life-size World of Warcraft character.

By the end of this chapter, you'll be building projects that do exactly these things. But before we can start on cool applications like these, we need to cover some of the basics of working in three dimensions in Processing. These principles will be fundamental for much of the rest of this book, not just for dealing with point clouds, but also in the next chapter when we start working with the skeleton data.

What You'll Learn in This Chapter

To start off, we'll learn how to orient ourselves in 3D. I'll cover how Processing positions the 3D axes relative to the screen and show you how to draw some basic 3D shapes in different positions in this space so you can get a feel for this system. Next, we'll start working with the Kinect point cloud data. I'll show you how SimpleOpenNI represents this 3D data as *vectors*, and we'll learn what vectors are and how to work with and display them. Once we've got a basic point cloud on the screen, the next step is to be able to move it around. I'll teach you the basics of moving in 3D, how to rotate and translate our points so that we can look at them from different angles and distances.

At this stage, we'll have a solid understanding of how to display and manipulate the point cloud, and it'll be time to use it to make our apps interactive. I'll teach you the simple logic you can perform with vectors to detect points in different parts of space. This is the trick we'll need to build our hot points, the areas in space that will be like buttons in our interface, triggering actions when the user reaches for them.

To build a workable user interface, we'll also need to be able to add our own graphics to the point cloud. How will users know where to move to trigger one of these hot points if we don't show them something on the screen indicating where they are? I'll teach you some additional 3D drawing techniques so that you can construct your own user interface elements. We'll move from drawing the 3D primitives that are built into Processing to creating some of our own shapes.

Finally, I'll cover a few things you can do to make your 3D sketches look a little nicer. Instead of moving the point cloud itself around, we'll start manipulating the virtual camera from which we see things. This will let us make really smooth transitions from one point of view to another and make it easier to display multiple objects in space. I'll also introduce the concepts of lighting and texturing 3D objects. These are advanced techniques that give us an enormous amount of control over how our 3D sketches will look. They're also pretty complicated and can take a long time to master. In this chapter, I'll just introduce the basic concepts that we'll continue working with throughout this book (and that you can spend ages mastering completely).

Let's get started!

Welcome to the Third Dimension

Probably the first thing you learned when you started playing with Processing was how Processing orients the coordinates of your sketch. You learned that if x and y were both 0, you were at the "origin" in the top-left corner of the sketch. Next you learned that as x increased, you moved to the right until it maxed out at the width of the sketch, and likewise as y increased, you moved down until you hit the sketch's height. Once you understood this arrangement, you could start to draw things wherever you wanted within the sketch's window. You've probably used your knowledge of this orientation so much now that it's become second nature to you. All of the work we did last chapter in learning how to iterate through the pixels in the depth image assumed you understood this setup and built on that knowledge.

But now we're going to add a third dimension to the mix. This third, z, axis points through the screen. Bigger z-values position objects closer to us, and smaller z-values move them farther away. But what do "farther" and "closer" really mean for us when drawing shapes? Just like in a photograph or a drawing, shapes that are closer will become larger and shapes that are farther away will get smaller. Likewise, drawing a shape at a position with a higher z-value will make that shape appear bigger even if its actual size doesn't change. And vice versa for smaller z-values.

Let's take a quick look at some simple sketches to make sure we understand what this means. Here's a sketch that's so simple it probably looks a lot like the first Processing program you ever wrote:

```
void setup(){
  size(640, 480, P3D);
}

void draw(){
  background(0);
  ellipse(width/2, height/2, 100, 100);
}
```

As you can see from Figure 3-1, this just draws a white ellipse at the center of the sketch over a black background. The only thing worth noting at all here is the call to size in setup. Notice that I passed P3D as the third argument. That tells Processing that we're going to be drawing in 3D. And since we've made that promise, let's fulfill it.

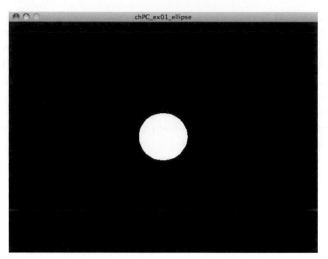

Figure 3-1. *Drawing a simple ellipse in 3D.*

Here's another version of the sketch that adds a single line of code, taking our first tentative steps into the third dimension:

```
void setup(){
  size(640, 480, P3D);
}

void draw(){
  background(0);

  // translate moves the position from which we draw
  // 100 in the third argument moves to z = 100
  translate(0,0,100);
  ellipse(width/2, height/2, 100, 100);
}
```

Behold the dramatic difference! (See Figure 3-2.)

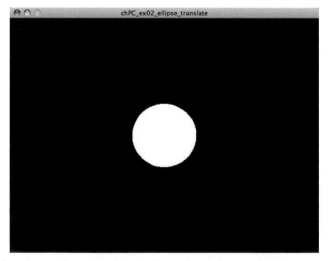

Figure 3-2. *Drawing an ellipse translated in three dimensions.*

Chapter 3

Hmm. Maybe not so dramatic. This seems to just be a slightly larger circle. But how did the circle get bigger? We didn't change our call to `ellipse` at all; it still draws a circle that's 100 by 100. By calling `translate(0,0,100)` we told Processing to move forward 100 units along the z-axis. Since we did that before calling `ellipse`, the circle was drawn closer to us and hence appears bigger. Try changing `translate` to give it a negative z-value: `translate(0,0,-100)`. Just as the larger z-value moved the circle closer and made it appear bigger, this negative value moves the circle farther away, making it look smaller than it originally did.

And, finally, if you leave the z-value as 0, by calling `translate(0,0,0)`, the circle will appear to be exactly its original size. This raises an important point about the relation of our z-axis to the two-dimensional world we're used to working in. When z is 0, everything is positioned exactly how it would be if we were only drawing in 2D. z-values greater than 0 move us in front of this original plane, and negative z-values move us behind it.

Now, in addition to poking about with different individual values, we can animate the z-position of our circle to make it appear to recede into space:

```
int z = 200;

void setup(){
  size(640, 480, P3D);
}

void draw(){
  background(0);

  // move to a further away z each time
  translate(0,0,z);
  ellipse(width/2, height/2, 100, 100);

  z = z - 1;
}
```

z starts off at 200 and then gets reduced by one every time `draw` runs. This creates the illusion that our circle is falling back into the screen, disappearing into the distance. Of course, we could create this same illusion by simply shrinking an ellipse in a two-dimensional sketch, but the point here is to understand how the third dimension works. By using the third dimension, we're making the circle appear smaller without changing its actual size. Now that we have a third dimension available to us, the appearance of every shape we draw will be determined not just by its actual size, but by how far away we draw it on the z-axis.

Drawing Our First Point Cloud

OK. Now that we're oriented, it's time to get back to the Kinect. We're going to access the Kinect's data as a set of 3D points so we can draw them in our sketch. The code for doing this will be similar in some ways to the code we've written in the past that accessed the Kinect's pixels, but it will be simpler. In that old code, we asked SimpleOpenNI for the depth values, and it gave them to us as a simple array of integers. We then had to translate from that one-dimensional array of depth values into x- and y- positions on screen.

This time, though, we're going to ask SimpleOpenNI for something more sophisticated. In addition to the simple array of depth values, SimpleOpenNI can give us the Kinect's data as a set of three-dimensional points. When we access these, instead of getting an array of integers, we get an array of *vectors*.

What is a vector? Vectors are a way of storing points with multiple coordinates in a single variable. When we're working in three dimensions, it takes three numbers to represent any given point in space: an x-coordinate, a y-coordinate, and a z-coordinate. Using only simple integers, we'd need three separate variables to represent this point, something like `pointX`, `pointY`, and `pointZ`. We saw this kind of thing constantly in our code in Chapter 2. We were constantly declaring pairs of variables, like `lastX` and `lastY` or `imageX` and `imageY`, to represent x-y coordinates that were meant to go together. In each case, these sets of numbers aren't really separate. Even though we stored `imageX` and `imageY` in two separate variables, they're really working together to store one single location in space. And this problem will only get worse as we start working in three dimensions. Instead of needing two variables for everything, we'll need three.

Vectors let us store all of the coordinates for a single point in a single variable. So instead of referring to `pointX`, `pointY`, and `pointZ`, we can declare a single vector and then access its x-, y-, and z-components.

What does this actually look like in Processing? Processing provides a vector class called `PVector` that allows exactly this functionality. Here's what it looks like to declare, initialize, and access a vector in Processing:

```
PVector p = new PVector(1,2,3);
println("x: " + p.x + " y: " + p.y + " z: " + p.z);
```

That first line declares a new vector as a local variable, `p`, and then populates it with a new `PVector`. The numbers passed in to create the `PVector` set the values for each of its components. So one gets set to p's x-component, two to its y-component, and three to its z-component. The second line of this fragment demonstrates how to access a vector's components. By calling `p.x`, `p.y`, and `p.z` we can access each component value individually as necessary. If you copy these lines into a blank Processing sketch and run it, you'll see the following output:

```
x: 1.0 y: 2.0 z: 3.0
```

So, what's the big advantage? We still have to set and access three different numbers—only now the syntax is slightly different. The big advantage comes when you're dealing with large sets of points, for example arrays of depth data from the Kinect. In the past, when we've gotten depth data from the Kinect it was stored as a one-dimensional array in which each element was an integer. This array was carefully crafted to store the two-dimensional data of the depth image, and we worked hard to untangle it back into rows and columns.

At that point, we only needed to access one piece of data per point: the depth reading. But, starting now, we're going to need three pieces of data per point: the x-, y-, and z-coordinates of each point in the point cloud. To access that information in a one-dimensional array, we'd either need to make the structure of the array even more complicated (requiring—the horror!—a triply nested loop) or use multiple arrays.

Luckily, we have vectors. We can simply populate our array with vectors instead of integers. Then each element in the array will contain all three of the coordinates of each point. We can just loop through the array once and at each point we'll have the x-,y-, and z-coordinates, everything we need to display a point in our point cloud. This is where the power of vectors really comes in handy. By letting us store all the information about each point in a single variable, we can dramatically simplify our code's logic.

Now that we understand what vectors are, let's dive in and draw a point cloud. Here's a sketch that accesses the depth data from the Kinect as an array of vectors and then uses these to draw points in three-dimensional space:

```
import processing.opengl.*;
import SimpleOpenNI.*;
SimpleOpenNI kinect;

void setup() {
  size(1024, 768, OPENGL);
  kinect = new SimpleOpenNI(this);
  kinect.enableDepth();
}

void draw() {
  background(0);

  kinect.update();

  // prepare to draw centered in x-y
  // pull it 1000 pixels closer on z
  translate(width/2, height/2, -1000); ❶
  rotateX(radians(180)); // flip y-axis from "realWorld" ❷

  stroke(255); ❸

  // get the depth data as 3D points
  PVector[] depthPoints = kinect.depthMapRealWorld(); ❹
  for(int i = 0; i < depthPoints.length; i++){

    // get the current point from the point array
    PVector currentPoint - depthPoints[i];

    // draw the current point
    point(currentPoint.x, currentPoint.y, currentPoint.z); ❺
  }
}
```

Figure 3-3 shows an example of what I see when I run the sketch.

I'll go through the interesting parts of this code in a bit, but since this is our first time looking at a point cloud, I want to make some observations that illustrate a few of the interesting properties of point clouds that will be relevant to the rest of the work we do with them.

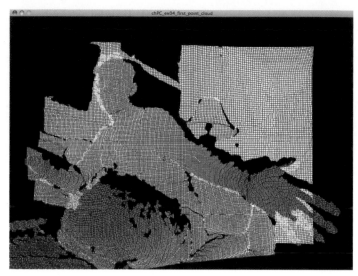

Figure 3-3. *Our first point cloud drawn from the Kinect's 3D data.*

On first glance, the point cloud might look pretty similar to the depth images we've seen before. It's a black and white image. It has the black shadows where closer objects obscure those that are farther away. On the other hand, it has a few differences. One obvious difference is the fact that the image no longer fits into a clean rectangle; it has a ragged border. My arm in the foreground extends beyond the straight edge of the wall behind it; the couch I'm sitting on sticks out below the bottom of the wall.

Why is this? Where does this effect come from? It's an artifact of capturing depth data as a two-dimensional image while displaying it in 3D. As you well know from earlier chapters, the Kinect is a depth camera. Like any other camera, its image squeezes the world into a flat rectangle. At the edges of this rectangle, everything gets cut off equally whether it's in the foreground or the background. For example, Figure 3-4 shows a simple depth image taken with the Kinect in the same position and me in the same pose as in the point cloud above.

Notice how my hand doesn't reach all the way to the edge of the image on the right or the bottom; there's quite a bit of wall visible to its right. And similarly, notice how the couch and the wall both get cut off equally at the bottom of the image underneath my hand. Anything cut off from this image will not be included in the point cloud. If the Kinect's camera can't see it, we don't have depth data about it, and so we can't draw the points that represent it.

Now, when we start to display things in 3D, things that are closer appear bigger than things that are farther away. That's why my hand extends beyond the edge of the wall in the point cloud. The wall is much farther back than my hand and so appears smaller. And the amount of wall we have data about is limited by what was included in the depth image. The result is that when you push the wall back into space, its edge shows up well inside the reach of my arm. Something similar happens with the couch at the bottom of the image. The couch is also well in front of the wall so it appears larger. Since both the couch and the wall were cut off at the same point in the depth image, the larger couch now sticks out beyond the wall in the background.

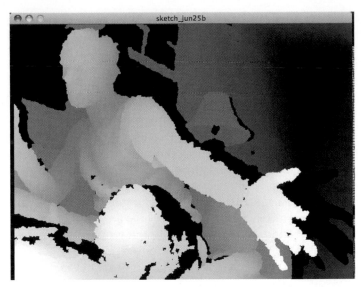

Figure 3-4. *A depth image from the same point of view as the previous point cloud. On first glance it might look somewhat similar, but there are key differences.*

There's another effect that distinguishes the point cloud from the straight depth image. In the point cloud, you can see through objects. Look closely at my hand on the right side of that image. You can see its shadow and the wall behind straight through it. The parts of my hand that are in front of the wall look brighter than the parts that are in front of its own shadow or the nothingness beyond the wall. The same effect is visible at the edge of my knee in the lower left of the image. Contrast these parts of the point cloud with the corresponding parts of the depth image. There, everything looks solid. What's going on here?

Imagine the point cloud as a plume of smoke that's in the room with you. From far away, where the smoke is dense, it might look like a solid object, completely obscuring what's behind it. But as you got closer or as the smoke spread out, you'd start to be able to see through it. This happens because the smoke isn't perfectly dense. Despite how it might appear from far away, it's not actually a solid thing at all. In fact, it's a bunch of tiny individual particles that have space between them. As you get closer or as the smoke diffuses, it gets to be easier to see between these particles.

This is exactly what's happening with the point cloud coming from the Kinect. The density of the point cloud is limited by the resolution of the Kinect's depth camera. We have a lot of depth points, but not an infinite number of them. So as parts of the point cloud get closer to us (like my hand is doing in the image above), we start to be able to see through the spaces between the individual points. Whatever's behind starts to show through.

OK, it's finally time; let's talk about the code. There are three interesting bits here:

❶ The first one comes on this line, where we call `translate`. Unlike the previous use of `translate` we saw at the beginning of this chapter, here we're translating on all three axes at once: x, y, and z. We're translating on x and y to center the point cloud within our sketch's window. Dividing both the sketch's `width` and `height` in half will give us a point that's exactly in the center. This logic is pretty straightforward, and you've probably seen things like it before when trying to draw shapes or images in the middle of your sketch. The z-value here is a little bit more interesting but should make sense to you after our earlier discussion of the orientation of the z-axis. In that discussion, we learned that positive z-values come toward us, making objects bigger, and negative z-values move away from us into the screen making objects smaller.

Here we translate 1000 pixels away from us along the z-axis. The z-values that come in from the Kinect are all positive. In the case of my particular scene, I found that they ranged from around 250 to a little over 1000. I was only sitting a few feet from my Kinect and there was a wall directly behind me. Your values may vary. You can figure them out by calling `println(currentPoint.z)` within your loop and noting what range of values you see (note: printing values like this is extremely slow, so you might want to alter your loop so that it only reads every 100th value while you're doing this; change the last part of your loop declaration from `i++` to `i += 100`).

Given this range of z-values coming in from the Kinect, if we just drew points at these locations, they'd all be so far in the positive z-direction that they'd be behind our point of view on the sketch and hence invisible. To get them situated somewhere we'll actually be able to see them, we translate by –1000 in the z-direction so that they're placed comfortably out in front of us.

❷   This line uses a function called `rotateX`. I want to mostly ignore what this line is doing for now. I will, however, tell you its purpose. To draw the point cloud, we're going to access a new function from SimpleOpenNI: `kinect.depthMapRealWorld`. As you'll see in a second, that function will give us the vectors we need to draw three-dimensional points that correspond to the scene in front of the Kinect. Unlike the functions we've used to access the Kinect's data before, `depthMapRealWorld` processes the data relatively heavily before giving it to us. In addition to organizing the depth data into vectors, this function processes the position of these vectors to remove distortion and project them into realistic 3D space. As part of this projection, `depthMapRealWorld` returns y-values that increase as the points move up in the y-direction. This sounds perfectly sensible: as things move up in the scene, their y-values should increase. Duh. But remember how Processing's axes are oriented. In Processing, the origin (i.e., 0 on the y-axis) is in the top-left corner of the sketch and positive y-values move down toward the bottom. Hence, if we leave these y-values alone, our point cloud will appear upside down! To fix this problem we have to rotate our sketch around the x-axis. I'm going to cover rotation more thoroughly in the next section, but for now, suffice it to say that this line uses `rotateX` to flip the points along the y-axis so that they'll be right side up.

❸   Note that the points only show up white because we called `stroke(255)` on line 20; it might be slightly counterintuitive, but points use the stroke color rather than the fill color and if you don't set that to white in your own sketches, you may end up very frustrated and with a lot of invisible points.

④ One more thing worth noticing is how we extract the vectors containing the point cloud information from SimpleOpenNI. That happens on this line, where we call `kinect.depthMapRealWorld`. That function returns an array of `PVectors`, which we store in the local variable `depthPoints`. Once we've got these vectors in an array, we loop over that array drawing a single point on the screen for each vector.

⑤ Processing's `point` function takes three arguments: the x-, y-, and z-coordinates of the point you want to draw. We then extract each component out of the `PVector` one at a time in order to pass them to `point`. Wash, rinse, repeat and voilà, a point cloud!

Making the Point Cloud Move

So, we've entered the third dimension. We've got a point cloud displaying our Kinect data in 3D space. And we've noticed a couple of interesting ways the point cloud differs from the depth images we'd seen before. But there's a lot more we can do with point clouds. Now that we've created a 3D representation of the Kinect's data inside of Processing, we can manipulate that in all kinds of ways. For example, if we move the location and orientation of the point cloud, we'll be able to view the scene from a different angle than where the Kinect is positioned. It's almost like having the ability to look around corners!

To gain control of where objects and points are positioned, we'll have to learn a few techniques for navigating in 3D. So far, we've only used `translate` to move our points into a comfortable position away from the screen. To look at the point cloud from different angles, we'll need to rotate these points around in addition to translating them. To accomplish this we'll learn about the three functions Processing provides for rotating around the different axes. We'll also need to control the center of our rotation. There's a difference between spinning in place and orbiting around the point cloud itself. Spinning in place would cause us to be looking away from the point cloud for half the time while orbiting around the point cloud will always keep it in the center of our view while constantly showing it to us from different sides. In order to control the center of rotation, we'll learn to use Processing's rotate functions in conjunction with `translate`.

One important thing to remember to keep yourself oriented is this: when we do translations and rotations, we're not moving our point of view. This is not like rotating a camera or moving it closer to some object. What we're really moving is the whole world: we're changing Processing's coordinate system itself. By default, Processing places the origin (the point where our sketch's x-, y-, and z-coordinates are all at 0) in the top-left corner of the sketch window. Positive x-values go to the right, positive y-values go toward the bottom, and positive z-values come forward straight out of the screen. When we call `translate`, we move this origin point to a different place based on the co-ordinates we pass in. When we use Processing's rotate functions, we change the angle of these axes. The result of these changes is that subsequent coordinate points refer to new places on the screen. For example, when we call `translate(width/2, height/2, 500)` as we did in this last sketch, we move the origin to the middle of the sketch on the x- and y-axes and pull it forward

Warning

It's extremely easy to get confused when you start doing complex navigation in 3D. You get just a few numbers a little bit wrong or do things in the wrong order and suddenly everything is far away or upside down or gone completely. Don't get frustrated! With time and practice you'll start to build up an intuition for how Processing organizes 3D space and how to use its navigation tools to get what you want.

500 pixels toward us. Then, when we draw our points, they will all be positioned relative to that new origin. They'll be shifted down, to the right, and toward us in depth.

Rotate has a similar effect. If we rotate our coordinate system by 180 degrees around the y-axis, we'll have essentially reversed the orientation of the x-axis. After this rotation, moving in a positive direction along x will be the reverse of what it would be in the original global coordinate system.

Remember the rotation line we included when we drew the point cloud? I told you at that point that it was used to flip the y-values so that they wouldn't be upside down. It looked like this:

```
rotateX(radians(180));
```

Based on what I just described, how this works should now make more sense to you. When we call this line, we rotate our coordinate system 180 degrees around the x-axis. The result is that the y-axis spins around and faces the opposite direction. Positive values along this axis, which previously pointed down in the default Processing orientation, now point up, which matches the real-world projection being given to us by SimpleOpenNI in `depthMapRealWorld`. (More about why we call that radians function when I go over the code in detail below.)

To make things even more confusing, these transformations and rotations are additive, each one picks up where the last one left off. Subsequent operations alter the coordinate system from within the current coordinate system rather than in reference to the original one. In other words if you rotate by 180 degrees around the y-axis and then translate by 100 pixels along x, it will have the same effect as if you'd translated in the opposite direction along the x-axis without the rotation, as if you'd simply called `translate` with a value of 100 pixels for x (with the difference that you'd be rotated in a different direction).

To deal with this confusing effect, Processing provides two functions, `pushMatrix` and `popMatrix`. When used together, these two functions can isolate a set of transformations and rotations so that they don't affect anything outside of them. Thankfully we won't get into any operations that are so complicated as to need `pushMatrix` and `popMatrix` quite yet. To rotate around the point cloud, all we'll need is a couple of calls to `rotate` and `translate`. However, after that we'll find ourselves using `pushMatrix` and `popMatrix` extensively as we proceed to do additional 3D drawing in order to add user interface elements to our point cloud.

For now, though, let's get on with the business of making this point cloud spin. As I mentioned above, we want to create the illusion that our point of view is orbiting around the point cloud. To accomplish this, we'll need to make two additions to our sketch. First, we'll need to get it rotating. To do that, we'll add a variable that stores the current angle of rotation, which we'll increment a little at a time on each run of `draw` and then use to rotate our coordinate system. Second, we'll need to ensure that this rotation is happening with the point cloud in the center of the coordinate system rather than at the edge. If we leave the coordinate system where it was when we drew the point cloud, then rotating as just described will cause it to move around our point of view, spending much of its time invisible behind us and not giving us much variety of vantage point even when it is visible. To prevent this, we'll need to do an additional `translate` to shift the coordinate system again so that it is centered within the point cloud before the rotation takes place. This translation will need to be somewhat the reverse of the one we already have in the sketch that pushes the points out into depth in front of us to make them visible. Along the z-axis at least, we want to put the coordinate system back where we found it, smack in the middle of the point cloud, so that the rotation is centered there. Doing so will create the appearance that our point of view is orbiting around the point cloud rather than vice versa, just what we want.

OK, that was pretty specific. Let's see what it looks like as code:

```
import processing.opengl.*;
import SimpleOpenNI.*;

SimpleOpenNI kinect;

// variable to hold our current rotation represented in degrees
float rotation = 0;

void setup() {
  size(1024, 768, OPENGL);
  kinect = new SimpleOpenNI(this);
  kinect.enableDepth();
}

void draw() {
  background(0);
  kinect.update();

  // prepare to draw centered in x-y
  // pull it 1000 pixels closer on z
  translate(width/2, height/2, -1000);
  // flip the point cloud vertically:
  rotateX(radians(180));

  // move the center of rotation
  // to inside the point cloud
  translate(0, 0, 1000);

  // rotate about the y-axis and bump the rotation
  rotateY(radians(rotation));
  rotation++;

  stroke(255);

  PVector[] depthPoints = kinect.depthMapRealWorld();

  // notice: "i+=10"
  // only draw every 10th point to make things faster
  for (int i = 0; i < depthPoints.length; i+=10) {
    PVector currentPoint = depthPoints[i];
    point(currentPoint.x, currentPoint.y, currentPoint.z);
  }
}
```

When you run this sketch, you'll see basically the same point cloud as before, but now your point of view will appear to be slowly circling it. Figure 3-5 shows a screen capture demonstrating what this sketch looked like for me when I ran it. In this image, I'm sitting directly in front of the Kinect, facing it. However, I've captured the output from the sketch while it was showing me from my right. The point of view it is presenting here is actually an impossible one in my apartment. This scene is presented as if you were looking at it through an external wall, hovering out over Avenue D. The semitransparent wavy lines you can see all the way on the left side of the sketch between me and the "camera"? Those are my window curtains.

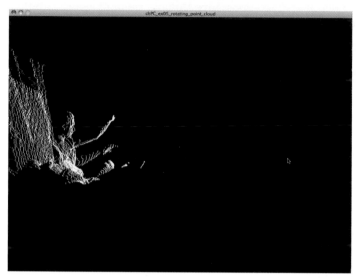

Figure 3-5. *The point cloud viewed from the side. The Kinect is directly in front of me, but we're viewing the point cloud from an alternate point of view.*

A few practical notes about this sketch. First of all, I've lowered the resolution at which we're displaying the point cloud. If you look at the first line of the loop, you'll notice that I'm skipping forward in the array of data from the Kinect 10 vectors at a time rather than 1:

```
for (int i = 0; i < depthPoints.length; i+=10) {
    ...
```

This makes the sketch run dramatically faster and smoother. Processing has to draw less than one tenth the number of points than in our previous example, which is a much easier job. Drawing fewer points also has the advantage of making our scene easier to see. As I noted when we were looking at first point cloud, the spaces between the points allow us to see through surfaces that would otherwise be solid, especially as they get up close to us. Only drawing a fraction of the available points makes every surface easy to see through, giving you a kind of x-ray vision over the whole scene.

One other technical detail here is the way we pass the current angle to Processing's rotation function. When we're working in 3D, Processing gives us three separate functions to control rotation: rotateX, rotateY, and rotateZ. Each function takes a single number as the argument. Each uses that number to rotate the coordinate system around the given access named in the function. So, rotateY, which we're using here, rotates the coordinates around the y-axis. Picture a pole pointing up in the y-direction and everything spinning around that. Our orientation will remain the same along the y-axis but change along both the x- and z-axes. The other two rotate functions work similarly, keeping the named axis fixed, while rotating the coordinates on the other two. Sometimes this naming scheme can be confusing because the function names the one axis whose coordinates it will not effect. If you find yourself getting confused, just picture a pole sticking out on the axis you're rotating and everything else dancing around that pole.

Warning

What about the argument we pass to rotateY*? Each of Processing's rotate functions takes its argument as radians. A radian is a unit of measuring rotation based on the proportions of a circle. It is different from the rotation unit you're probably used to thinking in: degrees. In order to convert from degrees to radians, Processing provides the convenient* radians *function. This function takes an argument in degrees and converts it to the radians that* rotateX*,* rotateY*, and* rotateZ *all demand. The formula that Processing uses to do this conversion is one you may have come across in high school geometry class: 360 degrees equals two times Pi radians.*

One thing you may have noticed while watching your point cloud spin is that things start to look a little bit weird about halfway through the rotation. As the points rotate around 180 degrees so that the back of the scene is facing you, it almost feels like the direction of motion reverses, things flip around, and you're again seeing the image from the front somehow.

For example, Figure 3-6 shows a screenshot of my copy of the sketch a few moments after the side view I showed in Figure 3-5.

Figure 3-6. *Point cloud rotated to be viewed from behind.*

Despite what it may look like on first glance, this actually shows the scene from directly behind me. Contrast it with Figure 3-7, which shows the point cloud from the front (from the Kinect's actual physical position), and you can start to see what I mean.

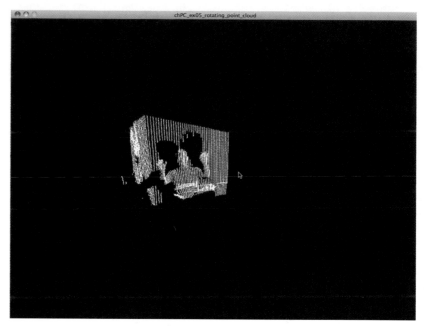

Figure 3-7. *Point cloud rotated to be viewed from the front.*

When you look at these two images closely in comparison, you can start to see which one's which. In the image taken from the front of the scene, you can clearly see my shadow in the depth data on the wall behind me. If you look carefully at the image taken from behind, you can see the wall and shadow are actually in front of me, between the scene's point of view.

What causes this effect? Due to how the Kinect works, we only have depth points for the surface of objects. The Kinect can't see inside of objects clearly, and at this stage we're not doing anything to reconstruct the objects we've detected into a solid form. Hence the points in our scene are all distributed over surfaces that are exactly one depth point thick. These types of surfaces suffer from an optical illusion similar to that of the classic wireframe cube. Look at a drawing of a cube that doesn't shade-in the outside walls (Figure 3-8, for example).

If you stare at this illustration long enough, the front and back faces of the cube will appear to swap: the face that was the front will become the back and vice versa. There's simply not enough visual information to fix the picture into a single state.

Something very similar happens with the Kinect point cloud data. Many views of the point cloud look very similar to their reverse. This is especially true for views that are largely vertically symmetrical so that flipping them provides no large-scale clue as to the change.

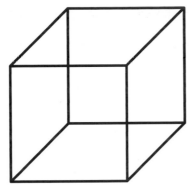

Figure 3-8. *A wireframe cube showing an optical illusion. Which face is the front and which is the back of this cube?*

Something very similar happens with the Kinect point cloud data. Many views of the point cloud look very similar to their reverse. This is especially true for views that are largely vertically symmetrical so that flipping them provides no large-scale clue as to the change.

Let's make a small change to the sketch that will make it more interactive and also lessen the impact of this effect. We're going to change our sketch so that instead of rotating automatically, its rotation will be controlled by the movement of your mouse. In order to do this, we have to change the value we're sending to rotateY. Replace the two lines immediately preceding stroke(255); in the sketch—where we were previously calling rotateY and incrementing our rotation variable—with these new lines:

```
float mouseRotation = map(mouseX, 0, width, -180, 180);
rotateY(radians(mouseRotation));
```

The first line here reads the x-coordinate of the mouse's position within the sketch and then maps its value to a range of −180 to 180. This means that when the mouse is all the way on the left side of this sketch, mouseRotation will be set to −180; as the mouse moves toward the center, its value will increase up toward 0; and then as we move toward the right edge, it will start to take on positive numbers up to 180. In the next line, we then take those values, convert them to radians, and pass them to rotateY.

The result of these lines will be that the position of your mouse controls the rotation of the coordinate system and hence the angle from which we see our point cloud. When your mouse is in the middle of the sketch, we'll rotate the sketch by 0 degrees (i.e., leave it alone). As you move the mouse to the left, it will rotate in the negative direction or counterclockwise, and as you move to the right it will rotate clockwise. If you leave your mouse still, the point cloud will stay in its current rotation. The mouse is now positioned very approximately at the origin of Processing's coordinate system, with the point cloud rotating around it as you move it.

This new interface should make the inside-out effect much less dramatic. Since you control the speed at which the point cloud moves, you can go slowly through the transition to the reverse side and your eye won't lose its bearings. Play around with this sketch while moving in front of your Kinect to get a feel for it.

Viewing the Point Cloud in Color

Up to this point, we've been looking at the point cloud in black and white. More accurately, we've only been looking at it in white. We've been drawing white points against a black background. Where the point cloud has appeared to be shades of gray, it's only been because of the density of white dots overlapping and creating an illusion.

We learned in the last chapter that the Kinect also has a color camera that we can access. Wouldn't it be great if we could use that color information to paint our point cloud so that it had realistic color? There's an obstacle to this, though. We also learned in that chapter that the color data and the depth data don't quite line up. In Figure 2-11, we compared the color image to the depth image side by side and saw how the framing and position of objects were slightly different. This happens because the Kinect's IR camera and color camera are slightly offset from each other on the front of the device. They both see the world from a slightly different point of view.

In order to give our point cloud the benefit of this color data (as shown in Figure 3-9), we need to find a way to overcome these distortions and offsets. We need to align both images so they match up. If we could do that, then we could simply access the pixels from the color image to figure out what color to make our depth points. Thankfully, SimpleOpenNI provides a method to do exactly that. It's called `alternativeViewPointDepthToImage`. All we have to do is call that method once on our `kinect` object during setup and then the depth and color data will be aligned. Here's a sketch based on our last example that does exactly that. Run this sketch, take a look at the changes, and then I'll go through and describe exactly how they work.

Figure 3-9. *The point cloud displayed with full color data from the RGB image. Shown here with full resolution so you can see the glory of the color point cloud.*

```
import processing.opengl.*;
import SimpleOpenNI.*;

SimpleOpenNI kinect;
float rotation = 0;

void setup() {
  size(1024, 768, OPENGL);
  kinect = new SimpleOpenNI(this);
  kinect.enableDepth();
  // access the color camera
  kinect.enableRGB(); ❶
  // tell OpenNI to line-up the color pixels
  // with the depth data
  kinect.alternativeViewPointDepthToImage(); ❷

}

void draw() {
  background(0);
  kinect.update();
  // load the color image from the Kinect
  PImage rgbImage = kinect.rgbImage(); ❸

  translate(width/2, height/2, -250);
  rotateX(radians(180));
  translate(0, 0, 1000);
  rotateY(radians(rotation));
  rotation++;

  PVector[] depthPoints = kinect.depthMapRealWorld();
  // don't skip any depth points
  for (int i = 0; i < depthPoints.length; i+=1) {
    PVector currentPoint = depthPoints[i];
    // set the stroke color based on the color pixel
    stroke(rgbImage.pixels[i]); ❹
    point(currentPoint.x, currentPoint.y, currentPoint.z);
  }
}
```

When you run this code, you should see something that at first looks like a flat color image from the Kinect; it will begin to rotate around and you'll see that it is three-dimensional like the other point clouds we've drawn in this chapter, only now the points all have the right colors. You might find that this code runs quite slowly. To demonstrate the qualities of the color point cloud, I set the loop through the depth points to not skip any points. As we discussed, this will make our sketch run quite slowly. But it also shows off the color point cloud to best effect, making it appear solid. If you change the amount the loop increments, you can make your sketch run much faster.

Even though the color point cloud appears solid when we look at it from far away like this, as it rotates around, you'll notice that there is still space between the points. Figure 3-10 shows an image capture as the point of view of the sketch spun around behind me. The dots representing me are close to the "camera" and the computer is far away. You can see the space between the close depth points, and you can see straight through them to the objects behind.

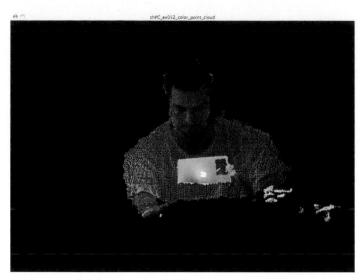

Figure 3-10. *The point cloud displayed with full color data from the RGB image. Even at full resolution, when you get up close you can see between the points.*

Now, let's look at exactly how we're calculating the color of the depth points. We'll examine the changes we made to this sketch to get the color information, align it with our depth data, and select the right color for each pixel.

❶ The changes start in `setup`. First of all, we call `kinect.enableRGB` so that we can access the color image. This is the first time we've used the RGB image since the first couple of examples in the first chapter.

❷ The next thing we need to do is to tell SimpleOpenNI that we want to align the color and depth data. We do this by calling `kinect.alternativeViewPointDepthToImage`. After that, our depth and color data will be correctly aligned. Now all we have to do is grab the right pixel from the color image for each depth point.

❸ The process of getting the color pixels starts at the beginning of `draw`. We access the color image from the Kinect with `kinect.rgbImage` and store the result in a `PImage`. As we saw in the last chapter, we can access the pixels of a `PImage` as an array. The idea here is to access the color of the pixel in this array that corresponds to each depth point and then to use that pixel to set the `stroke` color before we draw the corresponding depth point. The result will be that each depth point will take on the color of the equivalent pixel in the color image. The code for this happens near the bottom of the sketch inside the `for` loop that accesses all of the depth points.

❹ Just before we call `point` to draw the next depth point, there's a new line:

```
+stroke(rgbImage.pixels[i])+
```

This line does two things. First, it accesses the color of the current RGB pixel. We pass `i` the index we've been using to access the `depthPoints` into the pixel array belonging to `rgbImage`. That returns the color of the current pixel as a Processing `color` object. That object is then passed to `stroke` to set the color for the following depth point, which is drawn on the next line with `point`. And, boom, we've got a color point cloud.

Point clouds are a lot more exciting to look at in color than in monochrome. However, accessing the color image adds to the amount of data we have to retrieve from the Kinect on every frame. As our sketches get more complex (and especially in future chapters as they start to use other advanced features of OpenNI such as skeleton tracking), this can bog things down and even cause our sketches to run out of memory. Further, even though accessing the color data is quite straightforward, it still adds code to every sketch where it appears. That code can become a distraction as you're trying to understand the new concepts we're trying to learn, and it will certainly make the code for every sketch longer and more unwieldy on the page.

For all of these reasons, I'm going to skip coloring the point clouds for the rest of this chapter. If you ever want to add color to any project or example in this chapter (or anywhere else throughout the book), I encourage you to do so! We'll revisit the color data one more time next chapter in the context of user tracking. In addition to aligning the color image with the depth data, OpenNI can find individual people in the color image and give you just the pixels that are part of them. In other words OpenNI can remove people from images or replace the backgrounds behind them.

Making the Point Cloud Interactive

Now that we're oriented and we're starting to understand how to move around in 3D, let's make things interactive. To build a 3D interactive application we need to add two major tools to our growing 3D toolkit. First we need to be able to draw more sophisticated shapes in 3D. In order to give users an interface they'll actually understand, we need to give them some feedback on the screen about what they're supposed to do, how they're supposed to move to interact with our sketch. To do that, we need to draw shapes like cubes and spheres at positions of our own choosing. These will coexist with the points from the point cloud and act as areas of space the users can target to trigger interactions.

Second, we need to find out if the user is interacting with these areas of space that we've highlighted. To do so, we'll have to check to see how many of the points in the point cloud are within the area that we defined. This will involve processing the 3D points in the point cloud in much the same way as we did the 2D points of the depth image. We'll iterate through them and instead of simply drawing them to the screen, we'll look at their position in space and apply some logic to them to see if they meet our criteria. If they do, we'll give the user feedback by altering the appearance of our shapes and triggering other kinds of actions.

These floating 3D interactive elements are sometimes called *hot points*. They're a bit like the traditional buttons so commonly found in 2D interfaces, but translated into 3D. To activate a 2D button, you click while the mouse is within the button's bounds. To activate a 3D hot point, you move some number of the point cloud's points into the hot point's bounds. Unlike two 2D buttons, which are completely binary (i.e., they have only two states: on and off), 3D buttons are more continuous—we can measure not just whether any part of the point cloud is within the button, but how many of its points are within those bounds. We can use this attribute to our advantage, using hot points to give the user control of continuous values like the pitch of a sound, the brightness of an image, etc. On the other hand, if we want to reproduce the sharp on-off distinction of a 2D button, we can also do that with hot points by setting a threshold value. In other words, we would set up the hot point to treat any number of points less than, say, 100 within it as off and any number greater than that as on.

So, how would we go about implementing a hot point? As I've just described, there are two components to the process: indicating to users what part of space is interactive and checking to see if they've interacted with it. To accomplish the first, we'll need to learn a little more about drawing in 3D. We'll start by drawing a cube in the same space as the point cloud. This is a very primitive form of user interface. It requires users to look at the screen to know what part of the space around them is interactive. Really, we'd like them to be able to look at the actual space around them rather than the screen, but this will work as a starting point.

Once we've got our cube on the screen, we need to check to see if any of part of the point cloud is inside of it. Since we created the cube, we know its starting point and its dimensions. We can translate these values into a series of bounds on space. If the point satisfies all of these bounds, along each of its dimensions, then we know that it is inside of the cube. In other words, for a point to be inside the cube, its y-value needs to be greater than the cube's highest point, but less than the cube's lowest point; its x-value need to be greater than the cube's leftmost point but less than the cube's rightmost point; and its z-value needs to be greater than the cube's farthest point but less than its closest point. If all of these conditions are true, then the point is inside the cube. That might sound a bit complicated, but in practice the code ends up being a little repetitive, but mostly straightforward. Also, diagrams. It helps to look at diagrams when you're trying to figure out spatial code like this. We'll have some nice diagrams for you to look at.

And finally we'll need to give some form of feedback to reflect the user's interaction with our hot point. The simplest way to do that is to change the appearance of the cube in some way based on how many points we detect inside of it. Once we've got that down, we can try a slightly more complex form of feedback that will make the whole interaction stronger. If we use the user's interaction with the hot point to control the playback of a sound, for example, that might provide a more interesting interaction. Since the user would be getting feedback without having to look at the screen, he could concentrate on exploring the space around him and understanding the relationship between how he moves through it and the sounds that he hears.

Adding sound will also get us a big step closer to the awesome-sounding "air drums" app I mentioned in the introduction to this chapter. However, before we start pulling out our air drum sticks, we have to start at the beginning to build up this interaction, and that means displaying a cube in tandem with our point cloud.

Let's start with a sketch that just draws a cube in the same space as the point cloud. Starting with our existing point cloud sketch, adding this is easy. Here's the code:

```
import processing.opengl.*;
import SimpleOpenNI.*;

SimpleOpenNI kinect;

float rotation = 0;

// set the box size
int boxSize = 150; ❶
// a vector holding the center of the box
PVector boxCenter = new PVector(0, 0, 600); ❷

void setup() {
  size(1024, 768, OPENGL);
  kinect = new SimpleOpenNI(this);
  kinect.enableDepth();
}

void draw() {
  background(0);
  kinect.update();

  translate(width/2, height/2, -1000); ❸
  rotateX(radians(180));

  translate(0, 0, 1000);

  rotateY(radians(map(mouseX, 0, width, -180, 180)));

  stroke(255);

  PVector[] depthPoints = kinect.depthMapRealWorld();

  for (int i = 0; i < depthPoints.length; i+=10) {
    PVector currentPoint = depthPoints[i];

    point(currentPoint.x, currentPoint.y, currentPoint.z);
  }

  // We're ready to draw the cube ❹

  // move to the box center
  translate(boxCenter.x, boxCenter.y, boxCenter.z); ❺

  // set line color to red
  stroke(255, 0, 0);

  // leave the box unfilled so we can see through it
  noFill();

  // draw the box
  box(boxSize); ❻
}
```

If you run this, you should see the outline of a red cube in the sketch among the part of the point cloud that's about two to three feet in front of the Kinect. It will look something like Figure 3-11.

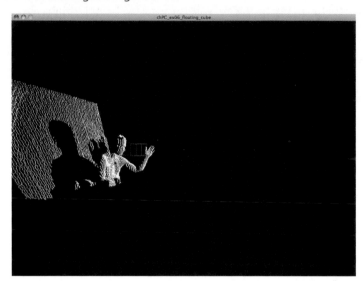

Figure 3-11. *A red cube floating amid the point cloud.*

It can be hard to tell exactly where an object on the screen is in relation to the rest of your space, so I've used the variation of our point cloud sketch that gives you control over the point of view by moving the mouse left and right to control the rotation. Notice that as you rotate the sketch around, the cube stays in a fixed position relative to the point cloud. It looks like it stays sitting a foot or so in front of me. Since we're drawing the cube after the translations and rotations we're applying to the rest of the points, it happens within the same coordinate system, and we didn't have to do anything special to get it to follow along.

A few notes to explain how this sketch positions and draws this cube. To draw a cube in Processing, we need to know two pieces of information: where the cube should be drawn and how big it should be. I set both of those pieces of information in variables at the top of this sketch. This may seem like overkill right now when they're only going to be used once to draw this cube, but we already know that we're planning on expanding this sketch to turn the cube into a touchable hot point. When we do that, the cube's size and position will be reused repeatedly throughout the sketch, so saving those in global variables will come in handy.

❶ The cube's size is a simple integer, and its position is a PVector with three components, one for each axis.

❷ I chose the position 0,0,600 based on the translation we do before drawing the point cloud. Moving 600 pixels along the positive z-axis from that point will put our cube comfortably in the front of the point cloud, a few feet in front of the Kinect. Other numbers might work better for you depending on where you have your Kinect and how far away from it you're sitting. If you move the cube too far forward in the positive z-direction, you won't be able to "touch" it. Don't forget that the Kinect won't detect anything closer than about 18 inches away from it. On the other hand, if you move it too far away, the cube might end up inside the wall or other furniture behind you. In that case it might be physically unreachable (unless you can walk through walls), or it might always have points inside of it (since the wall doesn't move), which will make it less helpful for interaction. Two to seven feet in front of the Kinect is usually a good range for user interaction.

❸ This statement performs the translation just mentioned, and will put the middle of the point cloud something like 1000 pixels away from the screen in the negative z-direction.

❹ Once we've got these variables set, we need to use them to draw the cube. Processing provides a function specifically for drawing cubes and other 3D solids: box. To draw a cube, we pass box a single argument representing the length of each side of the cube. When we call it, box will draw the cube at the origin of the current coordinate system. That means we have to use translate to position the box at the spot in space where we want it. This is just what we do in the last few lines of our sketch.

❺ As you can see here, I used the components of our boxCenter vector as arguments to translate to move the coordinate system to the center of the box. Then I set some basic color parameters and called box to finally draw the cube.

❻ It's important to note that box will draw our cube with its center at the origin of the current coordinate system. Since we want to detect the members of the point cloud that are within this cube, what we really care about are the positions of its edges, not its center. In the version of our sketch coming up next, we'll need to figure out the position of these edges relative to this center point in order to check if the points in our cloud are inside it.

Let's start on this next version. Now that we're displaying the cube, we need to start counting the number of points from the point cloud that are within it. And we need to add some kind of visual feedback based on that count.

How do we figure out which points are inside the cube? As I described above, the process for checking to see whether each point is inside the cube is going to come down to a series of greater-than and less-than statements. Is the point's x-component greater than the left edge of the cube? Is it less than the right edge of the box? If so, then it is within the box along the x-axis. Is its y-component greater than the lower edge of the cube? Is it less than the upper edge? Then it qualifies on the y-axis. And finally what about z? Is the point's z-component between the cube's closest edge and its farthest edge? If all of these things are true, then the point is inside of the cube and we'll count it toward our total.

We know how to access the x-, y-, and z-components of each point in our point cloud. We've been doing that all along in order to draw them. But how do we find the edges of our cube? We just learned that box draws the cube centered around the point we give it. In order to convert from this center point to the cube's edges in each dimension, we need to use the cube's size. The distance from the center of the cube to any edge is going to be exactly half of the length of each of the cube's edges. So, to find one edge of the cube, we'll subtract boxSize/2 from the component of the cube's center, and to find the other one, we'll add boxSize/2 (see Figure 3-12).

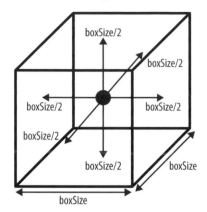

Figure 3-12. *An illustration showing the distance between the center of the cube and each of its sides.*

When we translate this logic into code, the result will be three nested if statements, one for each axis. Each of the if statements will have a less-than and a greater-than portion checking to make sure the point is within the bounds of the cube on that axis. Let's look at the code to see how this works in practice:

```
import processing.opengl.*;
import SimpleOpenNI.*;

SimpleOpenNI kinect;

float rotation = 0;

int boxSize = 150;
PVector boxCenter = new PVector(0, 0, 600);

// this will be used for zooming
// start at normal
float s = 1;

void setup() {
  size(1024, 768, OPENGL);
  kinect = new SimpleOpenNI(this);
  kinect.enableDepth();
}

void draw() {
  background(0);
  kinect.update();

  translate(width/2, height/2, -1000);
  rotateX(radians(180));

  // bumped up the translation
  // so that scale is better centered
  translate(0, 0, 1400);
  rotateY(radians(map(mouseX, 0, width, -180, 180)));

  // make everything bigger, i.e. zoom in
```

```
translate(0,0,s*-1000); ❶
scale(s);

println(s);

stroke(255);

PVector[] depthPoints = kinect.depthMapRealWorld();

// initialize a variable
// for storing the total
// points we find inside the box
// on this frame
int depthPointsInBox = 0;

for (int i = 0; i < depthPoints.length; i+=10) {
  PVector currentPoint = depthPoints[i];

  // The nested if statements inside of our loop ❷
  if (currentPoint.x > boxCenter.x - boxSize/2
      && currentPoint.x < boxCenter.x + boxSize/2)
  {
    if (currentPoint.y > boxCenter.y - boxSize/2
        && currentPoint.y < boxCenter.y + boxSize/2)
    {
      if (currentPoint.z > boxCenter.z - boxSize/2
          && currentPoint.z < boxCenter.z + boxSize/2)
      {
        depthPointsInBox++;
      }
    }
  }

  point(currentPoint.x, currentPoint.y, currentPoint.z);
}

println(depthPointsInBox);

// set the box color's transparency
// 0 is transparent, 1000 points is fully opaque red
float boxAlpha = map(depthPointsInBox, 0, 1000, 0, 255); ❸

translate(boxCenter.x, boxCenter.y, boxCenter.z);

// the fourth argument to fill() is "alpha"
// it determines the color's opacity
// we set it based on the number of points
fill(255, 0, 0, boxAlpha);
stroke(255, 0, 0);
box(boxSize);
}

// use keys to control zoom
// up-arrow zooms in
// down arrow zooms out
// s gets passed to scale() in draw()
void keyPressed(){ ❹
  if(keyCode == 38){
    s = s + 0.01;
  }
```

```
   if(keyCode == 40){
     s = s - 0.01;
   }
 }

void mousePressed(){
  save("touchedPoint.png");
}
```

This sketch makes the hot point active. It counts the number of points from the point cloud that are inside the hot point's cube and uses that to change the color of the hot point itself. The hot point will range from black on the inside to fully solid red depending on how much of the point cloud is inside of it. I've also added a few additional controls that let you zoom the view. I'll explain those at the end of this section.

❶ This line and the next are explained in "Zooming the Point Cloud" on page 138.

❷ So, we're heard a lot about these greater-than and less-than statements we're using to check to see if each point is within the cube. Here's how that ended up looking in practice.

That might look like a lot of code, but it's not really so bad. It's performing the same checks three times, once for each of our three axes. And each of those checks works just exactly the way I described. We make sure the current point is greater than the boxCenter minus one half the boxSize and less than the boxCenter plus one half the boxSize. We perform this comparison for each component of the currentPoint. If the point passes all of these comparisons, then it is in the cube, and so we increment the variable that's storing the count, depthPointsInBox.

❸ Once we have this count, we can use it to control the transparency of the cube. In Processing, every color can have a fourth ingredient just like red, green, and blue that sets how opaque it is. This is called the color's "alpha" value. We set it by passing a fourth value to fill after the RGB values. Just like those RGB values, our alpha value should be scaled between 0 and 255, with 0 being completely transparent and 255 completely opaque. So, in order to count how many of the points are inside the cube to control its transparency, we need to convert depth-PointsInBox to a value scaled between 0 and 255 so we can use it as the alpha component of our fill color. To do that, we'll use our trusty map function. To find out what values to use with map, I added a line to print out the boxAlpha and then looked at what values I got as I moved my hand into the hot point. I ended up deciding that 1000 was a good maximum value, but this may vary for you.

❹ This function is explained in "Zooming the Point Cloud" on page 138.

Run this sketch, and try interacting with the hot point. Rotate the point of view around if you're having trouble finding its position within your space. Since our sketch only shows us one angle at a time on the 3D scene, it helps to change your point of view to get a clearer sense of the relative position of objects in all three dimensions. Once you've located the cube, you should be able to get it to turn red by putting your hand into the space it represents. As you move into it more deeply, it will get more solidly red. And if you move other body parts

Chapter 3

that have more depth points in them (for example, I used my head), it will turn fully opaque. You can see this illustrated in Figure 3-13.

If you're having trouble getting this full range of colors, take a look at the values you're printing out for depthPointsInBox while you're interacting with the hot point. That will let you know the range of points you're managing to get in the box, and you can adjust the arguments to map appropriately.

OK, we've got our hot point working. We're drawing it to the screen, detecting how much the user is interacting with it, and displaying the output. What's next?

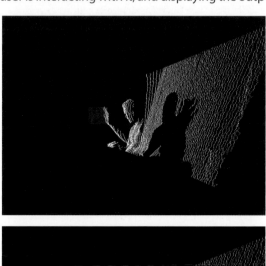

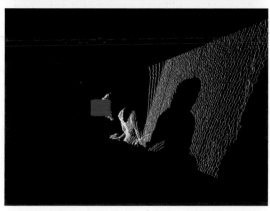

Figure 3-13. *Three screen captures showing the hotpoint increasing in color intensity based on how many depth points are inside of it.*

ZOOMING THE POINT CLOUD

I added an additional feature to this sketch to give you more control over your point of view on the point cloud: the ability to zoom by pressing the up and down arrows. To make it look like we're zooming in on the point cloud, we want all the distances between everything to get bigger while our point of view stays centered on its current center. To achieve this, we have to use an additional method for manipulating our coordinate system: scale. Just as translate changed the location of our coordinate system's origin and rotateX and rotateY changed the orientation of our system's axes, scale gives us control of another parameter: the distance between each tick on each axes. If we call scale with a number bigger than one, we're increasing the scale of our axes. For example, if we call scale(2), then after that, every translation and rotation we do will have twice the effect: calling translate(0,0,50) will move us forward by 100 along the z-axis as measured in the coordinate system from before scale was called. You can think of the values passed to scale as a percentage. One means don't change anything, keep the scale at 100 percent, 1.5 means increase the scale by 50 percent, and conversely 0.8 means decrease the scale by 20 percent. Since such small changes in the value of the argument passed to scale have such a large effect, we need to give the user fine-grained control over this value. To do this, I used keyPressed. Each time the user hits the up arrow, the value we pass to scale will be increased by 0.01, increasing the amount we scale by one percent. And conversely with the down arrow:

```
void keyPressed(){
  if(keyCode == 38){
    s = s + 0.01;
  }
  if(keyCode == 40){
    s = s - 0.01;
  }
}
```

(38 is the keyCode for the up arrow and 40 for down, s is a global variable we declared at the top of the sketch and use when we call scale within draw.)

So, this seems like an obvious way to zoom: just make everything bigger. However, scaling up like that will also move the position of all of our points relative to the origin of our coordinate system. This will affect how they are rotated. If we simply scale up without repositioning the origin, then the rotateY call we're using to let the user look at the point cloud from different angles will start to work differently. The point cloud will start to slip out of the center of the coordinate system, and so rotating will throw it out to the edges of the sketch rather than simply rotating it in place. To counteract this, I added another call to translate that repositions the origin based on the amount we're scaling. And the amount we translate needs to be based on the amount we've scaled. So, we used this s variable we set in keyPressed as part of our arguments to translate, but we'll need to multiply it by something to correct the units. As just discussed, scale takes its argument as a percentage, while translate takes its arguments as numbers of pixels. If we only change our translation by 0.01, we'll have nearly no effect. To get our scale value up to a level where it will have a meaningful impact on the position of our coordinate system, we need to multiply it by –1000, so that every change of 0.01 in s moves us 10 pixels forward along the z-axis:

```
translate(0,0,s*-1000);
scale(s);
```

Projects

To complete this chapter, we're going to do two projects. The first will extend what we've learned so far to complete the air drum kit I promised you at the start of this chapter. You'll start by learning how to play sound in Processing using the Minim library. Then we'll hook up these sounds to a series of hot points. To do this without making things repetitive and confusing, we'll reorganize the code you've seen so far into a hot point class that handles all the details of checking for interaction. You'll be able to reuse this hot point class in your own projects outside of this book as well. Once you've got multiple hot points hooked up to multiple sounds, you'll be ready to rock out on your air drums.

The second project will show you how to add 3D models to your sketch so that they appear to be in the scene with you. You'll learn how to work with multiple 3D file formats, how to load them into Processing, and how to display them. To position these 3D models precisely within our scene, we'll cover some more sophisticated tools for navigating in three dimensions. Once we've got our object positioned in the scene, we'll add a virtual camera to get more precise control over our angle of view. Introducing a virtual camera also means that we don't have to use translations, rotations, and scalings of the coordinate system to control what the user sees as we have up until now. This will let us focus on using those to control the position and orientation of our actual objects within the scene. And finally, we'll briefly discuss the concept of lighting 3D objects within Processing. Unlike the simple points we've worked with so far, complex models need lights to be visible. Controlling the lighting of 3D models is a rich and complex topic, and we'll only scratch the surface of it here.

By the time you complete these two projects, you should feel pretty confident working in 3D. You should know how to draw some basic shapes anywhere in 3D space, manipulate the point of view from which users see them, and alter them with user interaction. These will be important skills as we proceed through this book. Because the Kinect captures a three-dimensional picture of the world, we'll often want our projects to display their output to the user in 3D as well. Three-dimensional graphics are an incredibly deep topic and we've only scratched the surface here. We'll cover some additional topics later in this book, but you can spend a lifetime becoming an expert in this area. See the final chapter for some additional resources for learning more about programming 3D graphics.

Project 8: Air Drum Kit

An air drum kit is like the percussive version of an air guitar. Instead of waving your hands around in an over-enthusiastic strumming gesture when the power of a song overtakes you, you pretend to hit invisible snares, cymbals, and toms. The idea of this project is to use our floating hot points to make this kind of fantasy instrument playing come to life, to trigger actual sounds when you hit make believe drums that only you can see.

When we last left off, we had a working hot point. We displayed a cube correctly positioned within the point cloud, we detected any points that enter that cube, and we gave the user feedback based on this interaction. To get from there to a working air drum kit, we need to make three improvements to our sketch.

First, we need to trigger audio. We want to play a drum sound whenever the user sets off one of the hot points. To accomplish that, I'll show you how to use Minim, a popular library for working with sound in Processing. Second, we need to control exactly when and how the sounds are triggered. We want the drum sound to play just when the first part of the point cloud enters the hot point. Like a real drum, we want our air drums to sound only when you hit them. A real drum doesn't keep sounding if you leave your stick laying on it, and our hot points shouldn't trigger sounds whenever any parts of the point cloud are inside of them. They should only go off at the moment part of our hand passes inside them. The term for this kind of technique is edge detection. I'll show you how to implement it in Processing so that we can trigger our sound only when the user crosses the edge of the hot point. And finally, to create a fully featured air drum kit, we need to have multiple hot points that trigger multiple different sounds. Once we've got the first hot point all wired up and working, I'll show you how to convert the code into a `Hotpoint` class so that we can reuse it multiple times within our sketch. This `Hotpoint` class will be general enough that you'll be able to reuse it in your own sketches any time you need this kind of interaction.

Adding Audio with Minim

Minim is a Processing library that gives your sketches the ability to do things with sound. Using Minim, you can synthesize your own sounds, create generative melodies, and, most relevant for us, play back existing sound files like MP3s, WAVs, and AIFFs.

Before we dive in to integrating Minim with our hot point app, I'm going to show you the basics of using Minim. I'll show you how to include it in a sketch and walk you through a basic hello world sketch where we simply play back an existing sound file. Once you've got those basics down, we'll be ready to start attaching Minim to our point cloud code to give our air drums some sounds.

Minim comes with Processing. It's not part of Processing's core functionality but you don't have to download and install it either. If you have Processing you already have Minim installed. Let's dive in and write a hello world sketch with Minim. Our sketch is going to load up Minim and play a single WAV file once. Unsurprisingly, to run this app you'll ned a WAV file. If you want to follow along with me exactly, you can get the files I'm using here:

http://makingthingssee.com/files/air_drum_kit.zip

To use any WAV file, you need to put it in the same folder as your Processing sketch so that Processing can see it. Create a new sketch and save it. Processing will prompt you for where on your computer you want to save your sketch. Pick a location you like, and save the sketch with a memorable name. Processing will create a folder by that name with a .pde file inside of it with the same name. For example, if you called your sketch hello_sound, Processing would create a folder called *hello_sound* with a *hello_sound.pde* file inside of it. To use a sound file with that sketch, you need to put it into the *hello_sound* folder (to open the folder in Windows Explorer, Mac OS X Finder, or something similar on Linux, click Sketch→Show Sketch Folder). Grab one of the WAV files from the download or use your own.

Now, let's take a look at the code. Here's the simplest sketch that can play a sound file in Minim:

```
import ddf.minim.*; ❶

Minim minim; ❷
AudioSnippet player;

void setup() { ❸
  minim = new Minim(this);
  player = minim.loadSnippet("kick.wav");
  player.play();
}

void draw() { ❹
}

void stop() ❺
{
  player.close();
  minim.stop();

  super.stop();
}
```

❶ We start by importing the Minim library at the top of the sketch.

❷ Next, we declare two objects, `player` and `minim`. The `minim` object will set up Minim to use in general, `player` is an instance of the `AudioSnippet` class, which is used for playing short sound files like our drum samples. If we were going to use multiple sound files (cough, like for an air drum kit with multiple hot points, cough, cough) we'd need multiple `AudioSnippet` objects, one for each sound.

❸ In our `setup` function, we initialize the `minim` object and then use its `loadSnippet` function to load a sound file into our `AudioSnippet` object. In this case, I'm using the kick drum sound from my air drum kit sound sample set. One the sound file is loaded into the `player` object, we can play It by calling `play` on that object, which we do at the end of `setup`. Calling `play` here will mean that the sound plays once when the sketch starts up and that's all. Just what we want for now.

❹ The `draw` function of this sketch does nothing. It has no visible output and we're just playing our sound on startup, so we don't need to do anything here.

❺ The `stop` function at the bottom is just a little bit of cleanup. If we didn't carefully shut down our `player` and `minim` objects, our sketch would make a weird digital noise every time we quit it. We can just reuse this function almost verbatim in every sketch we write that uses Minim.

Being a basic example, this sketch doesn't cover a lot of what Minim can do. We'll get into its abilities a little bit more as we start to incorporate it into our hot point sketch, but for now I wanted to point out one specific thing about the way the AudioSnippet works.

As we saw here, AudioSnippet objects are how we control playing sound files with Minim. Each AudioSnippet object is like a tape deck. You start by loading a sound into it, like popping a cassette tape into the deck. Then, when you call play, you hear the sound play. As the sound plays, it's like the cassette turns, rolling its tape from one side to the other. If you stop the AudioSnippet (by calling its pause function, for example) and then start it playing again, it will pick up exactly from the point it left off. And when it gets to the end of the file, you have to rewind it before you can play the sound again. In all these ways, playing a sound with Minim's AudioSnippet is more like listening to a cassette in a tape deck than an MP3 in your iTunes library.

It will be helpful to keep this metaphor in mind as we move on to incorporating Minim into our Kinect point cloud sketch. To make our sounds play back any time the user interacts with the hot points, we'll need to play our sound files and rewind them.

Connecting Our First Air Drum

Let's get our hot point playing sounds. In addition to adding Minim to our sketch, we're going to have to make some changes to how our hot point works. First of all, we want it to act as a simple binary button. Unlike the output we gave it before of fading its color based on the number of points inside of it, when it comes to triggering the sounds, each hot point needs to be either entirely on or entirely off. As I mentioned before, we can turn our hot point into a binary button like this by setting a threshold. Once there's a certain number of points inside of its cube, the hot point will count as on. Instead of mapping the number of points to some output value, we'll write an if statement. To start with, we'll use a threshold of one. We'll start our sound playing if any part of the point cloud at all is found inside the hot point.

Applying a threshold will be enough to turn our hot point into a sound-triggering button. However, our code will have to be more complicated than a simple if statement. If all we did was check to see if any part of the point cloud was inside the hot point, it wouldn't act very much like a drum. If you swung at it, it would start playing its sound when you reached it, but then the sound would loop jerkily, constantly starting over from the beginning as long as any part of your hand was inside of the hot point. To prevent this problem, we need to implement edge detection. In other words, we want to trigger our sound only when our hot point goes from having no part of the point cloud inside of it to having at least one point inside. Only at that moment do we want to start the sound playing. In order to translate this into code, we'll need two new Boolean variables, one keeping track of whether there are currently any points inside the cube and one keeping track of whether there just were any last time we checked. We only want to trigger the sound when there are points inside now but weren't last time we checked.

This might sound confusing when we talk about it, but it will become clear just as soon as we look at the code. So, let's do that:

```
import processing.opengl.*;
import SimpleOpenNT.*;
import ddf.minim.*;

// minim objects
Minim minim;
AudioSnippet player;

SimpleOpenNI kinect;

float rotation = 0;

// used for edge detection
boolean wasJustInBox = false;  ❶

int boxSize = 150;
PVector boxCenter = new PVector(0, 0, 600);

float s = 1;

void setup() {
  size(1024, 768, OPENGL);
  kinect = new SimpleOpenNI(this);
  kinect.enableDepth();

  // initialize Minim
  // and AudioPlayer
  minim = new Minim(this);
  player = minim.loadSnippet("kick.wav");
}

void draw() {
  background(0);
  kinect.update();

  translate(width/2, height/2, -1000);
  rotateX(radians(180));

  translate(0, 0, 1400);
  rotateY(radians(map(mouseX, 0, width, -180, 180)));

  translate(0, 0, s*-1000);
  scale(s);

  stroke(255);

  PVector[] depthPoints = kinect.depthMapRealWorld();
  int depthPointsInBox = 0;

  for (int i = 0; i < depthPoints.length; i+=10) {
    PVector currentPoint = depthPoints[i];

    if (currentPoint.x > boxCenter.x - boxSize/2 &&
        currentPoint.x < boxCenter.x + boxSize/2) {
      if (currentPoint.y > boxCenter.y - boxSize/2 &&
          currentPoint.y < boxCenter.y + boxSize/2) {
```

```
            if (currentPoint.z > boxCenter.z - boxSize/2 &&
                currentPoint.z < boxCenter.z + boxSize/2) {
              depthPointsInBox++;
            }
          }
        }

        point(currentPoint.x, currentPoint.y, currentPoint.z);
      }

      float boxAlpha = map(depthPointsInBox, 0, 1000, 0, 255);

      // edge detection
      // are we in the box this time
      boolean isInBox = (depthPointsInBox > 0); ❷

      // if we just moved in from outside
      // start it playing
      if (isInBox && !wasJustInBox) { ❸
        player.play();
      }

      // if it's played all the way through
      // pause and rewind
      if (!player.isPlaying()) { ❹
        player.rewind();
        player.pause();
      }

      // save current status
      // for next time
      wasJustInBox = isInBox; ❺

      translate(boxCenter.x, boxCenter.y, boxCenter.z);

      fill(255, 0, 0, boxAlpha);
      stroke(255, 0, 0);
      box(boxSize);
    }

    void stop()
    {
      player.close();
      minim.stop();
      super.stop();
    }

    // use keys to control zoom
    // up-arrow zooms in
    // down arrow zooms out
    // s gets passed to scale() in draw()
    void keyPressed() {
      if (keyCode == 38) {
        s = s + 0.01;
      }
      if (keyCode == 40) {
        s = s - 0.01;
      }
    }
```

Most of this code is exactly what we had in previous examples: code that draws the point cloud in 3D, displays a cube, and fades the color of that cube based on how much of the point cloud is inside the cube. We've added the `minim` and `AudioSnippet` objects that are necessary to play sounds, as we've just seen. Both of those objects are declared at the top of the sketch and the initialized in `setup`. We're using the same kick drum sound, *kick.wav*, as we did in our Minim hello world. Don't forget that this will mean you need to save the sketch and stick the sound file in its folder as discussed earlier.

❶ A new variable that we declare and set at the top of this sketch is for edge detection, `wasJustInBox`. This Boolean variable will represent whether there were any points in the box on the last time we checked. We declare it as a global variable here so it can persist across multiple runs of `draw`. We set it to false initially because we're assuming that the hot point will be positioned in such a way that there are no depth points inside of it to start with.

❷ The real work of implementing edge detection begins here. On this line, we check to see if any depth points are inside the box. Remember from our discussion of the example on page 134 that `depthPointsInBox` is our count of how many point in the point cloud were found within the constraints of our hot point. This line checks to see if there were any points found at all. If there were, `isInBox` will be set to true; if not, it will be set to false.

❸ Now that we've got both `isInBox` and `wasJustInBox` set, we know enough to check if we should play the sound. We only want to trigger the sound at the very moment that our hot point switches from having no points inside of it to having some. In other words, we care about the brief moment when `isInBox` is true, but `wasInBox` is still false. This will be the moment when the depth points of your hand pass into the box from outside. Figure 3-14 shows a diagram to help you understand the logic of edge detection.

If there are depth points inside the box and they just arrived, then start playing our kick drum sound.

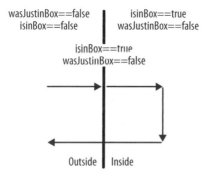

Figure 3-14. *A diagram illustrating the logic of edge detection. We only want our hot points to be triggered when the value crosses over the threshold for the first time.*

❹ Once we've correctly triggered our drum sound, we only have two other simple things we need to do. First, we need to make sure our `AudioSnippet` doesn't get stuck at the end of its cassette tape. Whenever it is not playing, we'll rewind it so that's cued up to start from the beginning and ready to go. This is just what our code does here.

❺ And then, last but not least, we need to save the current status of the hot point for next time. The only way our edge detection code works is if `wasJustInBox` stores the correct status of `isInBox` from the previous run of `draw`.

This is a lot like what we did in our drawing sketch at the end of last chapter. We needed two consecutive points to draw a line so we'd always save the current location of the closest point into a global variable so we'd have it around next time.

Filling Out Our Air Drum Kit

Now that we've got a single air drum working, it's time to add a few more. The most direct way of doing this is to add more variables. Instead of just having `isInBox` and `wasJustInBox`, we could have `isInFirstBox`, `isInSecondBox`, `isInThirdBox`, `wasInFirstBox`, `wasInSecondBox`, `wasInThirdBox`, etc. This would quickly become ridiculous. However, it is exactly what we did in past projects. For example, in the *Minority Report* photo viewer at the end of last chapter, we used multiple variables like this to store the x- and y-coordinates of each photo. This time around, though, the number of variables we'd need to duplicate would be crazy. To implement our hot points, we need not only the two Boolean variables we just added for edge detection, but also the `PVector` we used to store the position of the center of each box, the integer we used to store the number of points found in each box, and the integer we used to store the size of each box. Further, we'd need to duplicate not just variables, but code. We'd need a new copy of our three `if` statements that check each point in the point cloud to see if it's contained in the hot point. We'd need to set different colors and alpha values for each box. And on and on into madness.

Instead of going mad, we'll create a `Hotpoint` class. You may have learned a little bit about classes in previous work with Processing. The whole purpose of classes is to make code reusable in order to prevent this kind of maddening repetition. Instead of needing an additional set of variables for each hot point, we'll just create an instance of our class. And our class can also provide a bunch of functions that make it convenient to do common tasks that hot points need to do, like drawing cubes on the screen.

We'll start by looking at a new version of our sketch that uses the `Hotpoint` class to create multiple air drums. This will show us how using a class can simplify our code. Then, we'll take a look inside the `Hotpoint` class to see how it works. This class will mostly contain code that we've already written just reorganized into a new form. I'll explain that reorganization and point out a few other features of the `Hotpoint` class that make using it especially simple and convenient, like having the class set sensible defaults for some values while still allowing you to change them later if you want to. After we've looked at the `Hotpoint` class in depth, you should be able to reuse it your own code whenever you need to create an interactive hot point. Plus, you should also have some ideas for how you might be able to create your own classes in the future any time you find yourself doing something repetitive and maddening.

Here's the code of the sketch after I've updated it to use the Hotpoint class. Let's take a look at how it's changed. Don't try to run it yet, because you haven't seen the Hotpoint class.

```
import processing.opengl.*;
import SimpleOpenNI.*;
import ddf.minim.*;

SimpleOpenNI kinect;

float rotation = 0;

// two AudioSnippet objects this time
Minim minim;
AudioSnippet kick;  ❶
AudioSnippet snare;

// declare our two hotpoint objects
Hotpoint snareTrigger;  ❷
Hotpoint kickTrigger;

float s = 1;

void setup() {
  size(1024, 768, OPENGL);
  kinect = new SimpleOpenNI(this);
  kinect.enableDepth();

  minim = new Minim(this);
  // load both audio files
  snare = minim.loadSnippet("hat.wav");  ❸
  kick = minim.loadSnippet("kick.wav");

  // initialize hotpoints with their origins (x,y,z) and their size
  snareTrigger = new Hotpoint(200, 0, 600, 150);  ❹
  kickTrigger = new Hotpoint(-200, 0, 600, 150);

}

void draw() {
  background(0);
  kinect.update();

  translate(width/2, height/2, -1000);
  rotateX(radians(180));

  translate(0, 0, 1400);
  rotateY(radians(map(mouseX, 0, width, -180, 180)));

  translate(0, 0, s*-1000);
  scale(s);


  stroke(255);

  PVector[] depthPoints = kinect.depthMapRealWorld();
```

```
for (int i = 0; i < depthPoints.length; i+=10) {
  PVector currentPoint = depthPoints[i];

  // have each hotpoint check to see if it includes the currentPoint
  snareTrigger.check(currentPoint); ❺
  kickTrigger.check(currentPoint);

  point(currentPoint.x, currentPoint.y, currentPoint.z);
}

println(snareTrigger.pointsIncluded); ❻

if(snareTrigger.isHit()) { ❼
  snare.play();
}

if(!snare.isPlaying()) {
  snare.rewind();
}

if (kickTrigger.isHit()) {
  kick.play();
}

if(!kick.isPlaying()) {
  kick.rewind();
 }

// display each hotpoint and clear its points
snareTrigger.draw(); ❽
snareTrigger.clear();

kickTrigger.draw(); ❾
kickTrigger.clear();
}

void stop()
{
  // make sure to close
  // both AudioPlayer objects
  kick.close();
  snare.close();

  minim.stop();
  super.stop();
}

void keyPressed() {
  if (keyCode == 38) {
    s = s + 0.01;
  }
  if (keyCode == 40) {
    s = s - 0.01;
  }
}
```

❶ The changes start at the top of the sketch with the declarations. This
time, we declare two AudioSnippet objects, one for the kick drum and
one for the new snare sound we'll be adding.

❷ Here we declare our two `Hotpoint` objects, `snareTrigger` and `kick-Trigger`. I called these variables "triggers" because hitting each hot point is going to set off the playing of its sound.

❸ In setup, we load files into both of the `AudioSnippet` objects (don't forget to add the snare sound to your sketch's directory) and initialize the `Hotpoints`.

❹ Creating each `Hotpoint` takes four arguments. The first three represent the x-, y-, and z-coordinates of the hot point's center. And the last one represents its size. We already know that's the most basic information we need to create a hot point. These initializations replace the variables we'd set in previous versions of the sketch to represent this same information: `boxCenter` and `boxSize`. Notice that these two hot points are both positioned differently from the one we were previously using. Instead of being dead center within the Kinect's point of view, I've moved them off to the left and right. This will make them more convenient to play and prevent them from overlapping.

❺ Now, let's see how `draw` has changed. Inside the loop iterating over all of the points in the point cloud, our three nested `if` statements are gone. They've been replaced by two uses of our new `Hotpoint` objects.

Instead of doing all the geometric logic ourselves and storing the results in a series of variables, now we just tell each hot point to check to see if it includes the given point. The hot point will automatically do the right thing: it will figure out if it includes the `currentPoint` and keep a running total of how many points it's seen that did in fact fall inside of it.

❻ We can access that count of included points by calling each `Hotpoint`'s `pointsIncluded` method as we do just after the loop.

This line will show us how much of the point cloud was found inside of the `snareTrigger Hotpoint`. The `Hotpoint` does the work for us to keep track of how many points it included so we don't have to worry about or even see the details, but we can still access the result this way.

❼ Now, we're up to the point where we actually need to trigger the sounds. Instead of having to use multiple Boolean variables to check to see if we've just passed the edge of each hot point, we just ask the hot point if it was hit and play our sound.

This code is so much nicer than what we had before. It almost reads like an sentence in plain English: "if the `snareTrigger` is hit, play the snare sound." The function `isHit` does the edge detection check inside of itself, using however many variables it needs (we really don't care), and simply returns true or false. It will only return true at the exact moment that some part of the point cloud passes into the hot point, just when we want to play the sound.

❽ After this, there are two more uses of our `Hotpoint` objects right at the end of `draw`. The first of these represents one of the most convenient aspects of our `Hotpoint` class and the second a slight downside of it. First we tell each `Hotpoint` to draw. This handles all of the translations, rotations, calls to stroke and fill, etc., needed to draw our hot points at the position and size we initialized them. As you'll see when you run the sketch, this draw function even deals with creating different colors for both hot points and fading each hot point's alpha in and out based on how much of the point cloud is inside of it. This takes away so much that we previously had to worry about when displaying these by hand.

❾ The other line here, however, seems like a new burden.

What is this clear function? We didn't have to clear anything before. Having to explicitly clear our count like this is the cost of having moved so much complexity and messiness inside our Hotpoint object. Previously, we kept track of the number of points that fell inside our target areas using a local variable, depthPointsInBox. This variable had a limited scope. It was declared inside of draw so it automatically got reset back to 0 each time draw ran. Now, however, our hot points take care of the count themselves. Instead of being scoped to draw, this count is scoped to each Hotpoint object. And these Hotpoint objects stick around across multiple runs of draw. So, we need to explicitly tell our hot points to clear themselves. We need to let them know that we're done with the count they'd been keeping track of for us and we're ready to start over. We do that by calling clear.

OK. We've now seen how our sketch changed by using our Hotpoint class. Not only we were able to add a second air drum without making things dramatically messier, but we've actually made things simpler. That ugly triple-nested if statement is now gone, along with that confusing edge detection logic. This is another big advantage of using classes. For the complicated or messy bits, once you've gotten them working, you can hide them away inside a class so you don't have to constantly see them and be distracted by them.

But now let's tear open the Hotpoint class to see some of how its hiding these messy details from us. I'm not going to cover every detail of Java class syntax in general or even how this class works in particular. I just want to point out a few important techniques and ideas that might be helpful for you, both in using this class in your future projects and in designing your own classes whenever you find yourself with code that's getting repetitive.

Here's the code for our Hotpoint class:

```
class Hotpoint {
  PVector center;
  color fillColor;
  color strokeColor;
  int size;
  int pointsIncluded;
  int maxPoints;
  boolean wasJustHit;
  int threshold;

  Hotpoint(float centerX, float centerY, float centerZ, int boxSize) { ❶
    center = new PVector(centerX, centerY, centerZ);
    size = boxSize;
    pointsIncluded = 0;
    maxPoints = 1000;
    threshold = 0;
```

```
      fillColor = strokeColor = color(random(255), random(255), random(255));
  }

  void setThreshold( int newThreshold ){
    threshold = newThreshold;
  }

  void setMaxPoints(int newMaxPoints) {
    maxPoints = newMaxPoints;
  }

  void setColor(float red, float blue, float green){
    fillColor = strokeColor = color(red, blue, green);
  }

  boolean check(PVector point) { ❷
    boolean result = false;

    if (point.x > center.x - size/2 && point.x < center.x + size/2) {
      if (point.y > center.y - size/2 && point.y < center.y + size/2) {
        if (point.z > center.z - size/2 && point.z < center.z + size/2) {
          result = true;
          pointsIncluded++;
        }
      }
    }

    return result;
  }

  void draw() { ❸
    pushMatrix(); ❹
      translate(center.x, center.y, center.z);

      fill(red(fillColor), blue(fillColor), green(fillColor),
                        255 * percentIncluded());
      stroke(red(strokeColor), blue(strokeColor), green(strokeColor), 255);
      box(size);
    popMatrix();
  }

  float percentIncluded() {
    return map(pointsIncluded, 0, maxPoints, 0, 1);
  }


  boolean currentlyHit() { ❺
    return (pointsIncluded > threshold);
  }


  boolean isHit() { ❻
    return currentlyHit() && !wasJustHit;
  }

  void clear() { ❼
    wasJustHit = currentlyHit();
    pointsIncluded = 0;
  }
}
```

To add this code to your Processing project, click the arrow in the top right of your Processing window, as shown in Figure 3-15. Select New Tab from the menu that pops up. Processing will then prompt you to provide a name for the new file you're about to create. Call it *Hotpoint* and click OK. A new tab will appear in your Processing window with the title Hotpoint. Put the code for the Hotpoint class into this tab. You can move back and forth between this new file and your original sketch by clicking on the two tabs at the top of the window.

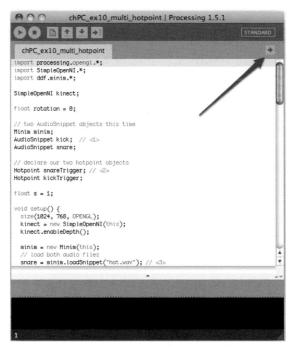

Figure 3-15. Click the arrow icon in the top right of your Processing window to add a new class to your project.

❶   The first thing to notice is the constructor. That's the function at top, the one that shares its name with the class itself. As we saw when we initialized our Hotpoints in the sketch, this function takes four arguments representing the position and size of the box we want to check. This constructor takes those arguments and saves them into instance variables. (As a refresher, *instance variables* are variables that can have different values for each object that you create; for example, in our sketch we created two hot points with different centers. We save that information into instance variables so that each hot point remembers its center without interfering with any other one.) However, the constructor does a bunch more beyond just saving the arguments that we passed to it. It sets five other instance variables as well: pointsIncluded, maxPoints, threshold, fillColor, and strokeColor. The first of these clearly needs to be set to 0 so it can be used in our count of included points from the point cloud. The rest are attributes of Hotpoint that we might think we would need to set manually. What if we want a hot point with a higher threshold or a different maximum number of points? For example, I could imagine wanting to use a hot point to make part of a wall interactive. In that case, you'd want to position the hot point so that it overlapped the wall, but you'd want to set its threshold and maxPoints values to take into account the part of the point cloud that represented the wall so that the hot point wouldn't be triggered until the user slapped the wall in that spot.

What we want is a compromise between automatically setting sensible defaults for these values that work for the majority of cases and making them changeable for those rare cases like this wall example where the defaults will need to be tweaked. This constructor function shows the first half of this balance, the setting of sensible defaults. But if you look below to the next three functions (setThreshold, setMaxPoints, and setColor), you can see that we also gave users of this class the ability to manually set these values themselves. So, in that rare case of the wall-bound hot point or some other strange situation, we'll be able to rejigger things so that our hot points will still work without having to open this class back up and alter it. It's the best of both worlds.

The only other thing to note about the constructor of our Hotpoint class is how we actually set the default color. It would be helpful if each new hot point would automatically have a new color. Different colors will make it easier to tell hot points apart in our sketch an to associate each one with the drum sound that it triggers. But our constructor doesn't know anything about any hot points that have previously been created. Its job is just to make a new hot point from the position and size parameters that the user passed in. How can we give each new hot point a unique color without knowing the colors of the existing hot points? I accomplish this by setting the hot point's color at random. For each of the red, blue, and green values, we call random(255), which will return some value between 0 and 255 and together create a random color. Using random doesn't guarantee that each hot point will have a unique color, but it makes it very unlikely that any two will come out the same. In practice, since we're only probably using a few hot points at a time in any sketch, this is plenty good enough.

OK. So that's the constructor. The rest of the class should look very familiar to you, as it basically does the same thing as our previous code. I'll point out a couple of items of interest that explain how the functions work together to make things simpler when you're using the class.

❷ The core of the class is the check and draw functions, both of which look nearly exactly like pieces of code we've seen before in our old sketches. In check, we take a single point and test to see if it's within the bounds of our box. These are the same old three if statements checking each dimension one at a time, only now they're using data stored in instance variables of our Hotpoint object rather than global variables in our sketch. For example, the pointsIncluded variable, which got initialized to 0 in our constructor, gets increased by one every time we find a point included within the bounds of our box. We'll use that variable in other functions. For example, we use pointsIncluded in draw.

❸ Even though it might look a little different, draw does exactly the same things as our previous code to position and display the hot point's box.

All the calls to `translate`, `fill`, `stroke`, and `box` are the same, they're just in a different context. First of all, they now use instance variables such as `center` and `fillColor`. But much more interestingly, all of these translation and drawing commands are wrapped within two new lines of code. This method begins by calling `pushMatrix` and ends by calling `popMatrix`. What do these two functions do, and why are we calling them here?

When we're working in 3D, the order in which we do things matters. As we've seen in our previous uses of Processing's translation and rotation functions, each time we call one of them, they alter Processing's coordinate system. This alters the results of all the following drawing and transformations commands. We've seen this over and over through this chapter as we've developed our control over the point cloud. If we call `scale` before `translate`, then we'll translate by a different amount based on whether `scale` expanded or shrunk things. When we call `translate`, it changes our center of rotation so that calling `rotateY` has a very different effect afterward. We had to account for both of these issues when giving the user control of the angle from which we viewed the point cloud.

But what if we want to do some drawing that requires using translations and rotations, but we don't our code to affect anything else outside of it? How can we make sure that we leave the coordinate system exactly as we found it?

❹ The answer is `pushMatrix` and `popMatrix`. Processing provides these functions to let us isolate a set of manipulations we make to the coordinate system so that they don't affect anything else outside of them. All calls to `translate`, `rotateX`, `rotateY`, `rotateZ`, and `scale` that happen after the call to `pushMatrix` will affect later code right up until we call `popMatrix` and then they will not affect anything after that. Between `pushMatrix` and `popMatrix`, we have a little private coordinate system that we can mess up without having to worry about how it will affect others.

This effect of `pushMatrix` and `popMatrix` is a little bit like the concept of `scope` we discussed in the last chapter. We use `scope` to limit the visibility of variables so that they are only available where they are needed. Using `pushMatrix` and `popMatrix` gives us similar control over our changes to the coordinate system. We can use this control to prevent code outside of our class from having to worry about the transformations we use inside of it.

In some ways, the whole purpose of a class is to hide the details of its workings so that people who use it from outside won't have to worry about them. One of the worst ways we could fail at this aim would be for code inside the class to have dramatic unexpected side effects on other code outside that uses it. This is why it's a really good idea to wrap any manipulations we make inside of `pushMatrix` and `popMatrix`. Without their ability to limit the scope of our changes to the coordinate system, our code could leave the coordinate system differently than we found it, confounding anyone using our class. For example, imagine if you were an innocent user of our Hotpoint library, but this time a version where we were irresponsible enough not to isolate our changes to the coordinate system. If you called draw on a Hotpoint all of a sudden everything you drew afterward might be displaced by 1000 pixels to the left or rotated to a strange angle or scaled up by triple. You'd probably get quite confused and frustrated and stop using the library.

Isolating our changes to the coordinate system lets other people use our code from outside without any danger of it screwing up anything else they're doing. On the other hand, it doesn't isolate our drawing code from them. If someone makes additional changes to the coordinate system before calling draw it will affect where the hot point is drawn and at what scale and rotation. This is just how it should be. We want the people who use our class to have as much control as possible over how they position and draw hot points. After all, frequently the people using this class will be us! We want to leave ourselves with the ability to move and position the hot point however we'll need later on.

Now that we understand draw, there are just a couple of other functions to look at and then we'll fully understand this Hotpoint class. We're going to look at the currentlyHit and isHit functions. Both of these reproduce ideas that were present in the earlier procedural version of this code, but with new twists.

⑤ In our previous version of this code, our ability to do edge detection was based around two Boolean variables: isInBox and wasJustInBox. The first of these was a local variable within draw. It stored the result of our check to see if there were currently any depth points within the hot point. At the end of draw, we then moved this value into wasJustInBox, which was a global variable. This variable stuck around until the next run of draw so we could compare it to the next value of isInBox. What we were really looking for was a change between these two values, for isInBox to be true while wasInBox was false. This meant that something had just entered an empty box and our hot point was triggered.

In our class, we've replaced these variables with two functions: currentlyHit and isHit. The first of these is nearly the same as isInBox. However, currentlyHit is a function. So instead of storing a value, it recalculates the result each time. Whenever it's called, currentlyHit checks to see if the pointsIncluded in the box exceed the threshold we've set. This change from a variable to a function makes currentlyHit much more useful to code outside of our class. A user of our class could call currentlyHit to check the status of a hot point whenever necessary. This would let users treat their hot points as more conventional buttons with simple on and off states instead of using the more complex edge detection triggering. Further, since currentlyHit recalculates its result whenever it's called, it is responsive to changes in both pointsIncluded and threshold. We could use this responsiveness to allow users to tune the threshold while interacting with the sketch. Changes to the threshold will immediately be reflected in the results from currentlyHit and therefore isHit. Or we could use it to exit the loop over the point cloud as soon as we detected the first hit. Since the rest of the points couldn't possibly change the result after we'd found a hit, this might make our code faster.

❻ Now, isHit has a different job: to perform the edge detection check and report the results. It relieves the user of any burden to keep track of the variables that were necessary in that check. It just returns true or false and the user can use that result however they like. Making this into a function hides the whole messy business of remembering the state of the hot point across multiple runs of draw. Its result is based both on currentlyHit and wasJustHit, which has become an instance variable of our Hotpoint object. But the users don't need (and probably shouldn't have) access to the details of how this result was obtained. In fact, wasJustHit should really be a private variable. We need it to do the edge detection, but we don't actually want any users of our class accessing it.

❼ However, there's one burden that we can't hide from people who use this code: the need to clear the points. Each time we want to start looking at a new set of depth points, we need to clear the previous count of pointsIncluded and we need to save the last result for use next time.

And there's no way to do these things without running code. That's why we had to add clear and require that users call it once in draw. In some ways this requirement is a downside of having moved this code into a class. That change made the resetting of our count into something that had to be done intentionally rather than something that happened automatically. Previously the local scope of our depthPointsInBox variable meant that it would be reset back to 0 on each run of draw. Moving our count to the pointsIncluded variable, which is internal to our Hotpoint object, removes this automatic reset and requires intentional action to reset the count. This is not entirely a bad thing. Even though having to call clear feels like an unnecessary burden, we can imagine times when being able to call it would be helpful. For example, if we connected clear to Processing's mousePressed or keyPressed functions, it might be useful as part of a calibration procedure. Or we could even connect it to a different Hotpoint's isHit function so that the first hot point would be inactive until the second one was hit.

One of the hallmarks of a well-written class is flexibility. You can use it in ways that its designers did not specifically imagine. The existence of currentlyHit and clear is a sign that Hotpoint has this kind of flexibility.

At this point, you know pretty much everything there is to know about the Hotpoint class. You should be able to use it in your own sketches in the future with confidence. We'll use it one more time before the end of this chapter just to make sure.

If you feel like testing your understanding of the Hotpoint class right now, I've got an exercise for you. Our air drums have one big way in which they are unlike real drums. No matter how hard you hit them, their sound stays the same volume. That makes them unresponsive and unnatural. The idea that how hard you hit an input should affect how that input sounds is called *velocity*. Real instruments have it, and so do many good keyboards and other computer music input devices.

With a little bit more code, we could give our air drums velocity. Minim lets you control how loud it plays back sounds using its `setVolume` function:

```
minim.setVolume(0.5);
```

When a hand or object is detected inside one of our hot points, how can we tell how fast its going or how hard it "hit" that hot point? Well, the faster the object was going or the bigger it is, the more points will be inside the hot point at the time that `isHit` returns true. You could use the `Hotpoint`'s `pointsIncluded` variable to check how many points are inside of `Hotpoint` at the moment it is triggered. If you then mapped this value to something in the right range and passed it as an argument to `setVolume`, your air drums would have something that sounded a little bit like real velocity.

See if you can modify your sketch to give your air drums this new level of realism.

Project 9: Virtual Kinect

To conclude this chapter, we'll do one more project. Where the Air Drum Kit exercised our skills at using the point cloud for interaction, this one will work on our ability to display in 3D. We'll learn how to load a 3D model from a file and display it within the point cloud so that it appears to be part of our scene. Specifically, we're going to load a 3D model of a Kinect and place it in our scene at the same location as our real Kinect.

We'll proceed in much the same way as we did in the last project. We'll start with a simple sketch that doesn't use the Kinect at all. This project will demonstrate how to load and display a 3D model within Processing using the OBJLoader library. Once we've covered the basics of working with 3D models, we'll integrate the Kinect model into our point cloud sketch. And we'll conclude by covering some slightly more advanced 3D drawing topics such as lighting and camera control.

Let's get started.

Displaying a 3D Object

The first step toward integrating a 3D object with our point cloud is figuring out how to work with 3D models in Processing at all. We'll start by writing a standalone sketch that will show you the ropes of using the Processing OBJLoader library. We'll install the library, download a model, and load and display it. Then we'll play around with the display code just a little bit to learn some things about how 3D drawing works.

OBJLoader is a Processing library like Minim. Unlike Minim, though, it doesn't come installed with Processing so we'll have to start by downloading it. You can find it from the list of contributed processing libraries:

http://processing.org/reference/libraries

or go directly to its page on Google Code:

http://code.google.com/p/saitoobjloader

Follow the instructions on Google Code to download the library. Extract the file, and rename the folder that results *OBJLoader*. Processing can be picky about the name of library folders on some platforms (especially Linux). Then move the folder into your Processing libraries folder. If you're not sure where to find your libraries folder, Processing will tell you. Open up Processing's preferences. There will be an entry there for "Sketchbook location." Your libraries folder will be inside of whatever folder you've selected for this location. Once you've moved the folder into your Processing libraries folder, quit and restart Processing. Open the Processing examples by choosing Examples from the File menu. If you scroll down and look inside of the Contributed Libraries folder, you should see a folder for OBJLoader with a bunch of examples in it. If these are there, that means you've gotten the library installed successfully. You're welcome to play with some of the examples that ship with OBJLoader, but be warned that they're all slightly more complicated than the basic hello world we're going to look at here. Once you've gotten the fundamentals of working with the library down, these examples are a great place to look to learn more advanced techniques.

Now, let's work on getting a basic example working with this library. The "hello world" of any 3D model library is loading a model from a file and displaying it. Hence, we'll need a 3D model. There are lots of great ways to get or make 3D models. You can download them from Google Warehouse, an amazing service Google provides as a companion to its SketchUp 3D modeling tool. Google Warehouse includes thousands of models built and contributed by people all around the world. It's an amazing resource when you're getting started working in 3D. You can also build your own models in a bunch of different 3D tools that range in complexity and power. Later on in this book, we're going to do some work with Blender, a free open source 3D modeling and animation tool. But for now, you can use a 3D model that I've specially prepared for use in this project. It's already in the right format, and you can download it here:

http://makingthingssee.com/assets/kinect_model.zip

Download that file, unzip it, and you'll find that it contains two files: *kinect.obj* and *kinect.obj.mtl*. This second file is a "material" file that we can use to give our 3D model a colorful skin. However, for now, we're not going to even use the *.mtl* file. Create a new Processing sketch and save it so that it has a folder. Move the *.obj* file into the folder (and the *.mtl* file as well, if you like; it won't do any harm).

Once you've got the *.obj* file in place, you're ready to write and run a sketch that loads and displays it. Here's the code. We'll go through it below to make sure that you understand it.

```
import processing.opengl.*;
import saito.objloader.*;  ❶

// declare an OBJModel object
OBJModel model;  ❷

float rotateX;
float rotateY;
```

```
void setup() {
  size(640, 480, OPENGL);

  // load the model file
  // use triangles as the basic geometry
  model = new OBJModel(this, "kinect.obj", "relative", TRIANGLES); ❸

  // tell the model to translate itself
  // to be centered at 0,0
  model.translateToCenter(); ❹
  noStroke();
}

void draw() { ❺
  background(255);

  // turn on the lights
  lights(); ❻

  translate(width/2, height/2, 0); ❼

  rotateX(rotateY); ❽
  rotateY(rotateX);

  // tell the model to draw itself
  model.draw(); ❾
}

void mouseDragged() {
  rotateX += (mouseX - pmouseX) * 0.01;
  rotateY -= (mouseY - pmouseY) * 0.01;
}
```

When you run that code for the first time, you should see a white sketch with a gray rectangle in the middle of it, as shown in Figure 3-16.

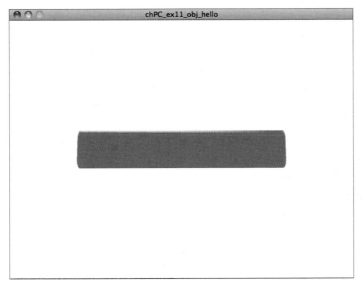

Figure 3-16. *First view of our Kinect 3D model displayed with flat lighting and from the top angle so that it looks like a boring rectangle.*

Not very exciting, is it? And doesn't look very much like a Kinect. What's going on here? Don't worry. Nothing has gone wrong. We're just looking at the top of the Kinect. By default, the model loaded into our sketch with a particular orientation. In our case here, the Kinect model was oriented so that its top was pointing up on the z-axis. In many 3D modeling programs, the z-axis points up away from the ground plane, which is defined by the x- and y-axes. However, in Processing, as we've seen, the z-axis points toward us, out of the screen. Figure 3-17 shows the difference.

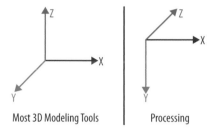

Most 3D Modeling Tools   Processing

Figure 3-17. *Processing orients its 3D axes differently from most modeling tools. This means that you have to rotate 3D models you import to get them to display in the correct orientation.*

That's why the top of the Kinect model ended up facing toward us when we loaded it in Processing. It was originally created so that its top faced up in the modeling program where it was created. The *.obj* file stored the information that the top of the Kinect should point up along the z-axis. So when we display it in Processing, that's just what we get.

To see the front of the Kinect, all you have to do is rotate the model. Click inside the sketch and drag your mouse up. You'll see the Kinect model turn up to face you, the three circles that represent its projector and cameras visible, as in Figure 3-18.

And if you drag your mouse around in different directions, you can rotate the model around to different angles so you can see all of its sides, as shown in Figure 3-19.

Let's take a look at the code to see how this works.

❶ The first thing to notice about this sketch is how it imports the OBJLoader library. This should look familiar from our work with Minim.

❷ Once the library is loaded, we declare an OBJModel. This will be the object we use to load our model file, display it, and control it.

❸ We initialize this object in setup. Out of the four arguments to the OBJModel constructor, there are two we really care about for now, the second and the last. The second argument is the name of our model file, *kinect.obj*. As long as this file is in the same folder as our sketch, OBJLoader will be able to find it and load up the geometry stored in there.

Figure 3-18. *Our Kinect 3D model rotated to face the right direction.*

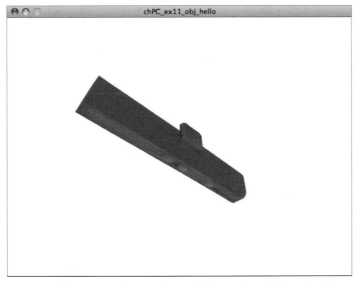

Figure 3-19. *Rotating the Kinect 3D model around shows it from different angles.*

The last argument tells OBJModel what kind of geometrical primitive we'd like to use to draw our model. To create any 3D shape, we always start with a set of points and then connect those points with a series of shapes. We might use lines, triangles, "quads" (i.e., four-sided shapes), or more complex patterns made up of these shapes. This argument determines what kind of shape we'll use to connect the points in our 3D model of the Kinect. We could choose from POINTS, LINES, TRI-ANGLES, QUADS, POLYGON, TRIANGLE_STRIP, or QUAD_STRIP. In Chapter 5, we'll cover 3D drawing in a great deal more depth and intimate detail.

For now, I only want to say enough to explain our choice of TRIANGLES over these other options. When it comes to drawing 3D geometry, triangles have a special status. There are certainly simpler shapes than the triangle. There are points and lines. We could use points or lines to draw our model, but then it wouldn't be solid. Points and lines don't fill in any part of space. They don't enclose anything, they just sit there. And all of the more complex shapes can be reduced to triangles. What's a rectangle? Just two triangles. What's a multisided polygon? Just a bunch of triangles. At a basic level, our 3D renderer is just a machine that draws triangles. That's what it's best at. That's why we choose TRIANGLES here as the fourth argument to create our OBJModel. Drawing our Kinect with triangles will cause the least surprises and the fewest problems if there's something not completely ideal about our model itself.

❹ Once we've loaded the .obj file into the model, we tell it to translate-ToCenter. That function resets the model's internal coordinate system so that the center of its geometry is at the origin—that is, 0,0. Without this function, the model's origin could be pretty much anywhere. It's determined by whatever software created the model file in the first place. It could be nowhere near the actual visible part of the model. Translating the model to the center of its own coordinate system will make it react to our own translations, rotations, and scalings in a more predictable manner. Think of the work we did in the last project within our Hotpoint class to keep our internal coordinate system manipulations from affecting any code outside. Calling model.translateToCenter tells this object to do something similar.

That's the end of the setup for working with a 3D model. Now we're ready to display our model. Displaying a 3D model is relatively straightforward.

❺ There are just two lines in our sketch's draw function that need explaining. Once we've understood those, we'll make a small addition to our sketch that will let us explore our options for displaying 3D models and teach us a little bit more about how 3D models work in Processing.

❻ The first new element in draw is this line.

Up until now we haven't used any lights when we've rendered our 3D scenes. We've always determined the appearance of things just with color and shapes. So then, what are lights and what do they do to our 3D geometry? Lighting is another rich and complicated topic that we'll only touch on here. Like the topic of drawing 3D shapes, we'll cover lighting them in more depth in the second half of this book. For now, we'll just learn enough to have some sense of what this light function does and why we need to call it here.

The system we use to render 3D geometry is, to some degree, a simulation of the real world. In the real world, we can see the shape of three-dimensional objects because of how they reflect light and cast shadows. With no light, or with extremely flat light, it can be difficult or impossible for us to perceive depth and comprehend the shape of objects. The same goes for 3D objects when we render them in Processing. Without lights,

Chapter 3

at best they will appear flat and at worst they can be completely invisible. In fact, try commenting out this line of code, eliminating any lights from this sketch. What do you find? Suddenly you can't see our 3D model of the Kinect at all. It's gone invisible. Now try changing the background color. Change the first line of `draw` from `background(255)` to `background(0)`. Leave the lights turned off. What do you see?

Figure 3-20 shows the results. It's our 3D model of the Kinect, but now it's just a white silhouette on a black background; none of the interior details are visible. Compare this with the model as we saw it previously, rendered with the lights turned on.

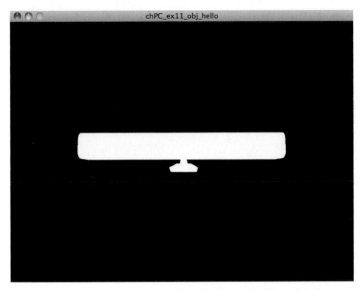

Figure 3-20. *Without lights, our 3D model will render flat and with no detail.*

Rendered without lights, the model looks flat. It has no shading to indicate the depth and angle of each of its surfaces. This is a key point about 3D rendering. The appearance of each object is determined by more than just the object itself. Its appearance is determined through a complex interaction between the object's geometry, its materials, and the lights in the scene. Further, there are different types of lights: ambient, diffuse, and specular. And different materials react different to each of these kinds of lights. All of these combinations and permutations give us extremely fine-grained control over the appearance of our 3D objects. However, it can also make 3D rendering complex and hard to work with. We'll explore these options in later chapters in some depth. For now, though, we just want a default lighting setup that lets us see our model without having to get an advanced degree in 3D rendering. This is exactly what `lights` provides. Its results won't be beautiful, but it will let us see what we're doing.

❼ After turning on the lights (Figure 3-21), our `draw` function continues to do a bit of translation and rotation. After the examples shown earlier in this chapter, you should be able to understand exactly what's going on here.

Figure 3-21. *With virtual lights, our 3D model becomes visible.*

⑧ The only new element is the function we're using to capture the user interaction and set our rotation values: mouseDragged. Anytime you drag the mouse, mouseDragged gets called with four variables set, mouseX and mouseY, which we're used to. They represent the current position of the mouse. And then there's also pmouseX and pmouseY. These are new. They represent the position from which the mouse just moved. The mouse dragged from pmouseX, pmouseY to mouseX, mouseY. As we learned back in the section "Making the Point Cloud Move" on page 119, Processing's rotateX, rotateY, and rotateZ functions each rotate the sketch's coordinate system around one axis. In other words, when we call rotateX, the x-axis will stay the same and the y- and z-axes will spin. The same goes for rotateY and rotateZ. In the case of this sketch, when the user drags the mouse left to right, we want our geometry to rotate around the y-axis, which will change its x- and z-positions. And, inversely, when the user drags up and down, we want to rotate around the x-axis.

Do you see why these lines are the way the are? Remember what you learned about rotating around the axes back when we were first drawing the point cloud.

⑨ After those translations and rotations, all we do to display the model is call its draw function. This function uses the parameters we've set in the model to draw it in our sketch. It figures out where all of the model's points should go within our current coordinate system and then connects them into shapes based on how we've configured our model object. In this case, that means connecting all of the model's points with triangles.

But, as we discussed above, there are other options as well. We could change the model's settings and it would display differently. Let's give ourselves the ability to change those settings interactively so we can see the differences between them and learn a little bit more about what they mean.

Add the following code to the bottom of your sketch:

```
boolean drawLines = false;

void keyPressed(){
  if(drawLines){
    model.shapeMode(LINES);
    stroke(0);
  } else {
   model.shapeMode(TRIANGLES);
   noStroke();
  }
  drawLines = !drawLines;
}
```

Here we're harnessing the `keyPressed` event to change the model's *shape mode*. The shape mode determines what shapes we use to connect the points in the model. The options are the same as those available in the constructor: `POINTS`, `LINES`, `TRIANGLES`, `QUADS`, `POLYGON`, `TRIANGLE_STRIP`, or `QUAD_STRIP`. This `keyPressed` function toggles between `LINES` mode and `TRIANGLES` mode. It also turns on and off the drawing of lines in general in Processing (via `stroke(0)` and `noStroke`, respectively) so that this change will be visible once it has taken effect.

When you run this code, what do you see? As you hit any key on the keyboard, the Kinect model toggles between solid shading and a kind of wireframe style. The wireframe style is what we get when we set `shapeMode` to `LINES`. OBJ-Model connects the points in our Kinect model with lines, but does not create any triangles or other shapes that can be solidly filled in. The result, shown in Figure 3-22, looks like an object shaped out of wire, an object that we can see through as we rotate it.

Figure 3-22. *Displaying our 3D model as a wireframe using the LINES shape mode.*

Unlike the solid surfaces of the `TRIANGLE` shape mode, when we draw lines, they do not obscure anything behind them. You can see through them. This is one effect of drawing a two-dimensional shape like a line within our sketch's three-dimensional space. The two-dimensional shape does not actually take up any space. It doesn't block us from seeing anything behind it. We've seen this effect before with the point cloud from the Kinect. Like lines, points are less than three-dimensional and so don't take up any space or obscure any thing behind them.

Try swapping out some of the other options into shapeMode to see what they look like. Some of these modes will look cool and teach you something about how the model is put together (hint: don't skip POINTS). A warning, though: some of the modes will make the model invisible. If you can't figure out why, look back to our original discussion of shape modes when I explained the arguments to OBJModel's constructor (hint: try adding stroke(0) so that you see the edges of the shapes rather than just their surfaces). There's a reason we chose triangles in the first place. And if your experiments leave you a little bit confused, that's good. Remember your questions. When we come back to learn more about 3D rendering in a later chapter, you'll have a head start.

For now, though, we can just revert to drawing our Kinect model with triangles. This will work reliably for the simple rendering we want to do right now. In fact, we've now covered enough about using OBJModel that we're ready to move on to incorporating it into our point cloud.

3D Model in the Point Cloud

Now that we understand the basics of rendering a 3D model, we can get back to the original goal of this project: displaying a model of the Kinect within our point cloud at the exact position of the real Kinect.

To do this, we'll have to find the right spot within our existing point cloud code to draw the model. We want the Kinect model to be positioned at the origin of the coordinate system in which we actually draw the point cloud. But remember that before we draw the point cloud, we conduct a series of translations, rotations, and scalings in order to center the points in our sketch and to give the user control over the point of view. We want to draw the Kinect model so that it feels like a part of the scene. That means our model should be subject to these same translations, rotations, and scalings. If we insert our code to draw the model after we've made these alterations to the coordinate system, then the Kinect will stay in a constant relationship to the point cloud just like we want. Let's look at the code:

```
import processing.opengl.*;
import SimpleOpenNI.*;
import saito.objloader.*;

SimpleOpenNI kinect;
OBJModel model;

float s = 1;

void setup() {
  size(1024, 768, OPENGL);
  kinect = new SimpleOpenNI(this);
  kinect.enableDepth();
```

```
    model = new OBJModel(this, "kinect.obj", "relative", TRIANGLES);
    model.translateToCenter(); ❶
    noStroke();
}

void draw() {
    background(0);
    kinect.update();

    translate(width/2, height/2, -1000); ❷
    rotateX(radians(180));

    translate(0, 0, 1400);
    rotateY(radians(map(mouseX, 0, width, -180, 180)));

    translate(0, 0, s*-1000);
    scale(s);

    lights(); ❸
    noStroke();

    // isolate model transformations
    pushMatrix();
      // adjust for default orientation
      // of the model
      rotateX(radians(-90)); ❹
      rotateZ(radians(180));
      model.draw();
    popMatrix();

    stroke(255);

    PVector[] depthPoints = kinect.depthMapRealWorld();

    for (int i = 0; i < depthPoints.length; i+=10) {
      PVector currentPoint = depthPoints[i];
      point(currentPoint.x, currentPoint.y, currentPoint.z);
    }
}

void keyPressed() {
    if (keyCode == 38) {
      s = s + 0.01;
    }
    if (keyCode == 40) {
      s = s - 0.01;
    }
}
```

Run this sketch (make sure you copied the *kinect.obj* into the sketch folder before you run it) and you should see the familiar point cloud, but this time with our Kinect model there pointing at it. If you rotate around and scale up and down, you'll see that the Kinect stays locked in its relation to the point cloud while you do so (see Figure 3-23).

Figure 3-23. *Our Kinect 3D model rendered with the live point cloud from the Kinect.*

Let's talk about the code. We started off by doing the basics to use OBJModel as we just learned them: import the class, declare an OBJModel object, and load our model file.

❶ We also called translateToCenter on the model, which ensures that our model is drawn around the origin of the coordinate system we set up before drawing it. That way we can control the position of the Kinect simply by moving the origin of our coordinate system with translate.

❷ In draw, we go through the same translations, rotations, and scalings as we always have. We center things along x and y, push them back along the z-axis, flip our points upside down on the y-axis, rotate based on the mouse, etc. We've been doing these since early on in this chapter. If you're having trouble figuring out why each step is there, jump back to our earlier discussion to remind yourself why these are here.

❸ Once we have everything in place to draw the point cloud, we stop and insert our code for displaying the model. This starts on this line. First we turn on the lights. Then we call noStroke to prevent our model's triangles from having outlines. Then comes the new and interesting part.

At this point, we're ready to draw the model. However, if we drew the model without any additional rotations, it would show up upside down and backward. Why? In our previous sketch the model seemed to draw right side up without any rotations. Why would we need to add them now? What changed?

Well, first of all, remember that the model in our previous sketch initially displayed with its top facing us rather than its front. When we first loaded the sketch, I explained that this was because of the difference between how the axes are conventionally oriented in most 3D modeling programs and how they're oriented in Processing. Most 3D modeling programs treat the z-axis as pointing up toward the sky away from the ground. Processing, on the other hand, treats the positive z-axis as pointing out of the screen toward the viewer. Because of this mismatch, 3D models will frequently show up facing the wrong way in Processing. In our earlier sketch, this mismatch wasn't a big problem because we gave users control over the orientation of the Kinect model. They could rotate it into a more useful orientation by just clicking and moving the mouse. This time, though, we want the Kinect to be fixed in place at its real location. Therefore, to correct this change, we need to rotate our coordinate system around the x-axis before we draw our model.

❹ And that's exactly what we do on this line of the sketch: `rotateX(radians(-90))`. That line of code will rotate the Kinect model by 90 degrees counterclockwise around the x-axis. The result is that the Kinect will be facing right way up with its little square base facing down.

In our previous sketch, once we rotated the model to face us, we saw the front of the Kinect. We were able to see the circles on its front representing the Kinect's IR projector and two cameras without having to do any rotations. Here, on the other hand, we want it to face away from us and toward the point cloud. Remember that our earlier translations positioned the point cloud a ways off into the distance along the z-axis. In order to get our Kinect model to face toward the point cloud rather than toward us, we need to reverse its orientation along the z-axis. Therefore, we need to rotate 180 degrees around the z-axis before we draw the model. This will orient it the opposite direction, into the screen and toward the point cloud.

Now that we've completed drawing the Kinect model, the rest of the sketch proceeds as before. We loop over all of the points in the point cloud and draw them to the screen. If you play with the sketch, you'll see that the Kinect appears to be realistically located in relation to the scene. It will also rotate and scale correctly as you control the point of view.

At this point, we've achieved most of the goals of this project. We've learned how to load and display a 3D model and we've discovered what it takes to integrate that model into the point cloud from the Kinect. We haven't talked much about scale. And in fact the Kinect is probably larger than life size in our point cloud right now. I'll leave this as an exercise for you. Try adding a call to `scale` within the `pushMatrix`/`popMatrix` context in which we draw the Kinect model. Maybe even set things up so that you can control the scaling factor with a variable that changes with a key press.

We're coming up on the end of this chapter. Before we reach it, though, we're going to look at two more variations to this project. First, we're going to do an experiment that lets us visualize the Kinect's line of sight. We've talked a lot about the idea of *occlusion*: what happens when an object in the foreground of the scene blocks the Kinect from seeing something behind it. This visualization will give us a new perspective on that problem, showing us a little bit more about how it actually comes about.

After that, we're going to add a virtual camera to our scene. Using a virtual camera is a way to dramatically simplify the process of controlling the point of view from which we render our 3D scene. Instead of moving around all of our 3D geometry whenever we want to change our point of view, we just manipulate the position of a camera and the direction in which that camera is looking. This will reduce the number and complexity of the translations, rotations, and scalings we'll need to execute to render our scene. More important, it will let us focus on using our control of the coordinate system to position our objects within the scene while the camera object controls the viewpoint from which we look at all of these objects. I'll introduce you to PeasyCam, a Processing library that implements a virtual camera. PeasyCam is very simple to get started with and provides robust controls that let the user move the camera interactively without us having to write any special code.

Variation: Visualizing the Kinect's Line of Sight

Now that we're reliably drawing our Kinect model within our point cloud, what more can we do with this sketch? We can use it to visualize how the Kinect works. In the previous chapter, we discussed the process the Kinect uses to capture depth information about the scene in front of it. We're going to review a little bit of that here and then we're going to make a small change to our existing sketch that lets us see these principles vividly.

In Chapter 2, we talked extensively about the issue of occlusion. We looked closely at the depth image from the Kinect and observed how objects cast a dark shadow on anything behind them. Because of these shadows, we found that we had no information about those parts of the scene that were trapped behind that closer object. This happens because of how the Kinect works. The Kinect projects a grid of IR dots out onto the scene. When one of these dots hits an object, it reflects back to be seen by the Kinect's IR camera. The Kinect uses the position of these IR dots to calculate the real-world distance of the object. However, anything behind that object is never reached by any IR dots. And so we don't end up with any information about its depth.

This should all be review from the preceding chapter. When described like this, it all sounds awfully abstract. But now that we have a 3D scene that includes both our Kinect and a point cloud representing what it sees, we can build a visualization that makes this process much more concrete. If we draw a line that connects each depth point to our 3D model of the Kinect, that line will show us approximately how the IR dot from the Kinect traveled to the object in the scene it ended up revealing. Infrared light is invisible, but with this sketch, we'll be able to get a sense of how the Kinect sees our scene. Figure 3-24 shows what it looks like.

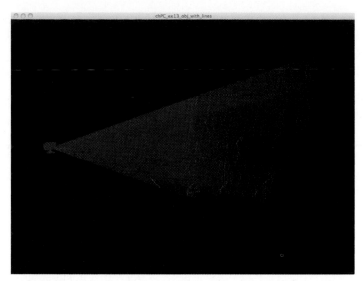

Figure 3-24. *Our point cloud with lines connecting each point to the Kinect 3D model. The result creates the illusion of rays of light passing through smoke or fog.*

To create this image, I only made a few small modifications to our previous sketch. All of the changes took place inside of the loop over all the depth points. Here's the new version of that code:

```
PVector[] depthPoints = kinect.depthMapRealWorld();

for (int i = 0; i < depthPoints.length; i+=100) {
  PVector currentPoint = depthPoints[i];

  // draw the lines darkly with alpha
  stroke(100, 30);
  line(0,0,0, currentPoint.x, currentPoint.y, currentPoint.z);

  // draw the dots bright green
  stroke(0,255,0);
  point(currentPoint.x, currentPoint.y, currentPoint.z);

}
```

What did I change? The main thing I added was the call to line. That line connects each point in the point cloud with the origin of the current coordinate system, which is where the Kinect is positioned.

The result is a series of lines that trace the path of the Kinect's IR projection. Or, more accurately, that trace the return path of these IR dots back to the Kinect from the objects they illuminated. Now that these lines are present, it becomes easy to see how objects in the scene obscure those that are behind them. Look, for example, at my left hand, the one closest to the right side of the sketch. You can see the lines from the Kinect run into it and stop dead so that the area behind, between my arm and the wall, is clear of lines altogether. The whole effect ends up resembling light projected through dense smoke like was seen in the famous scene in the movie theatre at the beginning of *Citizen Kane*. Just like the smoke makes the movement of conventional light through the air visible, these lines reveal the Kinect's line of sight. Run this sketch and move around in front of your Kinect. You'll see the shadows you cast clearly change as you occlude different parts of the background. The lines connecting your to the model of the Kinect should make this obvious.

A few notes about the changes I've made to our previous code in order to implement this effect. First of all, notice the change to the `for` loop statement itself. We're incrementing `i` by 100 on each iteration rather than 10. If we drew too many of these lines, they would obscure each other and our point cloud itself, rendering the whole thing into an incomprehensible mess. Reducing the number of lines reduces this problem. To reduce it further still, we also call `stroke` to change our drawing color before rendering the lines. Specifically, we draw each line at a dim gray and with an alpha value of 30. These two values work together to leave the lines visible but also allow you to see through them to the points behind. The alpha value is especially important in this capacity. Further, we also render the actual points in a fully bright green so that they stand out against the haze of lines. If you look carefully at the sketch you'll notice that each point is actually the terminus of one of the lines. That's obvious as we're drawing the lines between the origin and each of these points in turn. But an unintended side effect of this would be to render the points invisible if they were too similar in color to the lines. That's where the choice of this bright green color helps us.

Another interesting thing to note in this sketch is the strange patterns that seem to appear among the lines. If you look closely at the lines in the bottom half of the scene near the middle of our sketch, you'll see intricate curved and diamond-shaped patterns emerge. These are not coming from any specific shape we're intentionally drawing in our sketch, but instead from a natural optical illusion that comes from drawing many thin lines. When these lines cross each other at shallow angles, they produce a Moire effect, creating the illusion of filled-in areas and curved patterns. Similarly, as you rotate the sketch, you may notice areas of the lines disappear or suddenly increase in brightness. All of these effects occur as the lines interact with each other. As our angle on the sketch changes, you see different combinations of lines overlapping in different amounts. And since the lines are partially transparent, this results in different areas of the scene appearing more or less bright at the points of overlap and separation.

Camera Control with PeasyCam

In the last section of this chapter, we're going to add a virtual camera to our scene. Up to this point, we've been controlling our point of view through a series of explicit translations, rotations, and scalings. This has added a lot of extra lines to our sketch and, at times, interacted in a complex manner with the transformations we've used to position and draw our 3D objects and points. In this section I'll show you how to use the PeasyCam library for Processing to make the code that controls our sketch's point of view simpler and more robust. PeasyCam takes care of all of translations, rotations, and scalings that are required to apply a virtual camera to our geometry. We just tell PeasyCam where to put the camera and where the camera should look. Further, PeasyCam makes the camera's position interactive so that you can zoom the camera in and out, rotate it around, tilt it up and down, etc. with a series of simple mouse and key combinations. Using PeasyCam will give us richer control over the point of view of our sketch while also letting us eliminate a lot of the code we previously added to implement the rudimentary control our past sketches did have. Most important, using PeasyCam will eliminate any danger of accidental interactions between transformations meant to control the point of view and those used to actually position our objects in space. PeasyCam will take care of all the transformations necessary to create the illusion of a moving camera and we can trust it to cause no side effects to the coordinate system used by the rest of our sketch (you can guess PeasyCam must be using something like `pushMatrix` and `popMatrix` inside itself to get this job done). Therefore, we can apply whatever transformations we need to position our objects and points without any danger of cross-contamination with the viewing system. This separation of concerns will make our sketch significantly simpler.

We'll start by installing PeasyCam. At this point, the procedure for installing Processing libraries should be starting to get familiar to you. We need to download the library and put it into our Processing *libraries* folder. You can find the PeasyCam library available for download here: *http://mrfeinberg.com/ peasycam*.

Click the "download" link on that page and find the *.zip* file to download. Download that, unzip it, and stick the results in your Processing libraries folder. If you need more detailed instructions, jump back to the earlier section of this chapter where we installed the OBJLoader library.

Now we can add PeasyCam to our sketch and start using it. Here's the code. Once you've gotten it running, I'll point out a few things to observe about it, and then we'll look at the code. (If you're creating a new sketch for this example, be sure to copy the *kinect.obj* and *kinect.mtl* file into the sketch folder.)

```
import processing.opengl.*;
import SimpleOpenNI.*;
import saito.objloader.*;
import peasy.*;

PeasyCam cam;
SimpleOpenNI kinect;
OBJModel model;

void setup() {
  size(1024, 768, OPENGL);
  kinect = new SimpleOpenNI(this);
  kinect.enableDepth();

  model = new OBJModel(this, "kinect.obj", "relative", TRIANGLES);
  model.translateToCenter();
  noStroke();

  // create a camera
  // arguments set point to look at and distance from that point
  cam = new PeasyCam(this, 0, 0, 0, 1000); ❶
}

void draw() { ❷
  background(0);
  kinect.update();
```

```
    rotateX(radians(180));  ❸

    // NB: there used to be a bunch of transformations here

    lights();
    noStroke();

    pushMatrix();
      rotateX(radians(-90));
      rotateZ(radians(180));
      model.draw();
    popMatrix();

    stroke(255);

    PVector[] depthPoints = kinect.depthMapRealWorld();

    for (int i = 0; i < depthPoints.length; i+=10) {
      PVector currentPoint = depthPoints[i];
      point(currentPoint.x, currentPoint.y, currentPoint.z);
    }
  }
```

At first, this sketch will look indistinguishable from other recent sketches we've made that display the Kinect model and the point cloud. The differences here are in how we can interact with it. Try clicking and dragging within the sketch. You'll see that the entire scene rotates around as you drag. Dragging up seems to tilt the camera down, dragging down tilts it up, right makes it go left, and left makes it go right. It's like we're controlling a camera on a tripod, sweeping it around with an extended handle. However, we can move our virtual camera a lot farther than we could move a real one that was anchored to a tripod. Try moving the camera around the side of the point cloud. If you keep dragging the mouse to the side, you'll find that you can fly your point of view all the way around the point cloud to a position where you're looking straight back at the Kinect through yourself (or whatever else happens to be in front of the Kinect). The whole time you're moving, the camera stays fixed on the same point. Even though you're now looking at the scene from the opposite side, the camera is still facing toward the center. It's like you've flown around the scene on the surface of a sphere of fixed size and position. We'll learn more about how to control the size and center of that sphere in a minute.

But first, notice how smoothly our virtual camera moves. When we stop moving it around, it glides smoothly to a halt as if it were a real camera with momentum slowly skidding to a stop. There's none of the jerky and sudden repositioning that sometimes happened with our homemade transformations when the mouse would leave the sketch or return to it at a new position. On the downside, though, this smoothness can sometimes make it hard to get our camera into a precise position. Its orientation is so responsive that it will constantly slip and slide out from under you if you're not delicate in how you manipulate it.

And here's something cool. If you get the camera into a crazy position, you can double-click anywhere inside the sketch and the camera will jump back to the original orientation it started in. It will make this move smoothly, which looks really cool but is also helpful. Seeing the camera move continuously to get back to its starting position will reduce your disorientation, making it easier for you to navigate back to wherever you just were if necessary.

Now try scrolling up and down. The virtual camera will zoom in and out, getting closer and farther from the scene. Zoom out and swoop the camera far above your head to look down at yourself. If you do that, you might find that your image in the point cloud is actually off to the side of the sketch. Up to this point, we've never moved the center of our camera's field of view. It's always stayed locked on the Kinect itself. In a minute, we'll look at the code and see where that's set and how we can manipulate it. But for now, we can also change what the camera's looking at by moving the mouse while holding down the control key (or, on Windows, clicking and dragging with the middle mouse button). Once you've done that, try dragging and scrolling some more. You'll see that your rotations and zooming are now centered on a new point.

Using all of these controls in concert, it's now finally possible to get any perspective we want on our point cloud and model. Before when we rotated and zoomed we frequently ended up with empty space at the middle of our sketch and much of the stuff we actually cared about swung out to the edge. Now we can look at things from any angle while constantly repositioning our point of view to keep everything centered. For example, in Figure 3-25, I've rotated the point of view above my head to look down at me.

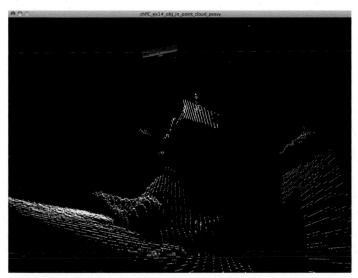

Figure 3-25. *Rotating around our point cloud while keeping it centered in the view lets us look at it from surprising angles such as from above. Here you can see me leaning against the wall with my hands behind my head.*

Play around for awhile until you get the hang of it.

Now let's look through the code. This is the first time we've added a feature to our sketch that actually results in fewer lines of code. So part of what we'll be looking at is the code we no longer have to write now that we're using PeasyCam.

❶ We'll start with the last line of `setup` where we create our PeasyCam object.

PeasyCam's constructor takes five arguments. The first one is always `this`, representing our sketch itself. Behind the scenes, PeasyCam is going to do some kind of magic to manipulate our sketch's output based on the current position and orientation of the camera. In order to do this, it needs direct access to our sketch. A lot of plug-ins do something similar, so `this` is frequently the first argument to the constructor of a Processing library.

The next three arguments describe the point at which the camera will look. They're the x-, y-, and z-coordinates of a point in three-dimensional space. PeasyCam calls this point the "look-at" point. In this case we're passing `0,0,0`, which is the origin of our coordinate system. In previous versions of this sketch, we intentionally positioned our point cloud and our Kinect model away from the origin. We used `translate` to center our x- and y-axes within our sketch and to push all of our geometry out along the negative z-axis so that everything would be visible. Now though anything that's in front of the camera will be visible. So we don't have to alter the position of our geometry in order to keep it on the screen. All we have to do is point the camera at it. Since Processing starts drawing everything at the origin by default, the easiest thing to do is just point our camera there. By doing that, we're guaranteed to get our model and points on camera, and we can eliminate all the transformations we previously included in our sketch simply to keep things on screen.

The final argument to the constructor tells PeasyCam how far away from this "look-at" point it should position the camera. In this case, we tell it 1000 pixels. We knew this was a good distance to capture all of the points in the point cloud from our previous versions of this sketch. But 1000 points away in what direction? To position our look-at point, we had to provide three values to specify the x-, y-, and z-coordinates. How can we position the camera using only a single number?

The answer comes from how PeasyCam constrains the motion of the virtual camera. PeasyCam uses the coordinates of our look-at point and this additional distance value to define a three-dimensional sphere. The sphere is centered on the look-at point and has a radius set by the camera distance. By using PeasyCam's interactive controls, we can move the virtual camera around to any position on this sphere. For example, when we drag the mouse down, the camera rotates toward the top of the sphere and then down the other side. Throughout its movement, it always points toward the center of the sphere, rotating its angle as necessary. And we can move the center of the sphere by holding command while we drag. As we saw above, this recenters our camera's point of view. In other words, it changes the look-at point, which moves the center of the sphere our camera can traverse.

❷ Let's move on to looking at our `draw` function. The most interesting change here is what's missing. In the sketches throughout this chapter, we've gradually added more and more transformations to the beginning of this function. Nearly none of these transformations were there to position our point cloud or our 3D model. Most of them were there to control the point of view from which the user saw the scene. We used translations to move everything away in depth so that it would be comfortably visible. We used other translations to set the center point around which everything would rotate under the user's control. We used rotations to give users control of the lateral angle from which they saw the scene and scalings to let them control how close they were to it.

❸ Now, none of these are necessary. We're no longer using the position and orientation of the geometry to control the viewer's point of view. That's exactly why we're using PeasyCam. Now, the only transformation we still need is the one that flips all of our depth points right side up. We call `rotateX(radians(180))` to correct the difference between how OpenNI orients the y-axis and how Processing does. This disjunction isn't affected by using PeasyCam. All of the rest of the transformations are simply gone from `draw`, leaving it a lot simpler.

In the absence of these transformations, what happens to our point cloud and our 3D model? Where do they end up located? Without any changes to the coordinate system, Processing draws everything starting at the origin. The first thing we draw is our 3D model of the Kinect. Before we draw that, we perform two rotations, but these don't move the model off of the origin of our coordinate system. They just orient it to face the right direction. Hence, our Kinect model is located at exactly 0,0,0, just where the camera is pointing. You may have noticed in interacting with the sketch that no matter how you rotated and scaled your point of view, the Kinect always stayed in the center of the screen with the camera aiming straight at it. That's because we're drawing the Kinect model at the exact position of the camera's point of interest.

What about the depth points? Why do they end up away from the origin even though we're not translating or rotating at all before we draw them? Remember back to the beginning of this chapter when we first drew the point cloud. At that point we saw that our depth points all came with z-values ranging in the negative direction from a few hundred back to about 1500–2000. Without any translations at all, they'll show up some distance away into the screen from the origin. Since our camera is centered on the origin, the point cloud will appear in front of us, a natural distance beyond the Kinect model.

What about the starting point of our camera? How did PeasyCam determine that? Every time we launch our sketch the camera starts off exactly lined up with the Kinect model along the x- and y-axes, but 1000 pixels in front of it. In other words, PeasyCam positioned the camera with the x- and y-coordinates of the look-at point. This ensures that whatever we told it to look at will, in fact, be in the center of our sketch window. Then, for the z-coordinate of the camera, PeasyCam used the starting distance from the object that we set, in this case 1000 pixels. So our camera starts off at 0, 0, 1000.

At this stage we've got the basics of PeasyCam down. We've seen how to use PeasyCam to add a virtual camera to our sketch, how to set where that camera looks, and how to use the controls PeasyCam gives us to let our users reposition the camera interactively. But what if we want to control the camera programmatically? We will frequently want our code to control what our camera looks at rather than just our user. Controlling how the camera frames our scene is one of the most powerful tools we have when making a 3D interactive application. What users see will give them a major hint about what we want them to think about and interact with. Think of 3D video games. When the game designers want to reveal an object or character that you can interact with, they will frequently swoop the virtual camera over to point at it so you have no choice but to see the object and to understand where it is in relation to your current position.

With PeasyCam we can do something similar. In addition to all of the automatic controls that PeasyCam gives us for letting our user control our sketch's point of view, it provides a set of functions that let us control the camera with our code. To explore this ability, we're going to try one last example that brings together everything we've learned in this chapter. We're going to add hot points to our scene and configure them to control our camera. When you interact with any individual hot point, it will tell PeasyCam to direct the camera at it. The camera will zoom from its current position to focus on the hot point. From that moment on all interactive movements of the camera will be centered around that hot point until the other point is touched or you manually move or reset the camera.

The code for this final iteration of our sketch is more complex than any we've seen in this chapter. After all, we're bringing together everything we've learned here. Thanks to PeasyCam it is not the longest code we've seen, but it is the densest. We'll be using three libraries as well as our own `Hotpoint` class. That means that our sketch has a lot of leverage: it can accomplish a lot in very few lines of code. It also means there's a lot going on behind the scenes. But almost none of what's going on should be new to you on its own. The only element we're adding here is control over the camera's look-at point. So I'm confident that you can understand everything that's going on.

In some ways, this is the most realistic sketch we've seen so far. In real-world programs, you often end up using many specialized libraries together to accomplish your goals. One of the best ways to approach a complex problem is to start with one simple piece of that problem, solve that, and then slowly add more features one at a time until your program does everything you want it to. This is exactly how we've worked in this chapter.

Here's the code. Read through it, enter it into Processing, and see how much of it you understand. Then continue reading below and I'll explain some of the trickier bits. To make this code work, you'll need the Hotpoint class that we created back in the example on page 150, as well as the Kinect model we've been using in the last few sketches. Create a new sketch in Processing, enter this code into it, save it, then copy the *kinect.obj* and *Hotpoint.pde* files from our earlier sketches into your sketch folder. Once you've done those things, you should be able to run the sketch and interact with the hot points. When you touch each hot point, you should see the camera center itself on that point and zoom in toward it.

```
import processing.opengl.*;  ❶
import SimpleOpenNI.*;
import saito.objloader.*;
import peasy.*;

PeasyCam cam;
SimpleOpenNI kinect;
OBJModel model;
Hotpoint hotpoint1;
Hotpoint hotpoint2;

void setup() {
  size(1024, 768, OPENGL);
  kinect = new SimpleOpenNI(this);
  kinect.enableDepth();

  model = new OBJModel(this, "kinect.obj", "relative", TRIANGLES);
  model.translateToCenter();
  noStroke();

  cam = new PeasyCam(this, 0, 0, 0, 1000);

  hotpoint1 = new Hotpoint(200, 200, 800, 150);
  hotpoint2 = new Hotpoint(-200, 200, 800, 150);
}

void draw() {  ❷
  background(0);
  kinect.update();

  rotateX(radians(180));   ❸

  lights();
  noStroke();

  pushMatrix();
    rotateX(radians(-90));
    rotateZ(radians(180));
    model.draw();
  popMatrix();


  stroke(255);
```

```
PVector[] depthPoints = kinect.depthMapRealWorld(); ❹

for (int i = 0; i < depthPoints.length; i+=10) {
  PVector currentPoint = depthPoints[i];
  point(currentPoint.x, currentPoint.y, currentPoint.z);

  hotpoint1.check(currentPoint);
  hotpoint2.check(currentPoint);
}

hotpoint1.draw();
hotpoint2.draw();

if (hotpoint1.isHit()) { ❺
  cam.lookAt(hotpoint1.center.x,
             hotpoint1.center.y * -1,
             hotpoint1.center.z * -1, 500, 500); ❻
}

if (hotpoint2.isHit()) {
  cam.lookAt(hotpoint2.center.x,
             hotpoint2.center.y * -1,
             hotpoint2.center.z * -1, 500, 500);
}

hotpoint1.clear(); ❼
hotpoint2.clear();
}
```

I'm going to go through and describe everything that happens in this sketch in plain English, much like I did at the start of this book. Recently we've been moving through code at a much faster rate, only discussing the new bits most recently added. However, at this point I think it's worth slowing down for a minute to review how far we've come and all the things we're doing to make this sketch work. I won't describe each line in detail (at this point, I trust that you can puzzle out the actual programming details yourself since we have covered all of them at least once), but I will point out what job it's doing and how it's contributing to the overall sketch.

❶   The top section of the sketch, before the start of setup, has gotten quite long. We're importing three different libraries and declaring five different objects now: two Hotpoints, an OBJModel, a PeasyCam, and our good old reliable SimpleOpenNI. Then, in setup itself, we initialize all these objects. The OBJModel loads up our *kinect.obj* file. The PeasyCam points itself at the origin with a rotation distance of 1000 pixels. And we add two Hotpoints, both 150 pixels on a side and both placed at the same height and depth 400 pixels apart from each other on either side of the y-axis.

❷   Similarly, much of draw is made up of code we've seen before. We start off by clearing the background to black, then we update the Kinect to get new depth data. Then we flip things around the x-axis in order to correct for the difference between the orientation of Processing's axes and those of OpenNI. Don't forget about this line of code. It is again going to prove important in this sketch. It has an impact on how we control our camera's look-at point.

❸ After the call to `rotateX` are the familiar lines for drawing the 3D model of the Kinect. We turn the lights on so that it will be visible and we call `noStroke` so the polygons that make up the model will be drawn without outlines. Then we set up a new coordinate system and, within it, we rotate around the x- and z-axes so that we can draw the Kinect 3D model right side up and facing toward our depth points. That done, we turn the stroke back on and set it to white so that we can draw out point cloud. Remember, points get drawn using Processing's `stroke` color rather than its `fill` color.

❹ To access the point cloud data, we call the SimpleOpenNI object's `depthMapRealWorld` function and store the array of `PVector`s it returns. Once we've got that array, we loop over it, using the x-, y-, and z-components of each `PVector` to draw the point using Processing's `point` function. We also tell both of the hot points to check to see if they include any of the points. Notice that we're skipping 10 depth points for every one that we process. This is to keep our sketch running fast and to prevent our point cloud from becoming too dense. After we've processed all of the depth points, we go ahead and draw both of the `Hotpoint`s. We do this using their own `draw` function, which we know will do the right thing and isolate us from the transformations that it uses internally to position the boxes it draws.

❺ Now, we finally reach the part of the sketch where we're doing something new. In a previous sketch, we used edge detection to trigger a sound whenever the user touched one of the hot points. To make this easier, we added a function to the `Hotpoint` class `isHit` that will return true only when the hot point detects an object or person entering it. This time, we use that same function to trigger a different action.

❻ Instead of playing a sound, we want the camera to focus in on the specific hot point that was touched. To accomplish this, we tell PeasyCam to "look at" the hot point.

This `lookAt` function takes five arguments. The first three arguments represent the x-, y-, and z-coordinates of the point we want the camera to look at. The fourth argument tells PeasyCam how close to that point it should get. Just like the fourth argument in PeasyCam's constructor, it defines the radius of the sphere PeasyCam establishes around the object it's looking at. This sets the initial position of the camera and also constrains when the user pans and tilts it. The last argument to this function is there for cosmetic purposes. It tells PeasyCam to make a smooth transition between the current look-at target and the one we just told it to go to. The number we pass for this argument is the amount of time we want this transition to take. Since we pass 500 here, PeasyCam will animate between the old look-at point and the new one we just set over the course of 500 milliseconds or half of one second.

I haven't yet mentioned the most important and confusing part of this line of code. Why are we multiplying the y- and z-coordinates of the `Hotpoint` by negative one before passing them as arguments to `lookAt`? Don't we want the camera to look at the actual position of the hot point?

We have to do this because of the one transformation we made to our coordinate system. As I mentioned above, at the start of `draw` we flipped our coordinate system 180 degrees around its x-axis. We had to do this to make Processing's coordinate system match the one the OpenNI uses, which orients its y- and z-axes in reverse to how Processing does. Without that rotation, our point cloud would draw upside down. However, PeasyCam doesn't know about that transformation. It still thinks of the y-axis as going toward the bottom of the sketch and the z-axis as pointing out of the screen. To get our camera to look at the right point, we have to reverse these two axes by multiplying the y- and z-values by negative one.

When I introduced PeasyCam, I promised that one of its advantages was separating the process of positioning and drawing 3D geometry from the process of placing a camera to view it. However, we still need to tell the camera the right place to look. Any time we pass coordinates into PeasyCam to set its look-at point (or manipulate it manually in any other way), we have to take into account what we've previously done to our own coordinate system and how that has altered the data we're about to send to PeasyCam. In this case, by rotating around the x-axis, we've reversed our y- and z-values. Hence we need to multiply them by −1 before passing them into PeasyCam to reverse them back.

Once we pass PeasyCam the right coordinates, it will zoom the camera in on each hot point whenever that point is triggered. After the camera has been repositioned, we can manipulate it interactively, zooming in and out rotating around and up and down. It will stay centered on the hot point until you manually move its look-at point by command-dragging or until you hit the other hot point, triggering it to look at that one. Notice that we have a nearly identical `if` statement and use of `lookAt` for `hotpoint2` after the one for `hotpoint1`.

❼ Then, finally, we complete our sketch by telling both `Hotpoints` to clear themselves. This resets the detection process and prepares them for the next run of `draw`.

Conclusion

This concludes both our discussion of PeasyCam and this chapter as a whole. You should now have the tools you need to work confidently in three dimensions within Processing. While much of this chapter explored various attributes of the point cloud data provided by the Kinect, very little of the actual code we wrote and concepts we learned were limited to data coming from the Kinect. To make useful visualizations of the Kinect data and to convert those into usable interactions, you need to become comfortable writing code that draws and makes measurements in 3D. The building blocks of this code are the translations, rotations, and scalings we've used throughout this chapter. I hope that at this point you are beginning to feel comfortable using each of these and have started to understand the strategies we use to combine them into meaningful manipulations of three-dimensional geometry.

Three-dimensional graphics is an incredibly rich topic, and this chapter has only covered the absolute basics. We will continue to build on this foundation as this book progresses. In the next chapter, as we start to work with the Kinect's skeleton data, we'll explore techniques for comparing 3D points: measuring the distance between them, tracking their movement over time, measuring their orientation, etc. The skeleton data is the Kinect's most direct and powerful way of representing the position of the user. Analyzing this data with these 3D comparison techniques will enable an amazing variety of interactions between the user and our sketches. In fact, the possibilities when working with the skeleton data are so rich that you may wonder why I even bothered dragging you through the depth image and the point cloud in these past two chapters. Hopefully, though, you'll find that the new skills you gained in these chapters will pay off handsomely when working with the skeleton data. Your newfound ability to process Kinect data over time to draw wider conclusions from it (learned in the Hand Waving Drawing project in the first chapter) and to navigate and draw in 3D (covered extensively here) should serve you well when diving into the complex, but extremely powerful, skeleton data.

Working with the Skeleton Data

In this chapter, we're going to learn how to work with OpenNI's user-tracking data. Up to this point, we've been working directly with the depth data from the Kinect. To make our sketches interactive, we've had to process this depth data so that it responds to the actions of our users. Since we didn't know the position of the user directly, we've had to infer it from the position of the depth points. In Chapter 2, we did this by tracking the closest point to the Kinect. Last chapter, we did it by looking for depth points in particular cubes of space.

Starting now, though, we can take a much more direct route. OpenNI has the ability to process the depth image for us in order to detect and track people. Instead of having to loop through depth points to check their position, we can simply access the position of each body part of each user that OpenNI tracks for us. Once OpenNI has detected a user, it will tell us the position of each of the user's visible "joints": head, neck, shoulders, elbows, hands, torso, hips, knees, feet. (Not everything on this list is a joint in the anatomical sense; OpenNI uses the term *joint* to refer to all of the points on a user's body the library is capable of tracking, whether or not they are actual joints.)

For building interactive applications user can control with their bodies, this is exactly the information we need. Think back to our Invisible Pencil application in Chapter 2. That application would have been so much easier to develop and so much more robust to use if we had access to the position of the user's hand. Rather than try to calculate the threshold of the depth image and then iterate through every point within it to find the closest one and assume that represented the user's outstretched hand, we could have simply gotten the position of his hand from OpenNI and used that to update the position of our line. And, further, using this joint data, we will now be able to implement much more sophisticated user interfaces that would have been previously impossible. We can base interactions on hand gestures and overall poses of the body, we can track body movements over time and compare them, and we can measure distances between parts of the body.

Why didn't we simply start off working with this data then if it's so much more effective? Why have I dragged you through two chapters of working with depth data directly? Because working with the joint data is dramatically more complex than either the depth image or the point clouds we've seen so far. Without the basic programming capabilities, in both working with arrays and understanding 3D, that you learned in the last two chapters, trying to work with the joint data from the Kinect would be an extremely high hurdle to jump over in a single leap. Further, to use the joint data in our applications, we'll have to learn a series of new programming tricks. First of all, we'll have to learn to use the functions that SimpleOpenNI provides for accessing the joint data. These functions are more complex and awkward to use than any Processing code we've worked with so far in this book. Beyond those basics, to get the joint data out of SimpleOpenNI, we'll have to master new programming concepts such as *setter methods* and *callbacks*. Most ambitiously, we'll have to learn some new mathematical techniques. In the previous chapter, we learned the basics of navigating and drawing in three dimensions. A lot of this effort involved understanding and working with vectors. Now, to compare points in three-dimensional space and analyze the movement of points over time, we'll need to learn how to do calculations with vectors in three dimensions. This will involve mathematical techniques such as vector subtraction, finding dot products, finding cross products, and other tools for performing calculations with vectors rather than simply drawing them as points.

In this chapter, I'll introduce these techniques to you one at a time. You'll learn a lot and you'll learn it quickly, but I'll do my best to keep things clear and straightforward. Compared to previous chapters, the code won't be as clean, and there will be a little bit more math to learn, but if you've come this far, you're totally ready for it. And the payoff will be huge; by the end of this chapter you'll have a programming vocabulary that will let you create a broad range of really compelling interactive applications.

We'll start by learning the ropes of the SimpleOpenNI functions needed to access the joint data. We'll write a sketch that detects a single user and moves a circle around the screen based on the position of the user's hand. In the process, we'll discuss the calibration procedure that we have to put users through in order to use the joint data. We'll talk about why this procedure exists and how to work with it in code. To access the joint data, we'll also get our first exposure to OpenNI's callbacks. Just like Processing itself gives us callbacks that make it easy for us to write code that runs when the user clicks the mouse or types a key, SimpleOpenNI provides its own callbacks that let us run code at critical moments in the user-tracking process: when a new user is discovered, when tracking first begins, when a user is lost, etc. Learning how to work with these callbacks is key to taking full advantage of OpenNI's tracking facilities.

Once we've learned how to access an individual joint, we'll scale our code up to access all of the joints in the user's skeleton. We'll use this data to draw a basic stickman that follows the pose of our user. SimpleOpenNI offers a set of helper functions that assist in the process of drawing "limbs," straight lines that connect the individual joints that the system has detected. Once we've got the stickman on screen, we can have our first lesson in OpenNI anatomy. We'll see all of the joints that we have access to and what parts of the user's body they represent. You'll see that OpenNI's sense of anatomy is just a little bit different than your local doctor's.

Having learned to access the full user skeleton, we'll be ready to start making our applications interactive. The next few sections of this chapter will focus on techniques we can use to analyze the position and movement of the user's joints. We'll start with the simplest of these techniques: measuring the distance between two joints. To accomplish this, we'll learn a little bit more about vectors. We'll see how vectors can represent both individual points in space as well as the distance between two points. And we'll learn how to do some basic vector subtraction to measure distances.

Next we'll look at the angles between the user's limbs. These angles are key in describing individual poses. For example, how can you tell if a user is sitting down? One big hint might be that there's something close to a 90-degree angle between her shins and her thighs. To calculate the angle between vectors, we use a mathematical technique called the *dot product*. I'll show you how to calculate the dot product and the *cross product* between two vectors in order to figure out the angle between them. These techniques also have another interesting use. Together they let us match the orientation of an object to a vector. This gives us a powerful new tool for manipulating 3D models. In the previous chapter, we learned how to load and display 3D models within our point cloud. Throughout that chapter, we treated 3D models as if they were part of the scenery. We set them in place within our coordinate system and then moved a camera around them. We saw them from different angles, but they stayed fixed relative to the coordinate system itself. With this new ability to use one vector to set the orientation of another, we can now start to move these 3D models around. We can map the orientation of our 3D models to the orientation of one or more of the user's limbs. For example, we can make it so that when the user moves his arms, 3D models of wings flap up and down behind him.

These techniques that use the skeleton data form our most powerful building blocks for creating user interfaces with the Kinect. However, OpenNI also has some other tricks it can do that don't require the complete calibration process. These tricks still use OpenNI's ability to analyze the depth image and detect objects and people within it. Knowing how to use them can supplement what we've already learned, giving us additional tools to analyze the scene and detect user movements. To finish this chapter, we'll cover three of these techniques: scene analysis, hand tracking, and finding the user's center of mass.

At the start of this chapter, I explained that OpenNI generates the skeleton data by processing the depth image captured by the Kinect. Well, it turns out that OpenNI can also extract other information from the depth image besides the locations of the user's joints. First of all, OpenNI can figure out which pixels in the depth image represent people and which ones represent the background of the scene. This information becomes available as soon as OpenNI detects that a person has entered the scene. OpenNI's algorithm detects that a person is present and keeps track of her continuously as she moves around. So we can distinguish individual users from each other as well as the background. OpenNI provides this information about which pixels belong to users in the form of a "map," an array of numbers corresponding to each pixel in the depth image. The map value for each pixel will be 0 if the pixel is part of the background. If the pixel is part of a user, the map value will be the user's ID: one, two, three, etc. In this chapter, I'll show you how to use this map to perform a technique called *background removal*. Background removal is the process of separating foreground elements, like people, from the background of the image that doesn't change. It works just like the green screen process in a special effects movie. We can use background removal to make it look like you're in an exotic location even when you're just standing in front of your Kinect in your room.

In addition to separating the user from the background of the scene, OpenNI can analyze the background itself, distinguishing different objects within it, such as furniture and walls. This feature is not nearly as reliable as the user tracking (after all, the Kinect was created to perform user tracking for games—these other scene analysis capabilities are just a happy side effect). That said, it can still come in handy for generating simple breakdowns of the scene similar to architectural diagrams. I'll show you how to access this extended scene map and display its data on top of the standard depth image.

Finally, we'll learn a couple of tricks for tracking users passively. Even without performing the calibration ritual, OpenNI can detect the position and movements of your hands. This is an especially useful interface for a person who cannot move his whole body, either because of a permanent debilitation or because of his current physical position or activity. I'll show you how to use OpenNI's built-in gesture recognition system to detect the presence of the user's hands and how to use the associated callbacks to begin tracking it. While skeleton and hand tracking are extremely useful for nearby users who are actively engaged with our applications, what about passersby who are farther away and possibly even unaware of our applications existence? OpenNI gives us a function that lets us track them as well. As soon as OpenNI detects any people in the scene, it will begin to report their *centers of mass*. We can use these points to track them in space and make our application responsive to them, whether they're ever aware of it or not.

To put all of this new information into action, we'll finish the chapter by building two complete projects. These projects will be slightly more sophisticated than the ones we've done in the previous two chapters. Having mastered so many skills at this point in the book, I believe you're ready for something more ambitious. Plus the joint data is so useful that we have the opportunity to make some applications that are dramatically more practical than some that we've built to this point. The result will be that the projects in this chapter will be a little bit more drawn out than those we've seen before but will also include more real-world code that you'll be able to reuse in your own projects outside of this book.

For the first project, we'll build a sketch that provides feedback on your exercise routine. For example, a physical trainer or occupational therapist will demonstrate an exercise with her own body while she helps you work out. Then, while you perform the exercise, copying the trainer's motions to the best of your ability, she will give you feedback, telling you to stretch farther or bend more deeply, or simply let you know when you've got it right.

This sketch will aspire to augment your trainer in this process, reminding you of her instructions while she's away. We'll start off by recording a series of motions that represent a particular exercise. This will involve storing the position of each joint over time as you perform the motion. Then, we'll play back the original motion. We'll use the recorded joint positions to animate a stickman that demonstrates the original correct motion. I'll introduce a Processing library I've created that makes it easy to record and play back joint data and explain a little bit about how it works.

At this point we'll have code that's more broadly useful than just this exercise app. Being able to record and play back joint data could be useful for all kinds of things from simple motion capture (imagine combining it with the 3D object animator I mentioned above) to instructional systems.

Once we've got our stickman performing the ideal version of the exercise, the final step will be to compare this ideal version with whatever our user is actually doing. We'll provide the user with live feedback that lets him know how he's diverging from the ideal version and what he can do to correct his motion. To accomplish this we'll use a lot of what we learned earlier in the chapter about comparing vectors. We'll measure the distance and angle between the ideal joint position and the user's actual position at every frame. And we'll draw connecting vectors that instruct the user in how to correct his motion to get closer to the ideal version.

In our second project, we'll focus more on static poses instead of moving joint positions. We'll build a sketch that detects famous dance poses and uses them to trigger the appropriate accompanying music. For example, you'll be able to use an outthrust hip and skyward-pointing finger to kick off *Saturday Night Fever*. Where our exercise app was all about comparing two recorded motions with each other in absolute space, this one will be about comparing the joints, relative positions to one another at any given moment. How can our sketch tell if you're in John Travolta's classic pose from *Saturday Night Fever*? It's all a matter of where your joints are in relation to one another. Is your right hand above your head? Is your left hand near your left hip? What is the angle between your left upper arm and your left forearm? If we define a pose as a set of relationships like these, then we can detect when the user has fulfilled all of them and we can reward her by triggering the corresponding music (of course, we already know how to play audio files from "Adding Audio with Minim"). This project was inspired by work created by Alex Vessels and Kimi Spencer, students at NYU's Interactive Telecommunications Program, and by the Michael Jackson Experience, a game created by Ubisoft for the Xbox 360 that uses the Kinect to test players' ability to dance like the King of Pop.

By the end of this chapter you will have a strong handle on how to use the joint data from OpenNI to build your own interactive applications that users can control with their bodies. You'll be able to display a user's body position on screen as a basic stickman and to use his motions to manipulate 3D objects. You'll be able to record motions to play back later. You'll be able to measure the distances and angles between parts of a user's body. You'll be able to describe individual poses and detect when the user has assumed them.

But before you can do all of this cool stuff, you have to start by accessing a single joint position on a single user. So, let's start there.

Unlike the initial code in our previous chapters, which always started out pretty simple, even the simplest joint-tracking sketch ends up being complicated. Working with the joint-tracking data involves a series of required steps that we just plain can't skip.

First among these is adding all of the callbacks to our sketch that handle the user-detection life cycle. As the user appears in front of the camera, presents herself for tracking, and is eventually detected and tracked, SimpleOpenNI will trigger a series of functions that we have to write to let us know about the passage of each step and its results. Within these functions we have to perform certain actions to keep the detection and tracking process going. To make things more complicated, the entire detection process happens asynchronously. In other words, our main draw function is also running the whole time in parallel. This means that in addition to handling these callbacks, we have to account for the possible presence or absence of tracked users throughout our actual code inside of draw.

Thankfully, after you understand these steps once, you'll be able to add them to all of your future sketches by simply copy and pasting them. The ritual dance of callback functions is the same for every sketch that performs user tracking. However, it's still important to understand each step in this dance. Getting a user to present himself for tracking and to assume the calibration pose necessary for OpenNI to lock on to him is a difficult user interface design challenge. Depending on how your app is meant to be used, you might need to give you users different instructions and feedback every step of the way. For example, if the user can see the screen, you might be able to use graphics and colors to show him what pose to take and to give him feedback indicating when he has successfully been tracked. On the other hand, maybe your application won't have a visual interface at all. Since the users can provide input to a Kinect application with just their bodies, maybe audio feedback would be more appropriate for your sketch. Either way, you'll have to understand the meaning of each callback function in the tracking workflow to know when to give the user what feedback.

Now that I've warned you about the difficulties involved, let's see what joint tracking actually looks like in practice. I'll present you with the code, explain how to use it, and then we'll walk through it. Along the way, we'll learn how to use these callbacks I've been telling you about, and I'll point out a few other tricks and quirks as well.

Here's the code:

```
import SimpleOpenNI.*;
SimpleOpenNI  kinect;

void setup() {
  size(640, 480);

  kinect = new SimpleOpenNI(this);
  kinect.enableDepth();

  // turn on user tracking
  kinect.enableUser(SimpleOpenNI.SKEL_PROFILE_ALL);
}

void draw() {
  kinect.update();
  PImage depth = kinect.depthImage();
  image(depth, 0, 0);

  // make a vector of ints to store the list of users
  IntVector userList = new IntVector();

  // write the list of detected users
  // into our vector
  kinect.getUsers(userList);

  // if we found any users
  if (userList.size() > 0) {
    // get the first user
    int userId = userList.get(0);

    // if we're successfully calibrated
    if ( kinect.isTrackingSkeleton(userId)) {
      // make a vector to store the left hand
      PVector rightHand = new PVector();
      // put the position of the left hand into that vector
      float confidence = kinect.getJointPositionSkeleton(userId,
                                    SimpleOpenNI.SKEL_LEFT_HAND,
                                    rightHand);

      // convert the detected hand position
      // to "projective" coordinates
      // that will match the depth image
      PVector convertedRightHand = new PVector();
      kinect.convertRealWorldToProjective(rightHand, convertedRightHand);
      // and display it
      fill(255,0,0);
      ellipse(convertedRightHand.x, convertedRightHand.y, 10, 10);
    }
  }
}

// user-tracking callbacks!
void onNewUser(int userId) {
  println("start pose detection");
  kinect.startPoseDetection("Psi", userId);
}
```

```
void onEndCalibration(int userId, boolean successful) {
  if (successful) {
    println("  User calibrated !!!");
    kinect.startTrackingSkeleton(userId);

  } else {
    println("  Failed to calibrate user !!!");
    kinect.startPoseDetection("Psi", userId);
  }
}

void onStartPose(String pose, int userId) {
  println("Started pose for user");
  kinect.stopPoseDetection(userId);
  kinect.requestCalibrationSkeleton(userId, true);
}
```

This sketch implements the necessary steps for performing user tracking. Once a user has been detected and successfully calibrated, it uses the joint position data to have a red circle track the user's right hand.

The first of these steps is to tell OpenNI that we want to turn on user tracking. That happens within setup with this line: kinect.enableUser(SimpleOpenNI. SKEL_PROFILE_ALL). Just as we've previously called kinect.enableDepth and kinect.enableRGB when we wanted to access the depth and color images from the Kinect, we're now telling OpenNI that we also want to access the skeleton data. Unlike those other enabling functions, this one takes an argument, SimpleOpenNI.SKEL_PROFILE_ALL. SimpleOpenNI.SKEL_PROFILE_ALL is a constant that tells SimpleOpenNI that we want to track all of the joints in the user's skeleton. There are some other options available for this, but in nearly all cases, you'll want to track the full skeleton, so you'll always pass this argument when you call enableUser.

This addition to setup is only the first of many new pieces of code that we'll explore as we come to understand how to work with the user-tracking data. We'll go through the code in this sketch thoroughly as we proceed through this chapter, but first you should actually run it and learn how to get OpenNI to track you. When you run this sketch, what you see looks like it's just the plain depth image. The sketch will only draw on top of this depth image once it has detected a user. Before anything as exciting as that happens, though, you have to perform the calibration ritual.

A Note About Calibration

In order for OpenNI's algorithm to begin tracking a person's joints, it needs the person to be standing in a known pose. Specifically, you have to stand with your feet together and your arms raised above your shoulders on the sides of your head. This pose is known by various names. In the technical literature and in PrimeSense's own documentation it is called the "Psi" pose. Other designers refer to it as the "submissive" pose because of its close resemblance to the position you'd assume if someone pointed a gun at you.

By whatever name, this calibration pose always stimulates a lot of discussion among designers working with the Kinect. Sometimes it is simply an inconvenience. If you have an idea that requires tracking people as they go about their normal activities, requiring them to stop and perform an explicit calibration can be an awkward obstacle. On the other hand, others are bothered by the potential for tracking without an explicit calibration. The idea that body-tracking cameras might observe your every move without your knowledge, perhaps while you're in a public space, is potentially disturbing. And the police or military resonances of the "submissive" pose don't do anything to calm this concern.

No matter your particular application or your particular interpretation of these issues, they deserve design attention. You may be surprised at how strongly users react to going through calibration.

There is one potential solution to this problem, however. OpenNI does have the ability to track users without the need for explicit calibration under certain circumstances. OpenNI can record the calibration data from a single user and then use that to calibrate other users of similar body type. This technique is somewhat complex and won't work in all situations—for example, if you expect a broad range of different people to use your application including both kids and adults, men and women, etc. Due to its complexity, we won't be covering the use of stored calibration data in this chapter. However, I have included two example sketches in the Appendix that demonstrate the process. The first example sketch, Example A-3, will record a *.skel* calibration file and the second, Example A-4, will load up that file in place of the usual calibration process.

So, how does the calibration actually work in practice? As users, what do we have to do to get OpenNI to track us? And what code do we have to write to get the process to take place? Let's walk through the process of calibration, looking both at the actions performed by the user and the parts of our sketch that run along the way.

Stages in the Calibration Process

Before we get into the nitty-gritty of code, I want to give you an overall picture of how calibration works (Figure 4-1). The diagram shows the flow of callbacks triggered by OpenNI and the actions that we have to take within them to continue the calibration process. I'll briefly explain the complete picture and then we'll dive into the actual code within our sketch to see how the whole system works in practice.

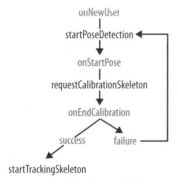

Figure 4-1. *Flow of OpenNI actions and callbacks needed to initiate joint tracking.*

Calibration is a back-and-forth process between our sketch and OpenNI. At each step, OpenNI will trigger one of our callback functions. Then, within that function, we need to perform an action to continue the process. This action will trigger the next callback in turn, and so on.

The three stages of tracking are basic user detection, calibration underway, and fully tracked user. When the sketch first starts running, OpenNI will not be tracking any users. The functions it provides for accessing users will return an empty list. The process begins when a user enters the scene. At that point, OpenNI detects that the user is present and is a candidate for tracking. It calls our sketch's onNewUser function. Within that function, we can initiate the tracking process by calling startPoseDetection. This function tells OpenNI to watch the user to see if she has assumed the calibration pose. Once we have detected a user, the list of users within our draw function will begin to be populated. However, joint data will not be available for these users until the calibration process has been completed. Sometime later, as soon as the user assumes the pose, OpenNI will call our sketch's onStartPose function. Then, to continue the calibration process, we need to call requestCalibrationSkeleton. This function triggers OpenNI's actual skeleton detection process. When this process completes, OpenNI will report back by calling yet another callback, our sketch's onEndCalibration function. The calibration process isn't always successful. Within this callback, OpenNI will report the status of the calibration. If it's successful, we can call startTrackingSkeleton to begin accessing the joint data from the user. If calibration fails, we can restart the process by calling startPoseDetection again. We might want to give the user additional onscreen feedback before doing so to improve the chances of a successful calibration.

So, now you know the overall steps: user detection followed by calibration, and finally initializing joint tracking. We're now going to dive more deeply into each step to look at the code that implements it, both in these callback functions and where we use the skeleton data within draw.

User Detection

As I indicated, the process begins when a user enters the view of the depth camera. When the user appears, OpenNI recognizes that a user is present. At this point, the user has not been calibrated and his joint data is not available. OpenNI basically has a hunch that someone is moving around within the view of the depth camera. OpenNI calls our sketch's onNewUser function.

Depending on the conditions of the scene, this can happen sooner than you might expect. OpenNI can detect the presence of a user even when not much of his body has entered the frame. For example, Figure 4-2 shows a screen capture from this sketch that was taken at the moment OpenNI first detected me. You can see that I've barely entered the frame on the left. My arm and part of my chest are visible, but not much else.

Let's look at the code for this callback. What does our sketch do when OpenNI detects a new user?

```
void onNewUser(int userId) {
  println("start pose detection");  ❶
  kinect.startPoseDetection("Psi", userId);  ❷
}
```

Figure 4-2. *OpenNI can tell that a user is in the scene very early. This screen capture was taken from within the onNewUser callback, and you can see I've barely entered the frame on the left.*

The first thing to note is that onNewUser takes an argument, an integer representing the ID of the user detected. OpenNI can track multiple people simultaneously. All users are given unique IDs to keep them distinct from the other users that you are tracking. In my experience, applications that track more than one or two users are relatively rare. However, you may have to work with the user ID if you want your sketch to track two people and give them different roles. For example, maybe you want the first user who arrives to control a particular graphic that represents her on screen and the second user to control a different one. To accomplish that, you'd just use the ID of each tracked user to position the graphic appropriately within your draw function.

Shortly, we'll look at how our draw function accesses the list of users that have been detected so we can get at those IDs. But first, let's look at what we actually need to do within onNewUser to keep the calibration process rolling.

❶ The first line within that function simply prints out a line to Processing's console to report what's happening. The calibration process can be frustrating without feedback. You can find yourself standing in front of your Kinect and fussing with your position and your pose, wondering if OpenNI can see you and is attempting to calibrate you. Having a println statement at each step gives us feedback to let us know where we are in the calibration process. It makes debugging dramatically less frustrating. When you begin to write an application that you intend for others to use, you will very likely want to substitute these calls to println with other code that provides onscreen feedback along with clear instructions so that your users don't experience this same frustration.

❷ After this status report, the only other line of code within onNewUser is this line, which tells OpenNI to begin checking to see if the given user is in the named pose. In this case, we're looking for the Psi calibration pose, the T-shaped pose I described earlier. OpenNI will look to see if the user has assumed this pose. When they have, it will call our next callback function, onStartPose.

Once onNewUser has been triggered, user data will become available within draw for the first time. Before we proceed to the next step in the calibration process, let's look at how we access this user data.

Take a look back at the draw function from the sketch. The first three lines of draw will look familiar to you from nearly every sketch in the first chapter of this book. We start off by getting the next frame of depth information from the Kinect and then we display the depth image on the screen. Once we've done that, we start into new territory. As I warned in the introduction to this chapter, accessing the joint data is going to involve a few new programming concepts. And here we're about to see one of them.

Up to this point, whenever we wanted data from a function, whether it be a function built into SimpleOpenNI for accessing Kinect data, a core Processing function, or a function from an external library like Minim, we've always gotten it using the same two steps: call the function, then store the return value into a variable. Take, for example, the second line of this draw function:

```
PImage depth = kinect.depthImage();
```

That line of code calls a function on the kinect object called depthImage. This function returns a PImage object containing the depth data captured from the Kinect. We then store this result into a local variable named depth. This should be the most mundane thing in the world to you. It's something we do constantly throughout each sketch to the point where we barely even notice it.

However, frequently with OpenNI we have to do things differently. Instead of calling a function and then storing its return value, OpenNI requires us to take a different approach. We have to create the variable where we want the results to be stored first. Then we hand that variable to an OpenNI function by passing it in as an argument. OpenNI will then store the data we wanted into that variable, and we can then proceed to use it as normal.

Dealing with this approach is like visiting a fried chicken restaurant where you are required to bring your own bucket. In most fried chicken restaurants, you place your order by naming an item from the menu (i.e., calling a function). When your order is ready, the restaurant's employees simply hand you a bucket with your order inside it (the return value), and you proceed to eat your fried chicken. In this alternate approach, however, the fried chicken restaurant does not provide its own buckets. When you place your order, you also have to hand them your own bucket that you brought from home (the variable that you've already declared and initialized). The restaurant employees will then take your bucket in the back, fill it with chicken, and return it to you. After this step, the two approaches converge. You take your chicken-filled bucket back to a table and proceed to eat the chicken (use the data in the rest of your application).

We've seen what the normal approach looks like in code. Now let's look at this second approach. The next lines in draw provide an example:

```
IntVector userList = new IntVector(); ❶
kinect.getUsers(userList); ❷
```

We want to ask OpenNI to give us a list of all of the users that it is currently tracking. OpenNI represents users as integers. Each user gets assigned a unique integer as his *user ID*. We've already seen user IDs in use within the

Chapter 4

onNewUser callback function. That function took an integer called userId as an argument. Once a user has been detected, the integer that was received in onNewUser will show up in the list of users OpenNI provides.

How do we get this list of users from OpenNI? Well, we know from the fried chicken metaphor that we'll have to provide our own bucket. So, the first thing we do is to initialize a variable that can hold a list of integers. We'll then pass this variable to one of SimpleOpenNI's functions, which will populate it for us with user IDs. These two actions are exactly what the code snippet above does.

❶ The first line creates a variable called userList to store the user IDs. This variable is declared as an IntVector. This is a special type of variable provided by OpenNI specifically to store lists of integers representing user IDs. We've encountered vectors before. In fact, we worked with them extensively last chapter. At that point, I told you that vectors are used to represent points in space. We used PVectors to store the x-, y-, and z-coordinates of the 3D position of each point in our point cloud. In this context, though, we're not using a vector to store a point in space. We're just using it to store a list of integers representing user IDs.

❷ Now that we've declared our IntVector, we need to give it to OpenNI so OpenNI call fill it with the IDs of the actual users being tracked. This is just what we do on this line. The getUsers function will put all of the user IDs that OpenNI knows about into the IntVector that's passed into it as an argument. Notice that there is no return value from this function. We don't assign our variable to the function's output. This is a fundamental difference to the conventional way of accessing data we've become used to. After this line, userList will contain whatever user IDs there were to be had from OpenNI. We've got our bucket back and we can go eat our fried chicken.

Warning

At first these two different uses might seem completely separate. However, they're more similar than they might initially appear. PVectors and IntVectors both store multiple numbers together in a single variable. PVectors gives names to these numbers. Rather than just storing a list of numbers, it gives each number a label: x, y, or z. When we're using a PVector, we can access each number by this label to read or set its value. IntVector doesn't label its values. There are no x, y, and z components of an IntVector to access. Instead an IntVector keeps its values in a set order. You can access the values by the order in which they were added to the vector, asking for the first, second, or sixth one specifically. This is something you can't do with a PVector. You may be asking yourself, how is an IntVector different from Processing's built-in array type? Why go to all this trouble to create a new type to just store an ordered list of numbers when array already does that? Processing's arrays store a fixed quantity of items. When you declare an array, you have to tell Processing how many items you plan to store in the array and then you can never exceed that number. However, we don't know in advance how many users OpenNI is going to end up tracking. It might start off with one then suddenly add three more in rapid succession. Unlike array, IntVector has the ability to grow in size with the addition of more elements. This makes it the perfect match for the list of user IDs tracked by the Kinect.

However, at this point in the calibration process, the fried chicken is not all that tasty. We have detected the presence of a user, but we don't actually have access to the position of her joints. We won't have that until we complete the calibration process. In draw, our code that accesses the user's joint positions is surrounded by two if statements. We can only access those positions if we are tracking a user and we have completed calibrating them. We've now made it past the first of these guards: we now have a userList that contains one user ID. However, we've yet to begin tracking any of the users represented by those IDs. The next three lines in draw implement these two if statements:

```
if (userList.size() > 0) { ❶
  int userId = userList.get(0); ❷

  if ( kinect.isTrackingSkeleton(userId)) { ❸
  ...
```

❶ At our current stage of calibration, the first if statement here will return true. Our userList will contain one integer representing the ID of the user we've detected.

❷ Here, we'll access that ID, pulling the first element out of our IntVector by calling userList.get(0). This userId will now be set to the same integer that was passed in to our onNewUser callback function.

❸ We now check to see if that user has been successfully calibrated. To do that, we call kinect.isTrackingSkeleton(userId). This function returns true only if the calibration process has been completed and joint data is available for the user. Since we have not completed the calibration process yet, it will return false for now, and draw will complete without accessing any of the joint information or drawing anything on top of the depth image.

Let's continue with the next steps of the calibration process so that we can begin tracking a user's skeleton and get this second if statement to return true. To do that, we have to implement two additional callbacks: onStartPose and onEndCalibration. We'll start by looking at onStartPose.

OpenNI triggers onStartPose as soon as it thinks the user has assumed the calibration pose. Figure 4-3 shows a screen capture taken of me at the moment of this event. You can see from looking at that image that my arms are not yet even fully above my head. Again, OpenNI is very fast on the draw. I haven't even fully assumed the calibration pose and OpenNI has already begun the calibration process.

What do we have to do within our onStartPose function? Let's take a look at the code to see:

```
void onStartPose(String pose, int userId) { ❶
  println("Saw start pose. Starting calibration"); ❷
  kinect.stopPoseDetection(userId); ❸
  kinect.requestCalibrationSkeleton(userId, true); ❹
}
```

Figure 4-3. *This screen capture was taken from within the onStartPose callback. OpenNI can tell that I'm in the start pose even though I don't have my arms fully in position.*

❶ The first thing to notice here is that unlike onNewUser, onStartPose takes two arguments. We still get passed the ID of the user being tracked, but now the first argument is the name of the pose in which the user has been found. In onNewUser we told OpenNI that we wanted to know when the user was in the Psi pose. We passed that in as an argument: kinect.startPoseDetection("Psi", userId). Hypothetically, this system can work with other calibration poses besides the Psi pose. For example, how would you calibrate a user who could not stand up or couldn't raise her arms because of a medical condition? In theory, OpenNI can use different calibration poses to overcome situations like these. The name of the pose that arrives here will correspond to the one set in onNewUser where we called kinect.startPoseDetection("Psi", userId). Since we always set Psi as the first argument to startPoseDetection, we'll always receive Psi as the argument here.

❷ As before, we begin the actual body of this function by printing out a line to the console as a signal that this event has begun. Just as we discussed with onNewUser, this would be a good thing to replace with more explicit visual feedback to let our users know that calibration has begun and that they should hold their pose.

❸ Next, we tell OpenNI to stop pose detection for the current user. If we don't call kinect.stopPoseDetection, OpenNI will continue checking to see if our user has assumed the calibration pose. Whenever it finds the user in that pose, it will call onStartPose again, causing significant confusion if we're already tracking that user successfully.

❹ The calibration "skeleton" is what we call the complete collection of the user's joints. When we call kinect.requestCalibrationSkeleton we tell OpenNI that we want it to begin finding all of this user's joint positions from here on out. Since OpenNI knows that the user is currently holding the calibration pose, it can use that information to calibrate its skeleton-tracking algorithm to the specifics of a user's body. Not everyone's arms are the same length, some people have longer torsos than others, some people are wider around the middle. All of these details affect OpenNI's ability to track a person's joints. By having a user stand in a known position during calibration, such as the Psi pose, OpenNI is able to adjust all of its assumptions about the shape of a person to fit the current user's actual body type. The standardization of the pose makes it so OpenNI can measure the length of your arms, the size of your torso, and how wide you are around. OpenNI will then use this information to make its tracking of all of the joints in your skeleton faster and more accurate.

This calibration process takes a little bit of time. When it is complete, OpenNI will trigger our final callback, onEndCalibration. The work we did in onStartPose didn't affect the results of our draw function at all. We have still not actually begun tracking any users, so kinect.isTrackingSkeleton will still return false, and none of the code that access the individual joint positions will run. After this last callback runs, that will change. When calibration ends, if it concludes successfully, we'll have begun tracking the user's skeleton, and the joint position data will become available to the rest of our sketch.

We'll start our discussion of onEndCalibration just as we have the last two callbacks: by looking at a screenshot of the depth image at the moment that the callback runs. Figure 4-4 shows me at the moment that onEndCalibration ran. I'm clearly in the Psi pose. My arms are raised so that they extend horizontally from my shoulders and they're bent at the elbows to complete the stick-'em-up appearance of the pose.

Figure 4-4. *This screen capture was taken from within the onEndCalibration callback. I'm clearly holding the calibration pose.*

Let's take a look at the code for this callback.

```
void onEndCalibration(int userId, boolean successful) { ❶
  if (successful) { ❷
    println(" User calibrated !!!");
    kinect.startTrackingSkeleton(userId);
  } else { ❸
    println(" Failed to calibrate user !!!");
    kinect.startPoseDetection("Psi", userId);
  }
}
```

❶ The first thing to notice is the arguments that get passed to this function. Like onStartPose, onEndCalibration takes two arguments. Unlike onStartPose, we actually need the information contained in both of these arguments. The first argument is the userId. Just as we've seen in the previous two callback functions (and within draw), this lets us distinguish which user just completed calibration if multiple users are on the scene. As before, we'll need to pass this userId through to other OpenNI functions to complete or continue the calibration process.

The second argument, successful, is the more interesting one. It is a Boolean variable that tells us whether or not the user was successfully calibrated. If the calibration was successful, then skeleton data will be available for the user, and we can begin using it in draw to build our actual interface. However, calibration can also fail. This can happen for a number of reasons. For example, a user might be positioned within the depth image in such a way that the Kinect can't see enough of his body for OpenNI to perform the calibration. If enough of the user's body is obscured, the process of matching up the specifics of this user's anatomy to OpenNI's basic idea of how a person should be shaped can fail. Less commonly, the calibration can fail if the user is of especially unusually stature, for example, if they are extraordinarily tall. I have a friend who is extraordinarily tall and skinny. He's 6'6" and under 200 pounds. Getting OpenNI to successfully calibrate his skeleton was extremely difficult. He would hold the calibration pose for a long time while multiple calibration attempts reported back failure. If you or your target user have an especially unusual body type and you find that you're having trouble with repeated failed calibrations, I recommend using a stored calibration file using the sketches provided in Examples A-3 and A-4. What we do in this function is going to depend on whether calibration succeeded or failed. The body of onEndCalibration is structured around an if statement based on the succeeded Boolean that OpenNI passes in to us.

❷ If calibration was successful, then we go into the first branch of the if statement. There, we kick off skeleton tracking by calling kinect.startTrackingSkeleton(userId). After calling that function, joint position data will become available for our user within draw. At this point, we have completed our journey through the calibration process and the attendant callback functions. They won't get triggered again during the running of the sketch unless a new user appears on the scene needing calibration (or our first user leaves the scene and needs to be recalibrated). Let's turn our attention back to draw to see how to work with the skeleton data after it finally becomes accessible.

❸ If calibration failed, succeeded will be false, and we'll go into the else branch of the if statement. What we do there is restart the calibration process. We call kinect.startPoseDetection("Psi", userId) to tell OpenNI to restart the process of checking to see if the user is in the calibration pose. If you look back at Figure 4-1, you can see that, in the case of failure, the calibration process becomes a loop. It jumps back to the pose detection phase and then continues again. When the user assumes the calibration pose (or continues to hold it), our onStartPose function will get called again, and if we keep the process going, eventually onEndCalibration will be called as well. However, if we don't instruct the user to move around or otherwise attempt to correct the problem, it is unlikely that the calibration process will achieve a different result. For that reason, it is once again a good idea to give users some visual feedback or instructions to make sure that they are fully visible within the depth image and standing still so that the calibration process has a chance to succeed.

This loop from startPoseDetection through to onEndCalibration will continue forever until we successfully calibrate the user or terminate the sketch.

Accessing Joint Positions

When we last left draw, we'd successfully accessed our tracked user from the list of users provided by OpenNI, but skeleton data was not yet available, so we were not able to proceed. Now that we've finished calibrating our user, the tables have turned—kinect.isTrackingSkeleton(userId) will return true and we'll be able to enter the inner if statement. From here on out, our job is to actually use the skeleton data provided by OpenNI to build an interface.

In this sketch, we're going to create the simplest interface possible: a red dot that follows your right hand. Creating this interface will take three steps. First we have to get the position of the right hand from OpenNI. OpenNI will give us this position in "real-world" coordinates. These are coordinates that are designed to correspond to the physical position of your body in the room. In other words, they would match the point clouds that we drew in the last chapter. If we positioned a sphere within one of those point clouds based on this joint data, it would show up where we expected it to, matching the position of your hand relative to the other objects in the point cloud. However, in this case, we're going to display the joint position on top of the two-dimensional depth image. We want the joint to show up over the corresponding body part in the depth image. To achieve this, we need to translate the real-world coordinates given to us by OpenNI into "projective" coordinates that match the two-dimensional depth image. We'll use one of SimpleOpenNI's helper functions to do this. Finally, once we have these converted coordinates in hand, we can use them to display a red dot on top of our depth image that will precisely match the position of the joint being tracked. You'll be able to wave your right hand around and the red dot will follow.

Let's look at the code for the first step:

```
PVector rightHand = new PVector();  ❶
kinect.getJointPositionSkeleton(userId,  ❷
                        SimpleOpenNI.SKEL_LEFT_HAND,
                        rightHand);
```

These two lines use the same pattern for accessing data from OpenNI that we observed above: first create a variable, then pass it into OpenNI to be populated.

❶ The first line creates a `PVector` to store the joint position.

❷ On the second line, we pass that variable into `getJointPositionSkeleton` along with the user ID and a constant indicating which joint we'd like to access. This function call tells OpenNI to grab the left hand joint from the user's skeleton and store its position in our `PVector`. After these lines, that variable will be set with the position of our skeleton's hand joint and we'll be able to use it in the next steps required to display our red dot.

One thing you might be asking is: didn't we say we were going to be tracking the right hand? This code seems to be asking for the position of the *left* hand. It passes the constant `SimpleOpenNI.SKEL_LEFT_HAND` to `kinect.getJointPositionSkeleton`. In other words, it's asking OpenNI for the position of the skeleton's left hand joint, but then saves this position into a variable named `rightHand`. What's going on here? Have I gotten dyslexic?

The answer is that OpenNI thinks of the orientation of the joints from the screen's point-of-view rather than the user's. Since the user is facing the Kinect, her right hand will show up on the left side of the screen. Therefore OpenNI refers to it as the left hand. This flipped orientation holds for all of the joints with left-right pairs: hands, arms, legs, etc. (We'll look more closely at OpenNI anatomy in the next section of this chapter when we learn how to draw the full skeleton.)

Now that we've got the position of the right hand, we need to convert it into coordinates that will match the depth image. How can there be two different sets of coordinates for the same object? And what does it mean to convert between the two?

Imagine that you have an object out in front of you in the real world, say a giant sphere as in Figure 4-5. And then imagine that you put a camera on a tripod somewhere in front of the sphere and snapped a picture. As you stood out in the field looking back and forth between the giant sphere itself and the picture you just took of it, what you would get is two representations of the same object in two different coordinate systems. First of all, there's the actual sphere out in space. You could describe its position in three dimensions relative to the wider world. This position corresponds to the `rightHand` variable that we just set. That `PVector` has three components that describe the position of the user's right hand relative to the full reconstructed 3D space that the Kinect can see. Those are the same as the coordinates that we worked with extensively in the last chapter while drawing point clouds.

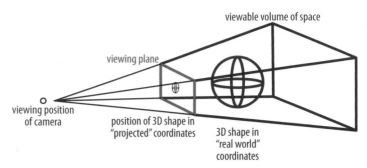

Figure 4-5. *The relationship between projective and real-world coordinates. Real-world coordinates locate the object in 3D space. Projective coordinates describe where you'd see it on the viewing plane.*

But we've also got a second representation of the position of that sphere: its location in the picture we just took with our make-believe camera. That picture is a two-dimensional image that represents the full three-dimensional space as seen from one particular point of view. That's why we call this kind of view a "projection." It collapses the scene onto a plane extending out from the camera. The x- and y-coordinates of the sphere on this plane will be determined by its x- and y-coordinates in the real world, but they won't correspond exactly. And the plane doesn't have a z-axis. Instead, as the sphere moves closer and farther from the plane, its image will grow and shrink and the rate at which its x- and y-coordinates change will increase and decrease.

Imagine you are standing at a window watching a dog run around in a yard outside. Put your finger on the window and move it around so it tracks the spot where you see the dog. While the dog moves around in three dimensions, your finger will track its position on the 2D surface of the window. As the dog runs left and right, your finger will move left and right along the window. If the dog turns and runs straight away from the window, your finger will move up slightly. If the dog runs side to side when it is far away, you won't have to move as far to track it as you did when it was close by. The dog's distance from the window affects how far it appears to move on the window even if it is actually covering the same amount of grass out there in the real yard.

So there's a relationship between the actual position of the dog in the real world and the position where you find it on the window. Or, in the vocabulary of coordinate systems, there's a relationship between the dog's location in the real world and its position in projective space. And this is also true of the objects we see in the Kinect's depth image.

This relationship is highly convenient since our goal is to draw the joint position on top of the depth image so that it matches up with the location of the user's right hand in the depth image. The depth image sits in the same position as the snapshot in our diagram, in projective space, whereas the joint position is behind the snapshot out there in real-world space. To get the two to line up, we need to translate the joint position from real-world coordinates to projective coordinates. Thankfully, SimpleOpenNI gives us a function for doing just that, unsurprisingly named `convertRealWorldToProjective`:

```
PVector convertedRightHand = new PVector();
kinect.convertRealWorldToProjective(rightHand, convertedRightHand);
```

This function works just like the last few we've seen. It takes our new PVector, convertedRightHand, and stores in it the result of the conversion of right-Hand into projective coordinates. This pattern should be starting to get familiar to you. After we've run convertRealWorldToProjective, convertedRight-Hand will match up with the position of the user's hand in the depth image. So, all we have left to do to finish our sketch is to use that vector to display a red dot. Doing this is the simplest code in the sketch, good old ellipse:

```
ellipse(convertedRightHand.x, convertedRightHand.y, 10, 10);
```

Figure 4-6 shows the results: the red ellipse appears exactly on top of my right hand. And as I swing my hand around, it stays locked to my hand perfectly.

Figure 4-6. *The red dot shows up immediately after the completion of calibration, and our sketch begins receiving joint data. Having been converted from real-world to projective coordinates, the joint position vector matches up with the position of the user's hand in the depth image.*

This completes our walkthrough of this sketch. I've explained every line of it and every detail of the skeleton-tracking process. You've learned how to calibrate users so that their skeletons can be tracked and how to access the positions of their joints after they become available. You've seen how to convert that data so you can work with it in 2D coordinates that match the depth image with which you're already thoroughly familiar. Some of these tasks, especially the calibration process, were somewhat complex and fiddly. But thankfully, they'll remain the same for all of our sketches that access the skeleton data from here on out. You'll never have to rewrite these calibration callbacks from scratch again; you can just copy and paste them from this sketch, though, as discussed, you might want to augment them so that they give the user additional feedback about the calibration process.

Shortly, we'll move on to doing some more advanced things with the joint data: displaying the full skeleton and learning how to make measurements between various joints. But first we have a few loose ends to tie up here. There are a couple of lingering questions from this first skeleton sketch, just beneath the surface of our current code. We'll explore these mysteries by putting together two variations of the current sketch.

The first question that arises when we look at our sketch in its current form is: what happened to the information about the distance of the user's right hand? As it currently stands, our red dot tracks the user's hand as it moves around left and right and up and down, but if the users moves his hand closer to the Kinect or farther away, the dot doesn't respond at all. We certainly have information about the distance of the user's hand. The PVector returned by getJointPositionSkeleton has x-, y-, and z-components. But right now, we're just ignoring the z-component of this vector.

How can we use the z-coordinate of the joint position when we're already projecting it onto a two-dimensional plane so that it corresponds with the depth image? We don't want to literally move the red dot forward or backward in space. That would cause it to lose its registration with the depth image. Instead, we could represent the recession of the user's hand in space using an old track from traditional perspective drawing: we can scale the size of the ellipse. The most basic principle of perspective is that objects that are closer appear larger than those that are farther away. We can recreate this effect without moving our ellipse out of the projective plane by simply making it larger as the user's hand gets closer and smaller as it gets farther away.

You may already be thinking to yourself: this sounds like a job for map. Exactamundo! We want to link the size of the ellipse to the distance of the user's hand from the Kinect, and map will let us do just that, outputting a number that corresponds to the distance of the hand but works as the size of the ellipse. Here's the code to add to the sketch:

```
float ellipseSize = map(convertedRightHand.z, 700, 2500,  50, 1);
ellipse(convertedRightHand.x, convertedRightHand.y,
        ellipseSize, ellipseSize);
```

Those two lines replace one line: the call to ellipse at the end of the inner if statement inside of draw (right below the comment // and display it). The numbers 700 and 2500 are relatively arbitrary. I discovered them by printing out convertedRightHand.z with println and observing the results as I moved my hand around. The 700 was around the smallest number I saw and 2500 around the largest. Notice that the smallest z-value represents the closest point to the Kinect and so corresponds to the largest size of the ellipse, and vice versa for the largest z-value: in perspective, closer objects appear larger than more distant ones.

Once I added this scaling code to my sketch, the red dot became responsive to the distance of my hand as well as its x-y position. Figure 4-7 shows two screen captures from this altered sketch. The left half shows the ellipse scaled down to nearly its smallest size as my hand is far away from the Kinect, and the right side shows me lunging forward, pushing the ellipse up to its largest size.

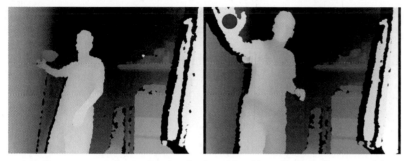

Figure 4-7. *Two screen captures showing the hand-tracking ellipse scaling up and down in size as the user's hand moves toward and away from the Kinect.*

This change solves the first of the two mysteries I described, but the second one still remains outstanding. That mystery is: what happens when OpenNI loses track of the user's right hand?

This mystery is easily solved with an experiment. Perform the calibration ritual so that the sketch is tracking your right hand. Then assume a pose where your hand is invisible to the depth camera. Figure 4-8 shows an example of me executing this experiment. In the screen capture on the left, my hand is clearly visible within the depth image and the red dot is correctly positioned right on top of my hand. In the screen capture on the left, on the other hand, I've hidden my right hand behind my back. What happened to the red dot that our code positions based on OpenNI's report on the position of my hand? It is floating off to the left, near where my hand was when it was last visible in the depth image. When OpenNI stopped being able to see my hand, it first froze in place. It kept reporting back a position near where it had last seen my hand. Then, after a little bit of time passed, it began reporting semirandom positions around the side of my torso, causing the red dot to jitter around the sketch.

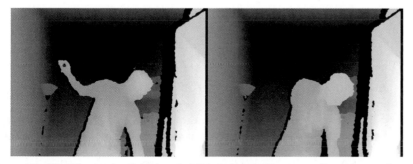

Figure 4-8. *When the tracked joint is not visible to the depth camera, OpenNI cannot update its position with new information. It reports back this problem as the "confidence" level of the joint.*

If OpenNI can't see the part of the depth image that includes the joint being tracked, it can't calculate the position of that joint. Skeleton tracking isn't magic. It is just code that processes the depth image just like the code that we wrote in the first chapter of this book, if much more sophisticated. OpenNI's skeleton tracking works so well most of the time that it can be easy to slip and forget this and treat it as a magical wonder that can see through objects and around corners. But, as we can see here, that's clearly not the case.

What can we do to deal with this problem? How can we tell if OpenNI is really successfully tracking a joint or has lost its position and is simply guessing? The answer is in `getJointPositionSkeleton`. In addition to telling us where OpenNI thinks the requested joint is currently positioned, this function will tell us how confident OpenNI is in its answer. This confidence value ranges from 0 to 1, with 1 being high confidence and 0 being low confidence. Its value also tends not to be especially subtle, it tends to jump between 0 and 1; either OpenNI knows where the joint is, or it hasn't got a clue.

But wait! How do we extract this confidence value from `getJointPosition-Skeleton`? We're already using that function to set our `rightHand` vector to the position of the user's right hand. How can we use it to simultaneously get the confidence value? OpenNI reports its confidence as the return value of `getJointPositionSkeleton`. When we've used `getJointPositionSkeleton` previously, we've passed our own vector to it so that it can store the joint's position in that variable. We've completely ignored the function's return value. It turns out that this troublesome technique of requiring that a variable be passed in to store a value has an unanticipated advantage. Since `getJoint-PositionSkeleton` doesn't have to use its return value to report the position of the joint, it can use it instead to report its confidence in that result. And if we find that we care about this confidence value, we can capture it by saving the return value into our own variable. Add this line just before the `ellipse` line you just added:

```
float confidence = kinect.getJointPositionSkeleton(userId,
                                     SimpleOpenNI.SKEL_LEFT_HAND,
                                     rightHand);
```

Once we've captured this confidence value, we can use it to correct the problem of the floating dot we observed in Figure 4-8. Now you need to change the code so that we only draw the dot if the confidence value is high enough. You can do this by wrapping the call to `ellipse` in this `if` statement:

```
if(confidence > 0.5){
  ellipse(convertedRightHand.x, convertedRightHand.y,
        ellipseSize, ellipseSize);
}
```

My choice of 0.5 as a threshold was relatively arbitrary. Again, I started by printing out the confidence value with `println(confidence)` and simply observing the output. I only ever saw values of 0.0 or 1.0. However, that doesn't mean that `confidence` wasn't rapidly passing through some other values close to 0 and 1 or that it couldn't do so in certain edge cases. We don't want the red dot to ever flicker on and off, so I chose 0.5 to give plenty of leeway on either side.

And that solves our second mystery. We now know how to defend ourselves the absence of information about a joint from OpenNI as well as how to apply the z-axis information about the joint's position even while operating on a 2D projection. Now we've truly mastered the basics of working with the skeleton data.

Having accomplished that, it is time to move on to more advanced topics. Our real goal is to use this skeleton data to build better interfaces with which people may use our sketches. Accessing the skeleton data is just the first step on the way to this goal. The next step is to understand the anatomy of the full skeleton. What joints are available? What names does OpenNI give to each joint? How are they connected to each other? How do they correspond to people's real bodies? In the next section I'll show you how to display the full skeleton, and we'll begin familiarizing ourselves with OpenNI's view of anatomy in order to answer these questions. Once we've done that, we'll be ready to learn our first tool for building skeleton-based interfaces: measuring the distance between joints. In the first chapter, we built the simplest gestural interfaces possible. Our sketches used the position of a single point to control them, letting you draw or move photos with your outstretched hand. Now that we have access to the skeleton data, we could recreate these exact applications. They would be even simpler to build and they'd be dramatically more robust. However, with just a little more work we can give our interfaces an additional dimension. Instead of simply basing our interactions on the position of a single joint, we can measure the distance between multiple joints. This distance is a surprisingly flexible and powerful basis for interfaces. It is exactly what lies behind the "pinch and zoom" gesture vocabulary of today's touch-based devices such as the iPhone. Finally, learning how to measure these distances will teach us a whole set of tools for working with vectors that will come in handy as we move toward more advanced work with the skeleton data.

But first, let's learn what goes where in the OpenNI skeleton.

Skeleton Anatomy Lesson

Now that we understand how to access a single joint, it's time to start looking at the whole skeleton. What parts of the user's body can we track? How accurately does OpenNI's sense of these joint positions correspond to a person's actual body?

To answer these questions, I've put together a sketch that accesses every joint in the user's skeleton. It also draws the user's "limbs": lines that connect adjacent joints in order to display the full skeleton. I'll start our skeleton anatomy lesson by showing you the output of this sketch with all of the joints labeled. I'll make some observations about this illustration, noting important details that will come into play as you begin to use the full skeleton in your applications. Then, we'll dive into the code behind this sketch. We'll examine the nitty-gritty details behind accessing each joint, and I'll demonstrate a helper function that's built into OpenNI for drawing limbs.

Let's get started.

Figure 4-9 shows me at the moment of calibration with my full skeleton drawn on top of me. There are red ellipses at the positions OpenNI has provided for my joints and black lines connecting these over my "limbs." This image was captured just after the `onEndCalibration` callback function of the sketch we'll be examining later in this chapter, so I am still holding the calibration pose.

The first thing to notice about this image is which joints I have chosen to connect with limbs. The pattern of connections shown here is the standard one. It is used by PrimeSense in their example applications. Most of these choices seem anatomically correct, but a few are somewhat surprising. For example, it's obviously right to connect the hands to the elbows and the elbows to the shoulders. The same goes for the legs: connecting the feet to the knees and the knees to the hips is a no brainer. But then things diverge somewhat from our usual idea of human anatomy. The torso seems to be made up of two triangles that come together at the center of the chest. We don't really have bones that traverse the torso in that way, let alone limbs. And I don't know about you, but I can't really bend my body at the point where OpenNI has found a joint in the middle of my chest. Also, It appears that my shoulders are connected directly to my neck, but my neck is not at all connected to my hips. In a real human skeleton, the head is connected to the spine, which goes down through the neck and is eventually connected to the pelvis, which makes up both of the hips.

Figure 4-9. *The full skeleton from OpenNI with limbs drawn as black lines and joints as red dots.*

I'm pointing out all of these divergences from medical anatomy to make a single simple point: the joints and limbs tracked by OpenNI are meant to be useful for building interactive applications, not to be anatomically correct. The joints that OpenNI provides are determined by two factors: what the algorithm is able to detect and what is useful to us as programmers. It's important to keep this in mind as you work with the skeleton data. Just as it is easy to slide into thinking of the depth data from the Kinect as magically complete and able to see around corners, when you start working with skeleton data, it's easy to think of it as perfectly matching the user's actual body. Your applications will work better and you'll be less frustrated with your results if you keep in mind the practical constraints and compromises at play.

To take a closer look at these constraints, let's examine how OpenNI names and classifies each joint.

Figure 4-10 starts with the same screen capture as Figure 4-9, but adds text labels to each joint indicating their name as given to them by OpenNI. Later in this chapter I'll show you how these names translate into constants that you can use to access all of these joints just like `SimpleOpenNI.SKEL_LEFT_HAND` (spoiler: just take the name shown here, connect the separate words with underscores, and append `SKEL_` to the front). But first, now that we've got the names of the joints handy, let's make some additional observations about the specifics of the skeleton data.

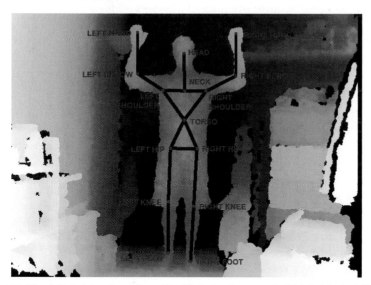

Figure 4-10. *The full skeleton from OpenNI with limbs drawn and all joints labeled. Notice that "left" and "right" refer to screen directions rather than body directions.*

The first thing to note is that some joints are not quite where you'd expect them to be. For example the elbows are too high. `RIGHT ELBOW` and `LEFT ELBOW` are both slightly above and inside of where my actual elbows appear to be in the depth image. On the other hand, the shoulders and the neck are both rather low, with `RIGHT SHOULDER` and `LEFT SHOULDER` a lot closer to where my nipples are than my shoulders. You'll find as you move around with the skeleton data displayed that OpenNI varies in how accurately its positions correspond to your actual body parts. The joint positions don't bounce around unless that's what your body is doing. They aren't noisy. It's just that sometimes they'll end up a little too low or too high or off to one side from the actual joint position. You can count on the joint positions from OpenNI to be within a sphere of about the size of a fist around whatever joint they're meant to represent. This is the limit of the system's accuracy (not counting moments in which OpenNI gets seriously confused and reports back a confidence level of less than `1.0` for a given joint).

The next question is: what about the torso? Now that we have all of the joints labeled, we can see that the two triangles I mentioned above actually connect the shoulders and hips to a joint in the middle of my chest labeled `TORSO`. Further, this `TORSO` "joint" is positioned at a spot in my body where I can't actually bend. What's the idea here? Why does OpenNI structure the data in that way?

Even though you might quibble about whether it should count as a "joint," `TORSO` turns out to be one of the most useful points on the body to be able to track. There are many scenarios where you might want to simply track a user as a whole without worrying about the details of her limbs or head. `TORSO` provides a convenient single point that is nearly always in the middle of the user's overall body area. Also, `TORSO` is probably the joint that is least likely to be obscured from OpenNI. As the user rotates around, hands, elbows, knees, and feet can easily become obscured behind each other or behind the torso itself. Put another way, the confidence level associated with these joints is highly variable. As the user turns around and interacts with objects, the confidence associated with her extremities is quite likely to fall. However, if the user is visible at all within the depth image, OpenNI probably knows the position of the TORSO with a high confidence.

Beyond the TORSO joint in particular, these two inverted triangles and the five joints that make them up (LEFT SHOULDER, RIGHT SHOULDER, LEFT HIP, RIGHT HIP, and TORSO) together describe the user's full torso as a single unit. By examining the orientation of this whole unit and comparing the joints within it, we can figure out a lot about a user's pose. For example, is this torso unit tipped dramatically forward or backward? If so, the user is probably quite off-balance. Are all of these joints oriented toward the left or right of the scene? Then the user is probably looking that way as well.

Moving down from the torso, we have the knees and feet. If you look closely at Figure 4-10, you'll notice that the joints labeled RIGHT FOOT and LEFT FOOT are actually a lot closer to my ankles than my feet. They are situated around my heel at the point where the line extending down from my knee reaches the floor. This is a subtle but important point. The position that OpenNI provides for the feet doesn't tend to capture the fact that our feet project out forward from our lower legs. For OpenNI, "foot" means something more like "bottom of leg." However, as we'll see later in this chapter, since OpenNI does provide orientation information for each joint, we can approximately recreate the presence of the feet by extending another joint out from the RIGHT FOOT and LEFT FOOT in the direction of those joints' orientations.

MORE JOINTS?

Now in addition to the 15 joints shown here, behind the scenes, OpenNI claims to be able to track nine additional joints. These are: WAIST, LEFT ANKLE, RIGHT ANKLE, LEFT COLLAR, RIGHT COLLAR, LEFT WRIST, RIGHT WRIST, LEFT FINGER-TIP, and RIGHT FINGERTIP. However, in my experience and in all of the demo applications I have seen, OpenNI never actually has any data about these joints. The confidence level associated with each of these joints is always 0, and they are never populated with position data. I believe that these joints are only present within OpenNI out of a spirit of future-proofing. All of these additional joints are matched to smaller features of the user's body that are more difficult to track than the 15 already mentioned. Right now, with the Kinect, OpenNI can not actually track these joints. However, there will likely come a time in the near future when higher resolution depth cameras and more sophisticated tracking algorithms make these joints accessible. Since OpenNI is designed to work on a variety of cameras and with a variety of skeleton-tracking algorithms, it supports these joints even though they are not actually trackable with today's technology. One day soon they will be, and OpenNI will be ready. For now, though, we'll ignore these additional joints. I left them off of the anatomy chart above, and we won't include them in any of our other code either.

That completes our skeleton anatomy lesson. Now it's time to look at the actual code behind these screen captures. This sketch builds on our first skeleton tracking example above. I'll present the full code listing, but much of it (especially the calibration callbacks) will be retained from that sketch. In explaining this version of the sketch, I'll focus on the functions that draw the limbs and the joints. When you read through the sketch below it will look at first like there's a lot of drawing code. The new drawSkeleton function has quite a lot of lines in it. However many of those lines are repetitive as there are just a lot of joints to be displayed and a lot of connections to be made between them. OpenNI provides us with data about 15 distinct joints, and the conventional way of connecting them draws 16 limbs between them. That adds up to a lot of lines of code that basically do the same thing over and over for different joints.

So, without further ado, Example 4-1 provides the sketch that draws the full skeleton on top of the depth image.

Example 4-1. skeleton_anatomy.pde

```
import SimpleOpenNI.*;
SimpleOpenNI  kinect;

void setup() {
  kinect = new SimpleOpenNI(this);
  kinect.enableDepth();
  kinect.enableUser(SimpleOpenNI.SKEL_PROFILE_ALL);

  size(640, 480);
  fill(255, 0, 0);
}

void draw() {
  kinect.update();
  image(kinect.depthImage(), 0, 0);

  IntVector userList = new IntVector();
  kinect.getUsers(userList);

  if (userList.size() > 0) {
    int userId = userList.get(0);

    if ( kinect.isTrackingSkeleton(userId)) {
      drawSkeleton(userId);
    }
  }
}

void drawSkeleton(int userId) {
  stroke(0);
  strokeWeight(5);

  kinect.drawLimb(userId, SimpleOpenNI.SKEL_HEAD, ❶
                          SimpleOpenNI.SKEL_NECK);
  kinect.drawLimb(userId, SimpleOpenNI.SKEL_NECK,
                          SimpleOpenNI.SKEL_LEFT_SHOULDER);
  kinect.drawLimb(userId, SimpleOpenNI.SKEL_LEFT_SHOULDER,
                          SimpleOpenNI.SKEL_LEFT_ELBOW);
```

```
        kinect.drawLimb(userId, SimpleOpenNI.SKEL_LEFT_ELBOW,
                        SimpleOpenNI.SKEL_LEFT_HAND);
        kinect.drawLimb(userId, SimpleOpenNI.SKEL_NECK,
                        SimpleOpenNI.SKEL_RIGHT_SHOULDER);
        kinect.drawLimb(userId, SimpleOpenNI.SKEL_RIGHT_SHOULDER,
                        SimpleOpenNI.SKEL_RIGHT_ELBOW);
        kinect.drawLimb(userId, SimpleOpenNI.SKEL_RIGHT_ELBOW,
                        SimpleOpenNI.SKEL_RIGHT_HAND);
        kinect.drawLimb(userId, SimpleOpenNI.SKEL_LEFT_SHOULDER,
                        SimpleOpenNI.SKEL_TORSO);
        kinect.drawLimb(userId, SimpleOpenNI.SKEL_RIGHT_SHOULDER,
                        SimpleOpenNI.SKEL_TORSO);
        kinect.drawLimb(userId, SimpleOpenNI.SKEL_TORSO,
                        SimpleOpenNI.SKEL_LEFT_HIP);
        kinect.drawLimb(userId, SimpleOpenNI.SKEL_LEFT_HIP,
                        SimpleOpenNI.SKEL_LEFT_KNEE);
        kinect.drawLimb(userId, SimpleOpenNI.SKEL_LEFT_KNEE,
                        SimpleOpenNI.SKEL_LEFT_FOOT);
        kinect.drawLimb(userId, SimpleOpenNI.SKEL_TORSO,
                        SimpleOpenNI.SKEL_RIGHT_HIP);
        kinect.drawLimb(userId, SimpleOpenNI.SKEL_RIGHT_HIP,
                        SimpleOpenNI.SKEL_RIGHT_KNEE);
        kinect.drawLimb(userId, SimpleOpenNI.SKEL_RIGHT_KNEE,
                        SimpleOpenNI.SKEL_RIGHT_FOOT);
        kinect.drawLimb(userId, SimpleOpenNI.SKEL_RIGHT_HIP,
                        SimpleOpenNI.SKEL_LEFT_HIP);

        noStroke();

        fill(255,0,0);
        drawJoint(userId, SimpleOpenNI.SKEL_HEAD); ❷
        drawJoint(userId, SimpleOpenNI.SKEL_NECK);
        drawJoint(userId, SimpleOpenNI.SKEL_LEFT_SHOULDER);
        drawJoint(userId, SimpleOpenNI.SKEL_LEFT_ELBOW);
        drawJoint(userId, SimpleOpenNI.SKEL_NECK);
        drawJoint(userId, SimpleOpenNI.SKEL_RIGHT_SHOULDER);
        drawJoint(userId, SimpleOpenNI.SKEL_RIGHT_ELBOW);
        drawJoint(userId, SimpleOpenNI.SKEL_TORSO);
        drawJoint(userId, SimpleOpenNI.SKEL_LEFT_HIP);
        drawJoint(userId, SimpleOpenNI.SKEL_LEFT_KNEE);
        drawJoint(userId, SimpleOpenNI.SKEL_RIGHT_HIP);
        drawJoint(userId, SimpleOpenNI.SKEL_LEFT_FOOT);
        drawJoint(userId, SimpleOpenNI.SKEL_RIGHT_KNEE);
        drawJoint(userId, SimpleOpenNI.SKEL_LEFT_HIP);
        drawJoint(userId, SimpleOpenNI.SKEL_RIGHT_FOOT);
        drawJoint(userId, SimpleOpenNI.SKEL_RIGHT_HAND);
        drawJoint(userId, SimpleOpenNI.SKEL_LEFT_HAND);
}

void drawJoint(int userId, int jointID) { ❸
  PVector joint = new PVector();

  ❹
  float confidence = kinect.getJointPositionSkeleton(userId, jointID,
joint);
  if(confidence < 0.5){
    return; ❺
  }
```

```
    PVector convertedJoint = new PVector();
    kinect.convertRealWorldToProjective(joint, convertedJoint);
    ellipse(convertedJoint.x, convertedJoint.y, 5, 5);
}

// user-tracking callbacks!
void onNewUser(int userId) {
  println("start pose detection");
  kinect.startPoseDetection("Psi", userId);
}

void onEndCalibration(int userId, boolean successful) {
  if (successful) {
    println("  User calibrated !!!");
    kinect.startTrackingSkeleton(userId);
  }
  else {
    println("  Failed to calibrate user !!!");
    kinect.startPoseDetection("Psi", userId);
  }
}

void onStartPose(String pose, int userId) {
  println("Started pose for user");
  kinect.stopPoseDetection(userId);
  kinect.requestCalibrationSkeleton(userId, true);
}
```

Even though the full sketch is quite long, one thing that can be said in its defense is that its draw function is actually dramatically simpler than our previous sketch. We still use two if statements to check to see that a user has been detected and the calibration process has been completed. But then, inside of these if statements, instead of the code that accessed a joint and converted its position into projective space, we find just a single function that takes the userId as an argument:

```
drawSkeleton(userId);
```

Even though this concision is an illusion (all the code we had before and more is still present within the sketch, it has just been shuffled off inside of the drawSkeleton function and another helper we'll examine shortly called draw-Joint), it is a productive one. Rarely in our future sketches will simply drawing the user's skeleton be sufficient. Even though we'll sometimes want to display the skeleton as user feedback (or sometimes only as a debugging mode), we'll always want to do something additional with the skeleton data to implement whatever interface we're using it to construct. Having packed all of the code for displaying the skeleton into this one function will keep our draw function tidy making it easier to add our other application logic. Further, keeping all of the drawing code in a single function like this will make it easy to turn the display of the skeleton on and off as needed with a simple if statement.

Let's look at how drawSkeleton actually works. As I mentioned before, even though it is a very long function, it is not a very complicated one. It only performs two actions (drawing limbs and drawing joints), it just performs each of them repeatedly. To understand it, we'll look at one example of each of these actions. First, let's learn how to draw limbs.

When displaying a user skeleton, a "limb" is just a line that connects two adjacent joints. This is a relatively simple task. In fact it's not much more complex than the drawing of a single joint-following dot that we took on in the last sketch. To draw a limb, all we'd have to do is access two different joint positions storing each one in its own PVector. Then we would pass the x-, y-, and z-components of both vectors as arguments to Processing's line function, which would draw a three-dimensional line connecting the two joints. While none of these steps is particularly complicated, there are a few of them. Drawing one limb would end up being around five lines of code. And don't forget we have 16 limbs to draw. So, we'd quickly end up with over 60 very repetitive lines of code to draw the full skeleton. Clearly, we'd never let this happen and would instead write our own function to handle this repeating need.

❶   Thankfully, the need to draw joints is so common that SimpleOpenNI already provides a helper function for it and we don't have even to go to the trouble of writing it ourselves. We can just call it like this. This is the line of our drawSkeleton function that draws the skeleton's neck, a limb that connects the head joint to the neck joint. Since it's a function provided by SimpleOpenNI itself, we call it on the SimpleOpenNI object that we initialized into our kinect variable. We've been using this variable so much throughout this book that it's easy to lose track of what it actually represents. In addition to providing the actual depth and skeleton data from the Kinect, our SimpleOpenNI object includes some helper functions that don't alter our object's internal state but are useful in different ways. In addition to drawLimb, we recently worked with kinect.convertRealWorldToProjective, which is another example of such a helper.

As you can see from this line, kinect.drawLimb takes three arguments: the ID of the tracked user and two constants that identify joints within the skeleton. Just like in other functions that we've seen, the user ID is a unique integer that OpenNI uses to distinguish between the potentially multiple users it could be tracking. We indicate the joints using a similar system to these numerical user IDs. However, rather than varying with each user we detect, the IDs for the joints are the same across all sketches that use SimpleOpenNI. SimpleOpenNI includes constants for all 15 of the joints that it is capable of accessing. In fact, I've already shown you all of the constants for these joints even though I didn't spell out that fact explicitly at the time. The joint labels in Figure 4-10 correspond directly to the constants by which SimpleOpenNI refers to the joints. To translate between each joint label in that diagram and the real official name of the joint, just add SKEL_ to the front and replace the spaces with underscores. Hence, LEFT ELBOW becomes SimpleOpenNI.SKEL_LEFT_ELBOW, TORSO becomes SimpleOpenNI.SKEL_TORSO, and so on.

Somewhere deep down within OpenNI, each of these constants is defined to be a particular integer. Just which integer is irrelevant. The key is that OpenNI's functions for accessing joint position and joint orientation know how to use these same numbers to give us back data about the right joint. We've already used these constants once in our previous sketch as an argument to kinect.getJointPositionSkeleton. Within drawLimb, SimpleOpenNI uses getJointPositionSkeleton itself to access the location of the joints. The order in which we choose to send the joints to `kinect.drawLimb` is irrelevant. A limb connecting `SimpleOpenNI.SKEL_HEAD` to `SimpleOpenNI.SKEL_NECK` will look exactly like one that connects `SimpleOpenNI.SKEL_NECK` to `SimpleOpenNI.SKEL_HEAD`. And actually there's nothing inside of `drawLimb` that restricts you to drawing sensible joints. If you wanted, you could pass `drawLimb` joints from totally different sides of the body (`SimpleOpenNI.SKEL_HEAD` and `SimpleOpenNI.SKEL_RIGHT_FOOT`, for example), and it would happily draw a line between them even though that line corresponds to no conceivable limb.

One additional nice feature of `drawLimb` is that it takes into consideration the confidence score for the joints that it is connecting. If either of the limbs has too low of a confidence level, `drawLimb` will simply not draw a line at all. This prevents the function from drawing errant limbs that fly all over our sketch. Instead, as you can see in Figure 4-11, limbs corresponding to parts of the user's body that are obscured will simply disappear. In Figure 4-11, you can see that I've hidden my left arm behind my back and am standing with my right leg back behind my left. The result is that my left elbow and hand and my right knee and foot do not show up in the depth image. Hence OpenNI cannot detect those joints with a high enough degree of confidence, so `drawLimb` does not display them.

Figure 4-11. *If the confidence score is too low for the given joints, SimpleOpenNI's drawLimb function will hide the affected limbs—in this case, my left upper and lower arm and my right thigh and shin.*

❷ But what about the joints themselves? SimpleOpenNI does not provide a helper function for displaying them. So, in this sketch, I wrote my own by adapting the code we developed in the previous example. In that sketch we accessed a single joint by name (the `LEFT_HAND`), converted it into projective space so it would match the depth image, and then drew it to the screen. Since we now need to draw 15 joints instead of just 1, I took the code we'd use to draw the `LEFT_HAND` and transformed it into a function. Just like SimpleOpenNI's own `drawLimb`, I defined my `drawJoint` function to use SimpleOpenNI's constants for indicating joint.

Since it's only going to draw the one joint, unlike drawLimb, drawJoint only needs a single joint ID in addition to the user ID in order to have enough information to ask SimpleOpenNI for the joint position.

As I mentioned, drawJoint basically reproduces the steps we had in our previous sketch to access the joint's position and draw it. However, there are a couple of changes that come into play when we move this code into its own helper function. Let's take a look at this function next.

❸ Read through this function, and you should be able to understand just about everything about it since it mostly reproduces lines of code we saw in our last example. The steps involved are: creating a PVector, passing it into SimpleOpenNI to be populated with the position information for the joint requested, confirming that the confidence associated with that position is high enough to continue, converting the joint position into projective coordinates so that it matches the depth image, and then, finally, drawing an ellipse based on those converted coordinates.

❹ The one idiom here that might be slightly confusing is how we perform the confidence check. When our joint drawing code was inside of our draw function, we simply wrapped our call to ellipse inside of an if statement. If confidence exceeded our threshold, we drew the ellipse, if not, we didn't. Now, however, we do that confidence check in the midst of this function. Once we've accessed the position information from getJointPositionSkeleton, we have a confidence value and we know whether or not we will want to draw the ellipse. If the confidence level is too low, there's no reason to proceed, no reason to bother converting the position vector to projective coordinates. What we really want to do is just pull the escape hatch and jump out of the function. And this is just what we do.

❺ So, instead of the if statement we call return, a special key word built into Processing that causes the current function to exit when it is called. If confidence is less than 0.5—in other words, if OpenNI is just guessing about the position of the joint—then this if statement returns true, we call return, and nothing below this point in the function ever happens. We bail out of the function and go on to whatever is next in the sketch. There are other ways of accomplishing this same result, but this technique of using return to exit the function is a common one because it is both clear and efficient. When you see it, you don't have to find your place among arbitrarily nested if statements to understand what will happen. You always know that the function will stop and none of the function's code below the return will get executed.

That brings us to the end of this example. You now understand the two main methods for displaying skeleton data: drawing joints and connecting them with limbs. You know which parts of the body OpenNI can track, you have a sense of how reliably it will report that data and an idea of how to deal with that unreliability in your own code. We've done everything possible with skeleton data besides actually using it for interactions. That's just what we're going to start now. In the next section of this chapter, we'll move from simply displaying the user's skeleton to beginning the building blocks for interaction from users' joint positions and how they move.

Chapter 4

Measuring the Distance Between Two Joints

The atomic unit of interaction is the user-controlled parameter. All satisfying interactions begin with a technique that lets the user directly control some behavior of the system. The button that turns on your lamp. The knob that sets your stereo's volume. The trackpad that positions the mouse pointer on screen. At their essence, most of these controls come down to a single number that is directly under the user's control. That number is then used within the system to determine some aspect of its internal operation. The button determines whether or not current flows to the bulb. The knob sets the amount of gain applied by the amplifier. The trackpad sets the x- and y-coordinates of the mouse pointer. These individual parameters are then combined into more complex elements creating the chemistry of user interaction. But no matter how sophisticated and capable they might get, the best interfaces always retain this sense of direct connection between aspects of the user's input and individual parameters in the system. Even the iPhone's highly advanced pinch-to-zoom gesture is basically keyed off of a single value: the distance between the user's two fingers on the screen.

To start incorporating the skeleton data into our own interactive applications, we need to reduce it down to a single number. We've already seen the suggestion of one technique for doing this earlier in the book. In the first chapter we built sketches that used the position of the user's hand to control a drawing line and to position photos. We could certainly reproduce those interfaces with the skeleton data. However, we also have the opportunity to do something more ambitious. Whereas that closest point technique could only track a single body part, the skeleton data gives us easy access to the user's whole body. We can produce our single interactive parameter from a slightly more complex source: the distance between two joints.

Specifically, we're going to start by measuring the distance between a user's two hands. This will give the user a single simple parameter that he can control in a completely intuitive manner that also lets him take advantage of a set of physical movements and intuitions that are deeply embedded in himself. We spend much of the day picking up objects with both hands, turning them around so we can manipulate and examine them, cradling them in a particular position, etc. We use the distance between our hands to indicate distance and size to each other. We gesture with them as we speak to enhance and underline our communication. And, best of all, the distance between our hands can be reduced to a single number that can easily be hooked up to a wide variety of parameters within our software. Once we've calculated this number, we'll have a plethora of options for how to display it back to the user in our Processing sketch, providing the necessary feedback for a fully interactive application.

So, how do we measure the distance between two joints? The short answer to that question is: vector subtraction. To understand that answer, though, we'll have to dig more deeply into vectors to understand a few subtleties about how they work and what they mean. We'll spend a little time doing that now so you'll have a strong basis for understanding this technique before we actually apply it in code. This work will pay off dramatically as we proceed through the rest of this chapter. After this most basic technique, the more advanced ones that we'll learn are also based in some of these fundamental properties of vectors. Learning enough about vectors to understand vector subtraction will prepare you for understanding the work we'll do later to transfer the angle of one vector to another using dot products and to work with the matrix of multiple vectors that OpenNI provides to represent the orientation of each joint.

Up to this point, we've used vectors to represent positions in space, especially three-dimensional ones. In our code, vectors have mainly been a convenient way of combining the x-, y-, and z-coordinates needed to represent a point in space in a single variable. But vectors can do more than this. Vectors are a general tool for describing distance and direction. I'm going to give you a quick and (hopefully) painless math lesson now that illustrates this idea and shows you some of the cool things that we can do with vectors once we start using them as such.

Before now, we've basically treated vectors as points in space. Each PVector that we've used in our sketches has defined a single point in 3D such as that shown in Figure 4-12. Each of these points has an x-, y-, and z-coordinate that is defined in terms of the larger coordinate system in which it is situated. We've talked extensively about how Processing's coordinate system is oriented, and we've had to deal with disjunctions between its coordinate system and that assumed by SimpleOpenNI. Remember how our point cloud data initially came in upside-down last chapter? That happened because of a mismatch in the coordinate systems. So we know well that a coordinate system consists of two things: an origin and three axes that have positive and negative direction.

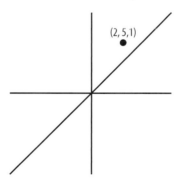

Figure 4-12. *A boring old point in 3D space.*

All this talk of origins and orientation implies a second way of describing a point in space. Instead of just describing it by its three coordinates, what if we thought of each point as a set of instructions that begin at the origin? Instead of treating the point's coordinates like an address, we'll break them down into a direction and distance of travel. Instead of saying "I live at 123 Maple Street," we'll say something like: "face northeast and travel for 1.2 miles."

Figure 4-13 shows a graphical version of this. We've added an arrow from the origin to our point. The direction of the arrow indicates the direction we need to travel to reach the point. The length of the arrow tells us how far we have to travel. This is a step in the right direction, but we need to break things down further. We need a way to describe this direction and distance so that we can work with them individually in code. Now that we're describing our point as a vector, we need to separate it into its constituent components of direction and distance. To do this, we'll use two tools: we'll measure our vector's *magnitude* and we'll calculate its *unit vector*.

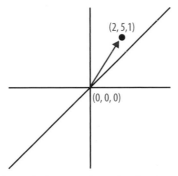

Figure 4-13. *A 3D point reinterpreted as a vector extending from the origin. The vector describes the position of the point as the combination of a direction and a distance.*

For any vector, we can measure its magnitude to figure out its size and we can create a unit vector that describes its direction. Figure 4-14 shows our vector with both its magnitude and unit vector displayed. Let's explore each concept a little bit more to make sure that you understand it.

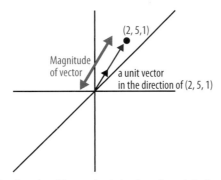

Figure 4-14. *A normalized vector. The vector is broken down into its unit vector, which describes its direction, and its magnitude, which describes the distance it covers.*

Magnitude is simple: it's just the vector's length. Forget that the vector is pointing in any particular direction and treat it as a simple line. How long is that line? That's the magnitude.

The unit vector is a little more complicated. How do you describe a vector's direction without including its magnitude? The answer is that you convert the vector to a standard length: you make it one unit long. The unit vector for our original vector points in the same direction as our original vector but only has a length of one. Since its length is standard, the only distinguishing feature left for a unit vector is its direction. Take any two vectors. Convert each to a unit vector. How will they differ? Only in their direction. They'll both have a length of one, but they'll be pointing in different directions.

Think of a vector as directions for how to get from one point to another. Imagine you were standing at the origin and I wanted to tell you how to walk to our point at 2,5,1. The first thing I would do is tell you what direction to walk. I'd calculate the unit vector in the direction of 2,5,1. The result I'd get would be: 0.365, 0.913, 0.183. If I gave you that, you'd know which direction to go.

You'd have to go mostly up on the y-axis, but a little bit more toward positive-x than positive-z. Once I gave you that unit vector and you turned to face it, you'd be pointing in the right direction, but you'd still be at the origin. Now I'd need to tell you how far to walk. To do that, I'd give you the magnitude. In this case, that would be 5.477. You'd just walk 5.477 steps straight ahead and you'd end up at your destination 2,5,1.

Now that you understand what a unit vector and magnitude are, let's take a look at what it feels like to work with in code. I think you'll be pleasantly surprised at how simple it is. Here's a short code fragment that initializes a PVector corresponding to the vector in our diagram and then breaks down both its magnitude and its unit vector:

```
PVector myVector = new PVector(2,5,1);
float magnitude = myVector.mag();
myVector.normalize();
println("magnitude: " + magnitude);
println("unit vector: " + myVector);
PVector myVector = new PVector(1,2,3);
PVector toNormalize = new PVector(myVector.x, myVector.y, myVector.z);
toNormalize.normalize();
println("before: " + myVector);
println("normalized: " + toNormalize);
```

Warning

Calling normalize *on a* PVector *alters that vector, shortening its length to 1 in order to convert it into a unit vector. If you try to use the vector after calling this function expecting it to be the same, you'll get surprising results. If you need both the original vector and its normalized version, create a second copy of your vector to normalize.*

After calling those two functions on myVector, we've got our two parameters ready to go for use in our interactions. The magnitude is a perfect example of a simple scalar parameter that can be hooked up to an output like we discussed in the beginning of this section. Along with the power of map, we could use it to change brightness, alter positions on screen, change the volume of a sound, or any of dozens of other outputs. Calling normalize on myVector transforms it into a unit vector. Unit vectors also have many uses. We can pass the components of myVector directly to Processing's rotate function to change the orientation of our view or of a 3D shape in space, we could use it to figure out where a virtual gun was pointing in a game, we could use each of its components individually to set the red, green, and blue elements of a color, etc.

But what about vector subtraction? I started this detour into vectors by promising that it would help us in measuring the distance between the user's hands as represented by OpenNI's skeleton data. Each joint in OpenNI is represented by a vector. To find out how two joints are related to each other in space, we subtract the vector representing one from the vector representing the other. The result is a third vector that contains both the distance between the joints and their direction from each other. Figure 4-15 illustrates this situation. That figure shows two vectors representing the theoretical positions of a user's left and right hands as reported by OpenNI. It also shows a third vector connecting these two. That vector is calculated by subtracting one of the hand vectors from the other. In this case, since the third vector is pointing toward the left hand vector, we can tell that it was calculated by subtracting the right hand from the left hand. Our subtraction vector tells us how to move from the right hand back to the left hand.

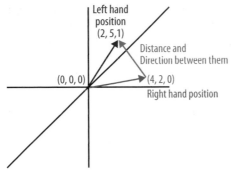

Figure 4-15. *The result of subtracting two vectors is a third vector that takes you from the end point of one to the end point of the other. In this case, it captures the distance and direction between two hands detected by OpenNI.*

There are two things we might want to know about the relative positions of the user's left and right hands: how far apart are they and in what direction? From our earlier discussion of vector normalization, we now know exactly how to extract these two answers from this subtraction vector. We get the distance by calculating the resulting vector's magnitude, and we get the direction by normalizing it into a unit vector.

Let's try using these techniques in an actual sketch with the joint data from OpenNI. We'll start by using what we've learned to access the vectors representing the left and right hands. Then we'll draw a third vector connecting them and we'll measure that vector's magnitude and calculate its direction in the form of a unit vector. Once we have these, we'll connect them to a series of outputs to make the sketch interactive.

Example 4-2 provides the code. Again, about two-thirds of this sketch is the standard skeleton-access code: the setup, the calibration callbacks, and the `if` statements guarding our `draw` loop against trying to access the skeleton data before it becomes available. I'm not going to discuss that stuff this time around. I'm just going to focus on the key bit in the middle where we access the hand positions and use them to create an interface. When you read through this for the first time, try to focus there. You should be able to understand what's happening given the material we just covered. I'll meet you after the code to explain it.

> *There's also a built-in method in* PVector *we can use if all we want to do is find the distance between the hands:* `leftHand.dist(rightHand)`.

Example 4-2. *joint_distance.pde*

```
import SimpleOpenNI.*;
SimpleOpenNI  kinect;

void setup() {
  kinect = new SimpleOpenNI(this);
  kinect.enableDepth();
  kinect.enableUser(SimpleOpenNI.SKEL_PROFILE_ALL);

  size(640, 480);
  stroke(255, 0, 0);
  strokeWeight(5);
  textSize(20);
}
```

```
void draw() {
  kinect.update();
  image(kinect.depthImage(), 0, 0);

  IntVector userList = new IntVector();
  kinect.getUsers(userList);

  if (userList.size() > 0) {
    int userId = userList.get(0);

    if ( kinect.isTrackingSkeleton(userId)) {
      PVector leftHand = new PVector();
      PVector rightHand = new PVector();

      kinect.getJointPositionSkeleton(userId,
                            SimpleOpenNI.SKEL_LEFT_HAND,
                            leftHand);

      kinect.getJointPositionSkeleton(userId,
                            SimpleOpenNI.SKEL_RIGHT_HAND,
                            rightHand);

      // calculate difference by subtracting one vector from another
      PVector differenceVector = PVector.sub(leftHand, rightHand); ❶

      // calculate the distance and direction of the difference vector
      float magnitude = differenceVector.mag(); ❷
      differenceVector.normalize(); ❸

      // draw a line between the two hands
      kinect.drawLimb(userId, SimpleOpenNI.SKEL_LEFT_HAND, ❹
      SimpleOpenNI.SKEL_RIGHT_HAND);
      // display
      pushMatrix(); ❺
        fill(abs(differenceVector.x) * 255, ❻
            abs(differenceVector.y) * 255,
            abs(differenceVector.z) * 255);

        text("m: " + magnitude, 10, 50); ❼
      popMatrix();
    }
  }
}


// user-tracking callbacks!
void onNewUser(int userId) {
  println("start pose detection");
  kinect.startPoseDetection("Psi", userId);
}

void onEndCalibration(int userId, boolean successful) {
  if (successful) {
    println(" User calibrated !!!");
    kinect.startTrackingSkeleton(userId);
  }
  else {
    println(" Failed to calibrate user !!!");
    kinect.startPoseDetection("Psi", userId);
  }
}
```

Chapter 4

```
void onStartPose(String pose, int userId) {
  println("Started pose for user");
  kinect.stopPoseDetection(userId);
  kinect.requestCalibrationSkeleton(userId, true);
}
```

When you run this sketch and perform the calibration ritual, a red line will suddenly connect your two hands and you'll see large text appear in the top left corner of the window. As you move your hands, the line will follow them, keeping them connected. As you move your hands apart, this number will increase, and as you move them together, it will decrease. Also as you rotate your hands around each other, the number will change color, rotating through the full color spectrum as your hands circle each other in three dimensions. Figure 4-16 shows two examples of the result. On the left, my hands are far apart and the number reads near 950. The line is also nearly vertical, which means its unit vector has a high y-component. Since our sketch uses the y-component of the unit vector to set the green component of the text's fill color, that makes the text green. On the right, my hands are closer together so the number is lower, only 630. My hands are also farthest apart in the z-axis, which results in blue text.

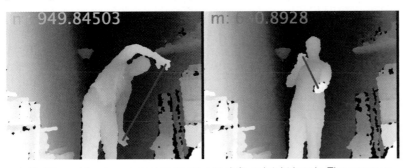

Figure 4-16. *The red line is a vector connecting my left and right hands. The onscreen number is the magnitude of this vector, its orientation determines the color of the text.*

Let's look at the code that creates this interface.

❶ We start in the middle of draw, after we've accessed the left and right hand joints from OpenNI, on line 31 of the sketch. Once we have the two hand vectors, we perform a subtraction between them to get the difference vector. We perform vector subtraction using a class method on PVector called sub. This method takes two vectors as arguments and returns a third one that represents the difference between the two. Just like in conventional subtraction, the order in which we pass the vectors matters. If we passed rightHand before leftHand, the resulting differenceVector would point in just the opposite direction. For now, we're only using the orientation of this differenceVector to set a color, so this issue doesn't matter as much as it might in other situations.

❷ Once we've calculated the differenceVector, we call mag on it to access its magnitude.

❸ Next, we call normalize on the differenceVector to convert it to a unit vector. We must access and store the magnitude of the differenceVector before we normalize it. Remember, normalizing a vector converts it to a unit vector, which means that its magnitude is set to one. normalize alters differenceVector in place instead of returning a different PVector to represent the unit vector, so if we called mag on differenceVector after normalizing it, we'd always get back 1.0 as the answer.

❹ Once we've got the magnitude and unit vector in hand, we're ready to use them in our interface. First, we draw the line connecting our right hand and left hand. This is mostly for the benefit of the users to make the sketch feel more vividly interactive by helping them visualize the distance and direction between their hands. To do this, we use kinect.drawLimb, which we discussed extensively in the last section when drawing the user skeleton.

❺ The rest of our interface takes the form of text in the top left corner of the sketch. Our drawing code for this text is contained in a pushMatrix/popMatrix pair. I did this because I wanted to increase the size of the text so that it would be clearly readable from far away.

❻ Since we just converted differenceVector into a unit vector, we know that each of its components ranges from 0 to 1. Hence we can use the components to scale the red, green, and blue values of a color by simply multiplying each component of the vector by 255 before passing it to fill.

❼ Then finally, we display some text on the screen using Processing's text function. The first argument is a string that we build out of the letter *m* (standing for magnitude) and the actual magnitude of the differenceVector. This means that the magnitude will be constantly displayed on the screen so we can see how it changes as we move our hands around. The other two arguments to this function specify the x- and y-coordinates at which the text should be placed. Since we called textSize(20) inside of setup, our text will be displayed large enough to see.

Now that you've got the hang of creating an interface based on the changes in a vector, let's use this technique to make something a little bit more creative. Right now the output of our sketch is simply an informational display. It uses a line to show the vector we're tracking, text to indicate its size, and color to specify its orientation. However, the ability to set the position, size, weight, and color of a line sounds an awful lot like the controls for a drawing application. With just a few simple changes to our existing sketch we can turn it into a program that lets us do some basic drawing by waving our hands around.

The first change is that we don't want to draw the depth image in the background every time. So remove image(kinect.depthImage, 0, 0) from the top of your draw function. Instead, we'd like to start with a blank canvas to draw on. So, in setup (not in draw!), clear the sketch to white by calling background(255);. While we're at it, let's also get rid of the informational display for the last version of this sketch. All of the lines between pushMatrix and popMatrix are just there to create the numerical display that formerly presented the magnitude and orientation information. Remove them.

Now that we've created a clean starting point for our sketch, we want to transfer all of the properties that we were previously tracking to our line. Just as we previously used the orientation of the differenceVector between the hands to determine the color of the text, we'll now use it to determine the color of our line. We'll still use `kinect.drawLimb` to draw the line, so it will still automatically reflect the distance between the hands in 2D. But now let's use the magnitude of our `differenceVector` to set the thickness of the line. Since `magnitude` reflects the length of `differenceVector` in all three dimensions, this will make our sketch more responsive to our movements in space.

OK, now that we know how we want to map the properties of our `differenceVector` onto our line, let's take a look at the code that implements it:

```
PVector differenceVector = PVector.sub(leftHand, rightHand);
float magnitude = differenceVector.mag();
differenceVector.normalize();
stroke(differenceVector.x * 255,
       differenceVector.y * 255,
       differenceVector.z * 255);
strokeWeight(map(magnitude, 100, 1200, 1, 8));
kinect.drawLimb(userId, SimpleOpenNI.SKEL_LEFT_HAND,
                SimpleOpenNI.SKEL_RIGHT_HAND);
```

These lines are meant to replace the lines immediately following the calls to `getJointPositionSkeleton` from our previous sketch. They are not too different from the lines that were previously there. They still find the `differenceVector` by subtracting the `rightHand` joint vector from the `leftHand` one. We still calculate the magnitude of the `differenceVector` and then convert it to a unit vector by calling `normalize`. Then, though, we diverge. The next two lines are the ones that implement our new artistic interpretation of the `differenceVector`. We use the x-, y-, and z-components to set the `stroke` color. Notice again that the values of these components are guaranteed to range between 0 and 1 because we converted `differenceVector` into a unit vector. That's why we know that multiplying each of these components by 255 will always result in a valid color value between 0 and 255. Once we set the stroke color, we go on to set its weight. The argument we pass to `strokeWeight` is determined by mapping `magnitude` to a range of values from 1 to 8. The input values for this use of `map` were, as usual, determined experimentally by trying a series of different options to see what worked. Since we printed the value of `magnitude` on the screen in our last sketch, I had a good sense of the range of the realistic values I was capable of creating by stretching out my hands. I sent these arguments to `map` based on those observations. And then finally, with the line's color and weight set, we use `kinect.drawLimb` to draw our line just as before.

Since we're no longer displaying the depth image in this sketch, it can be more difficult to calibrate. Without the depth image, it can be hard to tell if you're actually visible to the Kinect or if there are any objects in the way that could be preventing calibration. If you're having trouble calibrating, try running one of the early sketches from this chapter that shows the depth image. If you can calibrate with one of those, you should be able to calibrate with this one too by standing in the same spot.

You can see the results of this sketch in Figure 4-17. It's definitely not the most beautiful artwork I've ever seen, but it has some nice properties. Since we never clear the screen, each line that we draw ends up on top of the previous ones, creating a nice layering effect. The variations in the lines' width and length enhance this effect to give the illusion of three-dimensional swoops and arches in some places. Also, when I started using the sketch I discovered that I had an additional control over the drawing that I hadn't intentionally programmed in. The more quickly I moved my hands around, the more space resulted between adjacent lines. For example, look at the top right corner of the drawing where there is a set of tiny rotating dark lines. These lines have quite a lot of space between them. I specifically remember the rapid arm-waving gesture that produced those lines.

Figure 4-17. *A colorful abstract drawing made using our simple joint-tracking code. The color of the line is determined by the orientation of my hands, its width and length are determined by how far apart they are.*

And this brings me to a key point about this kind of gestural interface. This sketch's relatively primitive visual results don't capture everything about the experience of using it. As an interactive experience it was fun! The tight connection between the position and color of the line and my own hands made me experiment with trying to achieve different results. I found myself jumping and lunging around the room trying to get the lines to spread out or crossing my arms and tilting to one side trying to hit the exact angle that would yield the illusive long orange line. I felt like the interface was simultaneously in my control and pushing back against me, doing what I wanted but also surprising me. These are good properties for an interactive creative tool to have. Not everything good about such tools ends up visible in the final product.

Transferring Orientation in 3D

Up to this point, we've mainly been working with the skeleton tracking data in 2D. We've converted the joint positions from real world into projective coordinates so that they'd match the depth image. However, there is a whole other class of applications where we'll want to keep the tracking data in real-world coordinates in order to use it to provide 3D interfaces. If we are using the tracking data as the input to a 3D interface, we won't want to reduce it to two dimensions by converting it to projective coordinates. We'll want to keep it in 3D and apply the position as well as the orientation of various joints to our 3D elements.

In Chapter 3 we learned how to position and rotate objects in 3D coordinates for display. To build interfaces in 3D, we now need to learn how to transfer the position and orientation from one 3D vector to another. This will allow us to apply the motion of a user's joints to 3D elements in our display. We'll start out by working with the orientation of a single joint as captured by OpenNI.

We've worked extensively with joint positions, but we haven't yet accessed the orientation of a joint. We'll learn how SimpleOpenNI represents joint orientations and how we can apply these orientations to 3D objects that we draw in Processing. Orientation tracking is the ideal tool for matching the movement of 3D models to a user's body. In Chapter 3, we loaded a 3D model and fixed it in place within our scene. This time we'll make the model move by applying our joint orientations to it. This ability comes in handy for using the Kinect as a puppeteering tool. We can create a series of 3D models and then map them to the motions of our body. The most obvious use of this ability is to create a digital double of ourselves, a simple 3D character who moves around, matching our motions. We won't go quite that far here, but I'll show you enough of the technique that you will be prepared to build something like that yourself. We'll develop a sketch that loads in the same 3D model of the Kinect we worked with back in Chapter 2, but this time we'll make the Kinect move along with the user's body.

The ability to transfer joint angle and orientation is also a powerful tool for building interfaces in which users can intentionally manipulate and view 3D objects. We can use the position and orientation of a user's hands to control 3D objects within our sketch. Hands are the obvious choice for an interface like this, because they're the body parts we most frequently use to manipulate real objects in the physical world. Mapping those movements to digital objects will let users take advantage of all of the natural instincts and they already possess. Unfortunately we can't use joint orientation data to build this interface. As I'll explain in more depth below, orientation data is only available for inner joints in the user skeleton, joints that have two neighbors. OpenNI does not provide orientation data for joints that terminate limbs, like the hands. Even if it did, we want to use the relative position of the hands to each other as the source of our interface. When you pick up an object and turn it around to look at it, its position and angle are determined by both of your hands and how they move relative to each other, not just the orientation of either hand alone. What we really want is to represent how the hands are moving in relation to each other.

In the last section, we saw how vectors can be used to represent the difference between two points both in distance and direction. This means that we can calculate a single vector that represents the relative position of the user's hands to each other. We'll learn how to match the position and angle of the Kinect model to this vector that connects the user's hands using a technique called the Axis Angle method. In the latter part of this section, I'll show you how to implement that technique in just a few lines of code to get a 3D model to track the motion of one of the limbs from the OpenNI skeleton.

Orientation from a Single Joint

Before we get started working with joint orientation, it is worth noting some of the limitations in OpenNI's ability to track this data. It is surprising that OpenNI can calculate joint orientations at all. Even Microsoft's own SDK does not provide this feature, and if you think about it, you can see why it's a problem. Hold your arm out straight in front of you. Now rotate it as if you were turning a key in a lock. Keep an eye on your elbow. You'll notice that it's not moving much.

More specifically, its position is not changing. If you imagined a red dot over it where OpenNI would track its joint position, that dot would barely budge. And, further, imagine the changes that you would see in the depth image while performing this action. They would not be especially dramatic.

Given these constraints, OpenNI's ability to infer the orientation of joints is downright heroic. Unsurprisingly, it comes with a couple of caveats. Just like the OpenNI joint position data, the orientation data comes with a confidence score. This score is frequently low, indicating that orientation is not available. This is especially true for joints that form endpoints of the user's limbs (i.e., the hands, feet, and head). OpenNI seems to have a significantly harder time tracking the orientation of joints that only have a single neighboring joint. Orientation is rarely available for these joints.

Now that we're aware of the constraints on the orientation data, let's take a look at a sketch that accesses it. This sketch displays the user's skeleton. It then accesses the orientation information for the TORSO joint. It uses that information to draw three lines representing the orientation of the TORSO. These lines meet at the position of the TORSO and point along x-, y-, and z-axes representing the joint's orientation. In addition to displaying joint orientation, this sketch is our first to draw the skeleton in real-world 3D coordinates rather than in projective 2D. In our discussion of the code, I will briefly explain how this new drawLimb function works. It doesn't introduce any new concepts and should be almost completely familiar to you from drawing the line between two joints in our vector subtraction example earlier.

```
import processing.opengl.*;
import SimpleOpenNI.*;
SimpleOpenNI  kinect;

void setup() {
  size(1028, 768, OPENGL);

  kinect = new SimpleOpenNI(this);
  kinect.enableDepth();
  kinect.enableUser(SimpleOpenNI.SKEL_PROFILE_ALL);
  kinect.setMirror(true);

  fill(255, 0, 0);
}

void draw() {
  kinect.update();
  background(255);

  translate(width/2, height/2, 0);
  rotateX(radians(180));

  IntVector userList = new IntVector();
  kinect.getUsers(userList);
  if (userList.size() > 0) {
    int userId = userList.get(0);

    if ( kinect.isTrackingSkeleton(userId)) {
      PVector position = new PVector();
      kinect.getJointPositionSkeleton(userId,
                              SimpleOpenNI.SKEL_TORSO, position);
```

Chapter 4

```
      PMatrix3D orientation = new PMatrix3D(); ❶
      float confidence =
        kinect.getJointOrientationSkeleton(userId,
                                  SimpleOpenNI.SKEL_TORSO, ❷
                                  orientation);

      println(confidence);
      drawSkeleton(userId);

      pushMatrix();

      // move to the position of the TORSO
      translate(position.x, position.y, position.z);

      // adopt the TORSO's orientation
      // to be our coordinate system
      applyMatrix(orientation); ❸

      // draw x-axis in red
      stroke(255, 0, 0); ❹
      strokeWeight(3);
      line(0, 0, 0, 150, 0, 0);

      // draw y-axis in blue
      stroke(0, 255, 0);
      line(0, 0, 0, 0, 150, 0);

      // draw z-axis in green
      stroke(0, 0, 255);
      line(0, 0, 0, 0, 0, 150);

      popMatrix();

    }
  }
}

void drawSkeleton(int userId) {
  drawLimb(userId, SimpleOpenNI.SKEL_HEAD,
                   SimpleOpenNI.SKEL_NECK);
  drawLimb(userId, SimpleOpenNI.SKEL_NECK,
                   SimpleOpenNI.SKEL_LEFT_SHOULDER);
  drawLimb(userId, SimpleOpenNI.SKEL_LEFT_SHOULDER,
                   SimpleOpenNI.SKEL_LEFT_ELBOW);
  drawLimb(userId, SimpleOpenNI.SKEL_LEFT_ELBOW,
                   SimpleOpenNI.SKEL_LEFT_HAND);
  drawLimb(userId, SimpleOpenNI.SKEL_NECK,
                   SimpleOpenNI.SKEL_RIGHT_SHOULDER);
  drawLimb(userId, SimpleOpenNI.SKEL_RIGHT_SHOULDER,
                   SimpleOpenNI.SKEL_RIGHT_ELBOW);
  drawLimb(uscrId, SimpleOpenNI.SKEL_RIGHT_ELBOW,
                   SimpleOpenNI.SKEL_RIGHT_HAND);
  drawLimb(userId, SimpleOpenNI.SKEL_LEFT_SHOULDER,
                   SimpleOpenNI.SKEL_TORSO);
  drawLimb(userId, SimpleOpenNI.SKEL_RIGHT_SHOULDER,
                   SimpleOpenNI.SKEL_TORSO);
  drawLimb(userId, SimpleOpenNI.SKEL_TORSO,
                   SimpleOpenNI.SKEL_LEFT_HIP);
  drawLimb(userId, SimpleOpenNI.SKEL_LEFT_HIP,
                   SimpleOpenNI.SKEL_LEFT_KNEE);
```

```
        drawLimb(userId, SimpleOpenNI.SKEL_LEFT_KNEE,
                         SimpleOpenNI.SKEL_LEFT_FOOT);
        drawLimb(userId, SimpleOpenNI.SKEL_TORSO,
                         SimpleOpenNI.SKEL_RIGHT_HIP);
        drawLimb(userId, SimpleOpenNI.SKEL_RIGHT_HIP,
                         SimpleOpenNI.SKEL_RIGHT_KNEE);
        drawLimb(userId, SimpleOpenNI.SKEL_RIGHT_KNEE,
                         SimpleOpenNI.SKEL_RIGHT_FOOT);
        drawLimb(userId, SimpleOpenNI.SKEL_RIGHT_HIP,
                         SimpleOpenNI.SKEL_LEFT_HIP);
      }

      void drawLimb(int userId,int jointType1,int jointType2)
      {
        PVector jointPos1 = new PVector();
        PVector jointPos2 = new PVector();
        float   confidence;

        confidence = kinect.getJointPositionSkeleton(userId,jointType1,
                                                     jointPos1);
        confidence += kinect.getJointPositionSkeleton(userId,jointType2,
                                                      jointPos2);
        stroke(100);
        strokeWeight(5);
        if(confidence > 1){
          line(jointPos1.x, jointPos1.y,
               jointPos1.z, jointPos2.x,
               jointPos2.y, jointPos2.z);
        }
      }

      // user-tracking callbacks!
      void onNewUser(int userId) {
        println("start pose detection");
        kinect.startPoseDetection("Psi", userId);
      }

      void onEndCalibration(int userId, boolean successful) {
        if (successful) {
          println("  User calibrated !!!");
          kinect.startTrackingSkeleton(userId);
        }
        else {
          println("  Failed to calibrate user !!!");
          kinect.startPoseDetection("Psi", userId);
        }
      }

      void onStartPose(String pose, int userId) {
        println("Started pose for user");
        kinect.stopPoseDetection(userId);
        kinect.requestCalibrationSkeleton(userId, true);
      }
```

Let's start by looking at how this sketch accesses the orientation of the TORSO. These lines of the sketch should look quite similar to the familiar pattern for accessing joint position, albeit with a few twists:

❶ We've represented joint positions with a `PVector`, but here we're using a `PMatrix3D`.

❷ Just as we passed our `PVector` into `kinect.getJointPositionSkeleton`, we pass our `PMatrix3D` into `kinect.getJointOrientationSkeleton`, and afterward it will be populated with the orientation data for the joint we requested.

Again, as with `kinect.getJointPositionSkeleton`, `kinect.getJoint-OrientationSkeleton` returns a `float` representing OpenNI's confidence in the results of its calculation. These portions of this code should seem familiar.

But, what is a `PMatrix3D` and how does it represent the orientation of a joint? `PMatrix3D` is one example of a more general mathematical structure called a "matrix." Matrices store multiple vectors in a single grid of numbers. Theoretically, matrices can store an arbitrary number of vectors, but `PMatrix3D` happens to store four of them. Representing vectors collectively like this has some advantages. For example, we can store vectors that represent related concepts together in a single package so that they can be manipulated together. This is exactly what `PMatrix3D` does.

`PMatrix3D` stores four vectors that together can represent the full state of our coordinate system. It uses three vectors to represent the x-, y-, and z-axes. The components of each vector will store the results of any `scale` or `rotate` operations that we perform. The fourth vector stores the results of `translate`. Since `translate` affects the location of our entire coordinate system, you could also think of this fourth vector as defining our system's origin.

More specifically, the `PMatrix3D` set by `kinect.getJointOrientation-Skeleton` stores a set of transformations that change the default coordinate system to match the orientation of the joint we requested. Essentially, it is a shortcut for a bunch of `rotate`, `translate`, and `scale` operations that we'd otherwise have to perform on our current coordinate system to get it to match the orientation of the `TORSO`. Since `PMatrix3D` stores all of these transformations into a single convenient package, we can apply them to our coordinate system all at once using Processing's `applyMatrix` function. This is just what we do a few lines down in the sketch.

❸ Now we're starting to see how the definition of "matrix" we just learned connects with the `pushMatrix` and `popMatrix` functions that we've used constantly since Chapter 3. These two functions, used together, isolate a set of transformations we want to apply to our coordinate system. And we just saw that we can store a set of these same transformations in a `PMatrix3D` object and apply them using `applyMatrix`. Processing's entire coordinate system is just a single `PMatrix3D` whose values we're constantly changing behind the scenes when we perform our transformations. What we've gained here is the ability to alter the entire state of the coordinate system at once by passing in a `PMatrix3D`. Though we won't need to here, Processing also lets us access the current state of the coordinate system as a `PMatrix3D` so that we can manipulate it directly. The function to do that is called, appropriately, `getMatrix`.

❹ After we call `applyMatrix(orientation)`, our coordinate system is aligned with the orientation of our TORSO joint. To display that orientation, we want to draw lines pointing out in the direction of each axis. This is quite straightforward. We just use Processing's `line` function to draw three lines, each of which starts at the current origin, `0,0,0`, and heads out a short distance along one axis.

The first three arguments to `line` are the x-, y-, and z-coordinates of the line's starting point, and the last three are the coordinates of its ending point. Since the y- and z-coordinates of our line's ending point are 0, the line will only extend along the x-axis. We repeat this pattern for the other two axes, changing which argument to `line` is set to 150 each time along with the `stroke` color to indicate each axis in turn.

As you can see in Figure 4-18, the three axes correctly track the orientation of the plane of my chest as I move around. In the image on the left, I'm standing up almost completely straight facing the camera with a slight rotation toward camera-left. The x- and y-axes of my torso are facing straight up and to the right. The z-axis faces almost straight back, though I've turned just enough so that you can still see it. In the middle image, I'm bent over at the waist pretty far. The z-axis is now pointing up toward the ceiling and the y-axis is tilted far forward toward the screen. At first glance it appears that the x-axis is at a similar angle as in the first image, but if you look closely, you'll see that it is foreshortened. The x-axis is facing into the screen because I've turned toward screen right. In the final image on the right, I've turned even farther in that direction, and you can now see the alteration to the x-axis clearly. I've also straightened up significantly so the y-axis is now facing up. However, my turn to the right has taken me so far that I'm almost in profile. The z-axis, which points out of my back, is starting to point toward the left side of the scene.

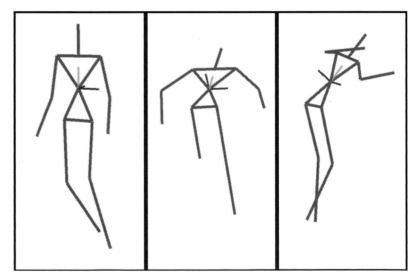

Figure 4-18. *Three user poses demonstrating the orientation of the TORSO joint as indicated by the red, green, and blue lines pointing along each axis out from that joint.*

This account of the changes to the orientation caused by my movements should give you some sense of how this data could be useful in an interactive application. For example, since my TORSO basically points toward where I'm looking, you could use its orientation to control the angle of a camera in a virtual environment, allowing me to look around by turning my body. Since we don't have any 3D environments handy, in this section, we'll examine another application for this data: controlling the display of a 3D model. We'll use the orientation of the user's elbow to rotate the 3D model of the Kinect we worked with extensively in the last chapter. As we learned in that chapter, navigating in 3D using two-dimensional tools such as a mouse can be quite confusing. Instead, if we can control the orientation and size of the model using our hands as we move them around in actual space, we might find that our body's built-in knowledge about the physical world around it translates into a more intuitive way of manipulating 3D graphics.

Before we explore that possibility, we have to briefly discuss some details about the process of drawing the skeleton in 3D, something we did for the first time in this sketch. If you look at this new version of drawSkeleton, you'll notice that it is almost identical to the function we've been using to do this job in the last few sketches. We still draw each of the 16 limbs in the skeleton. However, this time we're using our own drawLimb function instead of the one provided by SimpleOpenNI. SimpleOpenNI's version of this function draws the skeleton in projective coordinates. It is meant to be displayed on top of the depth image rather than in an empty 3D space. Our version of drawLimb uses the joint positions in real-world coordinates, which is more appropriate for displaying the skeleton in an empty 3D space like we're doing in this sketch. Since we're not trying to match a 2D depth image, there's no reason to throw away the z-axis information in the joint positions.

I'm not going to go into the implementation of drawLimb in too much depth. We've discussed every element in the function extensively, and you should be able to completely understand it on your own. That said, I wanted to point out one subtlety. Previously, we've used confidence reported by OpenNI to decide whether or not to draw each joint. When drawing a limb, though, two joints are involved with two separate confidence levels. If either joint's confidence level drops too low, we don't want to draw the limb. To enforce this constraint, our drawLimb function adds up the confidence score associated with each limb into a collective confidence variable:

```
confidence = kinect.getJointPositionSkeleton(userId,jointType1,jointPos1);
confidence += kinect.getJointPositionSkeleton(userId,jointType2,jointPos2);
```

Each individual confidence value will range from 0 to 1. In the past, we've treated any confidence score under 0.5 as too low to display. By that logic, here we'll only want to draw our limb if the final value of confidence is greater than one, in other words, if each limb contributes at least 0.5 to the total. If you look lower down in this function, you'll discover that we implement exactly that constraint, wrapping our drawing code in an if statement that checks to see if confidence is greater than one.

Now that we understand how to access joint orientation and have seen how it corresponds to the movement of our body, let's use it to build a simple interface. We'll revisit what we learned about displaying 3D models in the point cloud chapter, but now we'll put the model under the user's control. We'll access the orientation of a user's elbow and then apply that to the model so that it rotates around in space as the user moves her arm. We'd really like to access the orientation of the user's hand rather than her elbow. Our hands are the most natural joint to track for an intentional manipulation interface like this since we use them to pick up and manipulate objects all the time. However, we're constrained by the ability of OpenNI to calculate joint orientation. As I mentioned above, it is much more difficult for OpenNI to determine orientation of the outer joints on the skeleton such as the hand. Orientation data is almost never available for the hand. The elbow is the best we can do. Thankfully, your body's joints are attached to each other, so the orientation of your elbow won't be too far distant from the rest of the arm and hand.

Here's the code for our sketch. Read through it and remind yourself how we load up a 3D model and prepare it for display. Make sure you copy the `kinect.obj` file from one of your old projects (see Chapter 3) into this sketch's folder so that the OBJLoader library will be able to find it.

```
import processing.opengl.*;
import SimpleOpenNI.*;
SimpleOpenNI  kinect;
import saito.objloader.*;

OBJModel model;

void setup() {
  size(1028, 768, OPENGL);

  model = new OBJModel(this, "kinect.obj", "relative", TRIANGLES);
  model.translateToCenter();

  kinect = new SimpleOpenNI(this);
  kinect.enableDepth();
  kinect.enableUser(SimpleOpenNI.SKEL_PROFILE_ALL);
  kinect.setMirror(true);

  fill(255, 0, 0);
}

PImage colorImage;
boolean gotImage;

void draw() {
  kinect.update();
  background(0);

  translate(width/2, height/2, 0);
  rotateX(radians(180));

  scale(0.9);

  IntVector userList = new IntVector();
  kinect.getUsers(userList);
  if (userList.size() > 0) {
    int userId = userList.get(0);

    if ( kinect.isTrackingSkeleton(userId)) {

      PVector position = new PVector(); ❶
      kinect.getJointPositionSkeleton(userId,
                              SimpleOpenNI.SKEL_RIGHT_ELBOW,
                              position);
```

Chapter 4

```
        PMatrix3D orientation = new PMatrix3D();
        float confidence =
          kinect.getJointOrientationSkeleton(userId,
                                        SimpleOpenNI.SKEL_RIGHT_ELBOW,
                                        orientation);

        pushMatrix();
        translate(position.x, position.y, position.z); ❷
        applyMatrix(orientation);
        model.draw();
        popMatrix();
      }
    }
}

// user-tracking callbacks!
void onNewUser(int userId) {
  println("start pose detection");
  kinect.startPoseDetection("Psi", userId);
}

void onEndCalibration(int userId, boolean successful) {
  if (successful) {
    println("  User calibrated !!!");
    kinect.startTrackingSkeleton(userId);
  }
  else {
    println("  Failed to calibrate user !!!");
    kinect.startPoseDetection("Psi", userId);
  }
}

void onStartPose(String pose, int userId) {
  println("Started pose for user");
  kinect.stopPoseDetection(userId);
  kinect.requestCalibrationSkeleton(userId, true);
}
```

As usual, the majority of this code is made up of the verbose calibration call-backs that you're now probably sick of seeing. The core of it, though, is even simpler than in our previous sketch:

❶   We get the joint position and orientation by using `kinect.getJoint-PositionSkeleton` and `kinect.getJointOrientationSkeleton`.

❷   Next, we use these values to `translate` to the joint's position and apply its orientation system with `applyMatrix`. Lastly, we call `model.draw` to display the model in the correct position and orientation.

The result is that our Kinect model will float around in space as you move your arm and rotate it. Figure 4-19 shows an example of this in action. In these two screen captures, I've included the image from the Kinect's RGB camera as well as the rendering of the Kinect model so that you can see how the model's position relates to the pose that I'm holding. In the top image, my arm is up at angle in front of my face with my palm rotated to face to my right. The Kinect model is oriented at the same angle. It looks like a simple rectangle, because it is rotated along with my arm so that its base faces away from the camera. In the lower image, I've extended my arm out to my side and rotated it so that my palm faces toward the Kinect. And our 3D model has followed right along. You can now see the Kinect's base since it has turned toward us to match my arm's rotation.

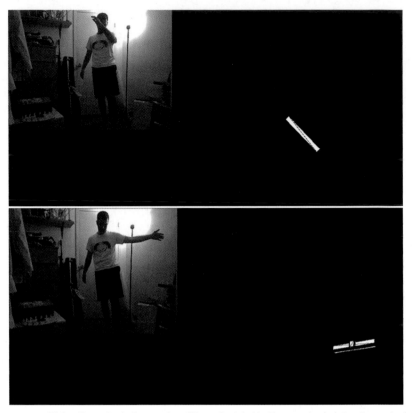

Figure 4-19. *Using the orientation and position of a joint in the user's skeleton to control the display of a 3D model. Note: even though this illustration shows the RGB image for comparison, the running sketch will not do so.*

Right about now, you should be jumping up and down a little bit in your chair imagining building a complete 3D puppet that you can control with your body. Imagine if you replaced the 3D model of the Kinect with one that represented your forearm and hand. Then supplement that with 15 more models, each one corresponding to one of the limbs we track with the Kinect. You could then use the technique we just demonstrated to apply the orientation and position of each joint from OpenNI to the correct limb model. The result would be a full 3D segmented puppet that would move and rotate along with your actual body. It would be like a toy version of the sophisticated motion capture systems that they use to make cutting-edge 3D animated movies and special effects.

Orientation from Any Vector with Axis-Angle

So we've seen how to use the orientation of a single joint to control a 3D model. But what if we want to use the relative position of two joints? For many applications, the most intuitive way for a user to interact with a 3D model on screen will be by using his hands. Our hands are our primary tool for interacting with real objects in our environment. So letting people use their hands to control virtual objects allows them to retain all of the instincts they already have. This can make interfaces more intuitive, more natural, and easier to learn.

To create a 3D interface based on a user's hands, we can't use the orientation data from SimpleOpenNI. SimpleOpenNI only provides orientation data for individual joints, and even that data is not available for the hands. We need data about how the hands are positioned in relation to each other. We learned earlier in this chapter that we can represent this relative position as a vector. If we subtract one hand position vector from the other, the result is a vector that captures the distance and angle between the hands. Now, to use the position of the hands to control a 3D model, we need to learn how to break this vector into components with which we can manipulate our coordinate system. Just as we reproduced the orientation of a single joint in our model by applying a `PMatrix3D` to our sketch, we now need to find a way to apply the angle and position of the vector between the hands to the 3D model itself. Applying the position is easy. We can simply `translate` the coordinates of one of our joints before drawing the model. But how can we get the model to be oriented in the right direction? We need to calculate the difference in angle between the hand vector and the original angle of the model. If we can do that, then we can call `rotate` with the right arguments, and the model will face the right way and be positioned correctly.

How can we calculate the angle between our model and our hand vector? We'll use an approach called the Axis-Angle method to accomplish this. This method describes the angle between two vectors in terms of two values: the angle and the axis in which that angle is defined. When working in three dimensions, a simple number is not enough to fully describe an angle. If I told you that my left arm was at an angle of 45 degrees to my right arm, you would immediately ask: in what direction? I could maintain a 45-degree angle between my arms while rotating one around the other into a many positions. To really know the angle between two vectors, we also need to specify the axis on which that angle sits. The Axis-Angle method provides us with a way with which to calculate both the angle and the axis needed to describe two vectors' relative rotation.

The Axis-Angle method uses two geometric techniques that are ubiquitous when working with vectors: the *dot product* and the *cross product*. The dot product gives us the angle between the vectors as a single number. And the cross product gives us a new vector that represents the axis in which this angle operates. Both of these techniques have wide uses within geometry, many of which are relevant to 3D graphics programming. For example, when building a mesh to represent a 3D surface, we can use the cross product to calculate the *normal* of each surface, a value that tells us which direction the surface is pointing and therefore in which direction it will reflect light. To use the Axis-Angle technique in code to orient a 3D model, you don't need to know anything about these advanced topics. In fact, this example probably represents the high watermark of geometric concepts that we'll be covering in this book. So if you feel confused or feel like you don't completely understand what a dot product or cross product means, that's OK. To understand this example, all you need to know is this: the dot product tells us the angle between the vectors and the cross product tells us the axis against which this angle is defined. We'll use the results of these calculations as arguments to rotate to position our 3D model so that it fits between the hands of our skeleton.

We'll be passing rotate different arguments than we have in the past. Instead of a single angle, this time we'll pass it four arguments: our angle and each of the x-, y-, and z-components that make up the vector that results from our cross product. The vector from our cross product represents a line in space, and the angle describes a rotation around that line. Let's try to visualize this. Hold your arm up with your elbow bent at a right angle. Think of the orientation of your forearm as the axis. Now, begin to rotate your forearm around while keeping your upper arm fixed in place. Move your forearm in a circle around the original direction it was pointing. That's the angle.

Now that I've laid out the theory, let's look at the code. Most of this sketch is quite similar to the last sketch where we worked with joint orientation. The difference comes at the heart of draw. There, we get the position of both hands from SimpleOpenNI and then proceed to implement the Axis-Angle method as I just described. After we've got the joint positions and the axis and angle between them, we use these values to translate and rotate our coordinate system before drawing the 3D model of the Kinect. This happens in a pushMatrix/popMatrix block near the end of the draw function. Read through this code, and then I'll go through it step by step to make sure it makes sense.

```
import processing.opengl.*;
import SimpleOpenNI.*;
SimpleOpenNI  kinect;
import saito.objloader.*;

OBJModel model;

void setup() { ❶
  size(1028, 768, OPENGL);

  model = new OBJModel(this, "kinect.obj", "relative", TRIANGLES);
  model.translateToCenter();

  // translate the model so its origin
  // is at its left side
  BoundingBox box = new BoundingBox(this, model); ❷
  model.translate(box.getMin()); ❸

  kinect = new SimpleOpenNI(this);
  kinect.enableDepth();
  kinect.enableUser(SimpleOpenNI.SKEL_PROFILE_ALL);
  kinect.setMirror(true);
}

void draw() { ❹
  kinect.update();
  background(255);

  translate(width/2, height/2, 0);
  rotateX(radians(180));
```

```
      IntVector userList = new IntVector();
      kinect.getUsers(userList);
      if (userList.size() > 0) {
        int userId = userList.get(0);

        if ( kinect.isTrackingSkeleton(userId)) {
          PVector leftHand = new PVector();
          kinect.getJointPositionSkeleton(userId,
                                  SimpleOpenNI.SKEL_LEFT_HAND, ❺
                                  leftHand);

          PVector rightHand = new PVector();
          kinect.getJointPositionSkeleton(userId,
                                  SimpleOpenNI.SKEL_RIGHT_HAND,
                                  rightHand);

          // subtract right from left hand
          // to turn leftHand into a vector representing
          // the difference between them
          leftHand.sub(rightHand); ❻

          // convert leftHand to a unit vector
          leftHand.normalize(); ❼

          // model is rotated so "up" is the x-axis
          PVector modelOrientation = new PVector(1, 0, 0); ❽

          // calculate angle and axis
          float angle = acos(modelOrientation.dot(leftHand)); ❾
          PVector axis = modelOrientation.cross(leftHand); ❿

          stroke(255, 0, 0);
          strokeWeight(5);
          drawSkeleton(userId);

          pushMatrix(); ⓫
            lights();
            stroke(175);
            strokeWeight(1);
            fill(250);

            translate(rightHand.x, rightHand.y, rightHand.z); ⓬

            // rotate angle amount around axis
            rotate(angle, axis.x, axis.y, axis.z); ⓭
            model.draw(); ⓮
          popMatrix();
        }
      }
    }

void drawSkeleton(int userId) {
  drawLimb(userId, SimpleOpenNI.SKEL_HEAD, SimpleOpenNI.SKEL_NECK);
  drawLimb(userId, SimpleOpenNI.SKEL_NECK,
          SimpleOpenNI.SKEL_LEFT_SHOULDER);
  drawLimb(userId, SimpleOpenNI.SKEL_LEFT_SHOULDER,
          SimpleOpenNI.SKEL_LEFT_ELBOW);
```

```
            drawLimb(userId, SimpleOpenNI.SKEL_LEFT_ELBOW,
                     SimpleOpenNI.SKEL_LEFT_HAND);
            drawLimb(userId, SimpleOpenNI.SKEL_NECK,
                     SimpleOpenNI.SKEL_RIGHT_SHOULDER);
            drawLimb(userId, SimpleOpenNI.SKEL_RIGHT_SHOULDER,
                     SimpleOpenNI.SKEL_RIGHT_ELBOW);
            drawLimb(userId, SimpleOpenNI.SKEL_RIGHT_ELBOW,
                     SimpleOpenNI.SKEL_RIGHT_HAND);
            drawLimb(userId, SimpleOpenNI.SKEL_LEFT_SHOULDER,
                     SimpleOpenNI.SKEL_TORSO);
            drawLimb(userId, SimpleOpenNI.SKEL_RIGHT_SHOULDER,
                     SimpleOpenNI.SKEL_TORSO);
            drawLimb(userId, SimpleOpenNI.SKEL_TORSO,
                     SimpleOpenNI.SKEL_LEFT_HIP);
            drawLimb(userId, SimpleOpenNI.SKEL_LEFT_HIP,
                     SimpleOpenNI.SKEL_LEFT_KNEE);
            drawLimb(userId, SimpleOpenNI.SKEL_LEFT_KNEE,
                     SimpleOpenNI.SKEL_LEFT_FOOT);
            drawLimb(userId, SimpleOpenNI.SKEL_TORSO,
                     SimpleOpenNI.SKEL_RIGHT_HIP);
            drawLimb(userId, SimpleOpenNI.SKEL_RIGHT_HIP,
                     SimpleOpenNI.SKEL_RIGHT_KNEE);
            drawLimb(userId, SimpleOpenNI.SKEL_RIGHT_KNEE,
                     SimpleOpenNI.SKEL_RIGHT_FOOT);
            drawLimb(userId, SimpleOpenNI.SKEL_RIGHT_HIP,
                     SimpleOpenNI.SKEL_LEFT_HIP);
        }

        void drawLimb(int userId, int jointType1, int jointType2)
        {
          PVector jointPos1 = new PVector();
          PVector jointPos2 = new PVector();
          float   confidence;

          // draw the joint position
          confidence = kinect.getJointPositionSkeleton(userId, jointType1, joint-
        Pos1);
          confidence = kinect.getJointPositionSkeleton(userId, jointType2, joint-
        Pos2);

          line(jointPos1.x, jointPos1.y, jointPos1.z,
          jointPos2.x, jointPos2.y, jointPos2.z);
        }

        // user-tracking callbacks!
        void onNewUser(int userId) {
          println("start pose detection");
          kinect.startPoseDetection("Psi", userId);
        }

        void onEndCalibration(int userId, boolean successful) {
          if (successful) {
            println("  User calibrated !!!");
            kinect.startTrackingSkeleton(userId);
          }
          else {
            println("  Failed to calibrate user !!!");
            kinect.startPoseDetection("Psi", userId);
          }
        }
```

```
void onStartPose(String pose, int userId) {
  println("Started pose for user");
  kinect.stopPoseDetection(userId);
  kinect.requestCalibrationSkeleton(userId, true);
}
```

When you run this sketch and perform the calibration ritual, you'll see the model of the Kinect appear between the hands of the stickman. As you move your hands, you'll see that one side of the model follows your right and the other side rotates toward your left. If you keep your hands close together the result is the illusion that the stickman is actually holding onto the model with both hands, as in Figure 4-20. If you move your hands farther apart, you'll discover that the model sticks to your right and constantly points toward your left. As you move your hands in relation to each other, the model will follow, rotating around and revealing its different sides just as if you were turning it over in your hands.

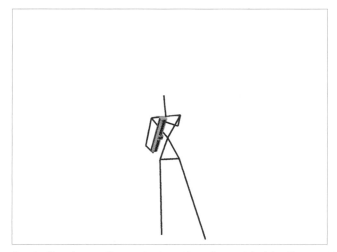

Figure 4-20. *Controlling the position and orientation of a model of the Kinect with my hands. This makes a natural interface for manipulating 3D models, because it builds on real-world experience.*

Let's examine how this sketch uses the Axis-Angle method described above to implement this interface.

❶ The process starts out in setup. When we previously worked with the OBJLoader library, we wanted to place our Kinect model at a fixed point within our 3D space. We used the translateToCenter method to move the origin of the model's internal coordinate system to the center of our Kinect model. This meant that all translation and rotations we applied to the model took place from its center and it was easy to control. This time, however, we want our stickman to be able to hold onto the Kinect model from its sides. We want to position the model at the location of one of our user's hands and then orient it toward the other hand. This is much easier to do if we move the model's origin so that it is all the way to one side.

❷ We do this in `setup`, immediately after the `model` is initialized, loaded, and translated to center. To find the side of the model, we have to first calculate model's bounding box. A bounding box is the smallest rectangular solid that can hold the whole model. 3D models can be all kinds of uneven blobby shapes, but there's always a bounding box that you can draw around them, going out as far as necessary in each direction to fully contain their geometry. Thankfully, OBJLoader provides a way to calculate the bounding box for our model. In fact, the library has a complete `BoundingBox` class for doing this kind of operation. All we have to do is pass the `BoundingBox` constructor our Kinect model and we'll then be able to use it to find the edges of the model.

❸ Once we have the bounding box, we call its `getMin` function, which returns a vector representing the edge of the model. Then we pass this vector to the model's `translate` function. Rather than moving the model around within our sketch's coordinate system, this method will move the model's internal origin to the given point.

❹ Having prepared the Kinect model, we're now ready to align it with our hands. In our `draw` function, we go through the normal checks to confirm that the calibration process has been successfully completed.

❺ Then we access the positions of the left and right hands using `getJoint-PositionSkeleton`, a process that should be second nature by now. Once we've got both of those vectors, we start in on applying the Axis-Angle method I described above to transfer the orientation of the vector between the hands to our Kinect 3D model.

❻ The first thing we do is calculate the vector that represents the difference between the positions of the two hands. This happens on this line, which subtracts the `rightHand` vector from the `leftHand` one, leaving the resulting difference value in our `leftHand` variable.

❼ Once we've got this difference vector, the first thing we do is `normalize` it. Converting a vector into a normal reduces it to information about direction. This is necessary before using `leftHand` in our Axis-Angle calculation.

We've got our difference vector ready to go. Our `leftHand` variable contains a `PVector` that represents exactly the direction from one hand to the other. Our eventual goal is to apply the orientation of this vector to our model. To use the Axis-Angle method to accomplish that, we need another vector that represents the orientation of our model. But what is the orientation of our model? How can we represent that with a vector?

We want our Kinect model to stretch across the distance between our stickman's two hands. In other words we want the width of the Kinect to point in the direction of the difference vector we just calculated. The Kinect model is much wider than it is tall. Its longest dimension is along the x-axis. Hence, we can think of the Kinect model as oriented in the positive x-direction. This is an orientation we can represent as a vector, specifically the unit vector: 1,0,0. The Kinect model points up along the x-axis with no turn toward the y- or z-axis.

⓼ After normalizing the `leftHand` vector, we initialize a new `PVector` to represent this orientation: `modelOrientation`. We create it to be a unit vector pointing along the positive direction of the x-axis to capture the orientation of the Kinect 3D model.

⓽ Now that we have both our `leftHand` vector and the `modelOrientation` that we want it to control, we're ready to start actually implementing the Axis-Angle method. We can use the dot product to calculate the angle between these two vectors and the cross product to generate the axis against which this angle has meaning. That's exactly what we do on the last two lines of this excerpt. First we call the `dot` function on our `modelOrientation` vector with `leftHand` as the argument.

⓾ We then call `acos` to calculate the arc cosine of the result. This is a mathematical function that converts the angle into the right units for use in our `rotate` function. Then, to calculate the axis that gives this angle meaning, we just call `cross` on the `modelOrientation` and pass in `leftHand` to perform the cross product. This returns a vector with the x-, y-, and z-components representing our axis.

⓫ With these two elements, we're ready to perform the rotation that will bring our Kinect model into alignment with the vector between our hands. This happens inside the `pushMatrix/popMatrix` block at the bottom of our `draw` function. Inside of there, we first set some display parameters. We turn on Processing's default 3D lighting setup with the `lights` function so that our 3D model will be visible. Then we set the `stroke` color and weight and the fill. I chose these values to make the Kinect model as visible as possible against the white background and the red lines of the stickman.

⓬ With those cosmetic moves out of the way, we're ready to position our 3D model. We start that process by calling `translate` with the x-, y-, and z-coordinates of our `rightHand` vector. Since we moved the internal origin of the Kinect all the way over to its right side, we want that origin to sit on the right hand as if the stickman was holding the Kinect. When the user moves her hand, the Kinect model will follow.

⓭ Now we come to the moment of truth: it's time to use the `angle` and `axis` values we just calculated to orient our coordinate system to point from the `rightHand` toward the `leftHand`. To do that we call Processing's `rotate`. We've used `rotate` extensively before, but this time we'll be sending different arguments to it. In the past we've simply sent a single angle value to `rotate` (or one of its siblings, `rotateX`, `rotateY`, and `rotateZ`) as a float. This time, though, we need to specify the axis around which we want the rotation to take place, so we'll pass the `angle` in along with each component of our `axis` vector: `rotate(angle, axis.x, axis.y, axis.z)`. With all four of these arguments, Processing can perform the rotation to align our coordinate system with the vector connecting the hands.

⓮ Afterward, all that's left is to display the model with `model.draw`. As we saw in Figure 4-20, this technique works effectively, and the model shows up naturally between the hands of our stickman.

> *None of the transformations we apply to the Kinect model to get it to match up with the user's hands rotate it around its own axis. Therefore its orientation along that axis will remain faithful to however it was set in the original model file. Refer back to review the rotations we applied to our model file to correct its orientation.*

You can take a deep breath now. This Axis-Angle technique represents the most complicated geometrical work we'll do in this book. The worst is over now. And hopefully it didn't turn out to be that bad. You learned that the dot product gives you the angle between two vectors and that the cross product tells you the axis defined by them, against which that angle is defined. We also covered how to represent sets of changes to the coordinate system as matrices. These are small steps into a set of geometric skills that will come in handy as you perform increasingly sophisticated work in 3D. If you're intrigued by this subject and want to learn more, I highly recommend Dan Shiffman's book *The Nature of Code* (Kickstarter, 2012), which provides a comprehensive overview of these kinds of techniques along with projects and concepts for using them to simulate natural systems in graphical software.

Background Removal, User Pixels, and the Scene Map

Up to this point in the chapter, we've been working with the skeleton data exclusively. However, there are some things that OpenNI can do without the full calibration process. These techniques aren't as universally useful as joint tracking, but they are handy to have in your toolkit while working with the Kinect. These alternate techniques break down into two categories: those that work with pixels and those that work with gestures. We'll get into gestures in the next section, but first we're going to look at what OpenNI lets us do with pixels.

In this section, we're going to learn how to combine OpenNI's user-tracking with the depth and RGB images. Think back to our discussion of the calibration process as shown way back in Figure 4-1. There is a point in that process when OpenNI has detected the presence of a user but not yet calibrated well enough to track his skeleton. What does it mean for OpenNI to have detected a user if it cannot yet locate his joints? It means that the system had recognized the part of the depth image taken up by the user, that a certain set of pixels within the depth image correspond to a user moving through the scene. Once that identification has been made, OpenNI begins processing those pixels further to locate the position of the user's joints. However, as soon as those pixels have been identified, we can use them for other purposes. We can separate out the part of the image that contains people from the background. Among other things, this will let us perform background replacement, a trick that's similar to the green screen process used in special effects movies or the fancier karaoke bars. Background replacement involves placing footage of a person over a different background than what is actually behind him.

Once we've achieved that effect, we'll look at an even more advanced breakdown of the scene that OpenNI makes available: the scene map. This includes a separation of the users from the background, but also a separation of the background itself into spatially distinct pieces. OpenNI breaks out each component identified in the scene map so that we can access the depth points belonging to each one separately. I'll demonstrate how to use the scene map to do some basic spatial analysis of a room.

But first, let's dive in and build our background replacement sketch. We'll start work on that by learning how to identify which pixels correspond to the user and which correspond to the background. To start, we'll just display that result as a simple silhouette. Then we'll move on to integrating the color data from the Kinect and a background image to achieve the full "green screen" look..

The key to removing the background is a function provided by SimpleOpenNI called getUsersPixels. This function returns a "map" of the scene. This map takes the form of an array of integers. The array has one element for each pixel in the depth image. The value of each element tells us whether the corresponding pixel in the depth image is part of a user or part of the background. Our first sketch here will take advantage of these values to draw the user's silhouette. If a pixel is part of a user, we'll draw it as a solid green. Otherwise, we'll leave it black. The result will look like Figure 4-21.

Figure 4-21. *Separating the user pixels from the background pixels using getUsersPixels.*

Here's the code:

```
import processing.opengl.*;
import SimpleOpenNI.*;

SimpleOpenNI  kinect;

PImage  userImage;
int userID;
int[] userMap;

PImage rgbImage;
void setup() {
  size(640, 480, OPENGL);

  kinect = new SimpleOpenNI(this);
  kinect.enableDepth();
  kinect.enableUser(SimpleOpenNI.SKEL_PROFILE_NONE); ❶
}
```

```
void draw() {
  background(0);  ❷
  kinect.update();

  // if we have detected any users
  if (kinect.getNumberOfUsers() > 0) {  ❸

    // find out which pixels have users in them
    userMap = kinect.getUsersPixels(SimpleOpenNI.USERS_ALL);  ❹

    // populate  the pixels array
    // from the sketch's current contents
    loadPixels();  ❺
    for (int i = 0; i < userMap.length; i++) {  ❻
      // if the current pixel is on a user
      if (userMap[i] != 0) {
        // make it green
        pixels[i] = color(0, 255, 0);  ❼
      }
    }
    // display the changed pixel array
    updatePixels();  ❽
  }
}
void onNewUser(int uID) {
  userID = uID;
  println("tracking");
}
```

If you're visible when the sketch starts up, you may need to move around a little bit before OpenNI will notice that you're there. Let's look at how this works.

❶   Just as with the other sketches in this chapter, we call kinect.enableUser
within setup to turn on user tracking. However, this time we don't actually
need the joint data, so we pass SimpleOpenNI.SKEL_PROFILE_NONE as an
argument.

❷   Next we start off draw by setting the background to black. I mention this
routine fact because it's going to become important in this sketch in a
way it hasn't been before.

❸   Once we've set the background, we call getNumberOfUsers to check to see
if any users have been detected. Notice at the bottom of the sketch that
we only had to implement one of the user-tracking callbacks, onNewUser.
Since we're not actually going to perform the calibration ritual, this is all
we need to get access to the user pixels.

❹   Once user tracking has begun, we're ready to grab the data indicating
which pixels belong to users and which are part of the background.
At the top of the sketch, we declared userMap as an array of integers.
Here, we load it with the map of the user pixels by calling kinect.get
UsersPixels(SimpleOpenNI.USERS_ALL). This argument is both the
only option for this function and a required part of calling it.

Our strategy for producing an image from this data is going to be a little
different from any we've used before. Once you get the hang of it, you'll
see that it's actually quite simple and elegant; however, it can seem a
little confusing at first. We're going to directly access the pixels of our

sketch itself. Just like a `PImage`, our sketch has an array of pixels that we can load, alter, and update. The difference is that when we set these pixels, we determine the final display of our sketch, rather than setting the appearance of an image that we can then scale and position. This approach can be inadequate when your drawing code becomes complex. Here it will be quite elegant.

⑤ Since we called `background(0)` at the top of `draw`, right now all of the pixels in the sketch are black. We call `loadPixels` to load up all of these black pixels into our sketch's pixel array. Now, as we loop through the depth image, all we have to do is update any pixels in this array that have a nonzero value in the `userMap`. These will be the pixels that correspond to the user. Since the rest of the sketch is already set to black, the result will be our user's silhouette set out in stark relief. Let's look at the details.

⑥ After we call `loadPixels`, we begin looping through the `userMap` array. Each point in the `userMap` corresponds to a single pixel in our sketch. Therefore we can use the same index to access both the `pixels` array and the `userMap`.

⑦ Inside this loop comes the key moment where we set the user pixels to green.

If multiple users are in the scene, the `userMap` will distinguish between them by setting each entry in the `userMap` to the ID of the user who is covered by the corresponding pixel. However, background pixels will always be set to 0, so the condition used here guarantees that we'll get all the user pixels and none of the background ones. We don't need an `else` statement here because all pixels started out life as black when we called `background(0)` at the top of `draw`.

⑧ At this point `pixels` now contains exactly what we want: green pixels for the user and black pixels everywhere else. To display this result, we call `updatePixels`, which tells the sketch to reload the pixel array for display. You can see the result in Figure 4-21.

Having successfully distinguished the user from the background, let's now work on swapping out the background for something more interesting and replacing this user silhouette with the RGB pixels that will show us what the user really looks like. We'll use a static image for the background. To do that, we need to load the image and then display it at the start of our `draw` function. Just as our code previously replaced the pixels of the black background with the user pixels, it will now replace parts of this image.

We also want to display an image of our user rather than the green silhouette we've been using up until now. To do that, we need to revisit our technique for aligning the RGB image with the depth image. We learned about this technique way back in the last chapter but haven't used it since. Here's a refresher: ordinarily the RGB and depth images are out of alignment with each other. The two cameras are set apart from each other on the front of the Kinect so they see the scene from different points of view. The result is two images that don't quite match up. Therefore, the user map we used in our last sketch will not successfully mask out the background in the color image. To get the user map to match the color image, we need to first align the color image to the depth image using SimpleOpenNI's `alternativeViewPointDepthToImage` function. This function will make the depth and color images match. We can then proceed with masking based on our user map. If we use those values to access the pixels in the RGB image, we'll end up with just the color pixels that show our user on top of our static background.

Here's the code. You'll need to save the sketch, open the sketch folder, and put in a file named *empire_state.jpg* before you can run it.

After the listing, I'll go over the specific lines that apply these changes.

```
import SimpleOpenNI.*;

SimpleOpenNI  kinect;

boolean tracking = false;
int userID;
int[] userMap;
// declare our background
PImage backgroundImage;

void setup() {
  size(640, 480);

  kinect = new SimpleOpenNI(this);
  kinect.enableDepth();

  // enable color image from the Kinect
  kinect.enableRGB(); ❶
  kinect.enableUser(SimpleOpenNI.SKEL_PROFILE_NONE);

  // turn on depth-color alignment
  kinect.alternativeViewPointDepthToImage(); ❷

  // load the background image
  backgroundImage = loadImage("empire_state.jpg"); ❸
}

void draw() {

  // display the background image
  image(backgroundImage, 0, 0); ❹
  kinect.update();
  if (tracking) {

    // get the Kinect color image
    PImage rgbImage = kinect.rgbImage(); ❺
    // prepare the color pixels
    rgbImage.loadPixels();
    loadPixels();

    userMap = kinect.getUsersPixels(SimpleOpenNI.USERS_ALL);
    for (int i =0; i < userMap.length; i++) {
      // if the pixel is part of the user
      if (userMap[i] != 0) {
        // set the sketch pixel to the color pixel
        pixels[i] = rgbImage.pixels[i]; ❻
      }
    }
```

```
    updatePixels();
  }
}

void onNewUser(int uID) {
  userID = uID;
  tracking = true;
  println("tracking");
}
```

❶ The changes start in `setup` where we enable the RGB image so that we can access the user's color pixels.

❷ We turn on the alignment of the depth and color images using `kinect.alternativeViewPointDepthToImage`.

❸ We need to load our background image into the `PImage` object we declared at the top of the sketch to hold it. In this case, I'm using a picture I took from the top of the Empire State Building on a cloudy day. You can use whatever image you like as long as it is at least 640 pixels wide and 480 pixels tall. Remember from the last sketch that we're going to loop over all of the pixels in the depth image. If your background image isn't at least 640 by 480, it won't have enough rows and columns for the loop, and your sketch will crash. If you don't happen to have a 640 by 480 image handy, you can resize whatever you want to use as your background image with one line of Processing code: `backgroundImage.resize(640,480);`.

Add that to the end of `setup`, just after you've loaded your `backgroundImage`. After resizing, your background image will definitely have the right number of pixels for our loop.

❹ Now that we have a background image that's the right size, we're ready to display it. At the beginning of `draw` we use `image` to display our `backgroundImage`. This replaces the spot in the previous sketch where we cleared the background to black. When we draw the `backgroundImage`, its pixels become part of the sketch's `pixel` array. So when we replace pixels in that array based on the `userMap`, we'll build a final image that has pixels from `backgroundImage` everywhere not occupied by the user. This creates the illusion that the user is in front of our background.

❺ Next we begin tracking. Once we're successfully tracking the user, we load up the color image from the Kinect using `kinect.rgbImage`. We need access to this image's pixels so that we can steal the ones that correspond to our user for our sketch's final image. We call `rgbImage.loadPixels` to prepare the image's pixel array. Then we tell the sketch to load its own pixels just as before. We also access the `userMap` just like in the last sketch. We load it, loop through its entries, and check to see which ones have nonzero values indicating the presence of a pixel that is part of the user.

❻ This time, though, when we find a user pixel, we're not just going to set it to green. Instead, we access the corresponding pixel in the Kinect's color image and use that to set our sketch's pixel.

Since our sketch is the same size as `rgbImage`, we can use the same index to access both pixel arrays, and they'll correspond to the same location in the image. This line fills in all of the pixels indicated by the `userMap` with the color pixels corresponding to the user. This completes the illusion that the user is standing in front of our background. In my case, the result made it look like I was taking a (somewhat dangerous) tourist snapshot from the top of the Empire State Building. Figure 4-22 shows a screenshot demonstrating the effect.

Figure 4-22. *Background removal using getUsersPixels. Using OpenNI's user tracking to extract the pixels representing the user from the background. Here I replaced the background with a picture I took from the top of the Empire State Building on a cloudy day.*

Warning

In these last two examples, we altered the pixels of our sketch itself. This made for quite concise and straightforward code, but it does have some downsides. Once you've altered the sketch's `pixels` *array, you've lost the data that was there before. While those pixels will be refreshed on the next frame for the course of each run of* `draw` *your changes are destructive. In practice, we frequently create a third* `PImage` *object to use as output, process that image's* `pixels` *array, and then simply display that image.*

In addition to tracking the user pixels, OpenNI can distinguish objects in the rest of the scene. Its ability to distinguish objects and walls is not nearly as sophisticated as its ability to track users. Don't forget that the Kinect was designed to track people as an input to games. Its capacity for comprehending the shape of a scene is a side-effect of technology that was intended to track people. Much less work and refinement has gone into scene analysis than user tracking. In this light, it is amazing that it works at all.

There are two ways that we can access the scene data: as an image or as a "scene map." The image will indicate what objects OpenNI has detected by displaying them in different colors. Figure 4-23 shows an example of this. The scene map works a lot like the user map we used in our previous sketches. It is an array of integers with one integer for each pixel in the depth image. The value of each element in the array indicates the object or person in the scene to which it belongs. Each user and object distinguished will have its own integer. The scene map includes the user pixels provided by `getUsersPixels` and adds the object pixels on top of that.

Figure 4-23. OpenNI's "scene map" breaks the depth map into spatially distinct pieces such as walls, people, and pieces of furniture. Here it is displayed mixed with the depth image to indicate separate objects.

The code for displaying the scene image is extremely simple. It resembles our first hello world programs more than anything we've seen since:

```
import processing.opengl.*;
import SimpleOpenNI.*;

SimpleOpenNI  kinect;

void setup() {
  size(640, 480, OPENGL);
  kinect = new SimpleOpenNI(this);
  kinect.enableDepth();
  // turn on access to the scene
  kinect.enableScene();
}

void draw() {
  background(0);
  kinect.update();
  // draw the scene image
  image(kinect.sceneImage(), 0, 0);
}
```

To access the scene image, you have to call kinect.enableScene in setup. Then within draw, you access the scene image with kinect.sceneImage, just like the other images available from the Kinect. When you run this sketch, you'll see a normal depth image at first. If you move the Kinect into a position where it can see a series of objects that are clearly separate from each other in space, you'll start to see those objects overlaid with different colors. I've found that if you don't move the Kinect around at least a little bit, sometimes the scene data will never become available. Figure 4-23 shows five distinct objects: the chair in red, the couch in blue, the table with flowers in orange, the wall in yellow, and the curtain in green. OpenNI's ability to distinguish between objects is far from perfect. Parts of objects will be left out, such as the bottom of the flower table, and parts of other surrounding objects will be erroneously included, such as the wall and doorframe adjacent to the window curtain.

You may have noticed that the highlighted objects in this image are not solid like the user silhouette we drew in Figure 4-21. Instead, they have shading based on the depth of the object they track. If you enable depth data, SimpleOpenNI automatically combines the scene data with the depth information to create the scene image. The color acts as an overlay on top of the depth image, as if it was drawn with less than complete opacity. If we comment out `kinect.enableDepth` from `setup`, then the image returned by `kinect.sceneImage` will no longer include depth information. Instead, it will have flat areas of color for each tracked object.

In addition to displaying this scene map, we can access it programmatically just as we did with the user map in our earlier sketches. In the user map the value of each element corresponds to the ID of the user that pixel is part of. In the scene map, it corresponds to whichever object has been detected: user, chair, table, wall, flowers, or other. Having called `kinect.enableScene` in `setup`, you can access the scene map like this:

```
int[] sceneMap = kinect.sceneMap();
for (int i =0; i < sceneMap.length; i++) {
  if(sceneMap[i] == 3){
    // we are tracking at least 3 objects
    // and this pixel belongs to the third object:
    rgbImage[i];
  }
}
```

I've seen the values of elements in the `sceneMap` range from 0 up to 6, but higher ones are possible if your scene is set up in such a way that OpenNI can distinguish more objects. This code sample shows how you would check to see which object in the `sceneMap` a particular pixel belongs to. It selects a pixel from an `rgbImage` that has been calibrated with the depth image using `kinect.alternativeViewPointDepthToImage` as in our previous sketch. This snippet doesn't actually do anything useful with the pixels, though. If you think of an application for this object tracking capability, this code would be a good place to start.

Tracking Without Calibration: Hand Tracking and Center of Mass

In this section we're going to look at two approaches to tracking users that don't require calibration: hand tracking and center of mass detection. These methods both go beyond simply accessing the user pixels. They use advanced functionality available from OpenNI to boil down the depth pixels into a simple position that will be useful in our application.

Hand Tracking

The first technique for tracking users without requiring calibration is hand tracking (Figure 4-24). This is the simplest use of OpenNI's wildly powerful and complex gesture recognition system, called *NITE*. This system allows us to detect the presence of the user's hand and to track its movement without needing the user to first perform the calibration ritual. The lack of the calibration ritual makes hand tracking much faster and more natural than the skeleton-based techniques we've used so far in this chapter. A user can move in front of the camera, raise her hand, and begin interacting with our application immediately. This results in faster startup times and much less opportunity for failure. It also enables user tracking in situations where it would otherwise be impossible, for example, where the camera is too close to a user to capture enough of her body to calibrate or, even more important, where the user can't actually move her body into the calibration pose due to physical disability or environmental constraints.

To perform hand tracking, we'll need to turn on OpenNI's gesture recognition system. This is a vast and complex system that has a lot of capabilities that require additional concepts to work with. We'll only scratch the surface of those here with this relatively simple example. However, this introduction should be enough for you to dive into learning more about NITE and OpenNI's more advanced gesture recognition capabilities on your own if you're interested.

Figure 4-24. *Hand tracking offers a gestural interface without the need for calibration. In this image I'm mostly offscreen, and OpenNI still has no problem finding my hand. The accuracy is nearly as reliable as the full skeleton data.*

How is gesture recognition related to hand tracking? To track the user's hand, OpenNI needs to know a starting place to begin searching for it. Thankfully, one of the gestures that NITE can detect is the act of raising your hand. By detecting this gesture, we'll have a starting location to kick off hand tracking. Further, this gives the user an explicit way to begin interacting with our sketch: raising your hand toward a screen is a natural method for indicating that you'd like to take control of it.

Like the skeleton tracking process, both the gesture recognition and hand tracking systems are based on callback functions. After we've configured our sketch to look for the RaiseHand gesture and to perform hand tracking, we'll have to implement a series of callback functions triggered by each process in order to receive its data. We'll write functions that get called when a user raises his hand, when we first lock onto this hand, whenever we get new data about the position of the hand, and then, finally, when we lose track of the hand.

Let's look at an example to see how this works. In the sketch below, I've built a new version of our Invisible Pencil project from the end of Chapter 2. This sketch waits for the user to raise his hand. When the hand is detected, the sketch adds its position to a growing ArrayList. Then, inside of draw, it uses this ArrayList to display a line that follows the user's hand. Take a look at the code, and then I'll explain some of its pertinent details.

```
import SimpleOpenNI.*;
SimpleOpenNI kinect;

ArrayList<PVector> handPositions;

PVector currentHand;
PVector previousHand;

void setup() {
  size(640, 480);

  kinect = new SimpleOpenNI(this);
  kinect.setMirror(true);

  //enable depthMap generation
  kinect.enableDepth();
  // enable hands + gesture generation  ❶
  kinect.enableGesture();
  kinect.enableHands();

  kinect.addGesture("RaiseHand");  ❷
  handPositions = new ArrayList();  ❸

  stroke(255, 0, 0);
  strokeWeight(2);
}

void draw() {
  kinect.update();
  image(kinect.depthImage(), 0, 0);

  for (int i = 1; i < handPositions.size(); i++) {  ❹
    currentHand = handPositions.get(i);
    previousHand = handPositions.get(i-1);
    line(previousHand.x, previousHand.y, currentHand.x, currentHand.y);
  }
}

// ----------------------------------------------------------------
// hand events  ❺
void onCreateHands(int handId, PVector position, float time) {
  kinect.convertRealWorldToProjective(position, position);
  handPositions.add(position);
}
```

```
void onUpdateHands(int handId, PVector position, float time) {
  kinect.convertRealWorldToProjective(position, position);
  handPositions.add(position);
}

void onDestroyHands(int handId, float time) {
  handPositions.clear();
  kinect.addGesture("RaiseHand");
}

// ----------------------------------------------------------------
// gesture events ❻
void onRecognizeGesture(String strGesture,
                        PVector idPosition,
                        PVector endPosition)
{
  kinect.startTrackingHands(endPosition);
  kinect.removeGesture("RaiseHand");
}
```

❶ The first new thing we have to do here is enable gestures and hand tracking. In setup, we call kinect.enableGesture and kinect.enableHands
to do just that.

❷ Once we've enabled the gesture recognition system, we need to tell
OpenNI what gesture we'd like to track. In our case, we're only interested
in finding out when a user raises her hands up from her sides. OpenNI
calls this gesture, RaiseHands. We tell SimpleOpenNI to track this gesture
by calling kinect.addGesture("RaiseHand").

❸ Here we initialize our ArrayList, called handPositions. We declared this
variable at the top of our sketch so it will be available in draw as well as
all of our callback functions. An ArrayList is similar to a normal array,
but it has a couple of major advantages. Most important, unlike an array,
an ArrayList can store an arbitrary number of items. We don't have
to know how many items it's going to store when we create it. We can
simply initialize it and then add items to it as we need. This is perfect for
our application here. We don't know how long we'll be tracking the user's
hand and so we don't know how many points we'll have to store to draw
our line. Therefore, there's no way we could create a normal array to store
these points. We know this ArrayList is going to store PVectors that
represent the position of our hand over time, so tell Processing that by
including the type inside of angle brackets: ArrayList<PVector>. This
is just like what we do when we create an array; we declare the type of
object that it will store like this: int[] myArrayOfInts.

❹ Now, let's look at the gesture and hand tracking callback functions. We'll
start with onRecognizeGesture. This function will be called whenever
the user performs a gesture that we've told OpenNI to watch out for. In
our case, that will only be RaiseHands. When this gesture occurs, we have
two steps to take. First, we want to tell OpenNI to start tracking the hand
it's found. The third argument that gets passed to onRecognizeGesture
is a PVector holding the current position of the hand. This is exactly the
data that we need to kick off the hand tracking process. We do that by
calling kinect.startTrackingHands(endPosition). This tells OpenNI
to start looking for a hand at the location indicated by endPosition.

Since we know that's just where the user's hand is located, this will work perfectly and we'll kick off hand tracking successfully. Once this is done, we can stop searching for the hand. We don't want to accidentally catch another `RaiseHand` gesture and reset our hand tracking process by calling `startTrackingHands` again. To avoid this, we call `kinect.removeGesture("RaiseHand")`. This tells OpenNI to stop looking for the raise-hands gesture. Our hand-tracking callbacks will take it from here.

❺ To perform hand tracking, we need to implement three functions: `on-CreateHands`, `onUpdateHands`, and `onDestroyHands`. The first of these gets called when we first begin tracking the user's hand, the second gets called over and over again for the duration of the time that we're tracking, and the third gets called once when we lose track of the user's hand because it's gone out of frame or been obscured by something else in the scene. In the first two of these functions, we get passed the same three arguments: which hand we're tracking, its position, and how long we've been tracking it. For this simple application, the action we want to take is also the same for both of these functions: we just want to add the current position of the hand to our `handPositions ArrayList`. We want `handPositions` to hold every location of the hand we've detected. In `draw` we'll be using that `ArrayList` to display a continuous line that follows the user's hand. To redraw this full line on each frame of our sketch so that it stays visible, we'll need to remember every point the hand has passed through. We save the `PVector position` passed to us in each of these functions into our `ArrayList` by calling: `handPositions.add(position)`. This sticks each new `position` onto the list at the end, maintaining the order in which they arrived. However, before we store the hand positions, we need to convert them to screen coordinates. Just like the joint position data we've been working with throughout this chapter, these hand positions arrive in real-world coordinates. Since we want our line to match the depth image, we need to convert them to projective coordinates so they'll match the screen. We do this with: `kinect.convertRealWorldToProjective(position, position)`. On previous occasions where we'd used this function, we introduced an additional `PVector` to hold the converted result. In this case, we're simply saving the new projective space version over our existing `PVector`. This saves us a couple of lines of code and is perfectly safe since we won't be using that `PVector` again in either of these short callback functions.

For `onDestroyHands` we want to do something different, obviously. This function gets called when the user's hand has disappeared from the scene and OpenNI can no longer track it. When that happens, we want to erase the line the user's been drawing and start searching for the hand again. This will let them start creating a new drawing simply by raising their hand into view again. Erasing the line is easy, we simply remove all of the vectors we've stored in our `handPositions ArrayList` by calling: `handPositions.clear`. Since our `draw` function is going to use this list to figure out what to draw, emptying it will immediately remove the line. We've already seen the function we use to trigger gesture detection: `kinect.addGesture("RaiseHand")`. Calling that again here ensures that `onRecognizeGesture` will be invoked again the next time the user raises her hand, beginning the whole process over.

❻ So, we've seen all the work we have to do to capture the position of a user's hand as she moves it around. But how do we display those positions in our sketch once we've got them? We want to make one long extended line that connects all the points we've collected. We'll do this by looping over all of the vectors stored in our `ArrayList` and drawing a series of line segments that connect each vector to the one immediately before it. This is the same approach we took in our Invisible Pencil example way back in Chapter 2.

Our loop starts right after we've displayed the depth image from the Kinect. This way our line will show up on top of the depth image, matching it. We use `handPositions.size` to loop over every element in our `ArrayList`. Inside the loop, we access the elements of `handPositions` in pairs, the `currentHand`, corresponding to the current index, `i`, and the `previousHand`, corresponding to the previous index, `i - 1`. In each case, we use `handPositions.get` to access the element. That function takes a position in the `ArrayList` and returns the element that it finds there.

Once we've got both of these vectors, it's simple to draw a line between them: `line(previousHand.x, previousHand.y, currentHand.x, currentHand.y)`. But what about the very first point that we detect? When we first start tracking the hand, there will only be one point in `handPositions`. Won't we have a problem finding the `previousHand`? We most certainly will. In fact, if we tried to call `handPositions.get(i-1)` for our very first vector, we'd end up crashing our sketch by failing to find anything. But look again at our `for` loop. Instead of starting our declaration with `int i = 0` as we usually would, this time we start it with `int i = 1`. We always start our loop on the second element in our `ArrayList`. This ensures that the previous hand position will always be available inside of our loop and our line will draw successfully without crashing our sketch (see Figure 4-25).

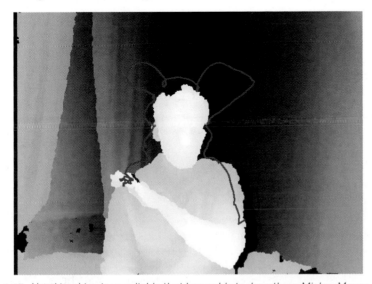

Figure 4-25. *Hand tracking is so reliable that I was able to draw these Mickey Mouse ears over my head.*

That brings me to the end of the discussion of hand tracking. While this new stack of callbacks to learn may seem fiddly, it's no worse than the skeleton tracking process with which you're now intimately familiar, and I think the results are more than worth it. The ability to perform hand tracking without the need for calibration is a terrific advantage that opens up interactive applications to whole groups of people who have limited ranges of motion that normally prevent them from using computer interfaces. These groups include both people with disabilities, older people with limited fine motor control, or simply anyone who's too constrained or distracted to use the complex traditional mouse-and-keyboard interface.

Center of Mass

Next, we're going to look at *center of mass detection*. This technique allows us to track users who are farther away from the Kinect and may not even know that they're on camera all. Once we've detected the presence of a user, OpenNI will report that user's *center of mass*. This vector locates the center of the user's body. It is based on the user pixels that we worked with above, but we don't need to access those pixels directly in order to obtain it. As soon as a user is detected within the scene, a center-of-mass vector will become available for him. Unlike the skeleton- and hand-tracking systems we've worked with before, the center of the mass is effective for tracking many users within the same scene. While hypothetically we can access skeleton data for up to four users, in practice it is difficult to fit more than two into the Kinect's view at a range where they are distinguishable enough for calibration to take place. Center-of-mass tracking eliminates this problem and so can be used to track larger number of users. Where nearly all of the other sketches in this book are tailored to detect only a single user, in this section, we'll develop a sketch that accesses multiple users and displays their centers of mass on the screen.

Here's the code:

```
import SimpleOpenNI.*;
SimpleOpenNI kinect;

void setup() {
  size(640, 480);

  kinect = new SimpleOpenNI(this);
  kinect.enableDepth();
  kinect.enableUser(SimpleOpenNI.SKEL_PROFILE_NONE); ❶

}

void draw() {
  kinect.update();
  image(kinect.depthImage(), 0, 0);

  IntVector userList = new IntVector();
  kinect.getUsers(userList);

  for (int i=0; i<userList.size(); i++) { ❷
    int userId = userList.get(i);
```

```
    PVector position = new PVector();
    kinect.getCoM(userId, position); ❸

    kinect.convertRealWorldToProjective(position, position);
    fill(255, 0, 0);
    ellipse(position.x, position.y, 25,25);
  }
}
```

This sketch detects all of the users that are visible in the scene, loops over them, and displays a red circle over the location OpenNI has determined is each user's center of mass. You can see its results in Figure 4-26. Let's walk through how it works.

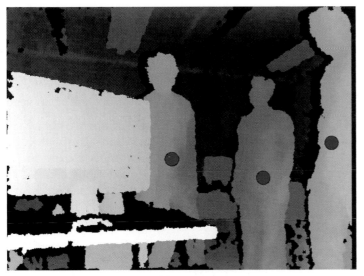

Figure 4-26. *Tracking multiple simultaneous users without calibration by their center of mass. This technique is especially effective for installations and projects in public space.*

❶ In setup, we call kinect.enableUser(SimpleOpenNI.SKEL_PROFILE_ NONE). This is the same function we use when doing skeleton tracking. It makes the user-tracking data that we need available to us. Passing SimpleOpenNI.SKEL_PROFILE_NONE tells OpenNI that we don't need all of the joint positions calculated. Since we're not planning on having our users calibrate, that data is unnecessary.

❷ Our draw function starts off as normal by updating the Kinect and displaying the depth image. Then, also as usual, we use kinect.getUsers to access all of the users that are currently known to OpenNI. In every other sketch in this chapter, we've specifically accessed only the first element in this list. We've only been tracking one user at a time (usually ourselves). But this time we want to track multiple users, as many as we can find in the scene. Therefore after populating our userList from kinect.getUsers, we loop over all of the user IDs that we found, working with each one in turn by calling int userId = userList.get(i) with the current index.

❸ To find each user's center of mass, we call `kinect.getCoM`. CoM stands for "center of mass." It's a badly named function, but it works. Just like `getJointPositionSkeleton` and many of the other SimpleOpenNI functions we've seen, `getCoM` takes a user ID and a `PVector`. It stores the user's center of mass into the `PVector`, which we can then use in the rest of our sketch. In the last two lines of `draw`, we convert this `position` into projective coordinates so it matches our depth image and then use it to display a circle.

As you can see in Figure 4-26, this code works to find the position of multiple users within the scene even when one of them is obscured by a desk and computer monitor and another is partially off camera. It's interesting to observe where the center of mass shows up on each user. It is approximately at the belly button.

An additional aspect of the center of mass that's obscured in this example is that it is actually correct in three dimensions. Each center of mass vector includes a z-coordinate that will position it inside the user's body. We discarded this information in this sketch by converting our center of mass vectors into screen coordinates, but if it suited your application, you could instead retain it and use it for something. For example, you could create a top-down representation of the people you'd detected. By simply using the center of mass x- and z-coordinates rather than the x- and y-coordinates to display our circles, they would begin to match the users' positions in the room rather than simply from the point of view of the camera. If you used these positions to draw lines, you could get a set of users to create a floorplan for a room simply by walking around it in view of the Kinect.

To complete this section, let's take a look at one small variation to this sketch. Replace `ellipse(position.x, position.y, 25,25)` from the end of `draw` with the following lines:

```
textSize(40);
text(userId, position.x, position.y);
```

This will display the actual ID of each user on top of their center of mass as shown in Figure 4-27. If you get a group of people to move around in front of your Kinect with this sketch running, you'll get a sense of the continuity OpenNI is able to maintain: when it can retain the identity of a single user and when it loses track of one it can't see and rejiggers the IDs. This exercise is especially vital if your application plans to distinguish individual users as they interact with your project. It will give you a sense of how well that will work in your particular space and situation.

Figure 4-27. *We can distinguish individual users in our scene as they move across each other in the space and even keep track of them if they briefly leave the frame and then return.*

Projects

To finish off this chapter, we're going to do two projects that exercise your ability to understand and work with the skeleton data. The first project will be practical, and the second will be silly and artistic.

For our first project we'll build an exercise training tool, letting you act as your own physical trainer. Physical trainers teach exercises by demonstrating them with their own bodies. Then as you try to copy their motions, they give you feedback about how you're doing. This project will record the position of one of your joints while you perform a series of physical motions. Then, with the click of a button, it will start playing back those motions as a target for you to follow. It will show you the current position of your joint and give you feedback about how far off you are from the target in the recorded exercise. If you try your best to respond to this feedback and conform your movements to the recording, over time you'll improve, performing the original action more and more accurately.

This sketch will have only a primitive visual user interface, but it will give you a set of powerful tools for comparing joint positions and recording skeleton motion that will come in quite handy as you start to build your own applications. We'll implement a SkeletonRecorder class that you can use in your own sketches just like the Hotpoint class from the last chapter. That class will record the position of one joint at each frame and then it will let us access that data to play back the joint's motion. We'll be able to use its recorded joint data along with the tools we've already learned in this book for comparing vectors to analyze how the user's current motions differ from what we recorded.

This will not be the sexiest or most fun project we'll complete in this book, but what you learn from it (as well as the code for the `SkeletonRecorder` class itself) will come in handy as you start to build more serious and powerful applications of your own. For example, you could expand this project to help with physical therapy for people who've experienced debilitating injuries. You could record a series of motions performed by a therapist and then turn them into a game that the patient would play as part of rehabilitation. Or you could use these techniques for sports training, using a similar approach to teach an athlete the proper technique for pitching a baseball or shooting a basketball. In a totally different direction, you could combine the `SkeletonRecorder` class with the 3D puppetry techniques we learned earlier to create a basic motion capture system. To accomplish that, you would record the position of all of your joints as you performed a motion, then play them back and apply their angle and orientation to 3D models representing each of your limbs. The result would be a 3D puppet that acted out your recorded motion. All of these advanced applications (and many more) start with the basic tools for recording the joint positions and playing them back that we'll cover in this project.

Our second project will be much sillier. We'll build a sketch that triggers music when you strike a dance pose. Specifically, we'll play "Stayin' Alive," the theme from disco classic *Saturday Night Fever*, when you hit the hips-out hand-up dance pose that John Travolta made famous in that movie. This project is inspired by work done by Alex Vessels and Kimi Spencer, students at the NYU Telecommunications Program in 2010. Where our Exercise Measurement project will teach us how to capture a user's motion over time, in this project, we'll explore techniques for analyzing the position of a user's joints relative to each other.

How can you tell if a user has struck the *Saturday Night Fever* pose? We'll define the pose as a series of spatial relationships between pairs of joints in a user's body. Is her left elbow bent away from her side? Is her left hand close to her left hip? Is her right elbow above her shoulders? Is her right hand extended above her right elbow? And so on. I'll show you how to break down a pose into a series of constraints such as these on the relative positions and angles between pairs of joints. I'll also provide another helper class that enables you to declare these constraints in code and then check to see if the user's current posture satisfies them and matches the pose. This helper class will pick up on some of the more advanced programming techniques demonstrated by the `SkeletonRecorder` from the Exercise Measurement project and extend them even further. The result will be a class that is sophisticated in its own code, but very easy to use from the outside. Again, you'll be able to use this class in your other sketches outside of this book to build applications that detect particular use poses.

After you've worked through these two projects, you'll have completed the tools section of this book. You'll know all the fundamentals for working with the Kinect, and you'll be ready to build some very sophisticated and powerful applications of your own devising. To give you some ideas for those and to give you some additional concepts for how you might use the Kinect data, the last three chapters of this book take the form of advanced case studies. Once you're done with these two projects, you'll be ready to dive into any of those, from building a game to help a stroke patient to making 3D scans you can print out on a MakerBot, to using your arm to control a robot arm powered by an Arduino.

Project 10: Exercise Measurement

Let's get started on the Exercise Measurement project (Figure 4-28). I explained the basic outline of this project earlier. Before we dive into looking at code, I'll walk through what our sketch has to do to make that outline come to life. This is frequently the best way to start on a project. Once you've defined the basic idea of what you want your sketch to do, go through it step by step and write down in words what your code will have to do to make those ideas real. This outline will then act as a map when you get to actually writing code, letting you dig into the details to solve individual problems without worrying that you'll lose your place in the overall plan for how you're going to get to a program that executes your idea. Creating the outline can also reveal flaws in your initial ideas for how to approach a problem, saving you lots of time by letting you rethink before you've written a bunch of useless code.

Figure 4-28. Two screen captures from the final Exercise Measurement sketch. The green sphere shows the recorded position of the user's hand, the red sphere shows its current position. The color of the line connecting them reflects the distance between them as seen in the number labeled "off by."

So, what's the outline for our Exercise Measurement project? We want to record a set of one of the user's joints. Then we want to play back those movements in a visual form while also showing the current movements of that same joint. And finally we want to compare the live movements to the recorded ones to give the user feedback about how he can correct his motions and to keep a running score of how good of a job he's doing. These are the requirements for our sketch. Now's let's talk about the individual steps we'll take to achieve them.

The first step is to display the motion of a single joint. This is something we've already done quite a bit in this chapter so we know exactly what's involved. We need to implement the callbacks and checks for the calibration process. Then, once the user skeleton becomes available, we can ask SimpleOpenNI to give us the position of any of the joints as a vector. Once we have that position, we want to display it on the screen in 3D. In our previous sketches that displayed individual joints, we used a projective coordinate system to get our joints to match the depth image. This time we want to display our joints in true 3D. We want to cue our users about when the joints are moving closer and farther from the Kinect, not just when they're moving side to side. Physical exercises can take advantage of the full range of the body's motion, not just sideways movements on a single plane. In order for the user to match the movement of the recorded exercise in depth, we'll give visual feedback about the z-axis position of our tracked joint. The easiest way to accomplish this is to display the joint's position as a sphere situated within a real-world 3D coordinate system. As the joint moves closer to the Kinect, the sphere will appear larger in our sketch, and as the joint recedes, the sphere will shrink.

Once we've displayed a single joint, we want to record its position. We'll do this by telling our SkeletonRecorder class to record the joint position on every frame starting when the user has completed calibration. We'll dive into how the SkeletonRecorder class works later on, but for now we'll just look at it from the point of view of our main sketch, defining what that SkeletonRecorder needs to do for us. Once the user has completed the motions that he wants recorded, we'll have him hit the space bar to indicate that recording has completed. When recording ends, we'll go into playback mode. In playback mode, we'll still want to display the current position of the user's hand; that shouldn't change. But now, in addition, we need to access the recorded joint position from the SkeletonRecorder and display that as well. We'll use a sphere to represent the recorded position for the same reason mentioned above. We'll want to make sure the recorded sphere is a different color than the one representing the user's real position so the difference is clear.

We also want to calculate and display some information about the difference between the recorded and live positions. We'll use vector subtraction for this. If we subtract the vector representing the recorded position from the one representing the current position, the result will be a vector that captures the angle and distance between the two. We'll display this vector as a line connecting our two spheres. This line will give the user an additional visual clue about the direction he needs to move to better match the recorded exercise. Then we'll calculate the magnitude of this vector, which will tell us exactly how far apart the two points are. We'll display this to the user in numerical form at the top of our sketch.

At this point, our sketch will be fully functional. Now that we've talked about how the sketch works, let's look at the code (listed in Example 4-3) and examine the results.

Example 4-3. *exercise_measurement.pde*

```
import processing.opengl.*;
import SimpleOpenNI.*;
SimpleOpenNI  kinect;

SkeletonRecorder recorder; ❶
boolean recording = false; ❷
float offByDistance = 0.0; ❸

void setup() {
  size(1028, 768, OPENGL);
  kinect = new SimpleOpenNI(this);
  kinect.enableDepth();
  kinect.enableUser(SimpleOpenNI.SKEL_PROFILE_ALL);
  kinect.setMirror(true); ❹
```

```
  // initialize our recorder and
  // tell it to track left hand
  recorder = new SkeletonRecorder(kinect, SimpleOpenNI.SKEL_LEFT_HAND); ❺

  // load a font
  PFont font = createFont("Verdana", 40); ❻
  textFont(font);
}

void draw() {
  background(0);
  kinect.update();

  // these are to make our spheres look nice
  lights(); ❼
  noStroke();

  // create heads-up display
  fill(255);
  text("totalFrames: " + recorder.frames.size(), 5, 50); ❽
  text("recording: " + recording, 5, 100);
  text("currentFrame: " + recorder.currentFrame, 5, 150 );

  // set text color as a gradient from red to green
  // based on distance between hands
  float c = map(offByDistance, 0, 1000, 0, 255); ❾
  fill(c, 255-c, 0);
  text("off by: " + offByDistance, 5, 200);

  translate(width/2, height/2, 0);
  rotateX(radians(180));

  IntVector userList = new IntVector();
  kinect.getUsers(userList);
  if (userList.size() > 0) {
    int userId = userList.get(0);
    recorder.setUser(userId);
    if ( kinect.isTrackingSkeleton(userId)) {

      PVector currentPosition = new PVector();
      kinect.getJointPositionSkeleton(userId, ❿
                                 SimpleOpenNI.SKEL_LEFT_HAND,
                                 currentPosition);

      // display the sphere for the current limb position
      pushMatrix();
        fill(255,0,0);
      ⓫translate(currentPosition.x, currentPosition.y, currentPosition.z);
        sphere(80); ⓬
      popMatrix();

      // if we're recording tell the recorder to capture this frame
      if (recording) { ⓭
        recorder.recordFrame();
      }
      else  { ⓮

        // if we're playing access the recorded joint position
        PVector recordedPosition = recorder.getPosition(); ⓯
```

```
                           // display the recorded joint position
                           pushMatrix();
                             fill(0, 255, 0);
                             translate(recordedPosition.x,
                                       recordedPosition.y,
                                       recordedPosition.z);
                               sphere(80); ⓰
                           popMatrix();

                           // draw a line between the current position and the recorded one
                           // set its color based on the distance between the two
                           stroke(c, 255-c, 0); ⓱
                           strokeWeight(20);
                           line(currentPosition.x, currentPosition.y,
                                currentPosition.z, recordedPosition.x,
                                recordedPosition.y, recordedPosition.z);

                           // calculate the vector between the current and recorded positions
                           // with vector subtraction
                           currentPosition.sub(recordedPosition); ⓲

                           // store the magnitude of that vector as
                           // the off-by distance for display
                           offByDistance = currentPosition.mag(); ⓳

                           // tell the recorder to load up the next frame
                           recorder.nextFrame(); ⓴
                  }
                }
              }
            }

void keyPressed() {
  recording = false;
}

// user-tracking callbacks!
void onNewUser(int userId) {
  println("start pose detection");
  kinect.startPoseDetection("Psi", userId);
}

void onEndCalibration(int userId, boolean successful) {
  if (successful) {
    println("  User calibrated !!!");
    kinect.startTrackingSkeleton(userId);
    recording = true;
  }
  else {
    println("  Failed to calibrate user !!!");
    kinect.startPoseDetection("Psi", userId);
  }
}

void onStartPose(String pose, int userId) {
  println("Started pose for user");
  kinect.stopPoseDetection(userId);
  kinect.requestCalibrationSkeleton(userId, true);
}
```

To run this sketch, you'll also need the `SkeletonRecorder` class. We haven't talked about the details of how that class works yet. We'll take that on after we discuss this sketch. You can find the code for the `SkeletonRecorder` class a few pages ahead in Example 4-4. Grab that code, create a new tab within your Processing sketch (by clicking the arrow at the top right of the Processing window), name your tab `SkeletonRecorder`, and paste the code into the new tab that Processing creates for you. This will add the code for the class to your Processing project and make it available in your sketch. Once you've got that class installed, the code here should run successfully. When you first run it, the screen will be blank except for some text in the top-left corner showing the values of a few key variables. Perform the calibration ritual. When you've been successfully tracked, a red sphere will show up on screen following the movements of your left hand. The `totalFrames` variable displayed at the top of the sketch will start running up as the `SkeletonRecorder` records your movements. Once you've performed the movement you wanted to record, hit the space bar on your computer to stop recording and start playback. You might want to get a friend to help you with this step since you'll probably have to step away from the Kinect to do it, distorting the motion you're recording. After you hit the space bar, the sketch will switch to playback mode. A green sphere will appear and begin to follow the track of your hand that you recorded. The red sphere tracking the current position of your hand will still be present, and there will be a line connecting the two telling you which way to move to keep up.

From this point, on the sketch will look something like the screen captures shown in Figure 4-28. That figure shows the sketch at two different moments. In the capture on the left, the user is doing a poor job following the recorded skeleton motions. You can see that the green sphere representing the recorded motion is above and to the left of the red sphere and also significantly larger. The user's current position is below, to the side, and behind where it should be. The result is that the "off by" distance displayed by the sketch is quite large, almost 1060. This is reflected in the red color of the line connecting the two spheres, which is solid red. In the image on the right, on the other hand, the spheres are quite close together. The red sphere representing the user's current position is following close behind the recorded motion. The line connecting them is short and green, reflecting the small off-by distance of less than 170.

This sketch is built on the familiar outline of most joint-tracking sketches we've seen in this chapter. It includes all the standard callback functions, declarations, and `if` statements for performing user calibration and setting up access to the skeleton data. As usual, I won't spend time on those, but will focus on the new additions here that implement our Exercise Measurement project.

❶ The first of these occurs at the top of the sketch as a set of three variable declarations. First, we declare `recorder` as an instance of our Skeleton-Recorder class. (After we've made our way through this sketch, I'll dive into how the `SkeletonRecorder` class works. But for now I'll just show you how we use it to make this sketch work.)

❷ After our `recorder`, we declare a Boolean, `recording`, to keep track of whether we're currently recording a motion or playing it back.

If you jump down to `onEndCalibration` near the bottom of the sketch, you'll see that when the user successfully completes calibration, we set `recording` to true. That way we can start recording automatically without the user needing to step forward to use the keyboard or mouse to trigger the recording. Then, within `draw`, we'll use the value of `recording` to decide whether to record or play back.

❸ The last variable we declare is a float called `offByDistance`. This variable will store the distance between our recorded hand position and our current one. We declare it as a global variable because we'll want it to carry across between multiple runs of `draw`. We'll use `offByDistance` to set the color of two separate parts of our display: the text output and the line connecting our two spheres. As we'll see when we look at the details of our `draw` function, we need to use the value of `offByDistance` before we've actually calculated it for the current frame. To overcome this problem, we simply use its value from the previous frame, which is still stored in `offByDistance` until we update it.

❹ Our `setup` function is mostly standard code for initiating skeleton tracking. The one bit of this that's worth noting is `kinect.setMirror(true)`. This function tells `SimpleOpenNI` to flip its data so that the screen will act as a mirror for the user looking at it. In other words, it will place the left hand on the left side of the screen and the right hand on the right side. This will make an interface that gives a user visual feedback about her body's position much more intuitive to use. It will be very hard for the user to match a recorded motion without it.

❺ The two new elements in `setup` that are key to this project happen at the bottom of the function. First we initialize our `SkeletonRecorder` object. To create the `SkeletonRecorder` instance, we have to pass in two arguments: our `SimpleOpenNI` object, `kinect`, and the `SimpleOpenNI` constant representing the ID of the joint we want to track, in this case `SimpleOpenNI.SKEL_LEFT_HAND`. As we'll see later, our `recorder` needs these so that it can access the joint positions in order to record them.

❻ The second new element here is the use of a font. This is our first time displaying text in a 3D sketch. When we created a heads-up display back in Example 4-2 we didn't use a font. We set the size of our text using `scale`. When we work in 3D, though, scaling up a font will cause it to become pixelated and ugly. The only way to make the font big enough to see, then, is to use a larger font size, which means using Processing's `createFont` and `textFont` methods. `createFont` takes two arguments: the name of the font we want to use and the size we want it to be. In this case we're using Verdana, which is a common sans-serif font. If you don't have Verdana on your system, substitute something else. `createFont` returns a `PFont` object, which we use to set the font by passing it to `textFont` on the next line.

❼ We've now got everything ready to go. Our `SkeletonRecorder` is armed and ready, we've set up our fonts, and we've initialized our variables. Let's look at `draw` to see how we use all this stuff to actually record and play back the skeleton data. Inside of `draw`, the first noteworthy additions are related to the fact that we're going to displaying our joint positions as 3D spheres. Near the top of `draw`, we call `lights` to turn on the lights and shadows so our geometry shows up as realistically 3D. We also call `noStroke` to prevent Processing from drawing all the inner lines of our sphere, which will dramatically improve its appearance.

❽ Next, we create the heads-up display that will show us data about our recording and how close our current movements are matching it. We use Processing's `text` function to display the total number of frames recorded, the current frame being shown in playback, whether or not we are currently recording, and how far apart our live hand position is from the recording. The first two of these pieces of information we get back by accessing variables within our `recorder` object: `recorder.totalFrames` tells us how many frames have been recorded, and `recorder.currentFrame` tells us which frame is currently being played back.

❾ Before we display the distance between the live and recorded hand positions, we calculate a next color for `fill`. We want to give the user feedback about how closely he is matching the recorded movement, and we want the feedback to be clear even some distance from the screen. To achieve this, we'll use the color of the text. Color is much easier to pick out from far away than the exact value of a number. We want the text displaying the distance to be green when the user is close to the recorded movement and then fade to red as the user gets farther away. We use `map` to make this happen. We use `map` to scale `offByDistance` from its real values down to 0–255, a range that's useful for setting color values. We want the red and green components of our color to scale opposite to each other, so we use the result from `map` twice: once to set the green component directly so that as that value goes up, the color will become more green, and once as an "inverse" by subtracting it from 255 so the color will become less red. The result will be a smooth transition between the two colors as our user gets farther from the recorded movement. Having set that color, we go ahead and display `offByDistance` using `text`, just as we had with our earlier values.

❿ After creating this heads-up display, we go through the usual boilerplate for accessing the skeleton data. Once this is done, we access the position of the user's left hand as usual via `kinect.getJointPositionSkeleton` and store it in our `currentPosition` variable. We then use this variable to display the joint position as a sphere in space.

⓫ Since we're working in 3D, we need to use `translate` to position our coordinate system where we want it before we draw our sphere. We'll pass `translate` the x-, y-, and z-coordinates of the `currentPosition` of the left hand. To prevent this translation from affecting the rest of our work, we'll wrap our work between calls to `pushMatrix` and `popMatrix` each time we want to display a sphere.

⑫ Having translated into position, we're ready to draw our sphere with Processing's very cleverly named sphere function. The value we pass to sphere will set its size. Through experimentation, I found the value 80 to be reasonable with the distances I normally stand from the Kinect. Regardless of its size, the sphere appears to shrink as you get farther away and grow as you get closer, since it is displayed in perspective.

⑬ **Recording joint positions.** We've now got the display representing the live hand in place. Next, our sketch will fork to do different things based on whether we're recording a motion or playing it back and comparing it. We'll start by examining what we do when we're recording and then we'll step back and look at playback.

If we're in the midst of recording, then our recording variable will be set to true. Hence, the if statement based on that variable will trigger its first branch. It turns out that recording the joint position is extremely easy. This is natural since this is exactly the task that SkeletonRecorder was designed to do. All we have to do to record the current joint position is call recorder.recordFrame. SkeletonRecorder will do all the necessary work to access the joint position and save it. Notice that we don't pass in the position of the joint even though we just accessed it ourselves. We accessed the joint position so that we could display it on the screen. We'll be doing this regardless of whether we're asking the SkeletonRecorder to record. As we'll see later, SkeletonRecorder accesses the joint position itself, so we don't have to worry about doing so. In a different application, we might want to skip getting the joint position ourselves, for example, if we were using the drawLimb function provided by SimpleOpenNI for our interface or simply not displaying the joint position at all. When we're in record mode, calling recorder.recordFrame completes our work. We're done with our draw function, and we move on to the next frame.

⑭ **Playing back joint positions.** When a user is done recording, she can hit any key to switch into playback mode. In our keyPressed callback function, we set recording to false. This will cause us to go down the alternate branch of the if statement. Let's now examine the code inside there to see how we play back the recorded joint positions and compare them with what the user is currently doing.

⑮ First, we access the recorded joint position with recorder.getPosition. When we call it initially, that function will give us the first joint position that was captured by the recorder. Once we've used that position, we can advance to the next recorded position by calling recorder.next-Frame. If you jump down to the last line in draw, you can see that we call nextFrame after we've finished all our other actions so that the next joint position will be ready for the next run.

⑯ We then store the recorded hand position in a PVector called recorded-Position. Once we've got that vector, we use it to draw a sphere just as we did with the live joint position. The only difference is that this time, we set our fill color to green so we'll be able to differentiate the recording from the live hand position, which will stay red.

Chapter 4

At this point, we've already got the recording playing back. This is the heart of the interface for this sketch. The user will be able to move his hand around to get the red ball to try to catch the green ball, and that will train him to reproduce the original recorded exercise motion. However, we'd also like to add some more feedback about how well they're doing, both visually and numerically. To do this, we have to use what we've learned about calculating the difference between vectors to determine the distance and direction between the recorded hand position and what the user is actually doing.

⑰ Before we get into vector math, though, we have some simple visual feedback we can give the user with the data we already have accessible. We can draw a line connecting our two spheres to indicate which direction the user should move to correct his position. The next three lines of our sketch do just this. First we set the stroke color using the same logic for fading between red and green discussed above. Our c variable still holds the mapped value of our offByDistance, which is ready to set colors. We use this to set our stroke and then set strokeWeight to a large value so that it is clearly visible. With our color set, we then call line to draw our line. The first three arguments to line are the components of the hand's currentPosition, and the last three are the components of the recordedPosition. This line will connect our two spheres.

⑱ Now it's time to get into our vector math. First we'll use vector subtraction to calculate the vector that connects our currentPosition to the recordedPosition. To do this, we call sub on our currentPosition vector with recordedPosition as the argument. This transforms the currentPosition vector into one that represents the difference between our two positions. If we used currentPosition to display the hand's position after this point, it would give us surprising and incorrect results. That's why we waited until the end of the sketch here to do this vector math. We've already used currentPosition for display, so this change to it won't affect our interface.

⑲ Once currentPosition represents the difference between our two vectors, we can take its magnitude to find out how far apart they are. This is the value we want to use to give users feedback about how well they're doing. We calculate the magnitude by calling the mag function on our currentPosition vector and storing the result in offByDistance. We've already seen how we use offByDistance in the heads-up display to set the color of our text and line. We initialized offByDistance to 0 so it will hold that value until we begin playback, but as soon as we reach this part of the sketch, its value will be set correctly to the distance between the current and recorded hand positions.

⑳ At this point, all our work for the playback portion of the sketch is done. The last step we've already mentioned: calling recorder.nextFrame so that our SkeletonRecorder advances to the next joint position that it captured for the next run of draw.

Having gone through it, this sketch doesn't seem that complex. It accomplishes quite a lot in a relatively small amount of code. It has multiple states: one for recording and one for playback. It displays information as text, as scaled color, and as 3D graphics. It performs vector math to analyze the difference between joint positions. Given all those objectives, the amount of code here (outside of the usual calibration callbacks) is actually relatively minimal. That's only possible because of how much work the `SkeletonRecorder` is doing for us. Up to this point, we've been pretending that the `SkeletonRecorder` was magic, simply using its functions without worrying about how they work. Now it's time to look inside the actual `SkeletonRecorder` class to see how it provides all of this useful functionality in such a simple interface. Understanding this is important not just because of the lessons you might learn for designing your own classes, but also to make it easier for you to use the `SkeletonRecorder` class in your own applications outside of this book. In the next section, I'll go through the class's implementation to show you how it works and then I'll conclude by suggesting some improvements you might make to the `SkeletonRecorder` to make it even more useful.

The SkeletonRecorder Class

Before we look at the actual code for the `SkeletonRecorder` class, let's talk about what it needs to do. We've already seen it from the perspective of our Exercise Measurement sketch. We've seen what functions the `SkeletonRecorder` needs to provide and how they'll be used in the workflow of our application. Now all we need to do is make those functions actually work. This can be an effective way of designing libraries, if a slightly counterintuitive one. Instead of starting from scratch and thinking about all the possible things that could go into the class, you start by thinking about how your external code will use the class. Write the code of your sketch to include the use of an imaginary class that doesn't exist yet. Initialize its objects, call its functions, and use the results in the way that seems most efficient and helpful for your application. This will show you the most useful functions for your class to provide and how it makes sense for them to work together. Then you can take those constraints and goals and do whatever it takes behind the scenes inside the class's code to make them work.

What are the specific demands our sketch makes on the `SkeletonRecorder` class? What functions does `SkeletonRecorder` need to provide, and how do those functions work together? To start, `SkeletonRecorder` needs to give the sketch a way to indicate which joint and user it wants to track. It does the first in initialization: the sketch initializes the recorder with `new SkeletonRecorder`, passing in an OpenNI context and a joint ID. It does the second in `recorder.setUser`, which the sketch calls to specify the user. We know what joint we want to track from the very beginning, because that's a decision we make at the time we write the code. That's why we can pass in the joint ID when we create our `SkeletonRecorder` within `setup`. However, we don't know the ID of the user until OpenNI begins to track a user and assigns an ID. That only happens once `draw` has been running for awhile and the user-detection process has begun. That's why we have this separate `setUser` function: so we can call it at that point when the user's ID finally becomes available.

Once the sketch is tracking the user, it needs to tell SkeletonRecorder to record a new frame when appropriate. This is done with recorder.recordFrame. When the recording is done and the sketch wants to play back the recorded joint positions, it needs to access the current position (recorder.getPosition) and then tell the SkeletonRecorder to move on to the next frame (recorder. nextFrame). That's it. That's all that our sketch needs from SkeletonRecorder. Whatever variables of functions the SkeletonRecorder has to use to get these jobs done don't matter as long as the constructor, setUser, recordFrame, getPosition, and nextFrame work as expected.

Let's go through these one at a time to see how they're implemented inside the class to fulfill this promise. Example 4-4 provides the full listing of *Skeleton-Recorder.pde* so you can follow along in the discussion.

Example 4-4. SkeletonRecorder.pde

```
class SkeletonRecorder {
  SimpleOpenNI context;
  int jointID;
  int userID;
  ArrayList<PVector> frames;
  int currentFrame = 0;

  SkeletonRecorder(SimpleOpenNI tempContext, int tempJointID ) { ❶
    context = tempContext; ❷
    jointID = tempJointID;
    frames = new ArrayList(); ❸
  }

  void setUser(int tempUserID) { ❹
    userID = tempUserID;
  }

  void recordFrame() { ❺
    PVector position = new PVector(); ❻
    context.getJointPositionSkeleton(userID, jointID, position);
    frames.add(position); ❼
  }

  PVector getPosition() {
    return frames.get(currentFrame); ❽
  }

  void nextFrame() { ❾
    currentFrame++; ❿
    if (currentFrame == frames.size()) { ⓫
      currentFrame = 0;
    }
  }

}
```

The first thing our sketch needs to tell SkeletonRecorder is which joint it wants to track. This happens inside of setup where our sketch initializes the SkeletonRecorder object:

```
recorder = new SkeletonRecorder(kinect, SimpleOpenNI.SKEL_LEFT_HAND);
```

The sketch indicates which joint it wants to track in the form of a `SimpleOpen-NI` joint ID, passed to the second argument of the constructor. It also passes along `kinect`, which is its `SimpleOpenNI` instance (also known as the *context*). `SkeletonRecorder` will need this to access the joint position data. Look at the constructor in our `SkeletonRecorder` class. The constructor is the function that creates new instances of any class. It's the function that gets called when we say `new SkeletonRecorder` in our sketch.

❶ In our `SkeletonRecorder` class, the constructor is the first function at the top, after the variable declarations at the top. Let's look at what our `SkeletonRecorder` class does in its constructor.

❷ These lines simply save the `SimpleOpenNI` object and the joint ID into instance variables. These values will be saved in our `SkeletonRecorder` object and will be available to us as long as we have that object around. We save the temporary variables passed to our function into instance variables that will be preserved in our object. You can see at the top of the class that there are declarations for `context` and `jointID`. Just like declaring a variable at the top of our sketch makes it available in the sketch's `setup` and `draw` functions, declaring variables like this inside our class will make them into instance variables that are available in all of our class's functions and that persist through the life of each object of the class that we make.

❸ In addition to saving the `context` and the `jointID`, our constructor declares a new `ArrayList` and saves it into another instance variable called `frames`. This variable is going to store the positions of the user's joints at each frame of the sketch. We'll fill it up with positions while we're recording and then read from it when we're doing playback. In the past when we've needed to save multiple values in a particular order, we've used a conventional array that we declare and access with square brackets. Conventional arrays hold a fixed number of items. When we declare them, we have to tell Processing exactly how big to make them like this: `int[] cats = new int[3];`.

That would tell Processing to create an array that can hold up to three elements. Once this array is initialized, that size can never change. When we're recording skeleton data from the Kinect, however, we don't know how many frames we're going to record in advance. We need an array that can grow in size over time as we add frames to it. That's exactly what the `ArrayList` is for. An `ArrayList` acts just like a conventional array except it can grow in size as we add elements to it. It also has special methods for adding and accessing elements rather than the square brackets used with a conventional array. We'll see those shortly when we look at how `recordFrame` works. For now though, we know that we've got our `frames` instance variable set up and ready to receive however many frames the user wants to record.

❹ The next time our sketch uses its `SkeletonRecorder` object is inside of its `draw` function. It calls `recorder.setUser(userId)`, where `userId` is the ID of the tracked user reported by `SimpleOpenNI`. The `SkeletonRecorder` will need the user ID so that it can access the joint position data for the right user. On first thought, it might make sense to pass in the user ID in the

Chapter 4

constructor. After all, it's part of the setup of the SkeletonRecorder object, and that object won't be able to access the joint data and hence won't be useful until it has the user ID. However, the sketch itself doesn't actually know the user ID within setup at the time it initialized the recorder object. That data only becomes available at the end of the calibration process inside of draw, hence the need to provide a separate setUser function that can be called at that point.

The implementation of setUser is trivial. All it does is assign the user ID passed in from the sketch to an internal instance variable called userID so that SkeletonRecorder can use that information later on to access the joint position. Even though this function couldn't be simpler, there is one subtle point worth mentioning about its operation. The side effect of needing to call setUser from inside the sketch's draw function is that setUser will get called over and over on every run of draw as the sketch is operating rather than just once at the beginning. If OpenNI is tracking multiple users, we might see strange results where the recorder switches which user's position it records if the initial user is lost. However, this is such an unusual edge case that we can simply ignore it. If it ever came up in a real application, we'd have a much better idea of how to solve it then with the actual application in front of us than we do right now.

⑤ Now, the sketch is into record mode. It has detected a user and is ready to begin recording the position of her joints. It calls recorder.recordFrame.

⑥ The first two lines of this function are comfortingly familiar. They create a PVector and then pass it to SimpleOpenNI to be populated with the position data for the joint. The userId and jointID variables used to specify which joint to access are the instance variables we assigned earlier. We'll access whichever joint the sketch requested.

⑦ Once we have the joint position in hand, we add it to our frames ArrayList by passing it to frames.add. This function sticks the PVector onto the end of the growing ArrayList where we'll be able to get it back later. Since we stick each new PVector onto the end of the ArrayList, it will preserve the order in which the joint positions arrived. We can read each frame out in order, and the result will look exactly like the motion as it was performed by the user.

There's something missing from this function that's worth noting. We're not doing anything with the confidence level that SimpleOpenNI reports from getJointPositionSkeleton. By ignoring the confidence value, we're actually losing information. There's no way that our sketch can recreate the confidence value after the fact if we don't save it here. We're not saving it because we have no convenient way to report the confidence level back to the sketch without making things significantly more complex. In other words, there's no way we can fulfill the demands set by how the sketch wants to use our library while also providing the confidence value. At the end of this section, I'll mention a series of improvements that could be made to this library, including an idea for capturing this confidence level.

At this point, we're ready to move on to playback. Our playback system is made up of two functions: getPosition and nextFrame. There's an implicit idea that makes these two functions work together: Skeleton-Recorder always keeps track of a currentFrame. Calling getPosition tells you the position that was captured at that frame. Calling nextFrame tells SkeletonRecorder to advance to the next frame, looping around and around the ArrayList of recorder frames.

❽ Near the top of the SkeletonRecorder class, we declared an instance variable called currentFrame and initialized it to 0. This variable will determine which frame we provide when the user calls getPosition. Let's take a look at how getPosition works and then we'll look at nextFrame to see how we maintain the correct value for currentFrame.

This function is very short, but it has one new element that you may never have seen before. Let me explain. This function grabs the position out of ArrayList that corresponds to the currentFrame. Unlike a conventional array, an ArrayList doesn't know what type of data it stores. When we declare a traditional array, we indicate what we'll be storing in it: an integer, a float, etc. However, an ArrayList is more flexible. We don't have to tell it up front what kind of data we're going to be storing in it. We can even store different types of data in different elements within a single ArrayList. The downside of this flexibility is that ArrayList doesn't know what it's storing. Therefore, when we access the elements of an ArrayList, we have to tell Processing what type of data we're expecting to get back. This process is called "casting." We take the element we get from our ArrayList and we cast it into the type of object we want. Let's take a look at how this works in our getPosition function.

In getPosition, we call frames.get(currentFrame) to access the appropriate element of our ArrayList. We then immediately return this value. That PVector will be exactly what our sketch wants: the position of the user's joint at the current frame.

But how do we make sure that currentFrame is set to the right value? The answer lies in nextFrame.

❾ Our sketch calls this function whenever it wants to advance the recording to the next joint position. You might expect that nextFrame would be almost as simple as setUser. It seems like all it has to do is increment currentFrame. However, its job is slightly more complicated than that. We want our recorded joint positions to play back in a loop. Every time we reach the last element of frames we want to start back over again at the beginning. Let's look at our code to see how we accomplish that.

❿ This function starts out by incrementing currentFrame. Usually that will be all it needs to do. currentFrame starts off at 0 and will increase every time we call this function, causing getPosition to step through each recorded joint position in turn. However, eventually currentFrame will reach the end of the number of frames that we actually recorded. If we don't do something, it will continue to run up, and getPosition will start trying to access elements of frame that aren't there, causing an error.

Chapter 4

⑪ To prevent this, we need to reset `currentFrame` back to 0 whenever it reaches the number of positions that are actually present in `frames`. And that's exactly what the last three lines of this function do. If `currentFrame` is equal to the size of our `ArrayList`, set `currentFrame` to 0.

Exercises

OK! We've made it all the way through our `SkeletonRecorder` class. You've seen how we implemented every function used in our Exercise Measurement sketch. Now, let's talk about things that you could do to extend `SkeletonRecorder`. First of all, you could extend the class so that it could record multiple joints. To accomplish this, it would be necessary to create a second class that works in collaboration with `SkeletonRecorder` to hold the position data for each individual joint. If we wanted to also capture the confidence value for each joint, we'd need a third class to represent the joint positions as well. All three of these classes would then work together to provide something close to the library functions I showed you here. Example A-6 in the Appendix shows an example of what this might look like in code. Another exercise would be to extend this `SkeletonRecorder` even further so that it could work with multiple users simultaneously. This would involve an additional helper class like the two we just discussed.

Finally, an advanced exercise that would be really useful would be to figure out how to save the recorded joint data to a file and then load it up again later so you can store the exercise for use in the future. To accomplish this, you'd choose a data format such as XML or JSON, and then you'd use a Processing library to convert the skeleton data captured by `SkeletonRecorder` into a string in this format, which you could then save to a file. If you want to attempt this, take a look at the "File I/O" example sketches that come with Processing for some ideas about how to get started.

Project 11: "Stayin' Alive": Dance Move Triggers MP3

The Exercise Measurement project was all about movement. We compared the position of a user's limb over time with a prerecorded movement and gave the user multiple forms of feedback so he could correct his motion. We based the interaction on a single limb because people have a limited ability to absorb and respond to visual feedback in real time. If we tried to correct the motion of multiple limbs simultaneously, users would find the experience overwhelming and end up incapable of following along at all.

In this project, on the other hand, we're going to look at the position of the entire body as a whole. Instead of tracking a user's motion over time, we'll check to see if she has assumed a particular predefined pose. We'll define this pose as a series of spatial relationships between the various parts of the user's body. Is her right hand above her left elbow? Is her left knee to the left of her left hip? And so on. When all of these relationships are found, we'll trigger an action. Specifically, we'll play a piece of music.

The seed for this project was planted by Alex Vessels, a classmate of mine at NYU's Interactive Telecommunications Program. Alex wanted to build DJ software that he could control by striking famous dance poses: Michael Jackson's moonwalk, a letter from the Village People's "YMCA" routine, and the disco finger point from "Stayin' Alive" by the Bee Gees. I collaborated with Alex to think through how to detect poses using the skeleton data from OpenNI. The ideas I'll show you in this project are the result of that work.

Describing a Pose as Joint Relationships

For this project, we'll focus on the disco-point move made famous by John Travolta in *Saturday Night Fever*. This is one of the most recognizable dance moves, and it's inextricably tied to one song: "Stayin' Alive" by the Bee Gees. Even better, it's a move that involves contorting the whole body into a pose with very clear relationships between different body parts.

To get an idea of what I mean, take a look at Figure 4-29. That figure shows a screen capture made with Example 4-1 from earlier in this chapter. In it, I'm copying John Travolta's famous pose from *Saturday Night Fever* while the sketch displays my skeleton. The skeleton display is annotated with notes showing the signature relationships between the joints that define this pose. For example, take a look at the raised right arm. In order for the whole arm to be in the right position, four things must be true: the hand must be above the elbow, the hand must be to the right of the elbow, the elbow must be above the shoulder, and the elbow must be to the right of the shoulder. If any of these relationships were not met, the user's arm would not be in the correct position. For example, if the user's elbow was below his shoulder, then his arm would be out to the side of his body as if he were flagging a cab, when instead it should be thrust skyward.

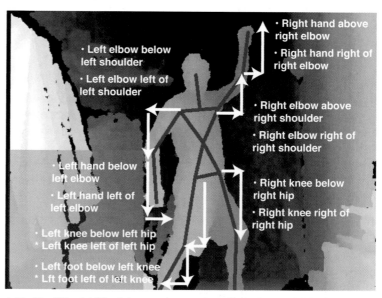

Figure 4-29. The "Stayin' Alive" dance pose expressed as a series of relationships between joint positions.

To fully describe the pose, we need similar sets of constraints on a number of other joints. In Figure 4-29, I've shown those for the left arm and both legs as well as the right arm. All of the constraints on those limbs are like those on the right arm: they describe spatial relationships between pairs of joints as indicated by the white arrows in the diagram. If all of these relationships are met, then we'll know that the user is in the correct pose, and we can trigger our song. The job of our code will be to access the position of the relevant joints and then to check to see if they are in these relationships.

We'll take on this project in two parts. In each part we'll use a different approach to specifying these relationships and checking to see if the user is fulfilling them. In the basic version, we'll break our dance pose into a series of if statements that compare components of the vectors supplied by SimpleOpenNI. In other words, we'll take constraints such as "right hand above right elbow" and "right hand right of right elbow" and turn them into expressions that compare x- and y-values of joint positions.

This procedural approach is quite straightforward. We'll write a series of if statements and if they all return true, then the user is in the pose. For the basic version of the sketch we'll use this approach to check the user's right arm, the one that should be pointing skyward. We'll give the user visible feedback for each limb to indicate when it's in the right position.

However, since we need two if statements for each joint relationship, this approach we will rapidly become unwieldy. For the advanced version of this project, we'll create two helper classes that together will let us specify the pose much more succinctly. These helper classes will contain all of the possible geometrical relationships between joints and will be able to check whether or not each relationship is being fulfilled. Instead of writing a series of if statements, our sketch will use these classes to declare the various relationships that make up the pose, making our code much more concise and comprehensible. The improvement will be so great that we'll be able to enforce all of the constraints that make up our "Stayin' Alive" dance pose, and we'll be able to play the song when the pose is detected.

After we've gotten to this point, I'll suggest some things you could do to improve our code so that it will have even more advanced features, such as the ability to check for multiple poses in a single sketch and the ability to give the user more sophisticated visible feedback.

Let's get started with the basic version.

Basic Version

For this first version of the project, we're going to focus on the right arm. According to OpenNI, the right arm is made up of three joints: the right shoulder, the right elbow, and the right hand.

We have four constraints we want to impose on these three joints:
- The right hand is above the right elbow.
- The right hand is to the right of the right elbow.
- The right elbow is above the right shoulder.
- The right elbow is to the right of the right shoulder.

Working with the Skeleton Data

Throughout this project, I'll refer to the right and left sides of the body from the point of view of OpenNI. In the past, this meant that our terminology was reversed from reality since the user's right hand showed up on the left side of the screen and vice versa. However, in this project we'll be displaying the depth data and the skeleton mirrored so that the interface is more intuitive for users. This means that OpenNI's right and left will correspond correctly with the actual left and right side of the user's body.

When all four of these constraints are met, then the user's right arm must be in the correct position for the "Stayin' Alive" pose: pointing up and away from the user's torso. In our code, we'll translate each constraint into a greater-than statement and then we'll apply each to the appropriate joint position provided by SimpleOpenNI. When all four of the comparison statements return true, we'll know that the arm is in the right position. We'll use the results of the statements to give the user visual feedback along the way. We'll display the limbs between each pair of joints; we'll color each limb red until the user gets it into the right position, at which point we'll turn it white to indicate success.

Before we dive into the code, let's talk through all of the steps required. We'll start with the familiar setup code and calibration callbacks. Then we'll get position data for all three of the joints we're interested in: the right shoulder, the right elbow, and the right hand. Once we've got this data, we'll look at two pairs of relationships: one between the hand and the elbow and one between the elbow and the shoulder. For each of these relationships, we need to compare the x- and y-components of the vectors representing each joint. We'll write four greater-than statements, two for each limb. We'll use the logical operator AND to make sure that both of the relationships have been met. Then we'll use the results of this comparison to set Processing's stroke color so that when we tell SimpleOpenNI to draw the limb, its appearance will tell users whether or not they're in the right position. Using SimpleOpenNI's `drawLimb` function means that our output will match the depth image from the Kinect so we'll display that to the user as well to provide further feedback. When the user's arm is in the correct position, both of these limb segments will turn white indicating success. If either limb segment is out of position, it will turn red, letting the user know it needs correcting, as shown in Figure 4-30.

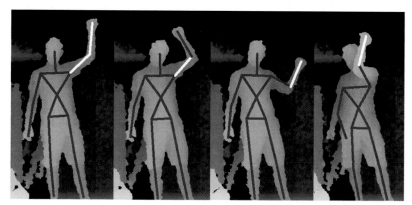

Figure 4-30. Checking the position of the right arm. The leftmost image shows the arm in the correct position where our sketch displays both limbs as white. The other three images show our sketch detecting different failed constraints in the joint relationships.

Chapter 4

That's the basic plan. Example 4-5 provides the code for the sketch that implements it. Run this sketch in Processing, perform the calibration ritual, and try moving your arm around to see the results.

Example 4-5. basic_dance_pose.pde

```
import SimpleOpenNI.*;
SimpleOpenNI  kinect;

void setup() {
  size(640, 480);
  kinect = new SimpleOpenNI(this);
  kinect.enableDepth();
  kinect.enableUser(SimpleOpenNI.SKEL_PROFILE_ALL);
  kinect.setMirror(true);
  strokeWeight(5);
}

void draw() {
  background(0);
  kinect.update();
  image(kinect.depthTmage(), 0, 0);

  IntVector userList = new IntVector();
  kinect.getUsers(userList);
  if (userList.size() > 0) {

    int userId = userList.get(0);
    if ( kinect.isTrackingSkeleton(userId)) {

      PVector rightHand = new PVector();
      PVector rightElbow = new PVector();
      PVector rightShoulder = new PVector();

      kinect.getJointPositionSkeleton(userId,
                          SimpleOpenNI.SKEL_RIGHT_HAND,
                          rightHand);
      kinect.getJointPositionSkeleton(userId,
                          SimpleOpenNT.SKFI_RTGHT_ELBOW,
                          rightElbow);
      kinect.getJointPositionSkeleton(userId,
                          SimpleOpenNI.SKEL_RIGHT_SHOULDER,
                          rightShoulder);

      // right elbow above right shoulder
      // AND
      // right elbow right of right shoulder
      //
      if(rightElbow.y > rightShoulder.y &&
         rightElbow.x > rightShoulder.x) { ❶
        stroke(255); ❷
      } else {
        stroke(255,0,0); ❸
      }
      kinect.drawLimb(userId, ❹
                   SimpleOpenNI.SKEL_RIGHT_SHOULDER,
                   SimpleOpenNI.SKEL_RIGHT_ELBOW);

      // right hand above right elbow
      // AND
```

```
        // right hand right of right elbow
        //
        if(rightHand.y > rightElbow.y && rightHand.x > rightElbow.x) {
          stroke(255);
        } else {
          stroke(255,0,0);
        }

        kinect.drawLimb(userId,
                        SimpleOpenNI.SKEL_RIGHT_HAND,
                        SimpleOpenNI.SKEL_RIGHT_ELBOW);
      }
    }
}

// user-tracking callbacks!
void onNewUser(int userId) {
  println("start pose detection");
  kinect.startPoseDetection("Psi", userId);
}

void onEndCalibration(int userId, boolean successful) {
  if (successful) {
    println("  User calibrated !!!");
    kinect.startTrackingSkeleton(userId);
  }
  else {
    println("  Failed to calibrate user !!!");
    kinect.startPoseDetection("Psi", userId);
  }
}

void onStartPose(String pose, int userId) {
  println("Started pose for user");
  kinect.stopPoseDetection(userId);
  kinect.requestCalibrationSkeleton(userId, true);
}
```

As usual, most of this code is familiar from our work throughout this chapter. In setup we enable the depth image as well as the user data. At the bottom of the sketch, we include all of the callback functions necessary to navigate the calibration process. We also make sure to call kinect.setMirror(true) so that the depth image will be shown facing the user. As discussed in the last project, this makes applications where we expect a user to respond to visual feedback much easier for her. At the top of draw, we clear the sketch to black, update the Kinect, and display the depth image. We're going to draw our skeleton data on top of the depth image, so we have to draw it first before we get started. Then we're into the usual code for checking to see if we've detected any users: we ask SimpleOpenNI for the list of tracked users; if there are any, we check to see if we've begun tracking their skeletons. This is all standard stuff.

Once a user has finished the calibration ritual, and our sketch has a calibrated user, we access the positions of three of his joints: rightHand, rightElbow, and rightShoulder. We declare a PVector for each of these and then pass them to kinect.getJointPositionSkeleton with the userId and appropriate joint constant. Now that all three of these positions are populated, we're ready to start in on the real work of comparing them.

Let's start by looking at the relationship between the `rightElbow` and the `rightShoulder`. We know from the discussion above that we need to enforce two constrains on this relationship:

- The right elbow is above the right shoulder.

- The right elbow is to the right of the right shoulder.

❶ Now that we've got the joint data handy, we can translate each constraint into a greater-than statement. The first of these constraints relates to the y-component of these vectors. To check to see if the right elbow is above the right shoulder, we need to make sure that the y-component of our `rightElbow` vector is greater than the y-component of our `rightShoulder` vector. Translated into code, that looks like this: `rightElbow.y > rightShoulder.y`.

That statement will return true when the right elbow is above the right shoulder and false when it is below. That deals with our first constraint. Now let's look at the second one. Our second constraint deals with the joints' positions on the x-axis. When the `rightElbow` is in the correct position, its x-component will be greater than that of `rightShoulder`. We can check for that with another greater than statement like this: `rightElbow.x > rightShoulder.x`.

At this point we've translated each constraint into code individually. But neither of them is sufficient on its own. This limb is only in the right position when both of these greater-than statements return true. We want to combine both of them into a single `if` statement that will be true if and only if both of these comparisons are. To do this, we use Processing's `&&` operator (pronounced "and and"). This operator lets us enforce multiple comparisons simultaneously. When we use `&&` in a condition, that condition will only return true if both of the comparisons it connects are true.

In our case, we use this combined `if` statement, to set the stroke color before we draw the limb that connects the user's right elbow and right shoulder.

❷ In the first branch of the `if` statement, we set the `stroke` to white to indicate that this part of the arm is in the right position.

❸ If our compound condition returned false because either (or both) of our greater than statements did, then we set the `stroke` to red to show the user what went wrong.

❹ After we've set the stroke color, we use `kinect.drawLimb` to draw a line connecting our two limbs. Why did we use this built-in SimpleOpenNI function rather than simple taking advantage of Processing's `line` function to connect the two `PVector`s that we already have? Don't forget that each `PVector` returned by `getJointPositionSkeleton` is in three-dimensional real-world coordinates. We want our display of the limbs to match the depth image. If we simply used the x- and y-coordinates of the vectors as they are, they wouldn't match the image. We need to convert them from real-world coordinates into the projective coordinates that will match the two-dimensional image. We could convert these vectors one at a time using SimpleOpenNI's `convertRealWorldToProjective` function. However, that would be awkward and verbose. Instead, we can use `drawLimb`, which performs the conversion to projective space itself, automatically making sure that our display will match the depth image without any additional work.

So that completes the check on the right upper arm. We then repeat this same procedure for the right lower arm. We make similar comparisons between the x- and y-components of the `rightElbow` and `rightHand` vectors, again using `&&` to ensure that both conditions are met before setting the color for that limb. With both of these `if` statements in place, the user will get complete feedback on whether they've positioned their arm correctly for the "Stayin' Alive" pose. Again, you can take a look at Figure 4-30 to see the full results in action.

Advanced Version

Now, we could proceed to implement all of the constraints for our full pose using `if` statements in this manner. However, the result would be ridiculously long and hard to maintain. For each of the 12 constraints illustrated in Figure 4-29, we'd need to add six more lines of code to our sketch to implement the `if` statement and color selection as we just did for each segment of our right arm. The result would be pages and pages of code in which it would be quite difficult to tell what constraints we were actually trying to enforce.

This situation screams out for a helper class. A helper class will let us enforce multiple constraints on the user's pose without repeating code. It will also let us declare these constraints in a manner that's much easier to read and understand. Consider an `if` statement that contains a condition like this:

```
rightKnee.y < rightHip.y && rightKnee.x > rightHip.x
```

Can you tell just from glancing at that code what joint relationships it enforces? Where should the right hip and right knee be in relationship to each other exactly?

What we'd really like is to be able to add rules to our pose declaratively in a manner that was easy to write and read and didn't require us to muck around with the `if` statements and greater-than comparisons through which these rules are actually enforced. Further, we'd like to be able to separate the declaration of these rules from their actual enforcement. In other words, we'd like to add these rules to our pose in `setup`. They will stay constant as the sketch runs, so having them in `draw` simply makes things messier and more complex, making it harder to add any other code that actually needs to be there. What we'd like to do is describe our pose in `setup` and then enforce it in `draw` where we can use the information about whether or not the user matched the pose to change our display and otherwise give the user feedback.

The two features of our helper class include:

- Providing an easy way to declare pose constraints.

- Separating adding pose constraints from checking for the pose.

Since we know that these are the main features that will be provided by our class, let's take a sneak preview of that class by looking at how these functions will appear in our sketch. The purpose of a helper class like this is to make the sketch's job easier. If we start by imagining the perfect functions for doing what the sketch needs, we can then work backward to figure out what our class needs to do to make those actually work.

We'll start with declaring pose constraints. In an ideal world, we'd like this to look something like so:

```
pose.addRule(SimpleOpenNI.SKEL_RIGHT_KNEE,
             SkeletonPoser.BELOW,
             SimpleOpenNI.SKEL_RIGHT_HIP);
pose.addRule(SimpleOpenNI.SKEL_RIGHT_KNEE,
             SkeletonPoser.RIGHT_OF,
             SimpleOpenNI.SKEL_RIGHT_HIP);
```

The `pose` variable used in both of these lines will be an instance of our `SkeletonPoser` class that we'll create. This `addRule` function takes three arguments to describe the constraint: a SimpleOpenNI joint, a spatial relationship, and another SimpleOpenNI joint. Together these arguments read like a sentence that describes the rule: "the RIGHT_KNEE is BELOW the RIGHT_HIP" or "the RIGHT_KNEE is RIGHT_OF the RIGHT_HIP." The function accepts the same constants as `getJointPositionSkeleton` and the other SimpleOpenNI functions to indicate which joints are involved in the rule. And `SkeletonPoser` provides its own constants to let us indicate the relationship between these joints.

But what about the second half of our functionality: checking to see if the user has assumed the pose? We'd like that to be even simpler:

```
if(pose.check(userId)){
  // play mp3
}
```

This fragment imagines a new `SkeletonPoser` function called `check`. This function would take a SimpleOpenNI user ID and return true or false based on whether or not the specified user was in the pose. As shown here, we can then use that in an `if` statement to play our "Stayin' Alive" MP3. The code in our `draw` function needed to check a pose just went from upward of 60 lines to check every limb down to one.

Doesn't that seem like a pleasant library to use? You could even imagine using it to check multiple poses within a single sketch. You'd simply declare two pose objects at the top of your sketch. Add constraints to both of them in `setup` using `addRule`, and then test each of them in `draw` with `check`, playing different MP3s based on which pose the user was actually in (or taking whatever other action you wanted). This is something that would be incredibly complex using the old nonclass system.

OK. Now that we've seen why we want to create a helper class and what exactly our `SkeletonPoser` class should do, let's look at Example 4-6 to see how it can be used. This sketch is slightly long, but that is due to repetition rather than complexity. Make sure you look closely at how the pose is declared at the top of the sketch. This is the key new component. We'll cover it thoroughly after the code.

Example 4-6. *advanced_dance_pose.pde*

```
import SimpleOpenNI.*;

// import and declarations for minim: ❶
import ddf.minim.*;
Minim minim;
AudioPlayer player;

// declare our poser object
SkeletonPoser pose;

SimpleOpenNI  kinect;

void setup() { ❷
  size(640, 480);
  kinect = new SimpleOpenNI(this);
  kinect.enableDepth();
  kinect.enableUser(SimpleOpenNI.SKEL_PROFILE_ALL);
  kinect.setMirror(true);

  // initialize the minim object
  minim = new Minim(this);

  // and load the stayin alive mp3 file
  player = minim.loadFile("stayin_alive.mp3");

  // initialize the pose object
  pose = new SkeletonPoser(kinect); ❸
  // rules for the right arm
  pose.addRule(SimpleOpenNI.SKEL_RIGHT_HAND,   ❹
               PoseRule.ABOVE,
               SimpleOpenNI.SKEL_RIGHT_ELBOW);
  pose.addRule(SimpleOpenNI.SKEL_RIGHT_HAND,
               PoseRule.RIGHT_OF,
               SimpleOpenNI.SKEL_RIGHT_ELBOW);
  pose.addRule(SimpleOpenNI.SKEL_RIGHT_ELBOW,
               PoseRule.ABOVE,
               SimpleOpenNI.SKEL_RIGHT_SHOULDER);
  pose.addRule(SimpleOpenNI.SKEL_RIGHT_ELBOW,
               PoseRule.RIGHT_OF,
               SimpleOpenNI.SKEL_RIGHT_SHOULDER);

  // rules for the left arm
  pose.addRule(SimpleOpenNI.SKEL_LEFT_ELBOW,
               PoseRule.BELOW,
               SimpleOpenNI.SKEL_LEFT_SHOULDER);
  pose.addRule(SimpleOpenNI.SKEL_LEFT_ELBOW,
               PoseRule.LEFT_OF,
               SimpleOpenNI.SKEL_LEFT_SHOULDER);
  pose.addRule(SimpleOpenNI.SKEL_LEFT_HAND,
               PoseRule.LEFT_OF,
               SimpleOpenNI.SKEL_LEFT_ELBOW);
  pose.addRule(SimpleOpenNI.SKEL_LEFT_HAND,
               PoseRule.BELOW,
               SimpleOpenNI.SKEL_LEFT_ELBOW);

  // rules for the right leg
  pose.addRule(SimpleOpenNI.SKEL_RIGHT_KNEE,
               PoseRule.BELOW,
               SimpleOpenNI.SKEL_RIGHT_HIP);
```

```
  pose.addRule(SimpleOpenNI.SKEL_RIGHT_KNEE,
               PoseRule.RIGHT_OF,
               SimpleOpenNI.SKEL_RIGHT_HIP);

  // rules for the left leg
  pose.addRule(SimpleOpenNI.SKEL_LEFT_KNEE,
               PoseRule.BELOW,
               SimpleOpenNI.SKEL_LEFT_HIP);
  pose.addRule(SimpleOpenNI.SKEL_LEFT_KNEE,
               PoseRule.LEFT_OF,
               SimpleOpenNI.SKEL_LEFT_HIP);
  pose.addRule(SimpleOpenNI.SKEL_LEFT_FOOT,
               PoseRule.BELOW,
               SimpleOpenNI.SKEL_LEFT_KNEE);
  pose.addRule(SimpleOpenNI.SKEL_LEFT_FOOT,
               PoseRule.LEFT_OF,
               SimpleOpenNI.SKEL_LEFT_KNEE);
  strokeWeight(5);
}

void draw() { ❺
  background(0);
  kinect.update();
  image(kinect.depthImage(), 0, 0);

  IntVector userList = new IntVector();
  kinect.getUsers(userList);
  if (userList.size() > 0) {

    int userId = userList.get(0);
    if( kinect.isTrackingSkeleton(userId)) {

      // check to see if the user
      // is in the pose
      if(pose.check(userId)){ ❻

        //if they are, set the color white
        stroke(255); ❼
        // and start the song playing
        if(!player.isPlaying()) {
          player.play();
        }

      } else {
        // otherwise set the color to red
        // and don't start the song
        stroke(255,0,0); ❽
      }

      // draw the skeleton in whatever color we chose
      drawSkeleton(userId); ❾
    }
  }
}

void drawSkeleton(int userId) {
  kinect.drawLimb(userId, SimpleOpenNI.SKEL_HEAD,
                  SimpleOpenNI.SKEL_NECK);
  kinect.drawLimb(userId, SimpleOpenNI.SKEL_NECK,
                  SimpleOpenNI.SKEL_LEFT_SHOULDER);
```

```
        kinect.drawLimb(userId, SimpleOpenNI.SKEL_LEFT_SHOULDER,
                       SimpleOpenNI.SKEL_LEFT_ELBOW);
        kinect.drawLimb(userId,
                       SimpleOpenNI.SKEL_LEFT_ELBOW,
                       SimpleOpenNI.SKEL_LEFT_HAND);
        kinect.drawLimb(userId,
                       SimpleOpenNI.SKEL_NECK,
                       SimpleOpenNI.SKEL_RIGHT_SHOULDER);
        kinect.drawLimb(userId,
                       SimpleOpenNI.SKEL_RIGHT_SHOULDER,
                       SimpleOpenNI.SKEL_RIGHT_ELBOW);
        kinect.drawLimb(userId,
                       SimpleOpenNI.SKEL_RIGHT_ELBOW,
                       SimpleOpenNI.SKEL_RIGHT_HAND);
        kinect.drawLimb(userId,
                       SimpleOpenNI.SKEL_LEFT_SHOULDER,
                       SimpleOpenNI.SKEL_TORSO);
        kinect.drawLimb(userId,
                       SimpleOpenNI.SKEL_RIGHT_SHOULDER,
                       SimpleOpenNI.SKEL_TORSO);
        kinect.drawLimb(userId, SimpleOpenNI.SKEL_TORSO,
                       SimpleOpenNI.SKEL_LEFT_HIP);
        kinect.drawLimb(userId, SimpleOpenNI.SKEL_LEFT_HIP,
                       SimpleOpenNI.SKEL_LEFT_KNEE);
        kinect.drawLimb(userId,
                       SimpleOpenNI.SKEL_LEFT_KNEE,
                       SimpleOpenNI.SKEL_LEFT_FOOT);
        kinect.drawLimb(userId, SimpleOpenNI.SKEL_TORSO,
                       SimpleOpenNI.SKEL_RIGHT_HIP);
        kinect.drawLimb(userId,
                       SimpleOpenNI.SKEL_RIGHT_HIP,
                       SimpleOpenNI.SKEL_RIGHT_KNEE);
        kinect.drawLimb(userId,
                       SimpleOpenNI.SKEL_RIGHT_KNEE,
                       SimpleOpenNI.SKEL_RIGHT_FOOT);
        kinect.drawLimb(userId, SimpleOpenNI.SKEL_RIGHT_HIP,
                       SimpleOpenNI.SKEL_LEFT_HIP);
    }

    void drawLimb(int userId, int jointType1, int jointType2)
    {
      PVector jointPos1 = new PVector();
      PVector jointPos2 = new PVector();
      float  confidence;

      // draw the joint position
      confidence = kinect.getJointPositionSkeleton(userId, jointType1, joint-
Pos1);
      confidence = kinect.getJointPositionSkeleton(userId, jointType2, joint-
Pos2);

      line(jointPos1.x, jointPos1.y, jointPos1.z,
      jointPos2.x, jointPos2.y, jointPos2.z);
    }

    // user-tracking callbacks!
    void onNewUser(int userId) {
      println("start pose detection");
      kinect.startPoseDetection("Psi", userId);
    }
```

Chapter 4

```
void onEndCalibration(int userId, boolean successful) {
  if (successful) {
    println("  User calibrated !!!");
    kinect.startTrackingSkeleton(userId);
  }
  else {
    println("  Failed to calibrate user !!!");
    kinect.startPoseDetection("Psi", userId);
  }
}

void onStartPose(String pose, int userId) {
  println("Started pose for user");
  kinect.stopPoseDetection(userId);
  kinect.requestCalibrationSkeleton(userId, true);
}
```

To run this sketch, you'll need to provide your own copy of "Stayin' Alive" by the Bee Gees. Save this code as a new sketch in Processing. Then move your copy of the MP3 into the new sketch folder. You'll also need to add the SkeletonPoser class to your sketch before you can run it. Here's the code for that class. In Processing, click on the arrow in the top right corner of the window to create a new tab. Name the tab SkeletonPoser. Place the code from Example 4-6 into it (we won't discuss the guts of this helper class for now, but we'll return to examine it after we've looked at how the SkeletonPoser class gets used within the main sketch).

At this point, you should be ready to run the sketch. Once it's up and running, stand way back from the Kinect so that your whole body is visible in the depth image. It helps to position your computer so you can see the depth image from across the room so you'll know when you're in the right spot. Once you're sure that you're completely visible, feet and all, perform the calibration ritual. When that is successfully completed, you should see a red skeleton drawn over your body in the depth image. Now, get into the "Stayin' Alive" pose. Refer to Figure 4-29 if you need a reminder of what exactly this pose should look like. When you get it right, the skeleton will turn white, and the song will start playing. (See Figure 4-31.) When this happens, boogie down.

Figure 4-31. Once we've declared all of the joint constraints, our SkeletonPoser object makes it easy to detect when the user has assumed our "Stayin' Alive" pose. On the left, the white skeleton indicates a correct pose, and on the right, the red skeleton indicates that one or more of the constraints has not been met.

Now, let's work on understanding all of this code. We'll start with the sketch itself. We've already seen the basic functions that are provided by our Skeleton-Poser class, but now it's time to see how we combine them in action to enforce our full pose and make it trigger an MP3.

❶ The work starts at the top of the sketch with some new declarations. We start by importing the Minim library and declaring the two objects we need to work with it: a Minim object and an AudioPlayer. Then we declare an instance of our SkeletonPoser class, which we call pose since it will contain a description of the "Stayin' Alive" pose.

❷ Proceeding on, our setup function starts with the normal SimpleOpenNI configuration. When that's done, we initialize our Minim object and load our MP3 into our player. With that out of the way, the rest of our setup is about declaring our pose.

❸ First we have to initialize our SkeletonPoser object. When doing that, we pass in the kinect object so that SkeletonPoser can access the joint positions it will need to check.

❹ Once our pose object is up and running, we can start adding rules to it to describe the "Stayin' Alive" dance move we want to capture. We'll use the pose.addRule function to tell our library about the constraints that make up the pose. As demonstrated in Figure 4-32, we can break these constraints out limb by limb. In fact, the way I came up with this code was to go through that diagram one limb at a time and add one line of code for each constraint mentioned in it. For example, here are the rules for the left leg as shown in Figure 4-32:

- Left knee below left hip.

- Left knee left of left hip.

- Left foot below left knee.

- Left foot left of left knee.

Isn't it nice how close this code is to the plain text version? Besides the ugly (but necessary) constants, it reads nearly the same as our bullet-point list. Our total list comes to 14 rules. We specify these for each limb except the right leg. For that leg, I left off the rules enforcing the constraint that the right foot should be below and to the right of the right knee. I couldn't figure out a way anyone could possibly violate that constraint while still keeping all the other limbs in place. If you were to lift your right leg high enough to get your foot above your knee while keeping everything else in place, you'd almost definitely fall over. You can specify a pose as completely as you want or as minimally, whatever you think makes sense physically.

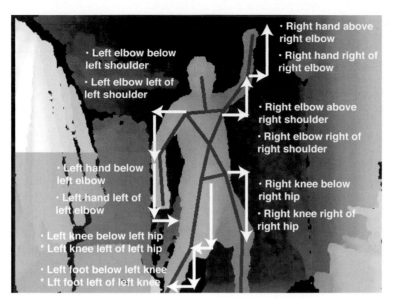

- Right hand above right elbow
- Right hand right of right elbow
- Left elbow below left shoulder
- Left elbow left of left shoulder
- Right elbow above right shoulder
- Right elbow right of right shoulder
- Left hand below left elbow
- Left hand left of left elbow
- Right knee below right hip
- Right knee right of right hip
- Left knee below left hip
- Left knee left of left hip
- Left foot below left knee
- Lft foot left of left knee

Figure 4-32. *The "Stayin' Alive" dance pose expressed as a series of relationships between joint positions. We can now implement these relationships using our SkeletonPoser class.*

⑤ Once the pose is specified, most of the rest of the sketch proceeds along familiar lines. We have the usual calibration callbacks and the drawSkeleton function to help us with display down at the bottom. Our draw function starts out by displaying the depth image and then does all the checks to see if we have a calibrated user. Inside of these checks, the heart of the sketch is almost embarrassingly simple.

⑥ We call pose.check and pass in the user ID of the currently tracked user. SkeletonPoser performs checks on all of the user's joints to see if they are, in fact, in the pose we specified. If all the joints are in the right place, this function returns true, if not it returns false.

⑦ If the check succeeds, we set the stroke color to white and then call player.play to start the MP3 playing. We guard this call in an if statement that checks to see if the MP3 is already playing. Since pose.check will return true over and over as long as the user holds the "Stayin' Alive" pose, we don't want our song to constantly restart. We only want to start it playing once when the user first assumes the pose. Then we want the song to play all the way through to the end no matter what the user does. This if statement only returns true if the song is not currently playing, preventing restarts midway through.

⑧ If the user is not in the pose, then pose.check returns false and we set the stroke color to red.

⑨ Once the stroke color is set, we call drawSkeleton to display the skeleton in the proper color on top of the depth image. The result is a sketch that stays silent until the user assumes the "Stayin' Alive" pose, showing the user's skeleton as red. Once the user gets into the correct pose and fulfills all of our declared rules, the sketch will start playing the Bee Gees and will show the skeleton in white. That's the whole thing. It works!

The SkeletonPoser and PoseRule Classes

Now let's dive inside the SkeletonPoser class to see how it works. Example 4-7 provides the code.

Example 4-7. SkeletonPoser.pde

```
class PoseRule { ❶
  int fromJoint;
  int toJoint;
  PVector fromJointVector;
  PVector toJointVector;
  SimpleOpenNI context;

  int jointRelation; // one of:
  static final int ABOVE    = 1;
  static final int BELOW    = 2;
  static final int LEFT_OF  = 3;
  static final int RIGHT_OF = 4;

  PoseRule(SimpleOpenNI tempContext, ❷
           int tempFromJoint,
           int tempJointRelation,
           int tempToJoint)
  {
    context = tempContext; ❸
    fromJoint = tempFromJoint;
    toJoint = tempToJoint;
    jointRelation = tempJointRelation;

    fromJointVector = new PVector(); ❹
    toJointVector = new PVector();
  }

  boolean check(int userID){ ❺

    // populate the joint vectors for the user we're checking
    context.getJointPositionSkeleton(userID, fromJoint, fromJointVector);❻
    context.getJointPositionSkeleton(userID, toJoint, toJointVector);

    boolean result= false;

    switch(jointRelation){ ❼
     case ABOVE:
       result = (fromJointVector.y > toJointVector.y);
       break;
     case BELOW:
       result = (fromJointVector.y < toJointVector.y);
       break;
     case LEFT_OF:
       result = (fromJointVector.x < toJointVector.x);
       break;
     case RIGHT_OF:
       result = (fromJointVector.x > toJointVector.x);
       break;
     }
```

```
      return result;  ❽
  }
}

class SkeletonPoser {  ❾
  SimpleOpenNI context;
  ArrayList rules;


  SkeletonPoser(SimpleOpenNI context){  ❿
    this.context = context;
    rules = new ArrayList();  ⓫
  }

  void addRule(int fromJoint, int jointRelation, int toJoint){  ⓬
    PoseRule rule = new PoseRule(context, fromJoint, jointRelation, to-
Joint);
    rules.add(rule);
  }

  boolean check(int userID){  ⓭

    boolean result = true;  ⓮
    for(int i = 0; i < rules.size(); i++){  ⓯
      PoseRule rule = (PoseRule)rules.get(i);  ⓰
      result = result && rule.check(userID);  ⓱
    }
    return result;  ⓲
  }

}
```

A big part of why this actual sketch became so simple and clear is how much work SkeletonPoser is doing on our behalf. Let's see how that work gets done and what we can learn from it in making good helper classes.

❶ The first thing you may notice when you look at the code for Skeleton-Poser in Example 4-7 is that it contains not one class, but two: Skeleton-Poser and PoseRule. These classes work together to provide the external functions of SkeletonPoser that we've been using so far. In our analysis of how to describe a pose, we learned that a single pose is made up of many rules. These two classes reflect that insight. The PoseRule class contains all of the data to describe a single rule and has a function to check to see if a particular user's skeleton obeys that rule. The SkeletonPoser class aggregates together multiple rules and has the ability to combine their individual checks into a single verdict on the user's complete posture.

Let's start by looking at PoseRule to see how it stores and enforces a single rule. Then we'll move to SkeletonPoser to see how it aggregates multiple PoseRule instances together to describe a complete pose.

❷ The PoseRule constructor takes four arguments. First it gets the SimpleOpenNI object. We'll need this in order to access the position of the user's joints. The other three arguments are all integers. The first and last of these, fromJoint and toJoint, correspond to SimpleOpenNI joint constants such as `SimpleOpenNI.SKEL_LEFT_HAND`. We'll pass these along to `getJointPositionSkeleton` to access the location of the joints. The third argument to this function, `jointRelation`, is also an integer, but it represents the spatial relationship between the two joints. Just as `SimpleOpenNI` uses constants to consistently identify joints by numbers, `PoseRule` does the same for spatial relationships. It provides its own constants for each possible relationship between the two joints: `PoseRule.ABOVE`, `PoseRule.BELOW`, `PoseRule.LEFT_OF`, and `PoseRule.RIGHT_OF`. These constants are declared near the top of the class as `static final int`. That complex declaration just means that they are class constants and they are integers. They are scoped to the class because, as unique identifiers, they're the same for every instance. Since they're declared this way, code outside the class can refer to them without having to know the actual number we're using to represent the relationship. This lets everything stay consistent and still have clear meaningful names that describe what every constant is actually for.

❸ The `PoseRule` constructor simply stores all three of these arguments into instance variables. Just like with the Exercise Measurement project, it uses Processing's `this` keyword to distinguish between the local variables that are passed in and its own instance variables.

❹ After saving that data we also initialize two vectors: `fromJointVector` and `toJointVector`. These vectors will hold the position of each joint from `SimpleOpenNI`. We don't want to populate them now, however. As we saw when we looked at the sketch, we declare the pose rules during setup when no user has been calibrated. If we tried to access the joint positions from `SimpleOpenNI` at that point the operation would fail. We have to wait for the calibration process to complete, which brings us to our `check` function.

❺ To check to see if the user is in the complete pose, each `PoseRule` needs to have its own individual `check` function to determine whether or not it is being met. Later on we'll see how `SkeletonPoser` combines all of these individual checks into a single result, but first lets look at how a single pose figures out whether or not the user matches it. The `PoseRule` `check` function takes the `userID` as an argument and returns a Boolean value letting `SkeletonPoser` know whether or not that rule was met.

❻ This function starts off by getting the position of the two joints whose relationship we'll be examining. The `userID`, `fromJoint`, and the `fromJointVector` make up the three arguments that we have to pass to `getJointPositionSkeleton` in order to populate `fromJointVector` with the position of the first joint. The same goes for the `toJoint`. We specifically asked for these pieces of data in the class's constructor so that we'd have enough information to pass to `SimpleOpenNI`. Here we take advantage of it.

❼ Once we've made our two calls to `getJointPositionSkeleton`, we have both of the joint positions, and we're ready to check the spatial relationship between them. As we saw in the basic version of this application, we can compare positions of joints with simple greater-than and less-than statements between individual components of their vectors. In this case, the value of `jointRelation` tells us exactly which comparison we need to make. There are four possible values of `jointRelation`, each one corresponding to a different comparison. Hence we use a `switch` statement to determine what to check. We'll store the final outcome in a Boolean variable called `result` so that we can return it at the end of this function. Since we want that variable to be accessible outside of the `switch` statement, we declare it before the statement begins. Then, within each branch of the `switch` statement, we set the value of `result` to the outcome of our comparison, `fromJointVector.y > toJointVector.y` for `ABOVE`, `fromJointVector.y < toJointVector.y` for `BELOW`, and so on.

The use of this `switch` statement allows us to enforce four different kinds of rules within a single function with only a single variable necessary to store the type of rule. This is a big part of why using classes is so much more elegant and compact than the approach we took in the basic version.

Notice that while code outside of our `PoseRule` *class has to refer to its constants using the class name (*`PoseRule.ABOVE, PoseRule.BELOW`*, etc.) within the class we can just use the constant names directly:* `ABOVE, BELOW, LEFT_OF`*, and* `RIGHT_OF`*. Since these constants are declare on this class itself, we can refer to them without having to refer to the class name, and Processing will still know what we're talking about.*

---

⑧ After the `switch` statement completes, our `result` variable will be set to true or false depending on whether the rule was met. We complete our `check` function by returning that result.

⑨ That completes our look at `PoseRule`. We've seen how it stores the information necessary to make up an individual rule and how it uses that information to check the current state of the user skeleton against that rule. Now let's examine how `PoseRule` interacts with `SkeletonPoser`. `SkeletonPoser` lets us combine multiple `PoseRule` instances into a single complex pose, such as the "Stayin' Alive" dance move we saw in our example. That process involves two steps:

- Adding multiple rules and storing them in an `ArrayList`.

- Checking all of the stored rules to determine the result.

⑩ The process starts with the class's constructor. As we saw in the sketch, the `SkeletonPoser` constructor only takes one argument: a `SimpleOpenNI` object. Each `PoseRule` will need access to that object in order to get the joint positions. Since `SkeletonPoser` is the class that talks to the outside world, it has to ask for this object on behalf of `PoseRule`.

⑪ Once the constructor has stored the `SimpleOpenNI` object into an instance variable, the only other task it performs is to initialize the `ArrayList` that it will use to store its set of `rules`. We saw `ArrayList` in action back in the Exercise Measurement project. We use it to store multiple objects when we don't know how many there are going to be and we need to add to the list dynamically. Our pose rules definitely fit these criteria.

⑫   Once our SkeletonPoser has been initialized, it's ready to receive rules. The addRule function is very straightforward. It simply creates a new PoseRule and then adds that to the growing rules ArrayList. This function takes nearly the same arguments as the PoseRule constructor, minus the SimpleOpenNI object, which SkeletonPoser already has handy and can simply pass along. The user of this code can call addRule as many times as he likes, and the rules ArrayList will smoothly grow in size every time add is called on it with the new rule.

⑬   At some point, though, we'll be done adding rules and we'll be ready to perform the check. This function gets passed a userID and it needs to tell every rule to check to see if that user's skeleton matches. Then it needs to combine these results, only returning true if all of the rules do, in fact, match.

⑭   To do this, we start off by declaring a Boolean variable, result, and setting it to true.

⑮   We're then going to update this value with the result of each PoseRule. And if it emerges as still true once we've checked all of the rules, then that means the user is in the pose. Otherwise, he's not. With this variable in hand, we loop through each PoseRule stored in rules.

⑯   We access the rule from the rules ArrayList, casting it to a PoseRule as it comes out. As explained in the Exercise Measurement project, this is necessary, because an ArrayList can store any kind of variable under the sun. Therefore, when we get our objects back out, we need to tell Processing what type they are.

⑰   When this is done, we have a single PoseRule and we call its check function, passing in the userID we've been asked to test. We want to combine the result from this one check with all of our previous checks. We only want the final result to be true if all of the individual checks return true. To achieve this, we use the logical AND operator we learned about in the basic version of this project: &&. We combine rule.check with our running result using && and we store the answer back into result. Since && only returns true if both of the expressions it combines are true, any single false rule.check will ensure that the final result comes out false. Just what we want.

⑱   Then, once we've looped through all of the rules, we return the final result so it can be used to play the MP3 or set the skeleton color. And that's it for our SkeletonPoser class. We can initialize it, we can add rules to it, and we can check them all to see if the user is really in the pose. We've completed this project!

Chapter 4

Exercises

This SkeletonPoser class is relatively sophisticated but there are number of things you could do to improve it. These exercises will test your knowledge of the SimpleOpenNI skeleton functions and give you a really powerful library for pose detection.

- Add the ability to create PoseRule instances that use the z-component of the user's joints. Start by adding constants for PoseRule.BEHIND and PoseRule.IN_FRONT_OF and then extend the switch statement to enforce these.

- Build a sketch that looks for multiple poses and plays different songs. Declare multiple SkeletonPoser objects, add rules to all of them, and then call each of their check functions in turn within your draw loop.

- In our basic version, we gave the user visual feedback about the results of each limb segment individually. However, when we converted to this class system, we lost that ability in favor of a simple true or false check for the whole user. Bring back this ability by storing the results of the pose check on the individual PoseRule so the sketch can report back to the user what failed.

- Add more types of rules that are based on the joint's orientation. For example, the "Stayin' Alive" pose should really require the user's hips to be pointed to one side. Combine this code with the joint orientation code from earlier in this chapter to add other types of rules.

Conclusion

At this point, you've finished learning all of the basic skills involved in writing programs with the Kinect. You can work with the depth image, you can draw point clouds in 3D, and you can do all kinds of things with the skeleton data. Now you're ready to move on to the rest of this book. For the last chapters, we'll explore applications of these skills. These skills only really become useful when you learn some background for the various application areas that they unlock. We'll explore three of these through extended projects in the next three chapters: 3D scanning for fabrication and kinematics for robotics. In each chapter, I'll introduce you to a some of the basic principles of the field, and then we'll work through a complete project that does something useful and fun within it. We'll scan and print our heads. We'll build a robot arm we can control with our bodies. With what you've learned so far, you're ready to go off and create all kinds of applications of your own imagining. These next chapters will give you some ideas and some additional skills to take those projects even further.

Scanning for Fabrication

Thus far, every project in this book has used the Kinect to translate the physical world into digital form. We've taken advantage of the Kinect's ability to scan its surroundings in order to build interfaces that translate our bodies and movements into actions on the computer screen. In this chapter, we're going to learn how to get the data that we've captured in the computer back out into the world in physical form. This chapter is going to explore techniques for using the Kinect as a 3D scanner for digital fabrication.

We'll take the data we capture from the Kinect, process it into a useful 3D representation, and then use it to manufacture new physical objects based on our originals, as shown in Figure 5-1. You'll learn:

- How to develop Processing sketches that can produce files that can be used in 3D design.

- How to work with those files in free 3D software such as MeshLab and ReplicatorG to improve them and modify them.

- How to produce actual objects from our Kinect scans using MakerBot and Shapeways.

While I'll be focusing on the MakerBot in this chapter, it is only one of many open source DIY 3D printers available today. For example, the RepRap (http://reprap.org) project, which seeks to build a 3D printer that can print its own parts, is a hotbed of DIY designs such as the Prusa Mendel (http://reprap.org/wiki/Prusa_Mendel), which is currently getting a lot of adoption among hobbyists and even 3D printer makers. Similarly, there are many other professional 3D fabrication services available beyond Shapeways, provided by local vendors with CNC mills and ZCorp printers but also from companies like Ponoko (http://www.ponoko.com/) and Sculpteo (http://www.sculpteo.com/). The scanning techniques covered in this chapter will create models that can be printed with any of these options.

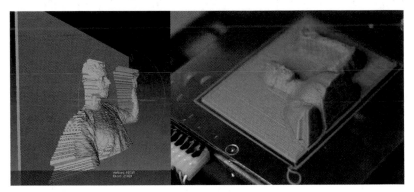

Figure 5-1. *A MakerBot printing out a scan of the author captured with the Kinect. The scan itself is shown on the left.*

Scan and Print: Rapid Prototyping Objects

The process is reminiscent of the workflow for importing paper documents into the digital domain. We start with the original piece of paper and capture an image of it using a scanner. Then we can manipulate that image using digital tools such as Adobe Photoshop. We alter the original, combine it with other scans, and add purely digital design elements until we've created what we want. Then we output the final result onto paper using a printer. With different printers, we can print with different inks on different papers at a variety of scales.

This digital workflow for documents has been around since the late 1960s and has been a staple of the modern office since the '80s. What's now newly possible is the ability to apply a similar workflow to the creation of physical objects. For awhile now, a variety of 3D fabrication technologies have been used in industry for rapid prototyping. If you're designing next year's model of Toyota, a children's toy for Hasbro, or the new Apple iPhone, you need to be able to test out your designs without having to tool up a whole factory. You could, of course, produce prototypes the old fashioned way out of hand-tooled blocks of wood and metal. However, since we had that digital revolution in the '80s, you're probably using software to produce your design. What you need is a technique for translating directly from your digital design to a physical object that you can hold in your hand and test. To fulfill this need, industry adopted the large-scale fabrication techniques they use to manufacture millions of identical objects at extremely low cost to create machines that could rapidly build individual copies of these prototype designs directly from the digital files. These machines all put some physical manufacturing process under the control of a computer: from deposition printers that build your object up out of plastic or resin to CNC mills and routers that can carve your design out of wood or metal.

For a long time, these rapid prototyping machines were themselves quite expensive. While they might have looked cheap by comparison with huge scale high precision industrial processes, they were still wildly beyond the budget of the home tinkerer or artist. In the past couple of years, that's begun to change as well. In 2009, a group of hardware hackers in New York—Bre Pettis, Adam Mayer, and Zach Smith—began selling a 3D printer for hobbyists they called the MakerBot. The MakerBot comes as a kit or fully assembled and costs around $1,300. It is small enough to fit on your desk or in the workshop of your local school or hackerspace. It prints in ABS plastic, the same material used to make Legos, but can also print with PLA (a thermoplastic material derived from organic sources). The MakerBot takes spools of this material (*filament*) and pulls it through a heated nozzle. The nozzle is positioned above a build platform that's connected to a set of three motors, one on each of the axes: x, y, and z. As the plastic melts out, a computer can control the motors to move the build platform around. The result is that the nozzle will lay down a series of layers of material one on top of the other to build up a three-dimensional object. You tell the MakerBot what to do with a software package that translates from the shapes in a 3D design file to instructions that tell the MakerBot to perform the set of movements needed to produce each layer of your model, one at a time on top of each other. The result is a printed version of the object you designed on your computer.

In addition to the MakerBot, there is now a series of other similar desktop 3D printers on the market ranging from other open source designs such as the RepRap project to more expensive models from companies such as ZCorp. Further, some other companies have begun to offer digital fabrication as an online service. Shapeways is a Dutch company, originally funded by Royal Philips Electronics, that recently relocated to New York. On their website, you can upload your 3D model files, chose materials ranging from food-safe ceramic to silver, and order copies to be printed out and sent to you or made available for sale to others in your own store. Shapeways uses a variety of different technologies in order to create prints in each material. The cost of the prints vary widely based on the material and size of your design, from $20 for a small plastic object to hundreds for larger objects in metal. While this is obviously more expensive than an individual print on a MakerBot, it has the advantage of needing no upfront investment in the printer and incurring no ongoing maintenance costs. A few other companies have begun to offer similar fabrication services as well, such as CloudFab.

Up until recently, the only way to generate objects that could be fabricated on a MakerBot or through Shapeways was to design them by hand. This involved learning complex 3D modeling software. The sophistication of the objects you could make was limited by your expertise as a modeler. It was a throwback to the era in printers before the invention of digital cameras and scanners when most people were limited to basic fonts and geometric shapes with the occasional piece of clip art. But now, with the advent of the Kinect, we have another way to create models for 3D printing: we can scan the physical world. We can

The approach to generating meshes from Kinect scans illustrated in this chapter is based on the work done by Kyle McDonald as artist-in-residence at MakerBot. In fact the code here was ported from one of the applications Kyle created there: KinectToSTL (http://github.com/kylemcdonald/ makerbot/tree/master/KinectToSTL). Many thanks to Kyle for his great work and his help in understanding his code.

use the Kinect to capture the three-dimensional shape of objects, spaces, and people. Then we can bring these shapes into our 3D modeling programs to manipulate them. We can remove parts of the scan or distort them, we can combine multiple scans into a single object, and we can merge scans with shapes created completely within the computer.

From a Point Cloud to an Object

In this chapter, we're going to develop a Processing sketch that acts as a 3D scanner. We've worked with the depth data from the Kinect in 3D before, especially in Chapter 3. In that chapter, we learned how to visualize the depth data as a point cloud on the screen. However, digital fabrication has very different constraints from computer graphics. Even though we can display a point cloud on the screen, it doesn't have the structure necessary to print it out as a physical object. The points in our point cloud are positioned within three-dimensional space, but they aren't sufficient to describe an actual surface that we could print in plastic or carve out of metal. To build such a surface, we have to sew our points together into a mesh. A three-dimensional mesh is the most common way to describe a solid object in 3D software.

So, we want to end up with a 3D mesh that corresponds to the surfaces of the actual objects that were in front of the Kinect at the time we took the scan. After all, the depth points all sit on the outside of solid objects that have real surfaces. We want our mesh to recreate these surfaces as closely as possible. However, a couple of challenges stand in the way of this goal. First, our scan did not capture the connections between these points. We'll have to invent some way of joining them together after the fact. And second, our scan missed many points on the surface of the objects (especially where they were occluded by closer objects). We'll have to figure out a way to fill in these gaps with something that produces a physically coherent object.

We want to end up with a 3D mesh made up of connected surfaces that closely match the shape of our subject. What we start out with is a set of isolated individual points that have position in space but no volume. How do we get from here to there? The first thing we do is combine multiple of these points into two-dimensional shapes. We'll go through all the points and define triangles that connect them to their neighbors. There are many different ways we could join our points into triangles, but not all of them are equally useful. The point cloud is like a giant connect-the-dots puzzle. The goal is for each triangle to correspond to one facet of the overall surface of our original object, not just arbitrarily connect three points at random. Some solutions to this puzzle will result in impossible objects that are partially inside out or tangled up into a mess. For example, imagine if you included one depth point in every single one of your triangles. You'd end up with a crazy spiky mess that had only a vague resemblance to your scanned object and was definitely not printable on a MakerBot. The correct solution will result in a smooth surface that is a close match with our original object.

Once we've created these triangles, we'll join them all together into a single 3D mesh. To do this, we'll need a data structure that lets us define meshes and slowly add triangles to it one at a time. Luckily, there's a great Processing library called Modelbuilder that does exactly this. Modelbuilder was created by artist Marius Watz when he was artist-in-residence at MakerBot, and it provides the data structures we need for building a mesh from our 3D points as long as we provide the algorithm, the strategy for choosing which points to combine into triangles. Modelbuilder also makes it easy to save our mesh as an STL after we're done building it. STL is one of many common file types for storing representations of 3D objects.

Simply building a mesh and saving it to a file is a necessary step for fabrication, but it is not sufficient. Not all 3D meshes are capable of being physically fabricated. We can specify and even display surfaces that can't possibly be constructed with a MakerBot or any other printing technology. I mentioned earlier that if we choose the wrong connections between points, we might end up with triangles that pass through each other, an effect that can't be rendered in plastic. We also still haven't discussed what we're going to do with the missing, occluded data. For some parts of the depth data captured by the Kinect, no actual 3D coordinates will be available. As I discussed extensively in Chapter 1, this happens when a closer object casts an IR shadow on the things behind it, preventing the Kinect from collecting any depth information about that part of the scene. If we don't do anything, these parts of the depth image will translate into holes in our mesh, some of which could be so large that they would render our object unprintable. Therefore, we'll have to decide on some way to fill in these areas. We'll have to intentionally set the depth value even though no data may be available. We'll do this by creating a *backplane*. For any point that's missing data, we'll set its depth to a predetermined value. That way, all of the missing points will become a solid plane behind the visible part of our object. This choice is somewhat arbitrary but has practical benefits, especially when printing on the MakerBot. The MakerBot builds its prints up layer by layer, starting with the flat surface of its build platform. Hence, there are great advantages to having your object be flat on one side: it will stop your object from falling over or sliding around as its being built up by the MakerBot's nozzle.

This brings up an important point in preparing files for printing: what makes a good mesh depends on the physical technique that's used for fabrication. Each fabrication technology has different restrictions and capabilities that arise out of how they work. For example, since the MakerBot builds up the model by putting thermoplastic material down one layer at a time, it can't have any "overhangs." Parts of the model that stick out beyond the layers beneath them will sag. There's nothing to support the heated material laid down by the nozzle—so instead of staying in place, those parts will slump downward. Many of the 3D printing technologies offered by Shapeways don't have this problem and can easily deal with overhangs. On the other hand, other printing technologies have their own limitations. For example, because of its flat build platform, the MakerBot is capable of printing meshes that are not fully closed. A mesh defines a surface, but it only truly defines a solid object if that surface is fully closed without any holes. Otherwise, how would you know which is the inside and which is the outside? Take a piece of unfolded paper and try to point to its inside and outside and you'll see the problem. Many printing technologies require an object to have a fully specified inside and outside in order to be fabricated, hence they can only deal with fully closed meshes. Since the Kinect only sees our objects from one side, it is impossible for its depth data alone to produce a fully closed mesh. We'll have to add some geometry to our mesh to make it possible to print with these systems.

Outline of This Chapter

This discussion of the issues involved in using the Kinect as a scanner for fabrication has given you a sense of what we'll be doing in this chapter, but here's the full plan step by step. We'll start by running a hello world program with Modelbuilder. We won't even use the Kinect. We'll just define a simple mesh and save it as an STL file. Once we've got that STL, we'll view it in a piece of free software called MeshLab. MeshLab is an amazing tool for viewing and processing 3D models. After we've gotten the hang of creating STLs, we'll start in on building our first mesh from the Kinect's depth data. We'll learn about the basic strategy for choosing which triangles to connect together. Then we'll see the problems with this basic strategy: the holes and other weird anomalies that result. We'll then go back and improve our code to clean up these problems and fill in the holes.

Once we have a workable mesh, we'll go through the steps necessary to prepare it for the MakerBot:

1. We'll use MeshLab to reduce the number of surfaces in our mesh. This will dramatically decrease the amount of time it take for the MakerBot to print out our object, and MeshLab can do it without losing a lot of detail in our mesh.

2. At this point, we'll have a file that's ready to print.

3. We'll import our file into ReplicatorG, a program provided by MakerBot that controls the actual printer.

4. Then we'll be ready to run our MakerBot and see the result.

And, finally, we'll go back to the editing stage to make a different version of our model that can be uploaded to Shapeways. We'll walk through the Shapeways upload process and talk about some of the wide range of materials and printing options they provide. We'll conclude the chapter by comparing the final results from both printing services.

Let's get started!

Intro to Modelbuilder

Before we start working with data from the Kinect, we need to learn the basics of creating 3D models in Processing. As I mentioned in the introduction to this chapter, we'll be using Marius Watz's Modelbuilder library for this purpose. Watz is an artist who creates sculptures and installations using *procedural geometry*. In other words, he writes programs that create complex 3D shapes. He controls the rules that determine the overall aesthetic of these shapes, and then his algorithms fill in the details.

Figure 5-2 shows some examples of his work that were created while he was artist-in-residence at MakerBot. Each of these individual sculptures is unique. Their geometry was created in Processing. He then printed each of them out on a MakerBot to create the finished object. To make physical sculptures from Processing, Watz created Modelbuilder. Modelbuilder provides tools that make it easier to create and manipulate 3D geometry in Processing and to export the resulting objects in a form that allows for fabrication. Modelbuilder is a rich library with all kinds of sophisticated tools for generating 3D forms. We'll only be scratching its surface in this chapter.

Figure 5-2. *Parametric form studies created by Marius Watz using his Modelbuilder Processing library as part of the MakerBot artist-in-residence project. Photo courtesy of Marius Watz.*

In this section, I'll give you an introduction to using Modelbuilder. We'll write a sketch that creates two faces of a cube, and then we'll save the resulting model into an STL file. In the next section, we'll open up that file in MeshLab so we can see the results of our work and start learning about the rest of the pipeline for 3D printing.

Before we dive into code, you need to download and install Modelbuilder. You can get it here: *http://code.google.com/p/codeandform/downloads/list*. Install it like any other Processing library by moving its folder into your Processing *libraries* folder.

Let's get started on our sketch. Creating 3D shapes in Modelbuilder consists of three steps:

- Initializing the model and adding geometry to it.
- Displaying the model.
- Saving the model as an STL.

In this example, we'll address each step in a different part our sketch. We'll initialize the model and add geometry in setup. We'll display it in draw. And we'll save an STL when the user hits a key. Later on in this chapter, the process of adding geometry to our model will become more sophisticated. We'll integrate our Modelbuilder code with the techniques we've already seen for accessing 3D points from the Kinect.

For now though, we'll start simple. We'll start by initializing our model using Modelbuilder's main class for representing shapes: UGeometry. Then, we'll start to create the faces of our cube. We'll break each face down into two triangles. As I explained at the start of this chapter, triangles are the basic atomic unit of 3D geometry and they're what we'll use to connect all of the depth point from the Kinect into a single smooth surface. Figure 5-3 illustrates the idea and shows some example coordinates for two sides of a 150 pixel cube. As you can see in the figure, we break each of these sides down into two triangles. Each triangle connects three of the four points that make up the side. The result is that each point ends up being part of multiple triangles.

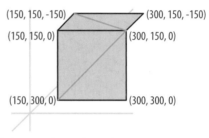

Figure 5-3. *Dividing each face on the surface of a cube up into triangles so that we can draw them with Modelbuilder.*

To create each triangle, we'll add points to our model in sets of three using Modelbuilder's addFace function. Once we've added all of our triangles, we'll close our shape and we'll be ready to display it and output it. In our draw function, we tell the model to display itself by calling its own draw function. We'll also include some coordinate system transformations so that our sketch will display the model from all different angles. Modelbuilder includes its own, quite sophisticated, system for interactively displaying 3D models. I won't cover this topic here as it would distract from our focus on fabrication, but I highly recommend reading about it in the Modelbuilder documentation, which is available at *http://workshop.evolutionzone.com/code/modelbuilder/javadoc/unlekker/ modelbuilder/package-summary.html*. Then, finally, we'll output our model to an STL file when the user hits any key. We'll accomplish this by calling the model's writeSTL function within our sketch's keyPressed callback.

Example 5-1 shows the code. Read through it, run it, and then I'll point out a few other important details and gotchas that you might have missed.

Example 5-1. modelbuilder_hello.pde

```
import processing.opengl.*;
// import both
import unlekker.util.*;
import unlekker.modelbuilder.*;
```

```
// declare our model object
UGeometry model; ❶

float x = 0;

void setup() { ❷
  size(400, 400, OPENGL);
  stroke(255, 0, 0);
  strokeWeight(3);
  fill(255);

  // initialize our model,
  model = new UGeometry(); ❸

  // set shape type to TRIANGLES and begin adding geometry
  model.beginShape(TRIANGLES); ❹

  // build a triangle out of three vectors
  model.addFace( ❺
   new UVec3(150, 150, 0),
   new UVec3(150, 150, -150),
   new UVec3(300, 150, 0)
  );

  model.addFace(
    new UVec3(300, 150, 0),
    new UVec3(150, 150, -150),
    new UVec3(300, 150, -150)
  );

   model.addFace(
    new UVec3(300, 150, -150),
    new UVec3(300, 300, 0),
    new UVec3(300, 150, 0)
  );

  model.addFace(
    new UVec3(300, 300, -150),
    new UVec3(300, 300, 0),
    new UVec3(300, 150, -150)
  );

  model.endShape(); ❻
}

void draw() {
  background(255);
  lights(); ❼

  translate(150, 150, -75); ❽
  rotateY(x);
  x+=0.01;
  translate(-150, -150, 75);

  model.draw(this);
}

void keyPressed() {
  model.writeSTL(this, "part_cube.stl");
}
```

Figure 5-4 shows some screen captures documenting the output of this sketch. When the sketch runs, you'll see a partial cube that looks a bit like an L-bracket. Red lines outline each of its triangular faces. This shape will rotate around the sketch so that you can see it from every angle. It's color will appear to gradually shift as it moves. As we learned back in Chapter 3, that happens because our virtual lights fall on the 3D model from different angles as it moves. When you hit any key on your keyboard, the sketch will hesitate for a second and then output the follow in Processing console:

```
01:28 Writing STL 'part_cube.stl' 4
01:28 Closing 'part_cube.stl'. 4 triangles written.
01:28
```

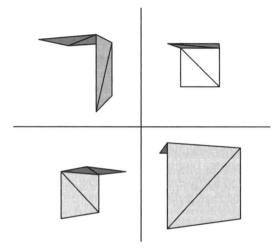

Figure 5-4. *Four views of a rotating quarter cube created with Modelbuilder. Each surface of the shape is made up of individual triangles. As the shape rotates, different parts of it are exposed to the virtual lights and so it appears different.*

This output tells us that Modelbuilder successfully saved an STL file called *part_cube.stl* that consisted of four triangles. In the next section, we'll open up that file and examine it outside of Processing. But first, let's take a closer look at the code for this sketch to make sure you've fully got the hang of working with Modelbuilder.

❶ Our work with Modelbuilder starts at the top of the sketch where we import the library and declare our UGeometry object. Modelbuilder comes in two parts: unlekker.util and unlekker.modelbuilder. We need both of them to create our geometry and save our STL file. As I mentioned above, UGeometry is Modelbuilder's chief class for describing 3D shapes. We'll be calling methods on this model object throughout the sketch.

❷ Unlike most of the sketches in this book, this one does most of its work inside of its setup function. Since our geometry is not changing, we only need to create it once when the sketch starts up. Therefore, all of our code that adds triangles to our model object goes into setup instead of draw. Once we've created our geometry, in draw we'll just focus on displaying the model, including the rotations and translations necessary to get it to spin in place.

❸ In `setup` we start by initializing our `model` as a new `UGeometry` object. With that out of the way, we're almost ready to start creating our cube.

❹ First, though, we've got to tell Modelbuilder what shape our faces are going to be. This is just like when we displayed a 3D model using OBJLoader back in Chapter 3. We had to tell OBJLoader what kind of geometrical primitives it should use to display the model. The options were: `POINTS`, `LINES`, `TRIANGLES`, `QUADS`, `POLYGON`, `TRIANGLE_STRIP`, or `QUAD_STRIP`. These same options are available to us now. We could define our geometry using any of these. We've chosen `TRIANGLES`. Therefore, we kick off the modeling process by calling `model.beginShape(TRIANGLES)`. This tells our `model` that we're going to start adding geometry to it and that this geometry will take the form of triangles.

❺ After we call `beginShape`, our `model` is ready to receive triangles. We'll build up our model using its `addFace` function. This function takes three points to define the triangle we want to add to the model. When we're talking about creating a 3D mesh, we call these points "vertices" because they exist at the intersection of multiple shapes. Each of our triangles is connected to others: they share vertices in common. We saw this illustrated in Figure 5-3 where each triangle shared at least two of its points in common with others. This sharing of vertices is what turns our set of points into a continuous surface and, eventually, a solid object.

Each time we call `model.addFace`, we pass it three arguments, one representing each vertex of the triangle we'd like to add to the model.

This call to `addFace` is creating the left triangle on the top face of our shape. In each argument to `addFace`, we use the three coordinates of our vertex (in the order x, y, z) as arguments to create a `UVec3`. `UVec3` is Modelbuilder's class for representing vertices.

The order in which we add these vertices to our face is important. Each of our triangles has a front and a back. The front is the side that reflects the virtual lights we shine on it. As we combine our faces into a closed surface, their front sides will determine which is the inside of our shape and which is the outside. To make a solid shape that can be successfully 3D printed, we want all of the faces to point toward the outside of the object.

But how does Modelbuilder determine which is the front side of our triangle? After all, we're only telling it three points. We don't seem to pass in any data about which side is which. The answer is that the orientation of each face is determined by the order in which we add its vertices. If we add the vertices in order, going counterclockwise around the face, then its top will be the front. If we reverse that order, then the reverse will be true. Figure 5-5 illustrates the principle. This is going to become quite important as we combine our triangles into a complete object based on the data from the Kinect. We need to orient all of the faces the same way so that our object is solid and can be 3D printed.

❻ Once we've added all our triangles, we complete our model by calling `model.endShape`. That completes the process of building our model and also finishes off our `setup` function.

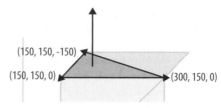

(150, 150, -150)

(150, 150, 0)

(300, 150, 0)

Figure 5-5. *The order of the vertices on each face determines its front and back. Connecting them in counterclockwise order ensures the front faces out.*

❼ In draw, we proceed to display the model. Just like when we worked with an OBJ file back in Chapter 3, in order to display this model, we need to position it and light it. Our draw function starts off by clearing the sketch to white and then turning on Processing's default lighting setup by calling lights. This will make our model appear shaded rather than flatly colored, making it much easier to discern its geometry.

❽ We position the model using translate to push it back into a comfortably visible location. Then we call rotateY with a slowly shifting rot variable so that we'll be able to see our model from every side. Once that rotation has completed and rot has been incremented to keep the model turning, we move back to our original position by passing the inverse values to translate. This will keep the model rotating around itself and in view within our sketch rather than orbiting around our point of view and ending up off screen half the time. After this counter-translation, we display the model with model.draw(this).

> *Here, this refers to our Processing sketch itself. To integrate itself into Processing's transformations, Modelbuilder needs access to the sketch itself and so we have to pass it in. This is a common pattern for libraries that want to do advanced things and need access to Processing itself to do them. We'll see Modelbuilder take advantage of it again shortly when we save our model to an STL file.*

The result, as demonstrated in Figure 5-5, will be two square surfaces, set at right angles to each other, rotating around our sketch.

Now how do we save this geometry as an STL? After all, we can already display the depth data from the Kinect. Half the point of using Modelbuilder is to be able to save our mesh to a standard file format that we can work with in other applications. Thankfully, Modelbuilder makes the process of creating an STL from our geometry almost too easy. As you saw when you first ran it, this sketch saves an STL whenever we hit a key. Let's look at the keyPressed function to see how it does this:

```
void keyPressed() {
  model.writeSTL(this, "part_cube.stl");
}
```

We simply call the writeSTL function on our model. This function takes two arguments. The first one is this, again representing the Processing sketch itself. Modelbuilder needs access to the sketch so that it can create a file. The second argument is a string representing the name we want to give our file. In our case, we call it *part_cube.stl*.

When the user hits a key, Modelbuilder will create a file called *part_cube.stl* in the sketch's folder and will populate it with the geometry that we've added to our model. Once that file is saved, we can view it and work with it in other applications. The first of these outside applications will be MeshLab. When we have a real scan from the Kinect, we'll need to use MeshLab to simplify our scan so that it prints out in a reasonable amount of time on the MakerBot. For now, though, let's bring our simple *part_cube.stl* file into MeshLab so we can learn the ropes.

Intro to MeshLab

MeshLab is a free cross-platform open source program for working with 3D models. MeshLab is extremely powerful but also highly unintuitive to use. Most 3D modeling programs provide an interface for you to create your own models by combining and manipulating geometric shapes and points with the mouse. MeshLab, on the other hand, lets you process your existing geometry using complex algorithms designed to achieve particular effects, such as "ScaleDependent Laplacian Smooth," "Mesh Aging and Chipping Simulation," and "Crease Marking with NonFaux Edges." As these highly technical names make clear, MeshLab makes these algorithms available directly. The program's interface mainly consists of menus that allow you to enter in the parameters needed by these algorithms to do their work. These options might be intuitive if you are a computer scientist who specializes in 3D geometry, but for others, they are largely impenetrable. That said, MeshLab does make it quite easy to experiment with these algorithms and to apply the few that you understand or find useful. Later on in this chapter, I'll demonstrate the use of one of these algorithms ("Quadric Edge Collapse Decimation") to reduce the size of our scan to make it easier to work with and print.

MeshLab is also a great interface for simply viewing 3D models. It can load in large sophisticated models with no problem and let you view them from multiple angles and at multiple scales. In this starting example, that's all we're going to use it for. We'll download and install MeshLab and then we'll use it to open up our *part_cube.stl* file so we can examine it and begin to familiarize ourselves with MeshLab's interface.

Your First Visit to MeshLab

MeshLab is available for download from SourceForge (*http://meshlab.source-forge.net*). There are installable binaries for both Mac OS and Windows. If you're on Linux you'll need to build from source. The SourceForge site contains complete instructions for installing. Follow those until you have MeshLab installed successfully. Once MeshLab is installed, launch it.

When MeshLab first launches, it will present you with a large window with a pleasant purple gradient and a pink bar across the bottom, as shown in Figure 5-6. In the center of that window is a pale circle with a crosshairs drawn over it. There's also a small square floating just above and to the right of this. These are the controls for rotating and scaling our 3D models so that we can look at them from different angles. Above the main window are a lot of small graphical icons that affect how models are displayed and how you can select parts of them. We won't need any of these for the things we'll be doing with MeshLab in this book.

Figure 5-6. *MeshLab is a program for manipulating 3D models. It provides access to powerful algorithms that will help us reduce the size of our Kinect scans so that we can print them.*

As mentioned above, we'll mainly use MeshLab to view and process the models that we create in Processing. The first thing we need to do to get started is load up the *part_cube.stl* model we just created. Click on the File menu and select Import Mesh. MeshLab will prompt you to select your STL file. Navigate to your Processing sketch's folder, select *part_cube.stl*, and click Open. When you open your STL, MeshLab will pop up a dialog box prompting you to Unify Duplicated Vertices, as shown in Figure 5-7. Click OK to agree.

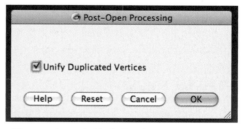

Figure 5-7. *MeshLab will prompt you to Unify Duplicated Vertices whenever you open an STL created in Processing.*

Once you've dismissed this dialog, MeshLab will display your model. When your model first pops up, though, you might have a hard time recognizing it. Upon first opening our *part_cube.stl* file, you'll see something that looks a lot like Figure 5-8, a flat black backward L-shape. Our model is upside down. We can correct this by rotating it around using the circle and crosshairs I mentioned earlier. Click somewhere inside that circle and drag up and to the left. You'll see the L-shape rotate and its surfaces turn a lighter gray (Figure 5-9). You'll also start to see some shading that will reveal the three-dimensional corner we saw in Processing. In Chapter 3 we discussed how Processing orients its axes. Well, MeshLab orients them differently. Specifically, it reverses the orientation of both the y- and z-axes. That's why our model appears upside down and flipped when we first open it. Since we're just using MeshLab to view our model, this mismatch doesn't make much difference. It's perfectly easy to rotate our models around after importing them. In fact, Processing's choice of orientation is different from most other 3D programs (which also frequently differ from each other), so it's something you'll always have to adjust for when using models created there.

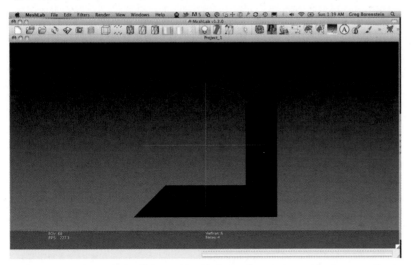

Figure 5-8. When we import the STL into MeshLab, it will come in upside-down and backward. This happens because MeshLab uses a different coordinate system than Processing.

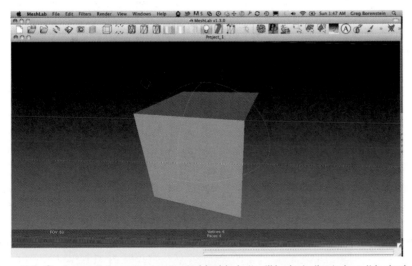

Figure 5-9. Once we rotate our geometry in MeshLab, it will look similar to how it looked in Processing, only with nicer shading and rendering. The order in which we draw the vertices determines which side is the front and back of each surface.

When we created this geometry, I explained the righthand rule (illustrated in Figure 5-5). The order in which we added our vertices to each of the triangles that make up our model determines which side of the model is considered the outside. Since we added the vertices in counterclockwise order, each of our triangles faces out away from the middle of the cube we began to create. In Modelbuilder, only the outside of our shape reflects light. These outside surfaces appear gray with shifting levels of brightness as we rotate our shape.

The inner surfaces appear solid black. The technical term for this property is the *surface normal*. Each triangle has an imaginary line that points away from it perpendicular to its outer surface. The direction of this normal determines how much light the surface will reflect in visualizations such as MeshLab. Also, important for us, the direction of the normals determines whether the object is solid and can be printed successfully. We need all of our triangles to have their normals facing toward the outside of our model. This will become crucial in the next section as we start to work on creating an STL from the Kinect point cloud.

So far we haven't taken advantage of nearly anything that MeshLab can do. We've just used it as a simple STL viewer. MeshLab will really come in handy once we start creating STLs from the Kinect depth data. Unlike this simple geometrical example, those STLs will have tens of thousands of vertices and faces. To print these STLs out on the MakerBot, submit them to Shapeways, or do anything else interesting with them, we'll need to use some of MeshLab's advanced algorithms to simplify them. But before we're ready for that, we need to learn how to make a mesh from the Kinect data to begin with.

Making a Mesh from the Kinect Data

Now that we've learned how to create geometry with Modelbuilder, it's time to apply that knowledge to our Kinect data. Instead of creating an STL that represents a simple geometrical shape, we're going to make one that represents the actual physical objects that are visible in front of our Kinect.

In the last section, we chose the positions of our vertices manually, selecting their coordinates so that they'd form triangles that made up the faces of a cube. This time we're going to create vertices based on the depth points captured by the Kinect. We'll loop through each depth point and create triangles that connect each one with its neighbors. Each of these triangles will make up one facet of a mesh that matches the surface of the objects in the scene in front of the Kinect. We'll add them to our model one at a time, and when we've covered all of the points in the point cloud, we'll have an STL that represents our complete scene (Figure 5-10).

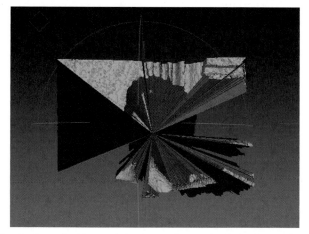

Figure 5-10. *The final result of the code in this section: a mesh that's built from the Kinect point cloud. This mesh will have holes and other geometrical problems that we'll need to clean up in the next section.*

We'll start this section by looking at the code that does this work. Then we'll look at the STL that's created by our code. We'll quickly discover that there are some problems with our model. I'll point these out and discuss their causes. Then, in the next section, we'll make some additions to our code to address these problems and create a clean mesh that we can use for fabrication.

Let's get started. Here's the code:

```
import processing.opengl.*; ❶
import unlekker.util.*;
import unlekker.modelbuilder.*;
import SimpleOpenNI.*;
SimpleOpenNI kinect;

boolean scanning = false; ❷
int spacing = 3;

UGeometry model;
UVertexList vertexList;

void setup() { ❸
  size(1024, 768, OPENGL);
  kinect = new SimpleOpenNI(this);
  kinect.enableDepth();

  model = new UGeometry();
  vertexList = new UVertexList();
}

void draw() { ❹
  background(0);

  kinect.update();

  translate(width/2, height/2, -1000);
  rotateX(radians(180));

  PVector[] depthPoints = kinect.depthMapRealWorld(); ❺

  if (scanning) {
    model.beginShape(TRIANGLES); ❻
  }

  for (int y = 0; y < 480 -spacing; y+=spacing) { ❼
    for (int x = 0; x < 640 -spacing; x+= spacing) {

      if (scanning) { ❽
        int nw = x + y * 640 ; ❾
        int ne = (x + spacing) + y * 640 ;
        int sw = x + (y + spacing) * 640;
        int se = (x + spacing) + (y + spacing) * 640;

        model.addFace(new UVec3(depthPoints[nw].x, ❿
                                depthPoints[nw].y,
                                depthPoints[nw].z),
        new UVec3(depthPoints[ne].x, depthPoints[ne].y, depthPoints[ne].z),
        new UVec3(depthPoints[sw].x, depthPoints[sw].y, depthPoints[sw].z));
```

```
        model.addFace(new UVec3(depthPoints[ne].x,
                                depthPoints[ne].y,
                                depthPoints[ne].z),
         new UVec3(depthPoints[se].x, depthPoints[se].y, depthPoints[se].z),
         new UVec3(depthPoints[sw].x, depthPoints[sw].y, depthPoints[sw].z));
        }
        else {
          stroke(255);
          int i = x + y * 640;
          PVector currentPoint = depthPoints[i];
          point(currentPoint.x, currentPoint.y, currentPoint.z);
        }
      }
    }
    if (scanning) { ⑪
      model.endShape();

      SimpleDateFormat logFileFmt =
        new SimpleDateFormat("'scan_'yyyyMMddHHmmss'.stl'");
      model.writeSTL(this, logFileFmt.format(new Date()));

      model.writeSTL(this, "scan_"+random(1000)+".stl");
      scanning = false;
    }
  }

  void keyPressed() {
    if (key == ' ') {
      scanning = true;
    }
  }
```

If you copy this code into Processing, save it, and run it, you'll be presented with an application that looks identical to the simple point cloud viewer we created back in Chapter 3. However, if you hit the space bar, the sketch will pause for a brief moment and then it will print out something like this in the console:

```
16:58 Writing STL 'scan_621.58685.stl' 67734
16:58 Closing 'scan_621.58685.stl'. 67734 triangles written.
```

If you look in your sketch folder, you'll discover that there's an STL there. The sketch saved a scan (Figure 5-11) based on the state of the depth data at the moment you hit the space bar. Later on, we'll take a look at the model that this sketch created and saved in that STL, but first let's dive into the code and learn how to create a mesh from depth points.

Figure 5-11. *Processing displaying the point cloud at the moment we create a mesh.*

This sketch is a combination of the Modelbuilder example we worked through earlier in this chapter and the code we wrote in Chapter 3 to display point clouds in 3D.

❶ The sketch starts off with the usual library import statements and variable declarations, including the UGeometry and UVertexList objects we saw in the Modelbuilder example.

❷ There are two new variables: a Boolean called scanning and an int called spacing. The first of these will let our sketch have two modes: one where we simply display the point cloud and one where we actually create geometry and build up our mesh. We set scanning to true in the sketch's keyPressed function so that whenever the user hits the space bar we know it's time to build up our mesh and save an STL file.

The second variable, spacing, we'll use to determine the resolution of our mesh. Meshes take a long time to build, and the STLs we store them in can end up as very large files. Depending on what we're doing with the STL, we may not need the full resolution that the Kinect is capable of providing. For example, when we're working with the MakerBot, a really high resolution mesh will take forever to process and print without actually adding that much more detail to our final product. We'll use this spacing variable to skip through the depth points, reducing the number of points we add to our mesh. I've found that setting spacing to three results in an STL that has a good balance of detail and file size.

❸ In setup, we set the size of our sketch, prepare to access the depth data from the Kinect and initialize our Modelbuilder objects.

❹ At the beginning of `draw`, we do the usual preamble work of clearing the sketch, updating the Kinect, and setting some rotations and translations to position the point cloud comfortably on the screen.

❺ With this out of the way, we access the depth points from the Kinect with `kinect.depthMapRealWorld` and store them into a `PVector` array called, creatively, `depthPoints`.

❻ What we do next depends on whether or not the user has initiated a scan by hitting the space bar. If so, then `scanning` will be true and we'll begin the process of creating our mesh.

Just like in our last Modelbuilder example, we tell our `model` to prepare itself for geometry and that we'll be adding that geometry in the form of `TRIANGLES`.

❼ Now, we begin our loop through the depth points. We will perform this loop regardless of whether we're in scanning mode (it's outside of our `if` statement), but what we do inside the loop will be different in each mode. Notice that we use our `spacing` variable in the declaration of our loops.

We loop over the depth points, incrementing both our row and column indices by the amount set in `spacing`. This means that we'll skip individual points as well as complete rows, keeping the density of the mesh down but also evenly spaced.

❽ The first thing we do inside the inner loop is check to see if we're currently in the process of performing a scan. We enter another `if` statement based on our `scanning` variable. The `else` branch of this statement (i.e., what we do when we're not scanning) is unchanged from our usual way of displaying point clouds. We set our stroke color to white, extract the `currentPoint` from the `depthPoints` array, and then use that vector's x-, y-, and z-components to draw a point in space.

❾ What happens when we are scanning is more interesting. We start with the index for a single depth point and we need to figure out how to connect that point to its neighbors in order to construct triangles that we can add to our mesh. How do we do this? How do we translate from the index of one depth point to the indices of its three adjacent neighbors?

Figure 5-12 illustrates the process. That diagram shows three rows of depth points with four points in each row. Since the depth points are meant to have come from the Kinect, they're not arranged in neat rows, but instead dispersed slightly based on where they fell on a surface of an object in the scene. The red point indicates the current point. We want to add two triangles to our `model` for each point. The two triangles will share one side so that together they form a single square. We'll refer to the corners of the square by the points on the compass rose: NW will be our current point; it will make up the top-left corner of the square. NE is the top-right corner of the square, the point immediately to the right of the NW. SW and SE will be the two points below these, respectively.

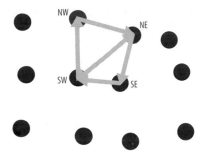

Figure 5-12. *We build a continuous mesh by connecting each point in the point cloud to its three adjacent neighbors with two triangles.*

So our job here is to calculate the index in the depthPoints array that corresponds to each of these four points: NE, NW, SW, and SE. The first of these is easy; it's just the current point in our loop. You'll remember the formula for that from way back in Chapter 2: int i = y * 640 + x. This formula translates from the x-y position of the depth point to its index in the depthPoints array. To find the other three points, we just have to replace x and y in this formula with new values that correspond to the NE point's three neighbors. The NW point is the next point in the same row after NE. The y-coordinate stays the same, but we have to add spacing to the x-coordinate: (x + spacing) + y * 640;. SW is at the same x-coordinate as NE but on the next row, so the reverse happens. The x-coordinate stays the same and the y-coordinate increases: x + (y + spacing) * 640;. And, finally, for SE, both the x-coordinate and y-coordinate are increased by spacing: (x + spacing) + (y + spacing) * 640.

To access the position of each of these points, we need to calculate their indices in the depthPoints array. We'll work off the index of the current point to accomplish this. Let's start with NE. NE is the point immediately to the right of our current point. Hence, to find its index, all we have to do is add spacing to the current point's index; that will give us the next point in the current row of depth points. SW, on the other hand, is one full row below our starting point. If we were including every row of depth points, then we could jump down one row simply by adding 640, the width of the depth image, to the index for the current point. However, since we're skipping rows to reduce the density of our scan, we need to multiply by spacing as well to account for the skipped rows. So, the index of SW is the current index plus 640 times spacing. Once we know the index for SW, it's easy to calculate it for SE as well. Just like NE is simply the next consecutive point after NW, the same goes for SE after SW. We can calculate the index for SE by simply adding spacing to the index of SW.

⑩ Once we've calculated these four indices we can access the depth points that will make up the vertices of the triangles we're going to add to our mesh. But now the question presents itself: which vertices should we connect to form each triangle and in what order? We know from our earlier experience working with MeshLab that we want to add vertices clockwise so that we follow the righthand rule as illustrated in Figure 5-5. So, in this case, we'll split the surface defined by our four vertices into two triangles: NW to NE to SW and NE to SE to SW, as shown in Figure 5-13.

Then we'll use Modelbuilder's `addFace` function to add each of these triangles to our growing `model`.

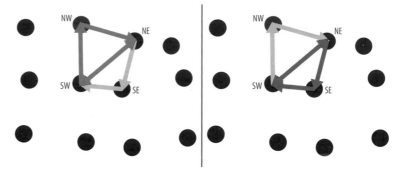

Figure 5-13. *The two triangles that connect a depth point with its neighbors.*

We'll add two triangles to our `model` in this manner for every point we process in the depth data. When we reach the end of our `for` loops, we'll have triangles that connect all of our selected depth points into a single shape.

⓫ As soon as the `for` loop completes, and if we're scanning, we'll end our shape, write out the STL file, and set `scanning` to false so that we don't produce another scan until the user hits the space bar again.

We use a timestamp to create the name of our STL file to prevent multiple scans from being saved with the same filename and hence overwriting each other. Setting `scanning` to false returns our sketch to display mode.

Looking at Our First Scan

Now that we've reviewed how the scanning code works, let's take a look at the final product. Figure 5-11 showed what the depth points looked like at the moment I took my scan. You can see me facing to the left of the point cloud in front of a window with a curtain hanging down behind me. Let's compare that with the mesh stored in our STL.

Launch MeshLab and select Import Mesh from the File menu. Navigate to the STL file you created with our scanning sketch and open it. When your mesh first comes into MeshLab, it will appear as a black silhouette. Click and drag to rotate your scan around to face you. You'll find that it looks something like Figure 5-14. What's going on here? Our mesh is a mess! If you zoom in and drag around, you'll discover that some parts of the mesh look right, like the folds of the curtain that are visible at the top of my mesh and the bit of my arm that's poking through at the bottom. But the mesh seems to be pinched together, many of its surfaces stretched toward a single point in front of the main body of the scan.

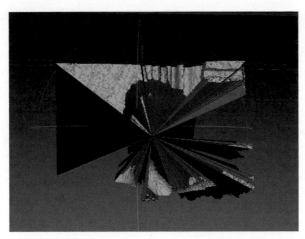

Figure 5-14. *Importing our scan into MeshLab reveals problems with its geometry. All of the points where the Kinect is lacking depth data due to my shadow are connected together into a single point.*

What caused this problem? Our approach in the last section was designed to connect each depth point to its neighbors, not some arbitrary point far in front of the rest of the scene. However, we forgot about a key attribute of the depth image: it has holes. As we learned way back at the beginning of Chapter 2, objects that are close to the Kinect will cast a "depth shadow" on those behind them, obscuring the infrared dots the Kinect uses to capture depth information. Hence many of the depth points we're iterating over will have zeros for all three of their coordinates. This explains what we're seeing in MeshLab. We included all of these zero points in our mesh. Any triangle that includes one or more zero points will stretch out to that point. The place in the mesh we're seeing where all the points come together? That's 0,0,0. Somewhere behind all of those stretched triangles the well-formed parts of our mesh are there, correctly in place..

In fact, we can even take a look at these parts through these stretched triangles. Zoom in toward the mesh by scrolling your mouse down. As the point of view passes through the foremost surfaces, MeshLab will start displaying them in cross-section, showing you what's behind them. If you zoom in far enough, you'll see something like Figure 5-15. In that figure, you can clearly see my profile and my extended arm in the mesh as well as the wall and curtain behind me. You can also see the gaps in the mesh where foreground objects cast depth shadows and the mesh's triangles ended up tangled together at 0,0,0.

Figure 5-15. *If we zoom in on our STL in MeshLab, we can see that the surface of my face has been correctly scanned. It is simply obscured by the facets of our model that are in front of it*

To solve this problem, we'll need to detect and do something with these empty points. In the next section, we'll look at an advanced version of our scanning sketch that does exactly that.

Cleaning Up the Mesh

In this section, we're going to improve our scanning sketch in a number of ways. We're going to preprocess the depth points to fix the "depth shadows" problem we just observed. We will also make a number of additions to the model designed to make it 3D printable. As we discussed at the start of this chapter, for a 3D model to be printable, it needs to be *watertight*. In other words, it needs to be a continuous solid surface with all of its normals pointing toward the outside. We'll make a number of additions to our sketch to ensure that the model we build from the Kinect depth points has these qualities. We'll deal carefully with the edges of the depth data we receive. We'll fill in all of the holes in the depth data with a backplane at a prechosen depth. We'll also attach our mesh to a rectangular solid to close its back. Since the Kinect only sees our scene from a single point of view, even a mesh that continuously connects all of the visible depth points without any holes will still not be watertight. Its entire back will be open. Adding a rectangular solid to our model fixes this problem. Thankfully, Modelbuilder makes it easy to define geometrical primitives and to add them to our model. We'll also add a few other niceties. We'll add the ability to change the maximum z-depth used in the scan. This will let users of the sketch isolate individual figures or objects from the background, which can prove really helpful. Finally we'll scale, position, and orient our model so that it's easier to work with in the other 3D programs we'll use on our way to fabrication.

Chapter 5

We'll proceed through the code for this improved version of the scanner covering each of these improvements in turn. Here's the code:

```
import processing.opengl.*;
import unlekker.util.*;
import unlekker.modelbuilder.*;
import SimpleOpenNI.*;
SimpleOpenNI kinect;

boolean scanning = false;

int maxZ = 2000; ❶
int spacing = 3;

UGeometry model;
UVertexList vertexList;

void setup() {
  size(1024, 768, OPENGL);
  kinect = new SimpleOpenNI(this);
  kinect.enableDepth();

  model = new UGeometry();
  vertexList = new UVertexList();
}

void draw() { ❷

  background(0);

  kinect.update();

  translate(width/2, height/2, -1000);
  rotateX(radians(180));

  if (scanning) {
    model.beginShape(TRIANGLES);
  }

  PVector[] depthPoints = kinect.depthMapRealWorld();

  // cleanup pass
  for (int y = 0; y < 480; y+=spacing) {
    for (int x = 0; x < 640; x+= spacing) {

      int i = y * 640 + x; ❸
      PVector p = depthPoints[i];

      // if the point is on the edge or if it has no depth
      if (p.z < 10 || p.z > maxZ
          || y == 0 || y == 480 - spacing
          || x == 0 || x == 640 - spacing) ❹
      {
        // replace it with a point at the depth of the
        // backplane (i.e. maxZ)
        PVector realWorld = new PVector(); ❺
        PVector projective = new PVector(x, y, maxZ);

        // to get the point in the right place, we need to translate
        // from x/y to realworld coordinates to match our other points:
        //
```

```
            kinect.convertProjectiveToRealWorld(projective, realWorld);

            depthPoints[i] = realWorld; ❻
          }
        }
      }

      for (int y = 0; y < 480 - spacing; y+=spacing) {
        for (int x = 0; x < 640 -spacing; x+= spacing) {

          if (scanning) {
            int nw = x + y * 640 ;
            int ne = (x + spacing) + y * 640;
            int sw = x + (y + spacing) * 640;
            int se = (x + spacing) + (y + spacing) * 640;

              model.addFace(new UVec3(depthPoints[nw].x, ❼
                                      depthPoints[nw].y,
                                      depthPoints[nw].z),
                            new UVec3(depthPoints[ne].x,
                                      depthPoints[ne].y,
                                      depthPoints[ne].z),
                            new UVec3(depthPoints[sw].x,
                                      depthPoints[sw].y,
                                      depthPoints[sw].z));

              model.addFace(new UVec3(depthPoints[ne].x,
                                      depthPoints[ne].y,
                                      depthPoints[ne].z),
                            new UVec3(depthPoints[se].x,
                                      depthPoints[se].y,
                                      depthPoints[se].z ),
                            new UVec3(depthPoints[sw].x,
                                      depthPoints[sw].y,
                                      depthPoints[sw].z));
          }
          else {
            stroke(255);
            int i = y * 640 + x;

            PVector currentPoint = depthPoints[i];
            if (currentPoint.z < maxZ) {
              point(currentPoint.x, currentPoint.y, currentPoint.z);
            }
          }
        }
      }

      if (scanning) { ❽
        model.calcBounds(); ❾
        model.translate(0, 0, -maxZ); ❿

        float modelWidth = (model.bb.max.x - model.bb.min.x); ⓫
        float modelHeight = (model.bb.max.y - model.bb.min.y);

        UGeometry backing = Primitive.box(modelWidth/2, modelHeight/2, 10); ⓬
        model.add(backing);

        model.scale(0.01); ⓭
```

```
    model.rotateY(radians(180));
    model.toOrigin();

    model.endShape(); ⓮

    SimpleDateFormat logFileFmt =
        new SimpleDateFormat("'scan_'yyyyMMddHHmmss'.stl'");
    model.writeSTL(this, logFileFmt.format(new Date()));

    scanning = false;
  }
}

void keyPressed() { ⓯
  println(maxZ); ⓰
  if (keyCode == UP) {
    maxZ += 100;
  }
  if (keyCode == DOWN) {
    maxZ -= 100;
  }
  if (key == ' ') {
    scanning = true;
    model.reset(); ⓱
  }
}
```

> *For best results, adjust the Kinect so it's pointing straight ahead. This way, you'll have a flat base under your scan, and your print will be able to stand up. Also, if you wear glasses, take them off because they interfere with the infrared light that the Kinect projects. Suck in your gut and stand up straight. The Kinect adds 20 pounds.*

You use this sketch exactly like our last version, only this time it has a few improvements. Specifically, this version has controls that let you restrict what part of the scene will be included in the scan, which are defined in the keyPressed function (more on that later).

❶   The preliminaries are nearly identical to the last version of the sketch. The only change among the library imports, the variable declarations, and the setup function is the addition of the maxZ variable we've just been discussing. We declare that as a global variable and initialize it to 2000.

❷   After these preliminaries, our draw function continues along the same path as in the last sketch. We still begin our shape when scanning is true, telling Modelbuilder that we'll be building our mesh out of TRIANGLES. We still load the depth points from the Kinect by calling kinect.depthMapRealWorld. Then, at this point, things start to change. Instead of proceeding straight into the loop where we add geometry to our model, we make an initial cleanup pass through the depth points.

In this cleanup pass, we're going to make a number of improvements to our depth data:

- Eliminate depth shadow areas with low or zero z-values

- Repair the edges of the depth image

- Apply the z-depth maximum value set by the user

For all of these cases, our strategy will be the same. When we detect a depth point that matches one of these criteria we'll replace its z-value with the maximum z-value selected by the user. In other words, we'll move the depth of the point to the z-value indicated by maxZ.

❸ This code takes iterates over the array of depthPoints acquired by calling kinect.depthMapRealWorld with x and y as the indices of the respective for statements.

❹ The main action in this snippet takes place in this long if statement. Each clause in that if statement selects a particular set of depth points that need to be repaired. Let's go through them one at a time.

- The first clause, p.z < 10, selects the depth points that caused the biggest problems we saw in the output from our last sketch: points that are hidden in the depth shadow of closer objects. Those points will have a very low z-value, so they'll be caught by this clause. The next clause does the opposite, it eliminates points whose z-values are greater than the maximum threshold set by the sketch's user: p.z > maxZ. This lets us reduce the total depth of our model since it will eliminate the background of the scene behind the threshold. This can produce better models by eliminating disconnected objects or simply allowing us to print the intended subject of our scan larger.

- The next four clauses are all about cleaning up the edges of the depth data. We're going to attach the mesh we build from the Kinect data to a rectangular solid. We'll position that solid at exactly our maxZ value so that it lines up with the backplane of our mesh. Hence, we need the edges of our mesh to be held down to that backplane, too. Imagine trying to glue a bumpy object down onto a surface. It would be a lot easier if the object's edges were flat. By selecting all of the depth points on the edges of our depth data and forcing them down to maxZ we're creating exactly those flat edges. Figure 5-16 demonstrates how we select each of these edges with a single clause.

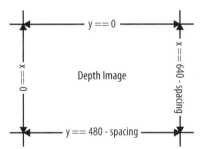

Figure 5-16. *We have to clean up the borders of the depth data so that our mesh will be continuous. This diagram demonstrates the indices necessary to select the borders for correction.*

Now what are we going to do with all of these bad points that we've selected? How are we going to repair them? As I explained, we want to place all of these points onto the backplane of our model. In other words, we want to set the depth for each of these points to the maxZ. How do we go about doing this? It's a slightly harder problem than it might seem at first thought. Some of these points (the ones lost in depth shadows) don't even have x- or y-components; they're all 0. Therefore, our strategy is to take advantage of the x and y indices we're using to loop through the depthPoints array. Each of these correspond to the x- and y-components of a depth point we're trying to replace. However, these x- and y-components are expressed in projective coordinates rather than the real-world coordinate of the rest of our depthPoints array.

Recall from Chapter 4 that projective coordinates indicate the location of part of the depth image from the point of view of the two-dimensional screen rather than the three-dimensional space of the real world. Projective coordinates match where a 3D object would show up when viewed through a flat 2D window. The x and y location of our indices within the depthPoints array are in projective, or screen, space. Therefore, we can create a PVector using these values along with our maxZ and then convert it into real-world coordinates, and it will fill in a slot within the rest of our depthPoints perfectly.

⑤ And so that's exactly what we do when we catch a point that needs repairing. We create a new vector, realWorld, where our final result will end up. Then we create a temporary PVector, projective, which we populate with x, y, and maxZ. Then we call kinect.convertProjective ToRealWorld(projective, realWorld), which will transform our projective, screen coordinate, vector into one in the real-world space with the rest of our depthPoints.

⑥ After that's done, we store the result back into the appropriate spot in the depthPoints array.

That completes our cleanup pass through the depth points. We've fixed a lot of problems with the depth data.

⑦ When it does return true, we proceed to access the neighboring depth points exactly as in the last sketch, calling model.addFace once for each of our two triangles.

At this point, we've finished adding geometry to our model based on the Kinect data. Now we have to perform a final cleanup to produce a solid and sensible model. As I explained above, we need to add a rectangular solid to the back of our model so that it is fully closed. While we're at it, we'll go ahead and scale, rotate, and position our model so that it is easier to work with outside of Processing.

⑧ The post-processing work comes after our double for loop has completed. It's wrapped inside an if statement to ensure that it only happens when we're in scanning mode.

⑨ The first thing we do is call mode.calcBounds, this tells the model to calculate its bounding box. As we covered when we displayed our OBJ in Chapter 3, every 3D model has a bounding box, the smallest box that contains all of its points. Once our model has determined its own bounding box, we'll be able to transform it more effectively. After all, how can you know how far you need to translate or scale a model to achieve some effect if you haven't figured out the model's full size?

⑩ Once we've had the model calculate its bounds, we start in on manipulating it. All of these manipulations will change the model's internal coordinate system. To implement them, we don't call Processing transformation commands that we've become so familiar with. Instead, we call a set of functions on our model object itself that parallel these same commands, but only affect the coordinates of the vertices that make up our model. The first transformation we apply is to simply translate the model to adjust for the z-offset of the points coming in from the Kinect: `model.translate(0, 0, -maxZ)`. This will pull our model forward so it's not so far away in depth, making it much more convenient to work with in the other software we'll use for prepping and printing it.

⑪ With that done, we're ready to start working on applying our backing rectangle. To do that, we need to calculate exactly how big our `model` is so far. Thankfully, Modelbuilder lets us access the bounding box it calculated around our geometry by calling: `model.bb`. This bounding box, in turn, has `max` and `min` properties that we can access to find its extent. Using the coordinates of these points, we can calculate the dimensions of our `model`.

⑫ With these numbers in hand, we can now create our backing shape. Modelbuilder has a built-in helper method for creating rectangular solids: `Primitive.box`. That function takes three arguments representing the size of the box from its center. In other words, whatever arguments we pass to this function, we'll end up with a rectangular solid of double the proportions. Taking that into account, we divide the `modelWidth` and `modelHeight` we just calculated in half before passing them in.

I chose a depth of 10 to create a substantial, but not bulky, backing. Having created this `UGeometry` object with our box, we attach it to our scan by passing it to `model.add`. Since we translate our model to the origin of its own coordinate system, the backing will line right up with it. After all of the effort we went through to create the surfaces of our main models, this step seems almost too easy.

⑬ Now all we have left to do is scale and rotate our model. I've found that scans made with the Kinect's real-world data tend to be gigantic when brought into the coordinate systems of other 3D programs. Hence, we scale the `model` down to 1/100 of its size. Also, as we noted in the last section, our models naturally come in facing backward. To fix this, we'll rotate the `model` 180 degrees around the y-axis. And finally, having made these transformations, we need to make sure that the `model` is still at the origin, so we'll call its `toOrigin` function, which will surely move it there.

⑭ Having completed these transformations, we're now ready to export our `model`. We do this in exactly the same way as in our last sketch: by calling `model.endShape` and `model.writeSTL`.

⑮ Once you launch the sketch, it will display the point cloud just like the previous version. If you press the down arrow the sketch will stop displaying some points at the farthest distance visible by the Kinect. Every time you hit the down arrow, the sketch will eliminate more points, bringing the threshold closer. If you go too far, you can reverse the process by hitting the up arrow to increase the maximum distance of points that will be included. Each time you hit either of these keys, the sketch will also print out the current maximum allowed z-value.

⑯ Inside of `draw`, we used this `maxZ` variable to place our backplane (i.e., we'll snap any points farther away than `maxZ` distance back to the backplane).

⑰ Another change to note here is the call to `model.reset` in the `if` statement that's triggered when you hit the space bar. I claimed that our previous sketch could be used to take multiple scans. However, if we don't reset our model like this, then the geometry we add to it when making each scan will simply accumulate. Our second scan will include whatever the Kinect saw that time as well as whatever was saved from the previous scan. Calling `reset` tells the `model` to clear out any geometry we'd previously added to it. The result is a sketch that can make multiple scans without needing to be restarted.

At this point, we've completed our improvements to our scanning sketch and we're ready to look at its output. Run the sketch, use the arrow keys to adjust the z-threshold until you've isolate yourself or whatever subject you're trying to scan, and then hit the space bar to save our your STL. In the next section, we'll open this STL in MeshLab and take a look at it to see how much things have improved.

Looking at Our Corrected Model

Let's take a look at the results of our improved sketch. Launch MeshLab and import the STL from your sketch into your project. When it comes in, it should look something like Figure 5-17. That figure shows a scan I captured of myself propped up against a stack of pillows. This is a huge improvement over our previous results!

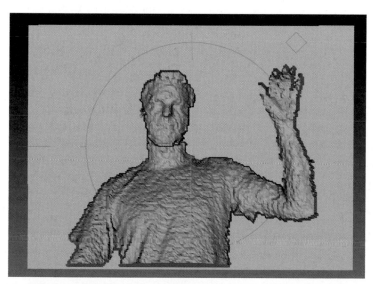

Figure 5-17. *An STL created from the updated version of our scanning sketch showing me waving at the Kinect. You can see how our sketch has connected the edges of my form to the backing plane.*

First of all, the model came in facing the right direction. When we opened it we didn't have to rotate it around before we could see our actual geometry. Second, those errant triangles connecting parts of the mesh to the origin are gone. We can now see the subject of our scan clearly. If you look carefully around the side of my head near the center of this figure or at the bottom of my torso, you can see what's become of those depth shadow areas that were previously linked together at the origin. Instead, they're now connected to the backplane.

If you'd like to learn more about these cleanup strategies, take a look at Kyle McDonald's work as artist-in-residence at MakerBot. It is available on Github (http://github.com/kylemcdonald/makerbot). The software he produced in that capacity (and continues to improve) demonstrates a number of these techniques.

This result is not completely ideal. If you look closely at my neck and a few other areas of the model, you can see gaps in the surface of the scan. Rather than puncturing all the way through the model as they did before cleanup, these gaps are now connected to the backplane as well, resulting in watertight printable geometry, but not necessarily the most beautiful possible result. We can imagine an approach that would fill in these gaps by connecting their adjacent sides to each other. That, and many other cleanup techniques, are certainly possible. For example, since these depth shadows tend to change rapidly, we could fill them in, and generally smooth out our scan, by averaging data captured over a period of a few frames. But implementing these kinds of improvements would make our code dramatically harder to read and less performant. So we'll leave them out.

As you rotate your model around in MeshLab, you'll discover that there are no parts of it that are black. The models created by our previous sketch were not fully closed. In essence, they were two-dimensional surfaces rather than real 3D objects. They weren't solid with an inside and outside. Instead they were more like pieces of paper crumpled up so that they took on volume, but not closed into complete shapes. Now, however, the back of our model is completely covered by the rectangular solid we added to our geometry as you can see in Figure 5-18. The result is a watertight model that has its insides on the inside and its outsides on the outside.

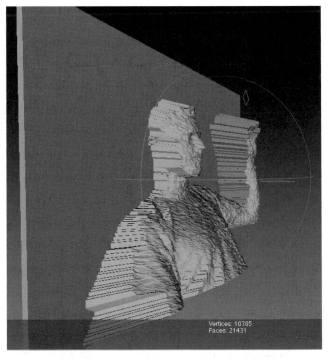

Figure 5-18. *An STL created from the updated version of our scanning sketch showing me waving at the Kinect. This side view shows the rectangular solid we've attached to the back of our mesh to make it into a solid object.*

Chapter 5

Prepping for Printing

Now that we've produced a good mesh, we need to process it to prepare it for printing. This processing includes two components. First we'll perform some operations on our geometry itself. The goal of these operations will be to simplify our mesh. We'll use MeshLab to discard as many polygons as possible without hurting the quality of our scan. Our scanning code was incredibly naive about the geometry that it created. It is quite likely that our models contain duplicate faces and vertices and other features that don't affect its appearance. By eliminating these we can create dramatically smaller *STL* files and significantly speed up the processing that will be necessary to prepare our models for printing with various different fabrication technology.

After we've simplified our model, the second step will be to prepare it for each of these different fabrication processes. The necessary steps will differ depending on the printing technology. To print on the MakerBot, we'll need to convert our STL file into *gcode*, a standard instruction format for controlling Computer Numerical Controlled (CNC) tools such as the MakerBot. To create this *gcode* from our STL we'll use ReplicatorG, software specifically designed for the purpose.

Printing our model through Shapeways is simpler but more mysterious. All we have to do is upload our STL to the Shapeways website, select the material out of which we'd like it made, and order a print. The print will arrive later in the mail. Shapeways provides a number of different fabrication technologies and materials and performs appropriate processing on our model to prepare it for whatever process we select. All of that happens at Shapeways without our having to worry about it.

Reduce Polygons in MeshLab

Regardless of whether we'll be fabricating our model on a MakerBot or through Shapeways, the first step is to reduce its polygon count. To accomplish that, we'll use MeshLab again. Launch MeshLab and import an STL file you created with the improved version of our scanner sketch.

Like it does every time, MeshLab will prompt you to Unify Duplicated Vertices. Click OK.

As I explained when I introduced it, MeshLab is basically a graphical interface for running a whole series of geometrical operations on 3D models. In this case, we want to run an operation that will reduce the number of polygons in our model. To do this we'll use an operation called Quadric Edge Collapse Decimation.

To run this operation, open MeshLab's Filters menu, select the "Remeshing, simplification and reconstruction" submenu, and choose Quadric Edge Collapse Decimation (see Figure 5-19).

Warning

Make sure that you don't import your STL file into a MeshLab project that already has geometry loaded into it (for example, your previous STL from earlier in this chapter). Doing so will create a project that combines the data from both models. Instead, close your existing project and select Create a New Empty Project from MeshLab's File menu. Then import your new model into this empty project.

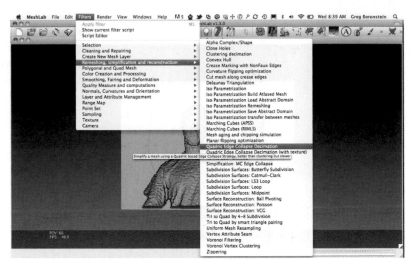

Figure 5-19. *To reduce our model's polygon count, we'll use MeshLab's Quadric Edge Collapse Decimation function.*

All operations in MeshLab are destructive. There is no undo. When you achieve a result that you like, export your mesh with a different descriptive filename (File→Export Mesh As, make sure you select STL from the pull-down menu). That way if something goes wrong, you can return to an older version by creating a new project and importing your saved mesh.

When you select this option, MeshLab displays a window with details about the operation and a number of parameters you can set for it (Figure 5-20). MeshLab describes this operation thusly: "Simplify a mesh using a Quadric based Edge Collapse Strategy, better than clustering but slower." Below this description are three text fields, a series of checkboxes, and four submit buttons. These are the controls you use to set the parameters for this operation. The only options we care about are "Target number of faces" and "Percent reduction (0..1)." We want to reduce the number of faces in our model, and these fields give us two ways to do that. We can either set the target for how many faces we want our simplified model to have, or we can simplify it by a percentage amount from its current state. I recommend the latter. That way, we can slowly reduce the complexity of our model while keeping an eye on it to ensure that the results aren't too obviously visible.

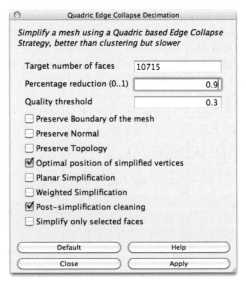

Figure 5-20. *Reduce the number of faces little by little while keeping an eye on your model. The goal is to reach a reasonable number (around 20,000) without visibly hurting the quality of your model too much.*

Let's start reducing the size of our mesh. Enter 0.9 into the box labeled "Percent reduction" and click Apply. Take a look at your model. You'll see that it looks subtly blockier, but not too bad. If you look at the purple ribbon at the bottom of MeshLab's main window, you'll see a display telling you how many vertices and faces are included in your model (see Figure 5-21). Our goal is to reduce the number of faces until it's around 20,000. My experience is that this is a ballpark figure for creating models with reasonable size files that print easily. However, it's not a hard and fast figure. Keep applying this reduction until you're in that area, but stop if you find that the quality of your model is dramatically degrading.

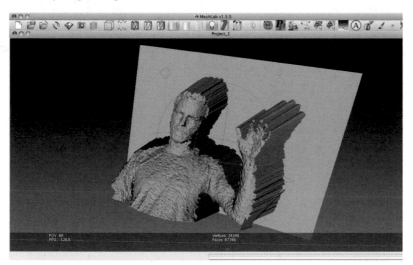

Figure 5-21. *MeshLab will show you the current number of faces and vertices in your model. Keep reducing it until this number is in the ballpark of 20,000, but stop before the quality degrades too badly.*

Once you've gotten the number of faces down to a reasonable level, you're ready to export your mesh. Select Export Mesh As from the File menu, give your file a name, set the format to STL File Format, and hit Save.

At this point, we could perform further processing on our model if we so desired. We could open our model in a 3D program and alter it in many ways. We could use Boolean operations to remove the backplane added by our sketch. We could combine our scan with other geometry to place your face on a sphere or other shape. We could combine multiple scans to create a full 360 degree model of a person. Many 3D programs exist for doing this kind of work, from the free and open source (but confusing to use) Blender (http://www.blender.org) to Rhino3D (http://www. rhino3d.com), which is preferred by many engineers to 123D (http://www.123dapp. com) from Autocad, which is specifically designed to be MakerBot friendly. The world of 3D modeling is rich and complex, too rich and complex to be explored here. The techniques demonstrated in the rest of this chapter should apply to models you create using these programs as long as they retain the watertight closed geometry of our model at this point.

Printing Our Model on a MakerBot

Now that we've got good geometry in a reasonably-sized file, we're ready to start printing. In this section, I'll take you through the steps that are necessary for printing out your scan on a MakerBot (Figure 5-22). We'll be using ReplicatorG (*http://replicat.org*) to process and position our STL file as well as to control the MakerBot during the print itself. I'll walk you through the basic steps required to make a print, including:

- Importing your model into ReplicatorG

- Positioning and scaling your model

- Generating *gcode*

- Driving the bot through the print

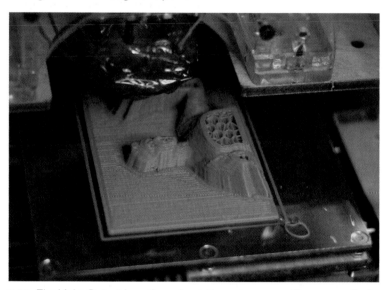

Figure 5-22. *The MakerBot midway through printing out our scan. You can see the honeycomb pattern MakerBot uses to fill in large areas.*

These instructions assume you have access to a fully assembled and operational MakerBot, RepRap, Prusa Mendel, or other 3D printer that can be controlled from ReplicatorG. (I'll be working on a MakerBot, so those are the details I'll refer to, but you should be able to translate them to the specifics of your machine with minimal changes.) They also assume you are familiar with the specifics of your particular printer: the size filament it prints, which build platform you have installed, etc. There are many details and complexities of using the Maker-Bot that I will not touch on or go into that could affect your outcomes. For a complete intro to working with the MakerBot, I recommend *Getting Started with MakerBot* by Bre Pettis, MakerBlock, and Anna Kaziunas France (*http://shop.oreilly.com/product/0636920015093.do*). MakerBot also has excellent online documentation for how to print (*http://www.makerbot.com/docs/how-to-print*) and how to troubleshoot (*http://wiki.makerbot.com/troubleshooting*). And, finally, with something as physical and detail-oriented as a MakerBot, having your own local specialist on hand to teach you and help solve problems can't be overrated.

Printing Our Scan

Printing our scan (Figure 5-23) will involve four steps: importing the STL file into ReplicatorG, scaling and position your model on the print bed, generating *gcode* from our model, and running the print. We'll start off by loading our STL.

Before you load your scan STL into ReplicatorG, make a copy of it. You may need to resize, rotate, or otherwise alter your model inside of ReplicatorG to optimize it for printing on the MakerBot. In order for ReplicatorG to generate the *gcode* required to print your model, it has to save these changes back to the STL file first. If you want to retain an unmodified version of your model, you'll want to work on a copy of it in ReplicatorG.

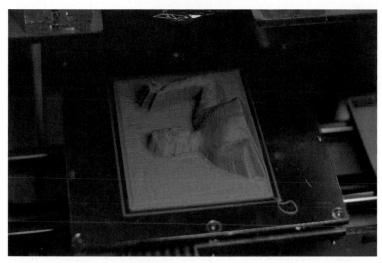

Figure 5-23. *Our final successful MakerBot print produced from our scan. See Figure 5-18 to compare the original model to this final result.*

Once you're ready, select Open from ReplicatorG's File menu. Navigate to your STL file and choose it. ReplicatorG will display your model in its window representing the print area of your MakerBot, as shown in Figure 5-24. Your scan should appear centered on the floor of the print area. You can click and drag within this viewer window to look at your scan from different angles.

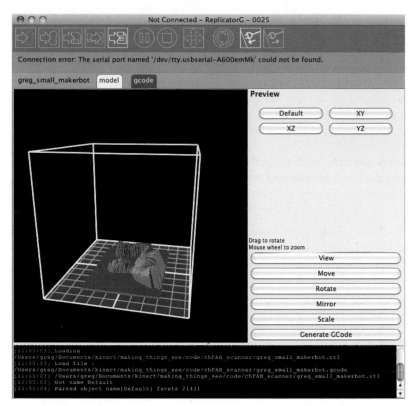

Figure 5-24. *The STL of our scan loaded in ReplicatorG. We can rotate it, resize it, and make other changes before printing it.*

Depending on the shape of your original scan, you may want to reposition, rescale, or resize it before printing. Click the Move button to the right of the viewing window to control the model's position. You'll see a series of buttons to make specific changes to the model's positions, such as Center and "Put on platform." While in this mode, you can also click and drag within the viewer window to reposition your model manually. Wherever you decide to place it, make sure that it is fully within the cage representing your printable area and that it is placed on the platform, or you might face problems when it comes time to actually print.

The two operations you'll most likely want to perform on your model are rotating and scaling. To print your model as big as possible, you'll need to rotate it so that its longest dimension is aligned with the longest dimension of the MakerBot build platform. Click the Rotate button on the right side of ReplicatorG's interface. You'll see buttons for rotating your model around each of its axes: Z+, Z-, X+, X-, Y+, and Y-. Since our scans have flat backings that we want to face down toward the build platform, you'll just want to rotate it around the z-axis by hitting Z+ or Z- until it is facing the right way.

Once you've aligned your model with the dimensions of the build platform, you can scale it up. Click the Scale button to open ReplicatorG's scale controls. You can either click and drag within the viewing window to manually control the size of your model, or you can enter numbers in the text box on the right and click Scale. These numbers will multiply the size of your model, so entering 1 will leave it unchanged, 1.2 will increase it in size by 20%, and 0.9 will reduce it in size by 10%.

Chapter 5

The larger you make your model, the more detail in it you'll be able to see, but the longer it will take to print and process. Printing time is significantly affected by how tall the model is in the z-axis. The MakerBot prints your model in a series of layers stacked on top of each other, and the more layers required, the longer it will take to print. STL files created from 3D scans also take longer to print than simpler models of equivalent size since they have very few straight lines or other simple geometric shapes that are easy for the MakerBot to print quickly. As a rule of thumb, I've found that it takes about an hour per vertical inch to print a scan.

When you've gotten your model to the size and position you want it, make sure you go back to the Move interface one more time to hit "Put on platform." It's easy to move the model off of the surface of the build platform while manually resizing and repositioning it, and this can cause build problems.

Now, connect to your MakerBot. Make sure it's plugged in via USB and turned on, and hit the Connect icon at the top of ReplicatorG's interface. If you configured the connection as I showed you in the last section, it should connect successfully and you'll see a green bar across the top of the interface.

Next, go ahead and generate the *gcode*. Click "Generate gcode" in the right panel of ReplicatorG's main window, make sure all of your settings are still correct, and then hit OK. If you made any changes to the position, rotation, or scale of your model, ReplicatorG will prompt you that it needs to save the model before it can generate *gcode*. Let it do so. Generating the *gcode* can take as longs as 10 minutes depending on the complexity and height of your scan.

When the *gcode* is complete, we're ready to print. Hit the print button and watch your MakerBot go! In just an hour or two (maybe less if you've got a MakerBot with the MK7 or later extruder), you'll have a print of your scan (Figure 5-25).

Figure 5-25. *Here's the final result of the print from my scan in closeup. You can see the topographical texture left from how the extruder moved around during the course of the print.*

Sending Our Model to Shapeways

So, we've learned how to create a 3D print from our file on a MakerBot, RepRap, or other desktop 3D printer. But what if you're not lucky enough to have one of these at your personal disposal? How can you get a physical copy of your scan in that case? One answer is by using Shapeways (*http://shapeways.com*).

As I explained in the introduction to this chapter, Shapeways (Figure 5-26) is an online service that lets you upload 3D model files and then purchase and sell copies of your design in a variety of different materials. In this section, I'll walk you through the steps for creating a print with Shapeways and point out some of the gotchas involved. Then we'll finish the chapter by comparing the results from Shapeways to what we got from our MakerBot print.

Figure 5-26. *Final print received from Shapeways. Compared to the MakerBot print, the smooth surface of this print makes for much better results in the face and other areas of fine detail.*

Creating prints with Shapeways takes four basic steps:

- Signing up for an account on the site
- Sizing and submitting your model
- Getting your model checked and approved by Shapeways
- Choosing a material and making your purchase

The process is much simpler than running your own MakerBot or RepRap. However, it also takes a lot longer, as you have to wait for Shapeways to approve and then create and ship your object. Let's get started.

Start off by visiting the site and creating an account. Shapeways will send you an email to confirm your address. Click the link to validate your account and follow the rest of their instructions to complete your registration.

Once you've registered for an account, you can start submitting models. However, before we upload our model file, we have to do a little bit of work to set its dimensions. Shapeways can only produce designs from 0.25 cm-cubed (0.098 inches cubed) up to 70 by 38 by 58 cm (27.56 by 14.96 by 22.83 inches). The larger your print, the more expensive it will be to fabricate. (As we'll see in a minute, Shapeways offers a wide variety of materials, and the final price will vary wildly based on what material you choose.) If you submit the same file you processed in ReplicatorG in the last section, you'll know exactly the dimensions of your print. If you want to make your model cheaper, you can use ReplicatorG or any other 3D modeling program to size it down before submitting it.

When your file is ready to go, click Create on the Shapeways website and select the "advanced" option to upload your own 3D model. Click the "choose file" button and select your STL file. In addition to selecting your file, you have to tell Shapeways what unit of measure it should use for your file. Select Millimeters. Give your model a title if you like, and then click the big Upload Model button. When your upload is complete, you'll land on a Shapeways page telling you it succeeded.

After you upload a model (Figure 5-27), Shapeways runs a series of automated checks to confirm that it is an appropriate size and that the geometry is sound enough to be printed. If anything goes wrong with your model, they'll send you an email letting you know. For example, if you selected the wrong units for your scan such as inches or meters, you'd get a message telling you there's a problem with your model and that you need to resize it.

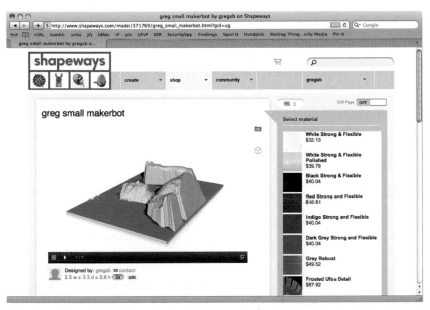

Figure 5-27. Our scan STL uploaded to Shapeways and ready to order. The White Strong & Flexible material is their cheapest option.

If your model passes these checks, you'll receive an email letting you know that it's now available. Once you've received this email, your model will appear in the list of your models on Shapeways (*http://www.shapeways.com/mymodels*), and you can select a material for it, place an order, and even make the model available for purchase by others.

The first step to making your model purchasable is to select a material for it. Shapeways offers a huge variety of materials with different properties at a huge range of costs. They provide a comprehensive list of all the materials they have available (*http://www.shapeways.com/materials/*). For my model, the options ranged from $20.82 for Sandstone to $510.20 for Silver Glossy. I chose the moderately priced White Strong & Flexible for $32.13.

Click on the material to select it. When this is done, you can click the big "Add to cart" button to buy a copy of your model. You can also click the privacy options to choose whether to make your model available to the public. You can choose to make it discoverable in the store or simply purchasable by people to whom you give the URL. You can also choose which materials shoppers can select for your model. If you're curious to see a Shapeways product page in action, I've made the example scan from this chapter public and available for sale here (*http://www.shapeways.com/model/371769/*).

That's it. In just those few simple steps, you've got a model that's ready to order for yourself or to sell to others. Despite its ease, one big downside to Shapeways is how long it takes them to produce and ship your prints. A lot of their printing equipment is located in Eindhoven in The Netherlands, so prints can take weeks to arrive after you order them.

Conclusion: Comparing Prints

Now that we've got both the MakerBot and Shapeways prints in hand, let's compare them. We'll look at the quality of results achieved by each process and compare that with the relative cost and complexity of each approach. We'll find that while the Shapeways results are, in many ways, more satisfying as objects, the immediacy and low cost of the MakerBot prints lend themselves better to experimentation and rapid iteration.

Figure 5-28 shows the results of printing my Kinect self-portrait scan on both the MakerBot and at Shapeways using their White Strong & Flexible material. The MakerBot print is at the top of the figure and the Shapeways print is at the bottom. (Figure 5-29 shows a side-by-side comparison.) The Shapeways print is visually superior in a number of ways. It retains enough detail in the face and hand areas to render them recognizable where the MakerBot's filament size eliminates much of the finest detail in our scan. In a face scan, this is especially critical as the lost detail in the MakerBot print essentially renders the subject unrecognizable as compared to the Shapeways print. The filament also gives the entire print a kind of dried spaghetti texture that is distracting from the shape of the whole scan. And finally, the MakerBot print has all kinds of strange textures in the backing plane that are artifacts of the particular path the print head took while laying down the filament. By contrast, the Shapeways print is perfectly smooth in this area, corresponding much better to what you'd expect looking at the 3D file that generated both of these prints.

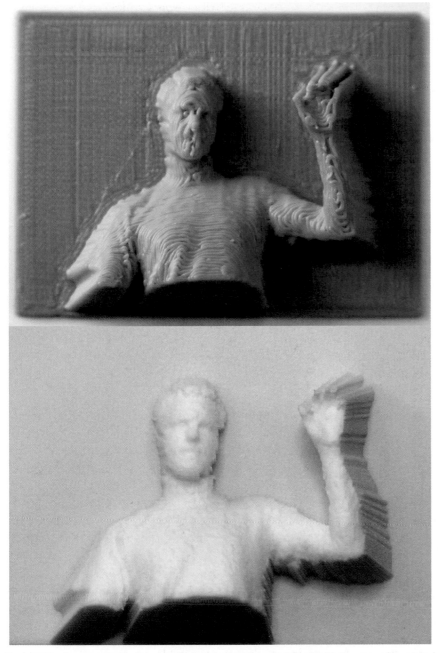

Figure 5-28. *A comparison of a scan printed on the MakerBot (top) with the same file printed at Shapeways (bottom). Notice all the additional detail that is visible in Shapeways print.*

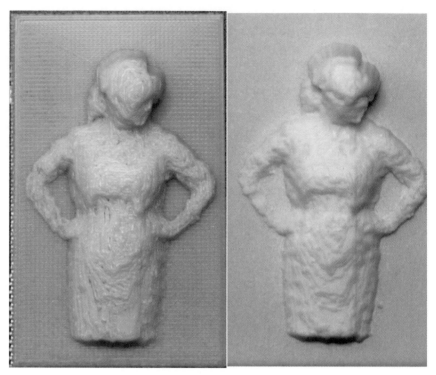

Figure 5-29. *Another comparison of a MakerBot print (left) with a Shapeways print (right).*

As a material, both prints are light and feel durable. The PLA used by the MakerBot is slightly more flexible than this particular material from Shapeways and also feels heavier (though, obviously, Shapeways offers a wide variety of materials, so this comparison is not by any means definitive).

So, Shapeways seems to win in terms of print quality and material options. On the other hand, the MakerBot provides a radically cheaper and more immediate experience. The final cost for my Shapeways print, all told, with shipping included, was more than $40. It also took more than two weeks to arrive. The MakerBot print cost essentially nothing (beyond some small share of the cost of the filament roll and the maintenance/lifespan of the MakerBot itself) and was ready within an hour.

The verdict on these radically different costs, timelines, and results is that the two processes are good for two completely different tasks. The MakerBot makes it possible to experiment and play with 3D printing. You can go from a scan or an idea for a model to a rough object sitting in your hand in an hour or less. You can find out what's wrong with your 3D file or your design idea right away and make a number of revisions over the course of a single sitting. You can also try printing files that you're not sure are actually technically feasible. After all, you'll be sitting right next to the machine as it prints, and you can always hit the stop button if anything is looking sketchy. However, once you've reached a design you're satisfied with, if it needs precise tolerances or a beautiful finish, those are much harder (or impossible) to achieve with the MakerBot. At that point, submitting your file to Shapeways, waiting a few weeks, and paying a few bucks for a really good quality print will produce a much superior outcome.

Chapter 5

Using the Kinect for Robotics

In the previous chapter, we took our Kinect data off of the computer screen and turned it into a physical object in the real world. In doing so, we turned the Kinect into a kind of still camera. We used it to capture 3D data about the world in front of it, freezing that data into a solid object preserved forever in plastic. The results were exciting, but they discarded one of the most important aspects of the Kinect's capacity: the ability to capture movement. In this chapter, we're going to take the motion captured by the Kinect off the screen and out into the physical world. We'll build a simple robotic arm and then explore two ways to control this arm with the movements of our own bodies.

The brain of our robotic arm will be an Arduino microcontroller (*http://arduino. cc*). The Arduino is a small computer that can control simple electronics and sensors. We'll hook up two servo motors to the Arduino, one making up each joint of our robotic arm. Then we'll communicate with the Arduino from Processing so we can position our robotic arm based on the data we capture from the Kinect. If you've never used an Arduino before, this project will be an exciting introduction, teaching you important techniques like serial communication and controlling servos. If you're looking for a general introduction to Arduino, I highly recommend *Getting Started with Arduino* by Massimo Banzi (*http://shop.oreilly.com/product/0636920021414.do*), one of the original creators of the Arduino project. For a more in-depth text that covers methods for connecting Arduinos with physical objects and computers of all types, you can't do better than *Making Things Talk* by Tom Igoe (*http://shop.oreilly.com/ product/0636920010920.do*), the spiritual ancestor of this book. If you feel totally intimidated by working with Arduino and yet still want to proceed with this project: take heart! The Arduino portion of this chapter will take the form of a recipe with detailed steps you can follow to get your robotic arm working. And once we get the arm up and running once, it will work for all of the Processing sketches in this chapter without needing further changes.

While the Arduino is a fun tool to learn, the real substance of this chapter comes in learning about *kinematics*, the study of motion. It derives from classical physics but has important applications in robotics and computer animation. It's the sense of kinematics meant in these later fields that is relevant to the Kinect. So what does kinematics mean in our context? For us, kinematics describes the relationship between the position of a joint and the angles of the other joints along the same limb. Look at your right arm. The position of your hand is determined by the angle of your shoulder and your elbow. Let's say your hand was resting on a table in front of you. If you wanted to bring it up to your face, one way to describe the operation would be as the following set of instructions:

- Rotate your upper arm, increasing the angle away from your torso until your upper arm is parallel to the line of your shoulders.

- Bend your elbow, decreasing the angle between your lower and upper arms until your hand reaches your face.

In these instructions, the position of the hand is determined by the changes we make to the angles of the joints above it in the arm. We wanted to get your right hand up to your face, but to get it there, we had to figure out what your shoulder and elbow should do. This approach is called *forward kinematics*. We start with the joint at the base of the limb and work forward toward the "end effector" that we actually care about positioning. The angle of each joint affects all of the joints below it on the arm, and treating them in this descending order keeps things sane.

In our first project for this chapter, I'll show you how to use this logic to control our robot arm with the Kinect joint data from your actual arm. We'll use what we learned in Chapter 4 to access the locations of your shoulder, elbow, and hand. From these, we'll calculate the angles of each part of your arm: the angle between your upper arm and your torso and the angle between your upper arm and your lower arm. Once we've calculated these angles, we'll send them down the serial connection to our Arduino, which will move our two servos to match. The result will be a small robot arm that copies the movements of your actual arm.

Besides the work with the Arduino, this project will consist almost entirely of techniques we've already learned. After Chapter 4, we're quite comfortable with finding joint positions and calculating the angles between them. This is the big advantage of forward kinematics: it is easy to implement in code and a natural match for the data we get from the Kinect.

However, forward kinematics is clearly not the way we usually think about moving our own bodies. When I want to reach up to scratch my nose, I don't start by figuring out how to rotate my shoulder. I think about where I want my hand to go and my elbow and shoulder get dragged along behind. It turns out we can use this same logic to control our robot arm. This alternate approach is called *inverse kinematics*. Where forward kinematics treats the position of the end effector as a side effect of the angle of the above joints, inverse kinematics starts with the position of the end effector and figures out the necessary joint angles to achieve that. One big advantage of inverse kinematics is that we can use it to get our robot arm to track any part of the body. When using forward kinematics, we needed our Kinect data to tell us the position of the shoulder and elbow as well as the hand so that we could calculate both of the angles needed to position our robot. Inverse kinematics lets us figure out these angles ourselves using geometry based solely on where we want to position our robot hand. Hence, we can use inverse kinematics to track our robot hand to any joint in the skeleton. For example, we could have our robot arm point a flashlight at a user's head. Even though the head's position is not determined by two joints in the same arrangement as our robot arm, we'll be able to calculate the angles we need to set the joints to get our robot arm to follow the head.

The downside of inverse kinematics is that it involves more sophisticated math than the forward variety. Whereas forward kinematics simply transfers the angles we calculate between the skeleton joints detected by the Kinect, inverse kinematics requires us to do some geometric trickery to determine those same angles. To keep this math from becoming overwhelming, we'll start the section on inverse kinematics with a Processing sketch that implements the algorithm for a graphical "arm" consisting of two lines and three circles. We'll use this example to explore the inverse kinematic calculations until they're clear. Only then will we move on to applying it to the actual Kinect input and Arduino output.

Forward Kinematics

We'll start off this chapter with the forward kinematics approach. We'll use the Kinect skeleton data to find the location of our user's shoulder, elbow, and hand. Then we'll calculate the angles between these joints. The joint angles are the values we'll want to send to our Arduino so that it can match them with the servos in our robot arm. Before we get into building our circuit, assembling our robot arm, or programming our Arduino, we'll start with the most familiar part of the project: the Processing sketch that uses SimpleOpenNI to calculate the joint angles. Then we'll proceed to add on these more advanced pieces of the project one at a time.

Calculating the Angles of Limbs

Let's get started by putting together a Processing sketch that calculates the two angles we need to control our robot arm. As you can see in Figure 6-1, we want to calculate the angles between each limb and the adjacent body part. Our robot's servos are going to reproduce the angles of the user's shoulder and elbow. When we refer to the angle of the shoulder, we mean the angle that the shoulder creates between the upper arm and the torso. And, likewise, when we talk about the elbow, we refer to the angle it creates between the upper arm and the lower arm. When you rotate your shoulder, the position of your elbow and your hand changes, but the angle between them stays the same. Similarly, when you tilt your torso left or right, the angle of your shoulder doesn't necessarily change even though its position will.

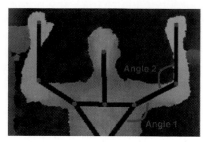

Figure 6-1. *The angles between the joints we want to calculate to control our robot arm.*

And the same goes for our robot arm. Figure 6-2 shows you the basic layout for how we plan to assemble our robot arm. Servo 1, representing our shoulder joint, will be affixed to the table. It will have a range of motion of 180 degrees ranging from pointing straight down to straight up. We'll attach a popsicle stick to the horn of Servo 1 that will rotate with its movement. At the end of this popsicle stick, we'll attach Servo 2, representing the elbow. This servo will be mounted so that its range of motion is aligned with the popsicle stick to which it is attached. When it rotates to an angle of 180 degrees, its popsicle stick will be pointing straight along in the same direction. When its angle falls toward 0, its popsicle will rotate back up toward the shoulder servo, like an upper arm being pulled by flexing bicep.

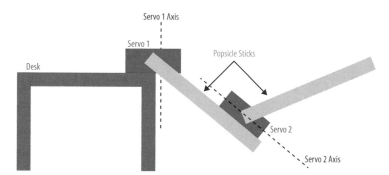

Figure 6-2. *Our plan for how to lay out the servos.*

This physical arrangement precisely corresponds to the angle calculation strategy we just set out for our sketch. We have to calculate the angles between our limbs relative to the correct axis so that they will translate correctly to the orientation of each of our servos. The shoulder angle should be calculated relative to the vertical angle of your torso since that corresponds to the table on which the servo is mounted. Likewise, we need to calculate the elbow angle relative to the orientation of the upper arm since that corresponds to the popsicle stick on which that servo is mounted.

Let's take a look at the full sketch. After the code, I'll go through the details of how we convert the positions of our joints into angles in exactly the right orientation that will fit our servos.

```
import SimpleOpenNI.*;
SimpleOpenNI  kinect;

void setup() { ❶
  size(640, 480);

  kinect = new SimpleOpenNI(this);
  kinect.enableDepth();
  kinect.enableUser(SimpleOpenNI.SKEL_PROFILE_ALL);
  kinect.setMirror(true);
}

void draw() {
  kinect.update();
  PImage depth = kinect.depthImage();
  image(depth, 0, 0);

  IntVector userList = new IntVector();
  kinect.getUsers(userList);

  if (userList.size() > 0) {
    int userId = userList.get(0);

    if ( kinect.isTrackingSkeleton(userId)) {
      // get the positions of the three joints of our arm
      PVector rightHand = new PVector();
      kinect.getJointPositionSkeleton(userId,
                                 SimpleOpenNI.SKEL_RIGHT_HAND,
                                 rightHand);

      PVector rightElbow = new PVector();
      kinect.getJointPositionSkeleton(userId,
                                 SimpleOpenNI.SKEL_RIGHT_ELBOW,
                                 rightElbow);

      PVector rightShoulder = new PVector();
      kinect.getJointPositionSkeleton(userId,
                                 SimpleOpenNI.SKEL_RIGHT_SHOULDER,
                                 rightShoulder);

      // we need right hip to orient the shoulder angle
      PVector rightHip = new PVector();
      kinect.getJointPositionSkeleton(userId,
                                 SimpleOpenNI.SKEL_RIGHT_HIP,
                                 rightHip);

      // reduce our joint vectors to two dimensions
      PVector rightHand2D = new PVector(rightHand.x, rightHand.y); ❷
      PVector rightElbow2D = new PVector(rightElbow.x, rightElbow.y);
      PVector rightShoulder2D = new PVector(rightShoulder.x,
                                            rightShoulder.y);
      PVector rightHip2D = new PVector(rightHip.x, rightHip.y);

      // calculate the axes against which we want to measure our angles
      PVector torsoOrientation =
        PVector.sub(rightShoulder2D, rightHip2D); ❸
      PVector upperArmOrientation =
        PVector.sub(rightElbow2D, rightShoulder2D);
```

```
            // calculate the angles between our joints
            float shoulderAngle = angleOf(rightElbow2D,        ❹
                                          rightShoulder2D,
                                          torsoOrientation);
            float elbowAngle    = angleOf(rightHand2D,
                                          rightElbow2D,
                                          upperArmOrientation);

            // show the angles on the screen for debugging
            fill(255,0,0);
            scale(3);
            text("shoulder: " + int(shoulderAngle) + "\n" +
                " elbow: " + int(elbowAngle), 20, 20);
        }
      }
    }

    float angleOf(PVector one, PVector two, PVector axis) {
      PVector limb = PVector.sub(two, one);
      return degrees(PVector.angleBetween(limb, axis));
    }

    // user-tracking callbacks!
    void onNewUser(int userId) {
      println("start pose detection");
      kinect.startPoseDetection("Psi", userId);
    }

    void onEndCalibration(int userId, boolean successful) {
      if (successful) {
        println("  User calibrated !!!");
        kinect.startTrackingSkeleton(userId);
      }
      else {
        println("  Failed to calibrate user !!!");
        kinect.startPoseDetection("Psi", userId);
      }
    }

    void onStartPose(String pose, int userId) {
      println("Started pose for user");
      kinect.stopPoseDetection(userId);
      kinect.requestCalibrationSkeleton(userId, true);
    }
```

❶ This sketch starts off with a lot of code that should be familiar to you from our work in Chapter 4. We initialize our SimpleOpenNI object, we enable the user data, we tell SimpleOpenNI to mirror the data, etc. It also has all of the usual skeleton-tracking callbacks at the bottom of the sketch: onNewUser, onStartPose, and onEndCalibration, as well as the if statements within draw that check to see when calibration has concluded successfully.

Once calibration is complete, we go ahead and access positions for four joints: the right hand, the right elbow, the right shoulder, and the right hip. Once we have all of these joint positions, we convert them from 3D vectors into 2D vectors. However, we don't do this using convertReal-WorldToProjective, the function we normally use for this purpose.

Our goal isn't to display these joints on top of the depth image, but instead to capture their motion.

Our robot arm can only move along a single plane. In robotics terminology, we'd say that it only has two *degrees of freedom* (i.e., it can only move in two axes). Obviously, real arms can move in more ways than this. In addition to bending, our shoulder can rotate in its socket, allowing the arm to move in front of and behind the body rather than simply alongside it. To keep things simple we're going to ignore any movement of our joints in the z-axis. To reproduce the full three axes of motion, both our robotic arm and our code would need to be significantly more complex.

❷ `convertRealWorldToProjective` does not simply discard the z-axis motion of our joints. Instead, it translates that motion into changes in the x- and y-axes. Joints that are farther away along the z-axis move more slowly along x and y. We don't want that distortion, so we need to simply discard the z-axis information altogether. We do this by creating a new vector using only the x- and y-components of the original three-dimensional vector.

We'll use these four 2D vectors in all of our angle calculations.

As I explained above, the first step in calculating the angle of our limbs is to figure out the axes against which these angles will be defined. Specifically, we want to calculate our shoulder angle against the vertical line of the torso and our elbow angle in reference to the orientation of the upper arm, as shown in Figure 6-3.

Figure 6-3. *The axes in reference to which we'll be calculating our arm angles. To find these axes, we'll need to do some vector subtraction.*

So, before we actually calculate our angles, we need to create vectors that correspond to each of these axes of orientation. As we learned back in Chapter 4, we can do this using vector subtraction. Subtracting two vectors produces a third vector representing the orientation between them. This concept is clearly illustrated in Figure 4-15.

❸ We'll create our axes of orientation by subtracting two pairs of skeleton joints. For our shoulder joint, we need a vertical axis that points up along the orientation of the user's torso. To calculate that, we'll subtract the right hip from the right shoulder. Since those joints are approximately vertically aligned on the body, the vector between them will capture how the user is leaning away from vertical. For our elbow joint, the choice is even more obvious. We want an axis that corresponds to the orientation of the user's upper arm. We can calculate that by simply subtracting the right shoulder from the right elbow.

❹ Now that we've got those orientation axes, we're ready to calculate the angles of our limbs in reference to them. To facilitate that process, I've written a helper function, angleOf. This function takes three arguments: the two vectors that represent the ends of the limb whose angle we want to find, and a third vector that represents the orientation axis.

The logic of this function is demonstrated in Figure 6-4. We start by subtracting one joint vector from the other. This gives us a new vector, limb, that represents the actual limb that connects these two joints. We then use Processing's PVector.angleBetween function to calculate the angle between limb and the axis against which we want to calculate our angle. This result comes back in radians, so we call degrees to convert it and return the result.

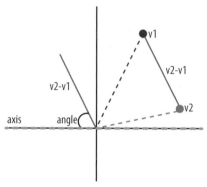

Figure 6-4. Converting the two vectors representing the ends of our limb into a single vector representing that limb in relation to a given orientation.

That's how our function works. Let's look at how we call it in this sketch. For our shoulder, we want to know the angle between the upper arm in reference to the orientation of the torso. And for the elbow, we want to know the lower arm in reference to the orientation of the upper arm.

These angles are exactly what we need. The last few lines of draw simply round them off and display them on the screen using Processing's text function.

Figure 6-5 shows the results of our sketch. In the first image, My shoulder is almost completely extended, raising my arm up alongside my head. We get an angle reading of 161 for the shoulder, close to 180. My elbow is bent at a right angle and we're seeing 91 for its value. In the center image, both my shoulder and elbow are bent at near right angles. We're reading 98 for the shoulder and 92 for the elbow, which is perfect. Finally, in the third image, I've extended my arm out straight to my right. We're still seeing near 90 for the shoulder (83), but now the elbow angle has increased to 169 just as we'd expect.

Figure 6-5. *Three screen captures from our forward kinematics angle calculation sketch. These angles are ready to be sent to the Arduino to control servos.*

These angles are perfect for sending to our servos. If we had a setup as described in Figure 6-2 and we sent it these angles, it would follow my arm correctly.

That said, there are some angles that my real arm can reach that our robotic arm will not be able to reproduce. Each of our servos only has a range of motion of 180 degrees, whereas both my shoulder and my elbow can rotate around 360, or at least they can appear to do so to the Kinect. By taking advantage of the ball joint in your shoulder, you can swing your whole arm around in a full windmilling circle or rotate your lower arm in a circle around your elbow. Even though we can translate these motions into two dimensions, our servos will not be able to reproduce them. As it currently stands, our sketch will still calculate angles successfully when my arm reaches positions that can't be replicated by the servos. For example, if I raised my right arm above my head and across my chest so that it was to the left of my head. As soon as my arm crossed the vertical axis we defined, the angle we calculate will start decreasing. If we sent these values to our servo arm it would immediately start moving in the reverse direction of my actual arm. We could eliminate this problem with a series of if statements that guarded against sending joint angles when either of the joints were in quadrants that the servos cannot access. However, this would make our sketch dramatically more complex and risks obscuring what I'm trying to show you, so I will leave it to you to do as an exercise if you're inclined to do so. In practice, once we've built our robotic arm, we'll find that such situations are easy to avoid simply by stopping our motion when the robotic arm reaches its limits.

Getting Started with Arduino: The Brain of Our Robot Arm

Now that we're successfully calculating the joint angles for our robot arm, we're ready to actually build and program the arm itself. The brain of our robot arm will be made up of an Arduino microcontroller. The Arduino's job will be to receive the joint angles from our Processing sketch over a serial connection. It will use these angles to position two servos, one for the elbow and one for the shoulder of the robot arm.

In this section, I'll tell you everything you need to know for the Arduino portion of this project. I'll show you where to get an Arduino and the other electronic supplies you'll need (Figure 6-6). I'll walk you through downloading and installing the Arduino development environment. Then I'll show you how to build the circuit you'll need to control the servos. Once everything's hooked up, we'll write the code to get our Arduino to read joint angles over a serial connection and use them to position the servos.

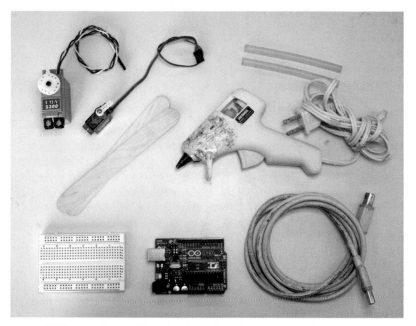

Figure 6-6. *All the supplies you'll need to build the robot arm: an Arduino, a breadboard, two servos, two popsicle sticks, a USB A/B cable, a hot glue gun, and some hot glue.*

Acquiring the Arduino and the Servos

There are lots of places online where you can buy an Arduino. The Arduino website has a definitive list of options (*http://arduino.cc/en/Main/Buy*). Similarly, there are lots of places online to buy servos. You'll want two servos of different sizes for our robot arm's shoulder and elbow joints. A standard size servo will work great for the shoulder, but you'll want to use a micro size for the elbow to reduce the weight. Make sure that both will operate at the five volts that Arduino supplies.

One source I recommend for both of these components is Adafruit (*http://www. adafruit.com*). As we discussed in Chapter 1, Limor Fried and Phil Torrone from Adafruit were early supporters of the open source community formed around the Kinect. Adafruit is one of the best sources for electronic components for DIY projects on the Web. In fact, in addition to selling the Arduino (*http://www.adafruit. com/products/50*), they carry servos that will work nicely for both our shoulder and elbow joints: their standard servo (*https://www.adafruit.com/products/155*) and their micro servo (*https://www.adafruit.com/products/169*).

Another great place to get an Arduino is O'Reilly's Maker Shed (*http://store. makezine.com*). They have all kinds of kits that package the Arduino with servos of various sizes and other useful components.

Wherever you purchase your servos, make sure that you get RC servos rather than continuous rotation servos. RC servos allow you to control their angle rather than just their speed. Since we want to use these servos as the joints for our robot arms, we'll need to send them joint angles. Continuous rotation servos won't work for this purpose.

In addition to the Arduino and the servo, you'll need a few other accessories that you can acquire online or at your local RadioShack: a pair of wire strippers/wire cutters, some solid core wire, a breadboard, and a USB A/B cable. The USB A/B cable is the one you'll use for connecting your Arduino to your computer to program it and for sending data to it from Processing. Even though we'll be using the serial protocol to communicate with our Arduino, we'll be doing it over a USB A/B cable, because that's what will plug into the ports on most modern computers.

Plugging in the Servos

Once you've got your hardware in hand, you're ready to plug it all in. We want to connect our two servo motors to our Arduino so that the Arduino can control them. Servos are really just small motors with built-in circuits that let other electronic components position them at a particular angle. Each of our servos has three wires coming off of it: one for power (almost definitely red), one for ground (most likely black), and one for control (blue, yellow, or white). We'll need to connect the power and ground to our Arduino's power and ground pins so that there's a complete circuit to the motor and it can draw power. We'll connect each motor's control wire to one of our Arduino's digital pins. The control pin is how the Arduino tells the servo what angle to move to. Each servo has a tiny circuit onboard that uses negative feedback to position itself at whatever angle gets sent over this control wire. Once you send it an angle, it will constantly double-check and adjust its position to make sure it is exactly that angle.

To learn more about servos, check out the ITP servo lab (http://itp.nyu.edu/physcomp/Labs/Servo).

With this in mind, let's plug in our servos. You'll need your Arduino, your servos, a breadboard, some solid core wire, and a good pair of wire strippers. Figure 6-7 shows the setup we'll be building. Follow these steps to recreate it yourself:

- Strip the ends of some lengths of red and black wire. Run the red wire from the pin on the Arduino labeled 5V to the red side rail on your breadboard. Run the black wire from the Arduino pin labeled GND to the blue or black side rail on your breadboard, right next to the red rail. This will connect the Arduino's power to every pin in that long row of the breadboard and likewise with the Arduino's ground to the neighboring row of pins. This gives us lots of options for where to plug in our servos.

If you use precut hookup wire, such as the Deluxe Breadboard Jumper Wires from Maker Shed (http://www.makershed.com/product_p/mk-seeed3.htm), you won't need to strip or cut it.

- Strip two short lengths each of red, black, and blue (or any color other than red or black—these will be your control wires) wire. Each of your servos has a female connector on the end with three holes—one for power, one for ground, and one for control. Since our breadboard and Arduino also have pins with holes, we'll need these wires to connect up our servos.

- Connect the red, black, and control wires to each of the holes in the servos' headers. Make sure to match the red wire to the hole corresponding to the servo's red wire, the black wire to the servo's black wire, etc. (Refer to Figure 6-7 if you need clarification.)

- Attach the servos to power and ground on the breadboard. The red wire from each servo should go to one of the pins in the row we just connected to the Arduino's 5V pin, and the black wire goes to one of the pins in the row connected to the Arduino's GND pin.

- Attach the servos' control pins to the Arduino. Plug the free end of each servo's control wire into one of the Arduino's digital pins. To make sure that your hardware matches mine exactly (and therefore that you'll be able to run exactly the same code I present later on in this chapter), plug the control wire from your micro servo into pin 10 on your Arduino and the control wire from your normal servo into pin 9. The micro servo will play the role of the elbow joint, and the full size servo will be our arm's shoulder.

- Finally, plug your USB A/B cable into your Arduino and connect the other end to one of your computer's USB ports.

Figure 6-7. *The Arduino connected to two servos.*

Now you're ready to move on to the software side of things.

Downloading the Arduino Development Environment

Now that our circuit is set up, the next step is to get up and running with the tools you'll need to program the Arduino. In addition to a microcontroller, the Arduino project provides a free Integrated Development Environment (IDE), a program for your main computer that will let you write programs for the Arduino and send them to the board to be run. You can find the instructions for downloading and installing the Arduino IDE on your operating system on the Arduino website (*http://arduino.cc/en/Guide/HomePage*). Make sure you follow all the instructions for your platform, including installing the necessary drivers.

Once you've installed the IDE and the drivers, run the hello world program of physical computing that's included in the Arduino instructions: blinking an LED on and off. When this works, you'll know that you've got everything installed correctly and you're ready to start on the Arduino code for our robot arm.

Programming the Arduino

With all of those preliminaries out of the way, we're finally ready to actually program our Arduino so that it will control our servos based off of the joint angles sent to it from our Processing sketch. Before we dive into the details of the code for our Arduino, I'll explain the ideas behind it.

Our Arduino sketch will establish a serial connection to our computer. Serial is a simple protocol that allows our Processing sketch (or other software on our computer) to send information to our Arduino and vice versa. The Arduino will open the serial connection and then listen for instructions. What form will these instructions take? Our Processing sketch needs to send us two numbers: the angle for the shoulder joint and the angle for the elbow joint. As its name implies, our serial connection can only send one value at a time (after all, it is serial rather than parallel). So, to get around this limitation, we'll have the Processing sketch alternate the values. First it will send the angle for the elbow, then for the shoulder, then for the elbow again, then the shoulder again, and so on. This means our Arduino code will have to keep track of which value is coming in when so that it can send the right values to each servo. We'll accomplish this by setting up an array to hold both servo values. Then we'll read in the next value from the serial connection, switch off which spot in the array we store it in. Finally, we'll update the position of both of our servos based on the values in this array, which will hold the most recent angles for each joint.

Let's take a look at the code, and then below it I'll call out how each of these steps is implemented.

> You may have noticed that the Arduino IDE looks almost identical to the Processing IDE that we've been working in throughout this book. That's not a coincidence! Arduino is a sister project to Processing, and the Arduino IDE is directly based on the Processing IDE. Hopefully, this will make it familiar to you and easier for you to learn.

```
#include <Servo.h>  ❶

// declare both servos
Servo shoulder;
Servo elbow;

// setup the array of servo positions  ❷
int nextServo = 0;
int servoAngles[] = {0,0};

void setup() {
  // attach servos to their pins  ❸
  shoulder.attach(9);
  elbow.attach(10);
  Serial.begin(9600);
}


void loop() {
  if(Serial.available()){  ❹
    int servoAngle = Serial.read();

    servoAngles[nextServo] = servoAngle;
```

```
    nextServo++;
    if(nextServo > 1){
      nextServo = 0;
    }

    shoulder.write(servoAngles[0]);  ❺
    elbow.write(servoAngles[1]);

  }
}
```

Paste this code into the Arduino IDE (Figure 6-8). Hit the right arrow button in the top row of icons to upload the sketch to your board. It should compile successfully. You'll then see lights blink on and off on your Arduino as it receives the code. We'll test the results shortly, but first let's go through this code to make sure you understand it.

Figure 6-8. *The Arduino IDE with our code visible in it.*

> *Unlike Processing code, which is Java, Arduino sketches are written in a variant of the C++ language. For simple examples such as this one, these two languages are quite similar, and you should be able to follow the code here with no problem if you've made it this far through this book. It is beyond the scope of this section to fully teach you the C++ programming language, so I'll gloss over a few spots where this code differs from what the equivalent would look like in Processing.*

❶ The sketch starts by including the Arduino Servo library. This library makes it easy for us to connect to servos and to control them. After we've included the library, we declare two Servo objects corresponding to each of the two joints of our robot arm: elbow and shoulder. We'll use each of these objects to control one of our two servos.

❷ Next, we set up the variables we'll use to keep track of the alternating servo positions that will be coming in from Processing. We use two variables to do this job: nextServo, an integer that keeps track of which of our two servos is getting updated next, and servoAngles[], an array of integers that will store the angles for each of our two servos. nextServo will alternate between 0 and 1, and we'll use it as an array to access the values that we store in servoAngles. We initialize both of the elements of servoAngles to 0. This will cause both servos to start at the 90-degree position. Hence, our robot arm will start off at a right angle with the lower arm facing up, just like our real arm at the moment that it completes calibration for skeleton tracking. This match is important, because it means that when our Processing sketch starts to send joint angles, the robot arm will already be pretty close to the first angles that it receives. This will prevent a violent rapid jerk at the start of each session, which would happen if the robot arm had to jump from some other starting position to match the position of the user's real arm.

❸ Having declared our servo objects, we need to tell Arduino what pins they're connected to. In our sketch's setup function, we call the attach function on each of our servo objects, passing in the correct pin number: 9 for the shoulder and 10 for the elbow. After that, we'll be able to use our servo objects to position the appropriate servos.

With that done, we're ready to initialize serial communication. We call Servo.begin(9600) to start things off; 9600 is the baud rate at which we'll be communicating. We could use pretty much any value as long as we're consistent between our Arduino and any other device that wants to communicate with it, but 9600 is a standard value for applications like this where we are just sending simple data. It's plenty fast enough that we won't notice any delay.

❹ Now we're into our sketch's loop function. Just like Processing has a setup function that runs once and a draw function that runs over and over, Arduino has the same system, only it calls the repeating function loop since Arduinos don't draw to the screen the way Processing sketches do.

The first thing we do inside our loop function is listen to see if anyone has sent us a message over serial. Serial.available will return true if any data is available for us to read and false if not. If no data is available, we have nothing to do, we only move the robot arm when the Processing sketch tells us where to move it. When serial data does come in, we read it using Serial.read and store the results into an variable called servoAngle.

We then take this value and store it into our array. We use our nextServo variable as the index in the array at which we'd like to store this new value. nextServo can be either 0 or 1, where 0 means that the angle is for the shoulder servo and 1 means that the angle is for the elbow servo. nextServo starts off as 0, so that means we're expecting the first value that comes in to be an angle for the shoulder. Once we've received this value, we increment nextServo so that it's ready to store the next value in the correct place in the array. However, just incrementing nextServo isn't enough. We want it to alternate between 0 and 1. So the next few lines of the sketch check to see if nextServo has risen above 1. If it has, we reset it to 0. The result is that nextServo will alternate back and forth between 0 and 1 as we wanted.

❺ Finally, all that's left for us to do is send the most recent values to each of the servos. To do this, we call each object's write function, passing the value in the servoAngles array that is appropriate: servoAngles[0] for our shoulder and servoAngles[1] for our elbow.

Testing Our Arduino Program: Serial in Processing

Now that we've got our program in place, we're ready to test it. But how can we send values over the serial connection to our Arduino? We have a couple of options. We could use the serial monitor that's built into Arduino. This lets us type values into a simple interface, as shown in Figure 6-9, which will then be sent immediately to our Arduino.

Figure 6-9. *The Arduino IDE's serial monitor. This is an easy way to send data over the serial connection to our Arduino, but it is difficult for us to type the ASCII characters representing the numbers that we actually want to send.*

However, if we use this interface, we'll have a problem with the encoding of the messages that we're sending to the Arduino. Our Arduino is expecting to receive the angles for the servos as numbers from 0 to 180 representing the degrees of the angle to which it should move each servo. However, when we type characters into Arduino's serial monitor, we're entering those characters as ASCII values. ASCII (*http://en.wikipedia.org/wiki/ASCII*) is a system for encoding individual characters as numbers for use in computers. It assigns each key on the keyboard its own unique number from 0 to 128, including the number keys and control keys such as Enter and the space bar. Unfortunately, the ASCII codes for the number keys on our keyboard don't correspond to the numbers themselves. For example, when you type the number 0 on your keyboard into the serial monitor, the Arduino IDE will convert that into the ASCII value for 0, which is the number 48, and then send that to your Arduino over the serial connection.

Since we need to send values between 0 and 180 to our Arduino in order to test our servo code, this ASCII encoding issue will make our life very difficult if we try to use the Arduino serial monitor. Thankfully, we have another tool that can send serial messages: Processing itself. We can write a simple Processing program that will send exactly the numbers that we want to our Arduino. This will serve both as a way to test your Arduino program and your circuit as well as to introduce you to performing serial communication in Processing, which we'll need to add to our joint-tracking sketch later in this chapter.

Here's the code for a simple Processing sketch that performs serial communication. It initiates a serial connection, and then it sends numbers to the Arduino based on keys that you type. Specifically,whenever you type a, it will send a 0 over the serial line; when you type s, it will send a 90; and when you type d, it will send 180. These three values will demonstrate the complete range of our servos. Plus, they'll let us calibrate our servos so we can figure out which direction to attach our popsicle sticks.

```
import processing.serial.*; ❶
Serial port;

void setup(){
  println(Serial.list()); ❷
  String portName = Serial.list()[0];
  port = new Serial(this, portName, 9600); ❸
}

void draw(){} ❹
void keyPressed(){ ❺

  if(key == 'a'){
    port.write(0);
  }

  if(key == 's'){
    port.write(90);
  }

  if(key == 'd'){
    port.write(180);
  }

}
```

❶   At the top of this sketch, we import the serial library and declare a serial object called port. We'll use this object for all of our communication with the Arduino.

❷   In our setup function, we want to initialize our Serial object. First we have to figure out which serial device we want to connect to. Each device has its own name, which will differ based on what operating system you're on and what devices are connected. The Processing serial library provides a function, Serial.list, that will enumerate all of the currently connected serial devices. On a Mac, it's likely that you only have one serial device (the Arduino) plugged into your computer, so you can probably use the first item (0) in list.

However, on Windows, you may have one or more additional serial ports, so run the sketch and check the output of `println(Serial.list)`, and adjust the array index on the next line if your Arduino is connected to another serial port. We'll save the serial port as `portName`, a `String` variable that we can use to initialize our `Serial` object.

❸ On this line, we go ahead and do just that. We initialize our `Serial` object, `port`, by calling the `Serial` constructor. We pass in the `portName` we just figured out as well as 9600, which is the baud rate we set in our Arduino code. As I mentioned before, this baud rate doesn't actually matter as long as we set the same rate here as we did in our Arduino sketch.

❹ Unusually in this sketch, we don't want to do anything at all in `draw`. This sketch isn't going to display anything, it's simply going to send values over the serial connection when we type. We still need to have a `draw` function so that our sketch will work, but we can leave it empty.

❺ The real action in this sketch happens in our `keyPressed` function. The whole point of this sketch is to let us send values to the Arduino by typing individual keys in our Processing sketch. In `keyPressed`, we provide a series of `if` statements based on the value of `key`, which holds the ASCII value of the key that the user typed. We test that value against the ASCII value for `'a'`, `'s'`, and `'d'` by enclosing each character in single quotes, which tells Processing that we're referring to the number that represents the ASCII code for the given letter. In each of these `if` statements, we call `port.write` to send a different value to the Arduino (0, 90, or 180) when that key is pressed.

With your Arduino plugged in and both servos connected, run this sketch and try typing different combinations of a, s, and d, slowly one at a time. You should notice that each servo is turning to a different position when you type a letter, alternating back and forth between the two. If you send the one servo the same letter twice in a row, you won't see it move at all: the servo knows that it's already at exactly the position to which you're trying to send it. If your servos aren't moving, double-check your circuit against Figure 6-7 to make sure you've got all your connections correct.

Building Our Robot Arm

Now I mentioned in the last section that we could use our test Processing sketch to calibrate our servos for attaching the popsicle sticks. What did I mean by that? Look back at Figure 6-2. Each of our servos needs to have its popsicle arm attached in a manner that will make it move along the correct axis. For example, our shoulder servo is going to be horizontal at the edge of our table so that its 0 position points its popsicle stick straight down and 180 points straight it up. Our elbow servo, conversely, needs to be attached to the shoulder popsicle stick in a manner where its 180-degree angle will make its popsicle stick point straight out in the same direction as the upper arm and 0 will make it point back the other way toward the shoulder servo. For another reference, look back at Figure 6-5. We want our servo arrangement to reproduce the arm positions shown there when at the angles indicated.

To help get things right, we can use this last Processing sketch to position each of our servos at 0, 90, or 180 degrees in turn before we attach popsicle sticks to them. Each servo has a range of motion of 180 degrees. Depending on how the servo's horn (the plastic bit that actually turns when the servo rotates) is attached, it will be pointing in different directions at each of these three positions. You can use your sketch to discover these positions and figure out if you need to unscrew the horn and reattach it so that it's pointing in a more useful direction.

Here's the procedure I followed to get my popsicle sticks attached successfully (Figure 6-10 shows the final result):

- Place the shoulder servo on the table flat side down as shown in Figure 6-2.

- Use the Processing sketch to set it to 0 degrees.

- Use your hot glue gun to glue a popsicle stick to the shoulder horn facing straight down.

- Now use the Processing sketch to move the servo to 90 and then 180 degrees while holding the servo still in the same position. At 90 degrees, the popsicle stick should be facing straight to the right. At 0 degrees, it should be facing straight up. See Figure 6-11.

- Hold the micro servo against the opposite end of the popsicle stick that's attached to the shoulder servo. It helps if this servo has a horn that lets you see what direction it's pointing. If it has a circular horn, draw a line on it with a marker so you can see how it's turning.

- Position the micro servo so that it points away from the shoulder servo at 180 degrees, straight up, at 90, and back toward the shoulder servo at 0. You may have to switch which side of the shoulder popsicle stick you attach it to achieve this result.

- Once you're sure you've got the micro servo moving the right way, hot glue another popsicle stick to its horn and then hot glue the bottom of the micro servo to the first popsicle stick.

- Finally, power down your Arduino so the motors don't resist you and rotate the second popsicle stick back toward the shoulder servo. If both your popsicle sticks are the same length, it will probably collide with the first shoulder servo before reaching the end of its range of motion. Trim the length of your second popsicle stick to prevent this collision.

> *Depending on the length of your popsicle sticks, you'll need to elevate your servos off your desk or lean them over the side of your desk so that your robot arm can go through its full range of motion without crashing into the desk and knocking itself over or pulling itself off of its supports. Likewise, be careful with how you arrange the servo wires, the Arduino, and the breadboard. You don't want the servo wires to get tangled up in the robot arm as it moves, which can be a danger since the wires need to extend out to reach the elbow servo, which will itself be moving at the end of the first arm section.*

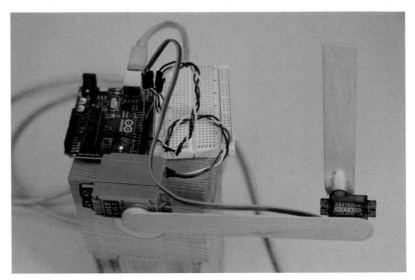

Figure 6-10. *The fully assembled robot arm in detail. Note that the elbow servo is attached to the opposite side of the popsicle stick as the shoulder servo so that it can achieve the correct range of motion.*

Figure 6-11. *Our servos with popsicle sticks attached. Make sure you attach your popsicle sticks facing the right direction to achieve the correct range of motion.*

When your robot arm is fully assembled, it should look like Figure 6-12. By sending values to each servo with your Processing sketch, you should be able to move the robot arm through its full range of motion, from extended straight down, where the shoulder is at 0 degrees and the elbow is at 180, to a right angle, where the shoulder and the elbow are both at 90, to completely vertical, where the shoulder is at 180 and the elbow is at 0.

Figure 8-12. *The fully assembled robot arm. Ready to move.*

Once all of these are working, we're ready to hook up the robot arm to our early Processing sketch that uses the Kinect to calculate these joint angles. We'll just make a few additions to that sketch to get it to send the joint angles over serial, and we'll have a robot arm that will copy our movements.

Putting It All Together: Connecting Our Robot Arm to Our Processing Sketch

We don't have to change the first Processing sketch in this chapter too dramatically to get it to control our robot arm. It's already calculating the shoulder and elbow joint angles in the perfect form for us, as numbers between 0 and 180. All we really need to do is add serial code to this sketch to get it to connect to our Arduino and then send these angles across in the format our Arduino is expecting. We've already seen a lot of this code in our Arduino helper sketch in the last section. Instead of reproducing the entire joint-tracking and angle-calculating Processing sketch here, I'll just describe the additions you need to make to the version of it we last left off. If you want to see the complete code all in one place, that's available in Example A-7 in the Appendix.

Our first addition will be at the top of the sketch, where we need to import the serial library and declare our `Serial` object:

```
import processing.serial.*;
Serial port;
```

Then, inside of `setup` we need to find the serial port to which our Arduino is connected and use that to initialize our `port` object. Remember to use 9600 as the baud rate so that it matches the one we set in our Arduino code, and also to change 0 to the appropriate serial port number if your Arduino isn't connected to the first serial port:

```
println(Serial.list());
String portName = Serial.list()[0];
port = new Serial(this, portName, 9600);
```

Now the real action happens inside of `draw`. Near the end of that function, just after we display the shoulder and elbow angles on the screen using `text`, we'll add some additional code to send the two joint angles over our serial connection to Processing. As we mentioned when we went through the Arduino code, we want to send the joint angles in an alternating manner: first the shoulder, then the elbow, rinse and repeat. The easiest way to do that in our Processing sketch is simply to send both angles every time consecutively. We do that by constructing an array of bytes representing both angle values in order and then sending that whole array over the serial port all at once. Here's what it looks like in code:

```
byte out[] = new byte[2];
out[0] = byte(shoulderAngle);
out[1] = byte(elbowAngle);
port.write(out);
```

One important thing to point out here is that we call the `byte` function on each of our angle values before storing them in our array. In addition to converting them to the right type to prevent an error, this rounds these values to the closest integer. This is how we'd been displaying our joint angles, and this is what we need for the values to makes sense as servo angles on the Arduino side.

With these changes in place, you're ready to try out your new robot puppet arm! Make sure your Arduino is plugged into your computer and start your Processing sketch. Once it starts up, perform the calibration ritual so that your sketch is tracking your skeleton. As soon as OpenNI locks on, you're sketch will start sending joint angles to the Arduino, and your robot arm will come alive, matching your motions. For a demo of what this looks like in action, take a look at this video of me demonstrating the robot arm (*http://vimeo.com/31698679*).

Having a robot arm copy your motions back to you like this is surprisingly fun. The servos give the arm a slightly jittery nervous quality that makes the whole thing take on its own personality. Plus the interaction of the robot arm copying your every gesture back to you is reminiscent of the famous Marx Brothers mirror scene from *Duck Soup*, where Harpo pretended to be Groucho's mirror image by copying and inverting his gestures.

Inverse Kinematics

Up to this point, we've been having our robot arm reproduce the motions of a real arm. This created a number of conveniences for us in our code. There was a natural match between the way the real arm moved and the data we needed to control the robot. We could simply measure the angles of the user's actual body and reproduce them with the robot. However, there are also many situations where we'd like our robot arm to be able to follow the motions of something that doesn't share its mechanics. For example, it would be great to have the arm be able to follow a single point, for example a user's head of center of mass. This ability would let the robot arm act as a flashlight or a pointer.

When we're tracking just a single point, however, we won't be able to determine the angles of our robot's two joints by measuring corresponding angles in the user's body. Instead we'll need an automated way of calculating these angles based solely on where we want to move the robot's hand. The term for this process is called inverse kinematics. In forward kinematics (which is what we've been doing so far), you set the angles for each of the joints one by one, and together they determine the position of the end the limb. On the contrary, with inverse kinematics, you start by setting just the position of the end of the limb, and your code determines the necessary angles for each of the intermediate joints in order to achieve that position. Imagine that I was standing in front of you with my arm extended. If you grabbed my hand and pulled it around into different positions, my arm would automatically adjust. I'd bend my elbow and my shoulder to accommodate the position into which you placed my hand. You wouldn't have to force these joints into particular angles yourself, and you also couldn't determine what angles they'd end up in exactly. You'd have inverse kinematic control over my arm.

Our inverse kinematic calculations will start with a few constraints. These include the fixed position of the shoulder that acts as the unmoving base of our limb, the length of each of our limb segments—the upper and lower arm—and the maximum range of angles we're willing to support. Given these constraints and the target position we want the arm to reach, we can calculate the angles that we need to control the arm. The math required to do these calculations is a little bit complicated, but you don't have to understand all of it in order to use the code. I'll give you the basic outline so you know what's going on, and I'll present a full walkthrough in Figure A-1 in the Appendix for the curious.

Inverse Kinematics Calculations without the Kinect

Diving straight into building a sketch that tracks the user, performs the inverse kinematics calculations, and uses the results to control our robot arm would be overwhelming. So, we're going to start by looking at a sketch that does inverse kinematics with some simple graphics. That way we can focus on understanding how to calculate our angles before we try to apply it the Kinect data. Then, in the next section, we'll integrate the code from this section with user-tracking data from the Kinect and serial communication with the Arduino to control the robot arm. Sine you've already seen those pieces of code, the final application will easy to understand once you've seen how inverse kinematics works.

To demonstrate inverse kinematics, let's look at a sketch that moves a graphical "arm" around in two dimensions. Even though it will be made of lines and circles instead of servos and popsicle sticks, our arm will have the same basic properties as our actual robot arm: its "shoulder" will be fixed in place. Its shoulder will be attached to its "elbow," and its elbow will be attached to its "hand." The popsicle sticks connecting each of these joints will be the same length. We'll use the mouse to simulate the real object we want our arm to track. As you move your mouse around the sketch, we'll figure out how to move the arm's joints so that its hand reaches toward your mouse. Figure 6-13 shows the visual results of this. The point at the center of the sketch is fixed. The point at the end of the arm sticks to my mouse. And as I move my mouse around the sketch, the elbow between bends and rotates to make sure the end point stays stuck to my mouse.

Figure 6-13. *Our sketch calculates the positions of the arm segments to make sure the end of the second segment always tracks the mouse.*

Here's the code. Copy it into Processing and run it yourself to get a feel for how it behaves, and then we'll discuss it below.

```
int segmentLength;

PVector shoulder;
PVector elbow;
PVector target;

void setup() {
  size(500, 500);
```

```
  segmentLength = width/5; ❶

  shoulder = new PVector();
  elbow = new PVector();
  target = new PVector();

  shoulder.x = width/2; ❷
  shoulder.y = height/2;
}

void draw() {
  background(255);

  target.x = mouseX; ❸
  target.y = mouseY;

  // begin complex inverse kinematics math ❹
  // find the length of longest side of the triangle
  PVector difference = PVector.sub(target, shoulder);
  float distance = difference.mag();

  // sides of the main triangle
  float a = segmentLength;
  float b = segmentLength;
  float c = min(distance, segmentLength + segmentLength);

  // angles of the main triangle ❺
  // via Law of Cosines
  float B = acos((a*a + c*c - b*b)/(2*a*c));
  float C = acos((a*a + b*b - c*c)/(2*a*b)); // C is also the elbow angle

  // angle of the shoulder joint ❻
  float D = atan2(difference.y, difference.x);
  float E = D + B + C - PI; // Pi is 180 degrees in rad

  float F = D + B;

  // use SOHCAHTOA to find rise and run from angles
  elbow.x = (cos(E) * segmentLength) + shoulder.x;
  elbow.y = (sin(E) * segmentLength) + shoulder.y;

  target.x = (cos(F) * segmentLength) + elbow.x;
  target.y = (sin(F) * segmentLength) + elbow.y;

  float shoulderAngle = degrees(PI/2 - E); ❼
  float elbowAngle = degrees(C);

  println("s: " + shoulderAngle + "\te: " + elbowAngle);

  stroke(255, 0, 0, 100); ❽
  fill(240, 0, 0, 200);
  ellipse(shoulder.x, shoulder.y, 10, 10);
  ellipse(elbow.x, elbow.y, 8, 8);
  ellipse(target.x, target.y, 6, 6);
  stroke(0);
  line(shoulder.x, shoulder.y, elbow.x, elbow.y);
  line(elbow.x, elbow.y, target.x, target.y);
}
```

I'm not going to try to explain every detail of this code. The math behind why we perform every operation here to calculate the angles and joint positions is too complex to cover quickly. Also you don't need to understand every last detail to make use of it. For a full explanation including all the geometrical details, see Figure A-1.

Run this code and play around with the results for a while so you get a feel for how this graphical version of our robot arm follows your mouse around. Now let's take a close look at the code to talk about how it works.

❶ As I mentioned above, one major constraint that helps us calculate the angles for our joints is the restriction that the length of the two segments of the arm are fixed and identical. Here, we set that segmentLength to be one fifth of the width of the screen. I chose this size to make sure that the arm stays comfortable on screen throughout its complete range of motion.

❷ We'll use three critical points to define our arm: the shoulder, the elbow, and the target. The shoulder will stay fixed and unmoving. The target will track the movement of the user's mouse. And we'll place the elbow based on the results of our calculations. We're using a PVector for each of these. Here we choose the fixed position for the shoulder to be the center of the sketch and set its x- and y-components accordingly.

❸ Now, we're into draw. The first thing we do is update the position of the target based on the position of the mouse. Once we know this position, our main job for the rest of the sketch is to figure out where to place the elbow to satisfy the fixed lengths of each limb segment.

❹ At this point, we start into the math for calculating the angles for our joints. We start with three known quantities: the position of the fixed shoulder, the position of the target as set by the user, and the length of both of the limb segments as determined before hand. Given these inputs, our job is to calculate the position of the elbow in such a way that it is exactly the length of one segment away from both the shoulder and the target. Or, put another way, we need to figure out how to flex the elbow to get the target into its specified position without distorting the arm in any other way.

Here's how we'll approach this problem. These three points—the shoulder, the elbow, and the target—make up a triangle, as shown in Figure 6-14. We have enough information about this triangle that we can calculate every angle and length related to it. We can do this using the tools of trigonometry, which is the science of triangles. We start out by finding the lengths of all three sides of the triangle. Two sides are simply the fixed segmentLength. The third side varies in length as the arm bends and straightens. We find its length using vector subtraction: by subtracting the position of the target from the shoulder and then calculating the magnitude of the resulting vector.

Chapter 6

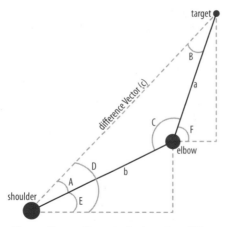

Figure 8-14. *Our inverse kinematics math works by knowing all the angles and lengths involved in the triangle made up of our three joints. With these values we can use trigonometry to calculate the angles we need for our robot arm. See Figure A-1 for a full explanation of how this works.*

❺ Once we have the lengths of all of these sides, we can use their values to calculate all three of the triangles inner angles (labeled A, B, and C) using a convenient geometrical rule known as the Law of Cosines (*http://en.wikipedia.org/wiki/Law_of_cosines*). Look at our triangle diagram again. The angle labeled C also happens to be exactly the angle of our arm's elbow. So we've already got one of our two angles down. However, the other angle, E, is not quite as easy to calculate since it's not an internal angle of our triangle.

❻ It turns out we can find the angle of E using two more trigonometric techniques. First we find the angle of our `difference` vector from the x-axis. Then we combine this with all of the other angles and PI to find the angle of E. This step is a hard to explain without a detailed proof. See Figure A-1 in the Appendix for the full story.

After we have these angles, we proceed to use them to find the positions of our `elbow` and `target` vectors using sine and cosine (and an old mnemonic you may remember from high school geometry: "SOHCAHTOA"). While we won't need these positions for our robot arm, we do them to create the graphical display of this sketch.

❼ Now, at long last, we convert our calculated angles from radians to degrees so they're in the units of 0-180 that we're used to. Also we have to convert our `shoudlerAngle`. The angle E that we calculated only measures the shoulder angle from the horizontal x-axis. We want to measure it from the vertical. And we want to do it in such a way that the angle will measure 0 when the arm is pointing straight down and 180 when it's pointing straight up. Subtracting E from PI/2 (the radian equivalent of 90 degrees) achieves this.

❽ And finally we use all of these measurements to display our arm. We draw ellipses at each of the positions represented by our three vectors and draw lines between them.

Controlling Our Robot Arm with Inverse Kinematics

So now you understand how inverse kinematics works in general. You've seen how we can go from two fixed points to a set of angles that arrange the limb segments between them. Now, we're ready to apply it to our robot arm. One cool thing about this is that we won't have to change our Arduino code at all. The Arduino simply receives angle values over serial from Processing and uses them to position the servos. This will work just as well for angles calculated with inverse kinematics as those calculated with forward kinematics as in our previous use.

However, we will have to update our hardware and our Processing code. You may have noticed that the "arm" displayed in our last sketch bends the opposite direction of our robot arm. Instead of bending up, the elbow bends down. Before we can send over the angles from our inverse kinematics calculations, we'll have to alter our hardware to match this configuration. When that's done we'll also have to integrate the inverse kinematics calculations we just looked at into code that uses the Kinect to do skeleton tracking. We'll use the Kinect to find the user's head, and we'll use that as the target for our arm to follow. Just like the graphical arm in our last sketch tracked the mouse as you moved it around the window, our robot arm will follow the user's head. Figure 6-15 gives you an idea of what the final sketch will look like. Of course, the really exciting results from this sketch can only be seen in person: the arm moving around to follow your head. The green arm in this sketch is simply an illustration. Here's a video (*http://vimeo.com/31739856*) of the final version of this sketch in action.

Figure 6-15. *The display from our sketch tracking my head using inverse kinematics. We position the base of the arm far off to the left so that the entire depth image is accessible in its range of motion.*

Chapter 6

Updating Our Hardware

We built our robot arm so that it would match the mechanics of a real arm. The elbow bends toward the shoulder, the shoulder raises the whole arm up and down, etc. Now, though, we're not using our robot arm like a real human arm. Instead, we're using it to embody the logic of our inverse kinematics calculations. And, as you've saw in the previous sketch, the result from that calculation points the lower arm down from its joint. Hence, we need to adjust our hardware to match this.

Thankfully, it's very easy to make this change. If you've been using your robot arm in forward kinematic mode, it will probably be stopped in a right angle pose with the elbow servo facing straight up. Simply remove the horn from the micro servo and reattach it so that the arm faces the opposite direction as shown in Figure 6-16. Now we've reversed the orientation of that joint in a way that will match up with the results of our inverse kinematics calculations. We'll be able to send the angles that result over to the Arduino and get it to reproduce the motions of the arm we're seeing on screen.

Figure 6-16. *To get our robot arm to match the angles generated by our inverse kinematic calculations, we need to reverse the orientation of our robot's lower arm, as shown here.*

Updating Our Code

Our hardware is ready to go. It's time to put all the pieces together. In this section, we'll look at a new sketch that tracks the user's head and then uses our inverse kinematics calculations to determine the angles needed for the robot arm to follow along.

Here's the code. Plug in your Arduino and run it with your updated hardware. After you've performed the calibration ritual, you'll see a green representation of the robot arm appear in your sketch and begin moving to keep its end joint lined up with your head, as shown in Figure 6-15. You should be able to understand nearly everything in this sketch. It just combines pieces of code that you've seen before in different contexts. Below the code listing, I'll point out a couple of changes and adjustments and some of the important parts where things come together.

```
import SimpleOpenNI.*;
SimpleOpenNI  kinect;

import processing.serial.*;
Serial port;

int segmentLength;

PVector shoulder;
PVector elbow;
PVector target;

void setup() {
  size(1200, 800);  ❶

  kinect = new SimpleOpenNI(this);
  kinect.enableDepth();
  kinect.enableUser(SimpleOpenNI.SKEL_PROFILE_ALL);
  kinect.setMirror(true);

  segmentLength = 400;

  shoulder = new PVector();
  elbow = new PVector();
  target = new PVector();

  shoulder.x = 0;
  shoulder.y = height/2;

  println(Serial.list());
  String portName = Serial.list()[0];
  port = new Serial(this, portName, 9600);
}

void draw() {
  background(255);
  kinect.update();

  image(kinect.depthImage(), 300, 100);  ❷

  IntVector userList = new IntVector();
  kinect.getUsers(userList);

  if (userList.size() > 0) {
    int userId = userList.get(0);

    if ( kinect.isTrackingSkeleton(userId)) {
      PVector head = new PVector();
      kinect.getJointPositionSkeleton(userId, SimpleOpenNI.SKEL_HEAD,
                                      head);
      kinect.convertRealWorldToProjective(head, head);

      head.y = head.y + 100;  ❸
      head.x = head.x + 300;
```

Chapter 6

```
    fill(0, 255, 0);
    ellipse(head.x, head.y, 20, 20);

    target.x = head.x; ❹
    target.y = head.y;

    // begin complex inverse kinematics math ❹
    PVector difference = PVector.sub(target, shoulder);
    float distance = difference.mag();

    // sides of the main triangle
    float a = segmentLength;
    float b = segmentLength;
    float c = min(distance, segmentLength + segmentLength);

    // angles of the main triangle
    float B = acos((a*a + c*c - b*b)/(2*a*c));
    float C = acos((a*a + b*b - c*c)/(2*a*b));
    // C is also the elbow angle
    float D = atan2(difference.y, difference.x);

    // angle of the shoulder joint
    float E = D + B + C - PI; // Pi is 180 degrees in rad

    float F = D + B;

    // use SOHCAHTOA to find rise and run from angles
    elbow.x = (cos(E) * segmentLength) + shoulder.x;
    elbow.y = (sin(E) * segmentLength) + shoulder.y;

    target.x = (cos(F) * segmentLength) + elbow.x;
    target.y = (sin(F) * segmentLength) + elbow.y;

    // adjust angles based on orientation of hardware ❺
    float shoulderAngle = constrain(degrees(PI/2 - E),0, 180);
    float elbowAngle = degrees(PI - C);

    fill(255, 0, 0);
    textSize(20);
    text("shoulder: " + int(shoulderAngle) +
        "\nelbow: " + int(elbowAngle), 20, 20);

    // ❻
    byte out[] = new byte[2];
    out[0] = byte(int(shoulderAngle));
    out[1] = byte(int(elbowAngle));
    port.write(out);

    fill(255, 0, 0);
    ellipse(shoulder.x, shoulder.y, 10, 10);
    ellipse(elbow.x, elbow.y, 8, 8);
    ellipse(target.x, target.y, 6, 6);
    stroke(0, 255, 0);
    strokeWeight(5);
    line(shoulder.x, shoulder.y, elbow.x, elbow.y);
    line(elbow.x, elbow.y, target.x, target.y);
  }
 }
}
```

```
// user-tracking callbacks!
void onNewUser(int userId) {
  println("start pose detection");
  kinect.startPoseDetection("Psi", userId);
}

void onEndCalibration(int userId, boolean successful) {
  if (successful) {
    println("  User calibrated !!!");
    kinect.startTrackingSkeleton(userId);
  }
  else {
    println("  Failed to calibrate user !!!");
    kinect.startPoseDetection("Psi", userId);
  }
}

void onStartPose(String pose, int userId) {
  println("Started pose for user");
  kinect.stopPoseDetection(userId);
  kinect.requestCalibrationSkeleton(userId, true);
}
```

❶ This sketch starts off with a series of variable declarations and a setup function that should be familiar. setup now configures our SimpleOpenNI object, initializes the variables for our inverse kinematics calculations, and opens up our serial connection to the Arduino. The new element here is the size of the sketch: 1200 by 800. Rather than just displaying the depth image, we also need to show the representation of the robot arm as it goes through its inverse kinematics machinations. (Remember to change the serial port index if necessary on the second-to-last line in setup).

Another thing worth pointing out in setup is how we position the shoulder. Just like in the last version of our sketch, the shoulder vector acts as the anchor for our arm. It needs to be fixed in place so that the other two joints can move freely to track our target. The particular spot at which we position the shoulder is somewhat arbitrary. No matter where we place it, our inverse kinematics algorithm will figure out the angles needed to move the arm into the right position. However, as we'll see shortly, placing the shoulder in the middle of the sketch and a ways off to the side of the depth image has some advantages for the real physical arm itself.

❷ As usual, we display the depth image; however, this time we don't show it at 0,0. Instead, we move it down and to the right to clear room for the lines and ellipses that will make up the representation of the robot arm. The need to create this space points out something interesting about inverse kinematics. Our robot arm will be able to move itself so that the end of its arm can reach anywhere within a rectangular range corresponding to the full depth image. However, the rest of the arm, its other joints and both of its segments, will frequently be outside of this range. So, we need to make extra room to accommodate them. This fact could become very important if you incorporate a robot arm with inverse kinematic control into some real-world application. While you may be focusing on movements of the end of the arm, you still have to allot space for the rest of the arm. For example, if you used this robot arm to draw on a piece of paper, you've have to have enough room around the paper for the rest of the arm to move without running into anything.

❸ Our draw function continues with some Kinect code we're used to: checking to make sure that we're tracking a user and that we've calibrated successfully. Once that's done, we get the head position and convert it into 2D so that it will match the depth image, as usual. However, this time, that 2D conversion won't be enough. We also have to adjust for the fact that we moved the depth image out of the top left corner of the sketch. We do this by adding the same values to the head vector's components as we used to position the depth image: we increase the x-component by 100 and the y-component by 300. This is important both to make the ellipse match your actual head in the depth image and so that the head position will have the right values for our inverse kinematics calculations.

❹ Once we've gotten the head position, we're ready to start our inverse kinematics calculations. These proceed exactly as they did last time.

❺ When our inverse kinematics calculations are complete, we have the values of E and C representing the angles of our elbow and our shoulder joints. This time, though, we have to do slightly more manipulation of them than we did in the last sketch. The first thing we have to do is constrain the values of the shoulder. As you saw when you ran the last sketch, our inverse kinematics calculations are perfectly happy to rotate the shoulder all the way around 360 degrees. However, our robot arm only has a range of 180 degrees. If we try to send it values above 180 or below 0, it will act erratically. To prevent this, we take advantage of Processing's handy constrain function. This function limits the values of a variable to a range that we specify. In this case, we constrain our shoulder angle (which we know from last time is PI/2 - E) to a range from 0 to 180, exactly what we need for the servo. After calling constrain, we're ready to convert our angle with degrees to prepare it for the servo

In the last sketch, we used the raw value of C as the angle of the elbow. However, this time we actually need the supplementary angle, i.e., the angle that adds up to 180 degrees (or PI, since we're working in radians). This is because of the way our servo is oriented on the end of our lower arm. We want it to extend straight out when the angle is at 90. To calculate this complementary angle, we simply subtract E from PI and then convert the result with degrees.

❻ Our last step is to send the data to the Arduino. This works exactly like in our forward kinematics example. We create a 2-byte array with each of our values stored in it and then send that out with port.write. Below this we also display the circles and lines that represent our arm on top of our sketch. I chose to use thick green lines so I could see this display from far away when I'm standing back and waving my arms. It's fun to be able to see the graphical arm on screen moving in parallel with your real robot arm as they both track your head.

When you run this code with your Arduino connected and your hardware all hooked up, you'll see results that look something like this video: *http:// vimeo.com/31739856*. After you've calibrated, the robot arm will follow your head around as you move. Congratulations! You've built an inverse kinematic-controlled robot arm.

Conclusion

Hopefully, this chapter has given you all kinds of ideas for how to integrate the Kinect into hardware projects as the vision system for interactive robots of different stripes. There's something incredibly satisfying about using the data from the Kinect in a physical interface. After all, the reason the Kinect is so exciting as a sensor is that it lets our programs sense the presence of people as more than just keystrokes and mouse movements. While it's great to use these motions to build graphical applications that live on a computer screen (and we've done quite a lot of that through this book), it feels somehow more complete and appropriate to send this data back out into the world to control a physical object. Our bodies respond to physical objects differently than graphics on a screen, and there's something powerful about closing that loop by making interactive objects that can see us move around the room and respond by moving in kind.

Rather than just waving at computers, now we've taught them to wave back.

Conclusion: What's Next?

We've come a long way since the start of this book. We started out by learning how to access the 2D depth image from the Kinect. We learned how to analyze an image by iterating through its pixels. Then we used this ability to build simple interfaces based on tracking the closest point to the Kinect. In the next chapter, we moved on to working in 3D. We learned how to use rotations, translations, and scaling to display the Kinect's depth data as a point cloud. Then we used this ability to build more sophisticated spatially situated interfaces and to integrate 3D models and graphics into them. After that, we moved on to working with the skeleton data. We learned how to access the joint positions of our users and how to use some basic 3D math to compare them. Then we used these skills to build sophisticated user interfaces based on tracking the user's whole body and on watching it move over time. And finally, in the last two chapters, we've applied these skills to the areas of 3D scanning and kinematics for robotics. We've used what we learned to turn the Kinect into a 3D scanner and into a pair of eyes for a robot arm.

IN THIS CHAPTER

Beyond Processing: Other Frameworks and Languages

Topics in 3D Programming to Explore

Ideas for Projects

Having accomplished all of this, you've probably got your own set of ideas for Kinect projects you're itching to try out. Go out and do them!

In addition to those, though, I want to use the rest of this conclusion to spur you on by suggesting avenues you can explore to take your work with the Kinect further. Those avenues branch out from your current knowledge in three different directions:

- New programming environments that have different abilities than Processing does

- Additional programming techniques that let you do more with the Kinect data

- Related tools and skills that will come in handy

After I cover each of these topics, I'll finish up with a list of suggested projects that you can try. Each project is designed to help you explore one or more of these new skills. In addition to your own ideas, working on any of these projects that strike your fancy will help move your Kinect skills beyond what we've covered in this book.

Beyond Processing: Other Frameworks and Languages

As we've seen throughout this book, Processing is a great environment for experimenting with the Kinect. Processing makes it easy to try out all of the techniques the Kinect enables, from skeleton tracking to point clouds, from background removal to hand tracking. However, there are many other environments in which it is also possible to work with the Kinect. In fact, because of the incredible growth of both the OpenKinect and OpenNI communities, there are libraries for working with the Kinect in a huge variety of languages and frameworks.

Each of these alternatives has its own virtues and capabilities. As you move beyond this book into further experiments, and maybe even some larger projects, there are good reasons for you to consider trying them out. In this section I'll briefly introduce some of the more prominent options, point out a little of why you might consider exploring them, and provide a few pointers toward resources that can help you get started.

Obviously there are a huge number of programming languages and environments available, and I make no claim that the options presented here are anything near definitive. I've chosen a few of the most prominent examples that I think represent a range of different approaches that will be useful for a variety of purposes and types of students.

Microsoft

The Kinect is, as you probably noticed when you bought yours, a Microsoft product. However, as I mentioned in Chapter 1, at the time of the Kinect's release, Microsoft did not provide tools for programmers to create their own applications using the Kinect. In the summer of 2011, that changed with the release of the Kinect for Windows Software Developer Kit. The Kinect for Windows SDK lets programmers write applications that run on a Windows computer using the Kinect. These programs are usually written using C#, but can use any language that works with Microsoft's .NET programming environment or with C++. At the time of this writing, the SDK program is still in beta, so applications written with it cannot be released commercially, though that will change with the release of the 1.0 version, which will allow commercial applications (scheduled for early 2012).

Chapter 7

Working with the Microsoft SDK offers a number of differences and advantages from other platforms:

- Microsoft provides their own driver for accessing the Kinect. This driver installs through the normal automated Windows device installation process, which is much simpler than the options available for OpenKinect and OpenNI.

- Microsoft implemented their own skeleton-tracking algorithm that does not require a calibration pose. Their algorithm is also less susceptible to certain failure modes that can affect the algorithm used by OpenNI, and it features a slightly different layout of the skeleton that includes a few additional joints.

- Microsoft provides access to the array of microphones in the Kinect, allowing programs to perform spatially aware detection of user's voices and other sounds. The Kinect contains four microphones. The Microsoft SDK accesses these and can use the difference between what each of them hear to identify the direction from which any sound is issuing. This allows programs to provide a voice control interface that can distinguish the voices of multiple different users simultaneously. Additionally, the SDK provides sophisticated tools for cleaning up the audio signal and removing the output of the PC that make it possible to do high-quality speech recognition while watching a movie or playing a game.

The chief limitation of the Microsoft SDK is that it can only be used on Windows—specifically, Windows 7 or later.

As usual with their developer tools, Microsoft provides rich documentation and example applications. To learn more about the Microsoft SDK, visit Kinect for Windows (*http://kinectforwindows.org*).

C++ Creative Coding Frameworks: openFrameworks and Cinder

One limitation you may reach in your Processing programs that work with the Kinect is performance. Processing emphasizes accessibility and ease of use over raw graphical performance. Processing uses Java, a relatively high-level programming language. It also provides functions that make it easy for beginners and students to achieve visually sophisticated results but do not provide the kind of low-level control required to make programs that can create complex graphics with blazing speed.

These limitations become a real problem when working in 3D. Drawing graphics in three dimensions is more computationally expensive, and Processing sketches that do so can quickly bog down, running at low frame rates that make animation jerky and interactivity frustrating. As we saw in Chapter 3, while it is certainly possible to create 3D graphics with Processing, we frequently find ourselves limiting the quality of what we create (reducing the number of points in our point cloud, for example) so that our sketches will run smoothly.

One way of overcoming these limitations is to work in a lower-level language such as C++. C++ provides improved performance over Java and Processing at the cost of having to deal with lower-level (and sometimes confusing) programming concepts such as pointers. Thankfully, there are creative coding toolkits, similar in spirit to Processing, that make it easier to write interactive graphical applications and can smooth the transition for a Processing programmer. The two most prominent of these are openFrameworks and Cinder.

openFrameworks (*http://openframeworks.cc*) was created by Zach Lieberman, Arturo Castro, and Theo Watson. Getting started with openFrameworks will feel familiar for an experienced Processing programmer. Your applications have `setup` and `draw` functions and can take advantage of a comprehensive built-in library that makes it easy to do common tasks such as selecting colors, drawing shapes, and performing transformations. openFrameworks also has a thriving community of contributors with hundreds of available libraries, called *add ons*, that provide tools for doing everything from computer vision to creating animated GIFs to working with the Kinect (for an extensive index of these, visit *http://ofxaddons.com*).

In addition to these Processing-like features, though, openFrameworks provides access to some of the advanced abilities of OpenGL, the industry standard graphics programming API (more about OpenGL below). These OpenGL features are designed to make it possible to build programs that produce rich sophisticated 3D graphics and perform at the high frame rates necessary for interactivity.

Cinder (*http://libcinder.org*) is another, more recent, C++ creative coding framework. It is targeted at experienced C++ programmers. Rather than resembling a translation of Processing into C++, Cinder employs more idiomatic C++ features. These features can make it more difficult for programmers who are new to C++, but make it more comfortable and expressive for advanced C++ developers. Like openFramework's add-ons, Cinder provides its own library system, called "Blocks." While there are not nearly as many CinderBlocks as Processing libraries or openFrameworks add-ons, there are Blocks for working with the Kinect through both OpenKinect and OpenNI.

One major downside to moving from Processing to any C++ environment is having to leave the creature comforts of the Processing IDE. The Processing IDE provides an incredibly simple experience of writing and running interactive graphical apps. You simply type your code, hit that "run" button, and your app launches. Installing libraries takes nothing more than dropping some code into a folder. As a Processing programmer transitioning to C++, you will have to abandon some of these conveniences. C++ code is written in more professional, and hence more complex, IDEs: frequently Xcode on the Mac and Code::Blocks or VisualStudio on Windows. While incredibly powerful, these environments can feel confusing and unfriendly at first. Also, the process of installing libraries and making sure their paths are correct for compilation is a much more manual process, which can frequently result in obscure error messages and frustration.

Data Flow: MAX/MSP and PureData

In a totally different direction from these C++ frameworks is the approach known as Data Flow Programming. In Data Flow environments, rather than creating your application by writing lines of code, you use a graphical interface to move and position a set of nodes and to create connections between them. The nodes perform various functions such as accepting user input, reading data from the Kinect, or filtering an audio signal. Each node then sends more data out to other nodes that can work with it in turn. You create your application by placing boxes representing these nodes and then dragging lines between them to establish the connections.

Frequently these data flow environments are more accessible to people who've never programmed before than even an education-focused traditional text-based programming environment like Processing. They require a different kind of thinking than traditional linear programming.

The two most prominent environments for data flow programming are MAX/MSP (*http://cycle79.com*) and PureData (*http://puredata.org*). Both MAX And PD (as they're colloquially known) share a common ancestry in the work of Miller Puckette. The biggest distinction between them is that PD is free and open source while MAX is a commercial product with the attendant slickness and level of support.

Both MAX and PD have tools for working with the Kinect. For example, see jit.freenect.grab (*http://jmpelletier.com/freenect/*) for MAX and pix_freenect (*http://www.matthiaskronlachner.com/?p=299*) for PD as well as OSCeleton (*https://github.com/Sensebloom/OSCeleton*), which broadcasts the skeleton data as OSC messages that can be accessed in MAX and PD.

Game Engines: Unity3D

In addition to all of these creative coding environments, it is possible to work with the Kinect in tools designed to create games. Unity3D (*http://unity3d.com*) is a professional-caliber game engine that has been adopted by artists and interactive designers looking to create 3D worlds and experiences with game-like mechanics and navigation. Unity includes a sophisticated 3D design tool that lets you create environments and design the rules that govern them. You can program it in JavaScript or C#, which makes it accessible to a broad range of developers.

Since Unity includes tools for controlling 3D characters and performing realistic physics simulations, it is a great match for the Kinect. In Unity, you can use skeleton tracking data to "puppet" a character within a realistic 3D world. Many of the tools to define the lighting, physics, and interobject interactions that you'd have to build yourself in a conventional graphics programming environment are already available and easy to use.

To learn more about using the Kinect with Unity, check out the chapter by Phoenix Perry in Meet the Kinect (*http://www.apress.com/978143028881*).

Topics in 3D Programming to Explore

Now that you've finished this book, you know a lot about how to work with the Kinect. You can access point clouds and skeleton data with ease. However, this new knowledge you've acquired is a bit like an isolated island in the middle of an ocean. You have a small area of solid ground underneath you, but all around are the dark seas of unknown programming topics. In order to make the most of your new knowledge, you'll need to explore some of these topics. Learning them will let you create more beautiful, sophisticated, and capable applications using the data you can already access from the Kinect. These subjects range from advanced topics in graphical programming to a plethora of techniques in computer vision to the craft of 3D modeling and animating. In this section, I'll briefly introduce you to a couple of these and point you toward some resources for getting started learning them. Each of these topics could fill a whole library of books, but with what you've learned here, you're ready to start learning them; you'll be able to apply each of these areas to what you've learned here right away.

Graphics Programming: OpenGL and Shaders

One of Processing's best features is how easy it makes it for us to create graphics. We can call simple functions such as `fill`, `translate`, and `sphere` to navigate and draw in 2D and 3D. But what really happens when we call these functions? How does Processing actually translate those commands into something that we see on the screen? Further, how does Processing make these same commands work on a diverse set of platforms that includes Mac OS X, Windows, Linux, and Android?

The full answer to these questions is complex and technical, but the short answer is: OpenGL. OpenGL is the industry standard interface for creating graphics. It provides a set of low-level functions that work consistently across different platforms. It provides an incredibly rich set of tools for doing everything from drawing simple shapes to creating sophisticated 3D environments with subtle lighting effects.

OpenGL is nearly ubiquitous in graphics programming environments. It underlies every one of the frameworks and environments I described above, including Processing. In fact, you've been using OpenGL throughout this book—in every single one of the 3D examples. Processing uses OpenGL for all of its 3D drawing capabilities.

Learning more advanced OpenGL skills is probably the single most effective thing you can do to increase your ability create more beautiful graphical applications that can do more sophisticated things in 3D, no matter what environment or language you use. In the rest of this section, I'll give you a brief intro to how OpenGL works and then I'll point you toward some resources for learning more about it. A word of warning: OpenGL is a gargantuan project, and mastering it can take years. However, everything you learn about graphics programming along the way will unlock new technical and aesthetic possibilities in your work, so the effort is well worth it.

Chapter 7

What does OpenGL provide? OpenGL provides standardized tools for drawing, creating geometry, and performing geometric manipulations in both 2D and 3D. You've already seen a lot of this functionality in a house-trained form in Processing's standard functions. OpenGL also includes a model for creating sophisticated 3D scenes and renders including lighting, texturing, fog, and a lot more. Further, it enables hardware acceleration for all of these graphics functions; in other words, it offers a set of abstractions that let programmers control the wildly powerful graphics cards included in modern computers to achieve the vast level of performance required to display rich and realistic 3D scenes.

The OpenGL programming model has two modes, referred to as "pipelines": the fixed-function pipeline and the programmable pipeline. The fixed-function pipeline is the older and more familiar of the two modes. This is the mode that we've been using under the hood in Processing. In fixed-function mode, you set a series of states that affect how your graphics are displayed. These states include things like Processing's `color`, `stroke`, and `fill` functions. Then, after you've set these states, you create geometry that is displayed with these properties. In general, unless you use special data structures and functions, most of the processing happens on the CPU rather than the GPU.

The programmable pipeline, on the other hand, works in a radically different manner. You define geometry and then send it all, en masse, to the GPU, where a series of programs known as *shaders* process it and convert it into the pixels of the final image. Instead of defining the appearance of your application procedurally from the top down, these shaders work from the bottom up, processing each vertex of your geometry or each pixel of your image in parallel. This makes for a new mode of programming that can feel quite foreign. It also makes for tremendously performant programs that can do feats of mass processing that would seem impossible in the fixed-pipeline/CPU-bound world.

Due to the ubiquitous nature of OpenGL, there are quite a number of resources for a student trying to learn about it. The classic overview text is the *OpenGL Super Bible* (*http://www.starstonesoftware.com/OpenGL/*), a doorstopper-sized book that covers both the fixed and programmable pipelines. For a more advanced text on programming shaders, I recommend *Graphics Shaders* by Mike Bailey and Steve Cunningham (*http://www.amazon.com/Graphics-Shaders-Practice-Mike-Bailey/dp/1568813341*), which provides a rigorous overview with examples. *Learning Modern 3D Graphics Programming* by Jason L. McKesson (*http://www.arcsynthesis.org/gltut/*) is another strong text that focuses on the programmable pipeline and is free online.

Finally, for any reader of this book trying to learn advanced OpenGL techniques, the GLGraphics (*http://glgraphics.sourceforge.net/*) library for Processing by Andres Colubri will serve as an irreplaceable tool. GLGraphics gives you access to the full suite of advanced OpenGL functionality within Processing including shaders, texturing geometry, off-screen rendering, filters, and effects. Nearly all OpenGL books give their examples using C++ code. Using GLGraphics will let you begin by translating some of these techniques into an environment with which you're already familiar.

Computer Vision: OpenCV, Feature Tracking, and Beyond

Computer vision is the academic and technical field that studies and invents techniques for analyzing the visible world with computers. Computer vision starts with the raw images from cameras and uses code to understand the objects, people, and motion in them.

The human vision system is an amazing thing. It does a lot more than simply show us images. Our vision system draws our attention to motion. It distinguishes objects. It focuses on people. It stabilizes what we see as we move. It transforms our distinct impressions into a complete image of our surroundings. It recognizes people and objects even when we see them from different points of view, with different lighting, and with some details changed. Each of these tasks is radically difficult for a computer. In the 1960s, the legendary Stanford artificial intelligence pioneer, John McCarthy, famously gave a graduate student the job of "solving" computer vision as a summer project. The problem has turned out to be a little bit more difficult than that. It has occupied an entire community of academic researchers for the past 40 years. And, in many ways, the first real breakthroughs have only come in the last decade or so, with the Kinect being one of the crown jewels of these recent developments.

Given the breadth and complexity of this field, it can be intimidating to get started. In this section I'll point you to one accessible tool, one ambitious technique, and one great book as just a few leads you can use to dive in.

One major product of the last 40 years of computer vision research is an open source library called OpenCV (*http://opencv.willowgarage.com*). Originally created by Intel, OpenCV packages up a large number of common computer vision techniques into a single shared library of code that can be used from many different languages and environments. OpenCV includes tools for altering the brightness and contrast of images, for comparing multiple images against each other to look for differences, for finding the edges of individual objects within the image, for detecting faces, and many other tasks. And, lucky for us, there's a great library that makes it really easy to use OpenCV with Processing: OpenCV for Processing (*http://ubaa.net/shared/processing/opencv/*). The documentation for that library will get you started, and O'Reilly's book on the topic is the definitive reference: *Learning OpenCV* by Gary Bradski and Adrian Kaehler (*http://shop.oreilly.com/product/9780596516130.do*).

Once you've mastered the basics of working with OpenCV, you'll be ready to take on some more advanced computer vision techniques. Many of these introduce a new dimension to the processing of images: time. OpenCV's tools are designed to process individual images. While we can use them to analyze recorded footage or live video, very few of them actually account for the movement of objects over time. In the last decade or so, though, researchers have developed new techniques that use the time dimension of moving images to extract additional information. This has led to a number of breakthrough techniques including camera tracking, panorama stitching, and 3D scene reconstruction. Camera tracking starts with a piece of 2D film or video footage and then tries to figure out how the camera moved to create the footage and where it was in relationship to the objects that were in the scene. This technique is used extensively In the visual effects industry for integrating 3D computer graphics such as animated monsters and exploding buildings into 2D film and video footage in order to make the 3D elements appear as if they were shot in the original 2D footage. Another breakthrough techniques is scene reconstruction. Scene reconstruction is the process of taking multiple images of the same space or object and blending them into a single more comprehensive image. You may have come across the 2D application of this technique in applications that perform "panorama stitching," combining multiple images taken side by side into a single wide panorama with no seams. There is also a parallel 3D technique that combines multiple depth images taken from different points of view into a single 3D model of a larger scene.

All of these applications are based on the fundamental idea called "feature detection." The software starts with a single still frame. It detects small pieces of this frame that are particularly recognizable, called "features." Then, when examining subsequent frames, the software looks for the same features in adjacent parts of the image to see if they've moved. If these features correspond to parts of the world that are themselves fixed (for example, the corner of a windowsill or the edge of fence post), then the movement of the features tells you about the movement of the camera itself. If you track enough of these features, you can combine the multiple frames into a single panorama, calculate the movement of the camera, or if your camera is a depth camera, build a full 3D reconstruction of the entire scene or room.

If you want to learn more about feature tracking and the other advanced techniques that have arisen in recent computer vision research, I highly recommend *Computer Vision: Algorithms and Applications* by Richard Szeliski of Microsoft Research (*http://szeliski.org/Book*). It presents a rigorous approach to the contemporary state of the art. The book arose from Szeliski's teaching work at the University of Washington computer science department and so definitely has some math in it. However, if you're excited about the field, and you go slowly and use the Internet to fill in the gaps in your background, there's no better way to really dive deeply into the field.

3D Modeling and Animation

In addition to creating 3D graphics with programming, there's a whole suite of tools that let you design them using a graphical user interface. These tools are tailored to creative artists such as animators, visual effects artists, and creators of motion graphics. They range widely in complexity, power, and ease of use, from simple applications such as Google SketchUp that are meant to be accessible to everyone to programs like Autodesk's Maya that are used by professional craftsmen as a full-time tool. Blender (*http://www.blender.org*) is a free and open source tool that has all the functionality of many of the professional tools.

No matter their level of complexity, however, each of these applications is built on the same foundations of computer graphics that you've started to learn in this book. They manipulate and display geometry in 3D. They apply lighting and use a camera to turn the 3D geometry into moving 2D images. They produce animation by altering all of these properties over time.

Working with 3D modeling and animation tools will inform your programming work and vice versa. In addition to the practical advantages of being able to create resources like 3D models that you can bring into your applications, the fields inform each other conceptually. It's like the relationship between traditional drawing and the study of anatomy or geometry. If you're a draftsman, learning anatomy will improve your figure drawing and learning geometry will improve your study of perspective. If you're an anatomist or mathematician, being able to draw is a great way to express and note your ideas quickly and clearly. The same goes for 3D modeling or animating and learning graphics programming. As a modeler or animator, understanding how OpenGL manipulates geometry and renders your scene will make you better at rigging your characters and positioning your lights. As a graphics programmer, being able to create your own 3D models will make your games and art pieces better; understanding how visual effects artists think about lighting a scene will help you make your own work more beautiful.

3D modeling and animation are also skills that have a large and growing professional application in various fields, from visual effects for movies and commercials to motion graphics to medical visualization. This means that there are a large range of training and education resources out there, but many of them cost money to access. Two of these that I've used extensively and highly recommend are FXPHD (*http://www.fxphd.com*) and Rigging Dojo (*http://www.riggingdojo.com*). FXPHD is a site that provides professional video training to visual effects artists in the movie industry. It offers rigorous training in many 3D programs and other related tools such as compositing and color correction. Rigging Dojo is narrowly focused on the art of rigging: the process of preparing a 3D model to be controlled in animation.

Ideas for Projects

In this section, I'll present four short project ideas that you can make with the Kinect. Each of these projects is designed be both creatively stimulating and also to encourage you to stretch the skills you've learned in this book and take them further. They each explore a different set of Kinect techniques that you learned in this book and also bring in additional areas from outside such as game design, robotics, and animation. Each project includes an estimate of its level of difficulty and the time investment required.

A Physical Therapy Game

Physical therapy is a type of medical treatment that helps people recover from injuries and other health problems that affect their ability to move around and perform everyday tasks. Physical therapy is a frequent and important part of recovery from surgery and other medical problems such as chronic pain.

The treatment usually consists of a set of exercises designed by a physical therapist, including stretching, core exercises, weight lifting, etc. Sometimes these exercises can be highly repetitive and boring, making it difficult for patients, especially kids, to stay motivated and committed to their treatment. It is also sometimes difficult for patients to perform these exercises correctly at home without the supervision of their physical therapist.

Since we can use the Kinect to track body movement, we can use it to detect if a patient is performing exercises correctly. Further, we can build a game around these exercises that will motivate a patient to perform them and also provide feedback that ensures that the patient is performing exercises correctly.

For this project, design a game that asks a user to exercise the range of motion of their arms. Create a set of graphics and game objectives that require the user to move her arms in wide circles around her body without tilting her shoulders. Use the graphical style of the game to reinforce what you want the user to do: maybe she's controlling a monkey that's climbing up a tree, or swimming through the ocean to chase fish, or reaching up to stop spinning plates from falling off of sticks. Use the skeleton-tracking data to ensure that the user is performing the motion correctly: give her feedback when her arms are properly extended or if her shoulders lean to the side incorrectly. You could make the game in a 2D style like *Angry Birds* (adding some simple physics using Dan Shiffman's Processing and Box2D tutorial [*http://www.shiffman.net/teaching/nature/box2d-processing/*] is a great way to achieve this kind of effect) or in 3D. Make the game fun and challenging enough that it keeps patients motivated through their exercises; gradually increasing the level of difficulty and providing enough graphical and aesthetic variety is key to this. Sound also really helps.

Level of difficulty: Easy

Skills: Skeleton tracking, collision detection, game design

Time required: 2 days, depending on how much investment you put into the art resources and physics

Kinect Stereo Viewer

Even though the Kinect sees the world in 3D, we usually display the results in 2D on a screen. There are, of course, also a set of techniques for viewing images in 3D. Known as *stereography*, these techniques work by capturing two images of a scene, one corresponding to each of the viewer's eyes, and then displaying them using some method that separates the images so that each one reaches the appropriate eye of the viewer. There are many methods for achieving this separation. Two of these are easiest to recreate using a normal computer screen. The first of these is to display one half of the stereo-pair in red and one half in blue and then have the viewer wear glasses with one red and one blue filter. Another option is to physically separate the two images so they appear side by side on the screen and then provide the viewer with an apparatus that uses lenses or mirrors to pull the appropriate image into the appropriate eye.

You can implement either of these techniques with relative ease based on the Kinect point cloud. Instead of displaying the point cloud from a single point of view as we did throughout this book, you capture it from two different points of view simultaneously. These points should be placed close together so as to reproduce the usual spacing of a person's eyes, known as the *interocular distance*. The Obsessive Camera Direction Processing library (*http://www.gdsstudios.com/processing/libraries/ocd/*) might come in handy for capturing these two images, as it provides the ability to capture and render a 3D scene within Processing with a high level of control.

Once you've captured these two images, you can display them as appropriate given the stereo approach of your choice. Either render them side by side if you have a stereograph mirror device or overlapping with color tints if you have red-blue glasses (either of these devices are easily ordered online). When you look at the image you produce with the appropriate optical aid, you'll see a live realistic 3D view of the scene captured by the Kinect, a combination of Victorian and 21st-century wonders!

Level of difficulty: Moderate

Skills: 3D graphics, 3D cameras

Time required: 2–4 hours

Animated 3D Puppet

In Chapter 4, we learned how to use the skeleton-tracking data to manipulate a 3D model. We built a sketch that rotated and moved a 3D model of the Kinect so that it appeared between users' hands as they moved around. The geometric approach we took to applying the orientation of the skeleton limbs to our 3D model is the basic ingredient we need to build a full 3D puppetry system that will let us animate 3D characters using our bodies.

In many advanced visual effects and animated films, movie makers create the performances of computer-generated characters by capturing the movements and expressions of real actors and then transferring to 3D models created in the computer. For this project, you'll implement your own simple DIY version of this technique.

Instead of animating a 3D model of a full body all at once, you can make things a lot simpler by splitting the body up into models that correspond to each of the limbs that we track with the Kinect. Use your favorite 3D modeling program to build models designed to sit between each adjacent pair of joints: head and neck, torso, upper arms, lower arms, upper legs, lower legs. After you've created each model, orient it so that it is facing straight up along the z-axis in your 3D modeling program. Export each model as an OBJ file. Then write a Processing sketch that uses the OBJLoader library to load in each model one at a time. Add skeleton tracking code. When a user's skeleton is detected, use the orientation transfer approach covered in Chapter 4 to move each limb segment model so that it matches the corresponding limb of the user. The result will be a 3D puppet that follows along with your body as you move and perform.

Level of difficulty: Moderate

Skills: 3D graphics, trigonometry, 3D modeling

Time required: 1 day

Rolling Person-Chasing Robot

In Chapter 6, we built a robot arm that responded to the movement of a person's arm. But what good robot can't move around on its own? The Kinect makes the perfect eyes for a mobile robot, providing a 3D picture of the scene around the robot that can help it navigate, avoid obstacles, and even track and seek people.

For this advanced project, create a robot that uses an Arduino to drive motors enabling it to move around the room in a direction determined by a Processing sketch you write that uses the Kinect to scan the room and determine where the robot should move. This project is ambitious enough that it is best approached in stages.

In the first stage, focus on making the robot and getting it to move. A great shortcut to building a rolling Arduino-powered robot is the 2WD Arduino Compatible Mobile Platform (*http://www.makershed.com/product_p/mk-seeed7.htm*) from the Maker Shed. The Platform provides two DC motors that are already connected to two wheels and attached to a platform that can carry your Arduino and other hardware such as the Kinect. You'll also need a motor shield (*http://www.makershed.com/product_p/mkad7.htm*) for your Arduino so you can control the motors. Start by hooking up your Arduino and motor shield to these motors and controlling the robot manually, with the Arduino tethered to your computer via a cable. You may need to chase your robot as it moves around the room, following along so that it doesn't run out of cable.

Once you have basic control of the robot, add the Kinect. Write a Processing sketch that access the depth image or tracks a user and figures out where the robot should move. Send that data to your robot over serial to control its motion. You'll now find yourself chasing after the robot with a computer and a Kinect in your arms. This will get awkward.

With this up and running, the next step is to start cutting the cord. The simplest way to do that is to have the Arduino on the robot communicate with the computer and the Kinect wirelessly via Bluetooth. You can use a Bluetooth add-in module such as the SparkFun's BlueSmirf (*http://www.sparkfun.com/products/582*) or The MDFLY Wireless Bluetooth TTL Transceiver Module (*http://www.mdfly.com/index.php?main_page=product_info&products_id=63*). You could even replace your Arduino with an Arduino BT (*http://www.arduino.cc/en/Main/ArduinoBoardBluetooth*). Any of these options let your Arduino communicate wirelessly to your computer so it can move around the room freely while the computer and Kinect stay fixed.

The final step is to attach the computer and Kinect to the robot so that its vision system can move along with it as it explores the space. To accomplish this, you may need a more robust robot platform that can support the weight of a laptop or other small computer as well as the Kinect. You'll also need to figure out a way to power the Kinect without having to plug it into the wall. Follow this tutorial for powering the Kinect from a battery (*http://www.ros.org/wiki/kinect/Tutorials/Adding%20a%20Kinect%20to%20an%20iRobot%20Create*).

When your robot can move freely and bring the Kinect and a computer along with it, you can start working on more sophisticated programming for it. For example, you can have it track a user's center of mass and then try to proceed toward the user while avoiding any intervening obstacles it detects in the depth image. This will stretch everything you've learned about user tracking, serial communication, kinematics, and many other topics as well. It is a truly advanced capstone project.

Level of difficulty: Advanced

Skills: Arduino, robotics, kinematics

Time required: 2–3 days for a simple version, can be tweaked and improved endlessly

Whether it's these projects or your own ideas, it's your turn now. Go off and make more things see!

Chapter 7

Appendix

A

This Appendix has code examples that did not fit inside the regular body text. They are here for your reference.

SimpleOpenNI Cheat Sheet

This section attempts to compile a condensed reference to every function and constant available in SimpleOpenNI.

Unless noted, all functions are member functions on a `SimpleOpenNI` object. Those labeled "PApplet functions" are functions that need to be implemented by the PApplet as part of various callback chains. These callback function signatures also include return types so they can be implemented correctly in your sketches. Those labeled "constructors" are constructors.

Return values are noted alongside each function. If no return value is noted, the function returns void. Arguments and their types are noted in the function signature.

Functions and constants are loosely grouped by use case.

No guarantees are made for completeness. Check the website (see "How to Contact Us" on page xviii) for updates since the publication of this book.

```
// constants

USERS_ALL

SKEL_PROFILE_NONE
SKEL_PROFILE_ALL
SKEL_PROFILE_UPPER
SKEL_PROFILE_LOWER
SKEL_PROFILE_HEAD_HANDS

// currently supported joint constants
SKEL_HEAD
SKEL_NECK
SKEL_TORSO
```

```
                              SKEL_LEFT_SHOULDER
                              SKEL_LEFT_ELBOW
                              SKEL_LEFT_HAND
                              SKEL_RIGHT_SHOULDER
                              SKEL_RIGHT_ELBOW
                              SKEL_RIGHT_HAND
                              SKEL_LEFT_HIP
                              SKEL_LEFT_KNEE
                              SKEL_LEFT_ANKLE
                              SKEL_RIGHT_HIP
                              SKEL_RIGHT_KNEE
                              SKEL_RIGHT_ANKLE

                              // present, but unsupported joint constants (maybe in the future)
                              SKEL_WAIST
                              SKEL_LEFT_COLLAR
                              SKEL_LEFT_WRIST
                              SKEL_LEFT_FINGERTIP
                              SKEL_RIGHT_COLLAR
                              SKEL_RIGHT_WRIST
                              SKEL_RIGHT_FINGERTIP
                              SKEL_LEFT_FOOT
                              SKEL_RIGHT_FOOT

                              // constant for enableRecorder
                              RECORD_MEDIUM_FILE

                              // constructors
                              SimpleOpenNI(PApplet parent)
                              SimpleOpenNI(PApplet parent,int runMode)
                              SimpleOpenNI(PApplet parent, String initXMLFile)
                              SimpleOpenNI(PApplet parent, String initXMLFile,int runMode)

                              // setup methods
                              enableDepth()
                              enableDepth(int width, int height,int fps)
                              enableRGB()
                              enableRGB(int width, int height, int fps)
                              enableIR()
                              enableIR(int width, int height, int fps)
                              enableScene()
                              enableScene(int width, int height, int fps)
                              enableUser(int flags)
                              enableGesture()
                              enableHands()
                              setMirror(boolean on)
                              enableRecorder(int recordMedium, String filePath)

                              update()

                              // display methods
                              depthImage() // return PImage
                              depthMap() // return int[]
                              depthMapRealWorld() // return PVector[]
                              rgbImage() // return PImage
                              irImage() // return PImage
                              sceneImage() // return PImage
                              sceneMap() // return int[]
                              getSceneFloor(PVector point, PVector normal)
                              getUsersPixels(int user) // return int[]
```

```
// calibration and recording
// all methods return boolean success
saveCalibrationDataSkeleton(int user, String calibrationFile)
loadCalibrationDataSkeleton(int user, String calibrationFile)
openFileRecording(String filePath)

// accessing position data
getCoM(int userId, PVector container) // returns boolean success
getJointPositionSkeleton(int userId, int jointId,
                         PVector container) // returns float confidence
getJointOrientationSkeleton(int userId, int jointId,
                         PMatrix3D orientation) // returns float confidence
getUsers(IntVEctor userList)
isTrackingSkeleton(int userId) // return boolean

// coordinate  system conversion
convertRealWorldToProjective(PVector world, PVector projective)
convertProjectiveToRealWorld(PVector projective, PVector world)

// display helper functions
drawLimb(int userId, int joint1, int joint2)
drawCamFrustum()

// skeleton calibration callback chain
startPoseDetection(String poseId, int userId)
startTrackingSkeleton(int userId);
startPoseDetection(String poseId, int userId);
stopPoseDetection(int userId);
requestCalibrationSkeleton(int userId, boolean somethingTrue);

// skeleton calibration PApplet functions
void onNewUser(int userId)
void onEndCalibration(int userId, boolean successful)
void onStartPose(String pose, int userId)
void onLostUser(int userId)
void onStartCalibration(int userId)

// gesture recognition PApplet functions
void onStartPose(String poseId, int userId)
void onEndPose(String poseId, int userId)
void onRecognizeGesture(String strGesture, PVector idPosition,
                        PVector endPosition)
void onProgressGesture(String strGesture, PVector idPosition,
                       float progress)
void onStartSession(PVector position)
void onEndSession(String string, PVector position, float progress)
void onFocusSession()

// gesture recognition setup
addGesture(String gestureId)

// hand-tracking PApplet functions
void onCreateHands(int handId, PVector position, float time)
void onUpdateHands(int handId, PVector position, float time)
void onDestroyHands(int handId, float time)

// hand tracking setup
startTrackingHands(PVector pos)
```

Chapter 2

Closest Pixel with Running Average

The sketch shown in Example A-1 uses two arrays declared as global variables to track the x- and y-components of the three most recent positions of the closest point seen by the Kinect. It then averages these three points to determine the current closest point. Performing this average smooths out the position of the point being tracked, making the tracking less responsive to outliers.

Example A-1. closest_pixel_running_average.pde

```
import SimpleOpenNI.*;
SimpleOpenNI  kinect;

// these will become a running average
// so they have to be floats
float closestX;
float closestY;

// create arrays to store recent
// closest x- and y-values for averaging
int[] recentXValues = new int[3];
int[] recentYValues = new int[3];

// keep track of which is the current
// value in the array to be changed
int currentIndex = 0;

void setup()
{
  size(640, 480);
  kinect = new SimpleOpenNI(this);
  kinect.enableDepth();
}

void draw()
{
  // declare these within the draw loop
  // so they change every time
  int closestValue = 8000;

  kinect.update();

  // get the depth array from the kinect
  int[] depthValues = kinect.depthMap();

    // for each row in the depth image
    for(int y = 0; y < 480; y++){
      // look at each pixel in the row
      for(int x = 0; x < 640; x++){
        // pull out the corresponding value from the depth array
        int i = x + y * 640;
        int currentDepthValue = depthValues[i];

        // if that pixel is the closest one we've seen so far
        if(currentDepthValue > 0 && currentDepthValue < closestValue){
          // save its value
          closestValue = currentDepthValue;
```

```
            // and save its position
            // into our recent values arrays
            recentXValues[currentIndex] = x;
            recentYValues[currentIndex] = y;
        }
      }
    }

    // cycle current index through 0,1,2:
    currentIndex++;
    if(currentIndex > 2){
      currentIndex = 0;
    }

    // closestX and closestY become
    // a running average with currentX and currentY
    closestX = (recentXValues[0] + recentXValues[1] + recentXValues[2]) / 3;
    closestY = (recentYValues[0] + recentYValues[1] + recentYValues[2]) / 3;

    //draw the depth image on the screen
    image(kinect.depthImage(),0,0);

    // draw a red circle over it,
    // positioned at the X and Y coordinates
    // we saved of the closest pixel.
    fill(255,0,0);
    ellipse(closestX, closestY, 25, 25);
}
```

Limiting the Depth Range

The sketch in Example A-2 displays a limited subrange of the depth image. For any points closer than a closestValue or further than a furthestValue, it shows black instead of the depth pixel. This is useful for determining a practical threshold for limiting the depth image to a range in which a user is likely to be moving his hand. Once you've determined the threshold values for your setup, you can then use them in others sketches like the Invisible Pencil project.

Example A-2. depth_range_limit.pde

```
import SimpleOpenNI.*;
SimpleOpenNI  kinect;

PImage depthImage;

float closestValue = 610;
float farthestValue = 1525;

void setup()
{
  size(640, 480);
  kinect = new SimpleOpenNI(this);
  kinect.enableDepth();
}

void draw()
{
  kinect.update();
```

```
    int[] depthValues = kinect.depthMap();
    depthImage = kinect.depthImage();
    for (int x = 0; x < 640; x++) {
      for (int y = 0; y < 480; y++) {
        int i = x + y * 640;
        int currentDepthValue = depthValues[i];
        if (currentDepthValue < closestValue
            || currentDepthValue > farthestValue) {
          depthImage.pixels[i] = 0;
        }
      }
    }

    image(depthImage, 0, 0);
}
```

Chapter 4

Save Calibration

Example A-3 presents a sketch that saves the calibration data into a file called *calibration.skel* in your sketch's *data* folder. After you have calibrated, hit any key to save the file.

Example A-3. save_calibration.pde

```
import SimpleOpenNI.*;
SimpleOpenNI  kinect;

int trackedUserID = 0;

void setup() {
  size(640, 480);

  kinect = new SimpleOpenNI(this);

  // enable depthMap generation
  kinect.enableDepth();
  // enable skeleton generation for all joints
  kinect.enableUser(SimpleOpenNI.SKEL_PROFILE_ALL);
}

void draw() {
  kinect.update();
  image(kinect.depthImage(), 0, 0);

  IntVector userList = new IntVector();
  kinect.getUsers(userList);

  if (userList.size() > 0) {
    int userId = userList.get(0);

    if (kinect.isTrackingSkeleton(userId)) {
      trackedUserID = userId;
      drawSkeleton(userId);
    }
  }
}
```

```
void keyPressed() {
  if (kinect.isTrackingSkeleton(trackedUserID)){
    kinect.saveCalibrationDataSkeleton(trackedUserID, "calibration.skel");
  }
}

void drawSkeleton(int userId) {
  kinect.drawLimb(userId,
                  SimpleOpenNI.SKEL_HEAD,
                  SimpleOpenNI.SKEL_NECK);
  kinect.drawLimb(userId,
                  SimpleOpenNI.SKEL_NECK,
                  SimpleOpenNI.SKEL_LEFT_SHOULDER);
  kinect.drawLimb(userId,
                  SimpleOpenNI.SKEL_LEFT_SHOULDER,
                  SimpleOpenNI.SKEL_LEFT_ELBOW);
  kinect.drawLimb(userId,
                  SimpleOpenNI.SKEL_LEFT_ELBOW,
                  SimpleOpenNI.SKEL_LEFT_HAND);
  kinect.drawLimb(userId,
                  SimpleOpenNI.SKEL_NECK,
                  SimpleOpenNI.SKEL_RIGHT_SHOULDER);
  kinect.drawLimb(userId,
                  SimpleOpenNI.SKEL_RIGHT_SHOULDER,
                  SimpleOpenNI.SKEL_RIGHT_ELBOW);
  kinect.drawLimb(userId,
                  SimpleOpenNI.SKEL_RIGHT_ELBOW,
                  SimpleOpenNI.SKEL_RIGHT_HAND);
  kinect.drawLimb(userId,
                  SimpleOpenNI.SKEL_LEFT_SHOULDER,
                  SimpleOpenNI.SKEL_TORSO);
  kinect.drawLimb(userId,
                  SimpleOpenNI.SKEL_RIGHT_SHOULDER,
                  SimpleOpenNI.SKEL_TORSO);
  kinect.drawLimb(userId,
                  SimpleOpenNI.SKEL_TORSO,
                  SimpleOpenNI.SKEL_LEFT_HIP);
  kinect.drawLimb(userId,
                  SimpleOpenNI.SKEL_LEFT_HIP,
                  SimpleOpenNI.SKEL_LEFT_KNEE);
  kinect.drawLimb(userId,
                  SimpleOpenNI.SKEL_LEFT_KNEE,
                  SimpleOpenNI.SKEL_LEFT_FOOT);
  kinect.drawLimb(userId,
                  SimpleOpenNI.SKEL_TORSO,
                  SimpleOpenNI.SKEL_RIGHT_HIP);
  kinect.drawLimb(userId,
                  SimpleOpenNI.SKEL_RIGHT_HIP,
                  SimpleOpenNI.SKEL_RIGHT_KNEE);
  kinect.drawLimb(userId,
                  SimpleOpenNI.SKEL_RIGHT_KNEE,
                  SimpleOpenNI.SKEL_RIGHT_FOOT);
}

// user-tracking callbacks!
void onNewUser(int userId) {
  println("start pose detection");
  kinect.startPoseDetection("Psi", userId);
}
```

```
void onEndCalibration(int userId, boolean successful) {
  if (successful) {
    println("  User calibrated !!!");
    kinect.startTrackingSkeleton(userId);
  }
  else {
    println("  Failed to calibrate user !!!");
    kinect.startPoseDetection("Psi", userId);
  }
}

void onStartPose(String pose, int userId) {
  println("Started pose for user");
  kinect.stopPoseDetection(userId);
  kinect.requestCalibrationSkeleton(userId, true);
}
```

Load Calibration

Example A-4 presents a sketch that loads the saved *calibration.skel* file and uses it to calibrate a user without her having to assume the calibration pose first. Create a *data* folder in your sketch and move a *calibration.skel* file (created with Example A-3) into it before running this sketch. It will begin tracking the skeleton of the calibrated user as soon as they become visible.

Example A-4. load_calibration.pde

```
import SimpleOpenNI.*;
SimpleOpenNI  kinect;

// IMPORTANT: calibration.skel needs to be in a folder called "data"
//            inside your sketch folder or SimpleOpenNI can't find it.

int calibratedUserID = 0;

void setup() {
  size(640, 480);

  kinect = new SimpleOpenNI(this);

  // enable depthMap generation
  kinect.enableDepth();
  // enable skeleton generation for all joints
  kinect.enableUser(SimpleOpenNI.SKEL_PROFILE_ALL);
}

void draw() {
  kinect.update();
  image(kinect.depthImage(), 0, 0);

  if (kinect.isTrackingSkeleton(calibratedUserID)) {
    drawSkeleton(calibratedUserID);
  }
}

void onNewUser(int userId) {
```

```
    println("start pose detection");
    if (kinect.loadCalibrationDataSkeleton(userId, "calibration.skel")) {
        println("calibration succeeded");

      calibratedUserID = userId;
      kinect.startTrackingSkeleton(calibratedUserID);
    } else {
      println("calibration failed");
    }
}

void drawSkeleton(int userId) {
  kinect.drawLimb(userId,
                  SimpleOpenNI.SKEL_HEAD,
                  SimpleOpenNI.SKEL_NECK);
  kinect.drawLimb(userId,
                  SimpleOpenNI.SKEL_NECK,
                  SimpleOpenNI.SKEL_LEFT_SHOULDER);
  kinect.drawLimb(userId,
                  SimpleOpenNI.SKEL_LEFT_SHOULDER,
                  SimpleOpenNI.SKEL_LEFT_ELBOW);
  kinect.drawLimb(userId,
                  SimpleOpenNI.SKEL_LEFT_ELBOW,
                  SimpleOpenNI.SKEL_LEFT_HAND);
  kinect.drawLimb(userId,
                  SimpleOpenNI.SKEL_NECK,
                  SimpleOpenNI.SKEL_RIGHT_SHOULDER);
  kinect.drawLimb(userId,
                  SimpleOpenNI.SKEL_RIGHT_SHOULDER,
                  SimpleOpenNI.SKEL_RIGHT_ELBOW);
  kinect.drawLimb(userId,
                  SimpleOpenNI.SKEL_RIGHT_ELBOW,
                  SimpleOpenNI.SKEL_RIGHT_HAND);
  kinect.drawLimb(userId,
                  SimpleOpenNI.SKEL_LEFT_SHOULDER,
                  SimpleOpenNI.SKEL_TORSO);
  kinect.drawLimb(userId,
                  SimpleOpenNI.SKEL_RIGHT_SHOULDER,
                  SimpleOpenNI.SKEL_TORSO);
  kinect.drawLimb(userId,
                  SimpleOpenNI.SKEL_TORSO,
                  SimpleOpenNI.SKEL_LEFT_HIP);
  kinect.drawLimb(userId,
                  SimpleOpenNI.SKEL_LEFT_HIP,
                  SimpleOpenNI.SKEL_LEFT_KNEE);
  kinect.drawLimb(userId,
                  SimpleOpenNI.SKEL_LEFT_KNEE,
                  SimpleOpenNI.SKEL_LEFT_FOOT);
  kinect.drawLimb(userId,
                  SimpleOpenNI.SKEL_TORSO,
                  SimpleOpenNI.SKEL_RIGHT_HIP);
  kinect.drawLimb(userId,
                  SimpleOpenNI.SKEL_RIGHT_HIP,
                  SimpleOpenNI.SKEL_RIGHT_KNEE);
  kinect.drawLimb(userId,
                  SimpleOpenNI.SKEL_RIGHT_KNEE,
                  SimpleOpenNI.SKEL_RIGHT_FOOT);
}
```

Extended SkeletonRecorder That Can Track Multiple Joints

Example A-5 presents the extended `SkeletonRecorder.pde` code that can track multiple joints.

Example A-5. SkeletonRecorder.pde

```
class SkeletonRecorder {
  private SimpleOpenNI context;
  TrackedJoint[] trackedJoints;
  int userID;
  int currentFrame = 0;
  int[] jointIDsToTrack;
  int totalFrames;
  boolean hasUser;

  SkeletonRecorder(SimpleOpenNI context, int[] jointIDsToTrack) {
    init(context, jointIDsToTrack);
  }

  SkeletonRecorder(SimpleOpenNI context, int jointIDToTrack) {
    int[] joints = new int[1];
    joints[0] = jointIDToTrack;
    init(context, joints);
  }

  void init(SimpleOpenNI context, int[] jointIDsToTrack ) {
    this.context = context;
    this.jointIDsToTrack = jointIDsToTrack;
  }

  void setUser(int userID) {
    if (!hasUser) {
      this.userID = userID;
      hasUser = true;
      trackedJoints = new TrackedJoint[jointIDsToTrack.length];

      for (int i = 0; i < trackedJoints.length; i++) {
        trackedJoints[i] =
          new TrackedJoint(this, context, userID, jointIDsToTrack[i]);
      }
    }
  }

  void recordFrame() {
    for (int i = 0; i < trackedJoints.length; i++) {
      trackedJoints[i].recordFrame();
    }
    totalFrames++;
  }


  void nextFrame() {
    currentFrame++;
```

```
    if (currentFrame >= totalFrames) {
      currentFrame = 0;
    }
  }
}

class TrackedJoint {
  int jointID;
  SimpleOpenNI context;
  ArrayList frames;
  int userID;
  SkeletonRecorder recorder;

  TrackedJoint(SkeletonRecorder recorder,
  SimpleOpenNI context,
  int userID,
  int jointID )
  {
    this.recorder = recorder;
    this.context = context;
    this.userID = userID;
    this.jointID = jointID;

    frames = new ArrayList();
  }

  JointPosition getPosition() {
    return getPositionAtFrame(recorder.currentFrame);
  }

  JointPosition getPositionAtFrame(int frameNum) {
    return (JointPosition) frames.get(frameNum);
  }

  void recordFrame() {
    PVector position = new PVector();
    float confidence =
      context.getJointPositionSkeleton(userID, jointID, position);
    JointPosition frame = new JointPosition(position, confidence);
    frames.add(frame);
  }
}


class JointPosition {
  PVector position;
  float confidence;

  JointPosition(PVector position, float confidence) {
    this.position = position;
    this.confidence = confidence;
  }
}
```

And Example A-6 presents an example sketch that uses this new Skeleton-Recorder to recreate the functionality of the Exercise Measurement example from the chapter. Modify that sketch to accept multiple joints by adding joints to the jointsToTrack array inside of setup and then using the results inside of draw.

Example A-6. exercise_measurement_advanced.pde

```
import processing.opengl.*;
import SimpleOpenNI.*;
SimpleOpenNI  kinect;

SkeletonRecorder recorder;

boolean recording = false;
boolean playing = false;

float offByDistance = 0.0;
PFont font;

void setup() {
  size(1028, 768, OPENGL);
  kinect = new SimpleOpenNI(this);
  kinect.enableDepth();
  kinect.enableUser(SimpleOpenNI.SKEL_PROFILE_ALL);
  kinect.setMirror(true);

  // initialize our recorder and tell it to track left hand
  // it takes an array because it can track multiple joints
  int[] jointsToTrack = {
    SimpleOpenNI.SKEL_LEFT_HAND
  };
  recorder = new SkeletonRecorder(kinect, jointsToTrack);

  font = createFont("Verdana", 40);
  textFont(font);
}

void draw() {
  background(0);
  kinect.update();

  // display text information
  pushMatrix();
  //    scale(4);

    fill(255);
    translate(0, 50, 0);
    text("totalFrames: " + recorder.totalFrames, 5, 0);
    text("recording: " + recording, 5, 50);
    text("currentFrame: " + recorder.currentFrame, 5, 100 );
    float c = map(offByDistance, 0, 1000, 0, 255);
    fill(c, 255-c, 0);
    text("off by: " + offByDistance, 5, 150);
  popMatrix();

  translate(width/2, height/2, 0);
  rotateX(radians(180));
```

```
IntVector userList = new IntVector();
kinect.getUsers(userList);
if (userList.size() > 0) {
  int userId = userList.get(0);
  recorder.setUser(userId);
  if ( kinect.isTrackingSkeleton(userId)) {
    PVector currentPosition = new PVector();
    kinect.getJointPositionSkeleton(userId,
                              SimpleOpenNI.SKEL_LEFT_HAND,
                              currentPosition);

    pushMatrix();
      stroke(255, 0, 0);
      strokeWeight(50);
      point(currentPosition.x, currentPosition.y, currentPosition.z);
    popMatrix();

    // if we're recording
    // tell the record to capture this frame
    if (recording) {
      recorder.recordFrame();
    }
    else if (playing) {


      // if we're playing access the recorded joint position
      PVector recordedPosition =
        recorder.trackedJoints[0].getPosition().position;

      // display the recorded joint position
      pushMatrix();
        stroke(0, 255, 0);
        strokeWeight(30);
        point(recordedPosition.x, recordedPosition.y,
              recordedPosition.z);
      popMatrix();

      // draw a line between the current position and the recorded one
      // set its color based on the distance between the two
      stroke(c, 255-c, 0);
      strokeWeight(20);
      line(currentPosition.x, currentPosition.y, currentPosition.z,
          recordedPosition.x, recordedPosition.y, recordedPosition.z);

      // calculate the vector between the current and recorded positions
      // with vector subtraction
      currentPosition.sub(recordedPosition);

      // store the magnitude of that vector as the off-by distance
      // for display
      offByDistance = currentPosition.mag();
      // tell the recorder to load up
      // the next frame
      recorder.nextFrame();

    }
  }
}
}
```

```
void keyPressed() {
  if (key == ' ') {
    recording = !recording;
    playing = !playing;
  }
}

// user-tracking callbacks!
void onNewUser(int userId) {
  println("start pose detection");
  kinect.startPoseDetection("Psi", userId);
}

void onEndCalibration(int userId, boolean successful) {
  if (successful) {
    println("  User calibrated !!!");
    kinect.startTrackingSkeleton(userId);
    recording = true;
  }
  else {
    println("  Failed to calibrate user !!!");
    kinect.startPoseDetection("Psi", userId);
  }
}

void onStartPose(String pose, int userId) {
  println("Started pose for user");
  kinect.stopPoseDetection(userId);
  kinect.requestCalibrationSkeleton(userId, true);
}
```

Chapter 6

Complete Forward Kinematics Example

Example A-7 presents the complete Processing sketch for forward kinematics. It calculates both joint angles and then sends the results over serial to the Arduino.

Example A-7. forward_kinematics_serial.pde

```
import SimpleOpenNI.*;
SimpleOpenNI  kinect;

// import the processing serial library
import processing.serial.*;
// and declare an object for our serial port
Serial port;

void setup() {
  size(640, 480);

  kinect = new SimpleOpenNI(this);
  kinect.enableDepth();
  kinect.enableUser(SimpleOpenNI.SKEL_PROFILE_ALL);
  kinect.setMirror(true);

  // Get the name of the first serial port
  // where we assume the Arduino is connected.
```

```
    // If it doesn't work, examine the output of
    // the println, and replace 0 with the correct
    // serial port index.
    println(Serial.list());
    String portName = Serial.list()[0];

    // initialize our serial object with this port
    // and the baud rate of 9600
    port = new Serial(this, portName, 9600);
}

void draw() {
  kinect.update();
  PImage depth = kinect.depthImage();
  image(depth, 0, 0);

  IntVector userList = new IntVector();
  kinect.getUsers(userList);

  if (userList.size() > 0) {
    int userId = userList.get(0);

    if ( kinect.isTrackingSkeleton(userId)) {
      // get the positions of the three joints of our arm
      PVector rightHand = new PVector();
      kinect.getJointPositionSkeleton(userId,
        SimpleOpenNI.SKEL_RIGHT_HAND, rightHand);

      PVector rightElbow = new PVector();
      kinect.getJointPositionSkeleton(userId,
          SimpleOpenNI.SKEL_RIGHT_ELBOW, rightElbow);

      PVector rightShoulder = new PVector();
      kinect.getJointPositionSkeleton(userId,
          SimpleOpenNI.SKEL_RIGHT_SHOULDER, rightShoulder);

      // convert our arm joints into screen space coordinates
      PVector convertedRightHand = new PVector();
      kinect.convertRealWorldToProjective(rightHand, convertedRightHand);

      PVector convertedRightElbow = new PVector();
      kinect.convertRealWorldToProjective(rightElbow, convertedRightElbow);

      PVector convertedRightShoulder = new PVector();
      kinect.convertRealWorldToProjective(rightShoulder,
                                          convertedRightShoulder);

      // we need right hip to orient the shoulder angle
      PVector rightHip = new PVector();
      kinect.getJointPositionSkeleton(userId,
        SimpleOpenNI.SKEL_RIGHT_HIP, rightHip);

      // reduce our joint vectors to two dimensions
      PVector rightHand2D = new PVector(rightHand.x, rightHand.y);
      PVector rightElbow2D = new PVector(rightElbow.x, rightElbow.y);
      PVector rightShoulder2D = new PVector(rightShoulder.x,
                                            rightShoulder.y);
      PVector rightHip2D = new PVector(rightHip.x, rightHip.y);
```

```
        // calculate the axes against which we want to measure our angles
        PVector torsoOrientation = PVector.sub(rightShoulder2D, rightHip2D);
        PVector upperArmOrientation =
          PVector.sub(rightElbow2D, rightShoulder2D);

        // calculate the angles of each of our arms
        float shoulderAngle =
          angleOf(rightElbow2D, rightShoulder2D, torsoOrientation);
        float elbowAngle =
          angleOf(rightHand2D, rightElbow2D, upperArmOrientation);

        // show the angles on the screen for debugging
        fill(255,0,0);
        scale(3);
        text("shoulder: " + int(shoulderAngle) + "\n" +
             " elbow: " + int(elbowAngle), 20, 20);

        byte out[] = new byte[2];
        out[0] = byte(shoulderAngle);
        out[1] = byte(elbowAngle);
        port.write(out);
      }
    }
}

float angleOf(PVector one, PVector two, PVector axis) {
  PVector limb = PVector.sub(two, one);
  return degrees(PVector.angleBetween(limb, axis));
}

// user-tracking callbacks!
void onNewUser(int userId) {
  println("start pose detection");
  kinect.startPoseDetection("Psi", userId);
}

void onEndCalibration(int userId, boolean successful) {
  if (successful) {
    println("  User calibrated !!!");
    kinect.startTrackingSkeleton(userId);
  }
  else {
    println("  Failed to calibrate user !!!");
    kinect.startPoseDetection("Psi", userId);
  }
}

void onStartPose(String pose, int userId) {
  println("Started pose for user");
  kinect.stopPoseDetection(userId);
  kinect.requestCalibrationSkeleton(userId, true);
}
```

Inverse Kinematics Geometrical Proof

<u>Law of Cosines</u>
C = arcos(a*a + b*b - c*c)/2ab
B = acrosa*a + b*b c*c)/2ac

<u>Triangle Angles</u>
// D is the angle of difference where
// difference = target - shoulder
D = atan2(difference.x, difference.y)
// Pi radians in a triangle
A + B + C = Pi
// sub angles sum
D = A + E
// solve for A
A = D - E
// plug this into triangle
D - E + B + C = Pi
// solve for E
E = D + B + C - Pi

<u>Supplementary Angles</u>
// angles in a triangle add to P
// D is parallel to D below
D + B + C = Pi
// F and C are supplementary
F + C = Pi
// solve for F
F = D + B

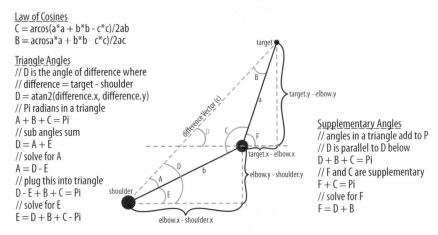

Deriving Joint Positions from Angles with SOHCAHTOA

cos(E) = (elbow.x - shoulder.x)/b
cos(E)*b = elbow.x - shoulder.x
cos(E)*b + shoulder.x = elbow.x

sin(E) = (elbow.y - shoulder.y)/b
sin(E)*b = elbow.y - shoulder.y
sin(E)*b + shoulder.y = elbow.y

All of this is repeated for target.x and target.y
in relation to elbow.x and elbow.y and the
angle D+B. The result is:

target.x = (cos(D+B)*a) + elbow.x;
target.y = (sin(D+B)*a) + elbow.y;

Figure A-1. *An explanation of the geometric proof behind our inverse kinematics calculations.*

Index

Symbols

Colophon

The heading and cover font are BentonSans, the text font is Myriad Pro, and the code font is TheSansMonoCondensed.

About the Author

After a decade as a musician, web programmer, and startup founder, **Greg Borenstein** recently moved to New York to become an artist and teacher. His work explores the use of special effects as an artistic medium. He is fascinated by how special effects techniques cross the boundary between images and the physical objects that make them: miniatures, motion capture, 3D animation, animatronics, and digital fabrication. He is currently a resident researcher at NYU's Interactive Telecommunications Program.

Get even more for your money.

Join the O'Reilly Community, and register the O'Reilly books you own. It's free, and you'll get:

- $4.99 ebook upgrade offer
- 40% upgrade offer on O'Reilly print books
- Membership discounts on books and events
- Free lifetime updates to ebooks and videos
- Multiple ebook formats, DRM FREE
- Participation in the O'Reilly community
- Newsletters
- Account management
- 100% Satisfaction Guarantee

Signing up is easy:

1. Go to: oreilly.com/go/register
2. Create an O'Reilly login.
3. Provide your address.
4. Register your books.

Note: English-language books only

To order books online:

oreilly.com/store

For questions about products or an order:

orders@oreilly.com

To sign up to get topic-specific email announcements and/or news about upcoming books, conferences, special offers, and new technologies:

elists@oreilly.com

For technical questions about book content:

booktech@oreilly.com

To submit new book proposals to our editors:

proposals@oreilly.com

O'Reilly books are available in multiple DRM-free ebook formats. For more information:

oreilly.com/ebooks

O'REILLY®

Spreading the knowledge of innovators   oreilly.com

Have it your way.

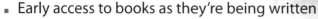